Classroom Teaching Skills

James M. Cooper, GENERAL EDITOR

University of Virginia

Sandra Sokolove Garrett
Medifacts, Ltd.

Mary S. Leighton
Policy Studies Associates, Washington, D.C.

Peter H. Martorella
North Carolina State University, Raleigh

Greta G. Morine-Dershimer
University of Virginia

David Sadker
The American University

Myra Sadker
The American University

Robert Shostak
Florida International University

Terry D. TenBrink
Kirksville College of Osteopathic Medicine

Wilford A. Weber
University of Houston

D. C. HEATH AND COMPANY

Lexington, Massachusetts   Toronto

Classroom
Teaching
Skills

FIFTH EDITION

Address editorial correspondence to
D. C. Heath and Company
125 Spring Street
Lexington, MA 02173

Acquisitions Editor: Walter Cunningham
Production Editor: Heather L. Garrison
Designer: Judith Miller
Photo Researcher: Judy Mason
Production Coordinator: Charles Dutton
Permissions Editor: Margaret Roll

Photo Credits: p. iii, Monkmeyer/Paul Conklin; p. 1, The Picture Cube/Robert Finken; p. 19, The Picture Cube/David Strickler; p. 55, Monkmeyer/Mimi Forsyth; p. 89, Elizabeth Crews; p. 115, Stock Boston/Richard Sobol; p. 153, The Picture Cube/Julie O'Neil; p. 189, The Image Works/Nina Winter; p. 233, The Image Works/Elizabeth Crews; p. 281, The Image Works/Weisbrot; p. 327, The Image Works/Elizabeth Crews.

Cover Photo: © Richard Hutchings/PhotoEdit

International Standard Book Number: 0-669-34963-1

Library of Congress Catalog Number: 93-78766

10 9 8 7 6 5 4 3 2 1

Preface

At one time in the not-too-distant past, teacher education consisted of a few courses on education theory, some courses on methods, and a topping of student teaching. Except for the student teaching, and maybe a little observation experience, the program consisted of campus-based courses.

Teacher education today differs considerably from the preceding description. Programs are much more field-oriented than ever before, requiring prospective teachers to spend more time working with students in schools. The present emphasis on practical experience with students should not be interpreted as a movement away from theory. Rather, educational theory is being integrated with practice. This integration recognizes that theory, to be internalized, must be learned in the context in which it is to be applied. In the past, prospective teachers were expected to translate theory into practice with little help. Usually they were unsuccessful. Today, with the help of newly developed curriculum materials, teacher educators help prospective teachers apply the theory in field contexts and give them feedback on their efforts.

The fifth edition of *Classroom Teaching Skills* will help beginning teachers meld theory with practice. The book conceptualizes the teacher as a decision maker — one who makes planning, implementing, evaluation, and management decisions as part of the instructional role. To make and carry out these decisions the teacher needs certain teaching skills. The conceptual framework of the teacher as a decision maker is presented in Chapter 1. Each subsequent chapter addresses a particular skill by first discussing the theory behind the skill and then giving the reader practice situations in which knowledge about the skill can be applied and feedback received. Because each chapter presents specific learning objectives as well as mastery tests, the reader receives immediate feedback on this learning.

After students have completed the chapters, the instructor may want to set up microteaching experiences that will enable the students to practice the skills with actual learners. Ultimate acquisition of the skill must, of course, take place in actual classroom situations.

From the outset our goal was to produce instructional materials that are (1) important, (2) flexible, (3) readable, and (4) scholarly. A word about each of these features follows.

First, the *importance* of the teaching skills contained in this book has been dramatically demonstrated during the last three decades by the millions of dollars spent on researching the skills and the multitude of publications on each skill. Our experience indicates that students emphatically want to master practical teaching skills that will enable them to cope successfully with their classroom responsibilities. Consequently, it is our belief that these instructional materials, dedicated as they are to the mastery of basic teaching skills, will be retained and used by most students as an ongoing self-evaluation tool — to be referred to both during and after their field experiences.

Our second goal, to produce a highly *flexible* text, has been met in two ways. First, the content itself — the skills — is ubiquitous, reaching into virtually every course in the teacher-education curriculum. Second, the book has been designed as a self-contained teacher-education learning package, thus permitting use in a variety of capacities in many parts of the curriculum. Instructors may choose to focus on particular chapters for one course and different chapters for another course. How the book is used will depend on the structure and organization of a given teacher-education program.

Our third goal, *readability*, has been achieved through editing the manuscripts of the various authors. While each author's unique writing style has been consciously preserved, the level and structure of writing has been adjusted to conform to preplanned standards. In each chapter we have tried to present a relatively simple presentation within a four-step, self-teaching format: (1) a statement of objectives, (2) a presentation of written information, (3) practice exercises with answers, and (4) a mastery test with an answer key.

Our fourth goal, developing materials representative of the best current *scholarship*, has been met by experienced authors, each a recognized authority on the particular skill about which he or she has written. Further information on each author is presented following the Contents.

Before revising *Classroom Teaching Skills*, questionnaires were mailed to professors who had used the book in their classes, asking them to evaluate the various chapters and to suggest changes for improvement. These evaluations and comments were mailed to each author, along with my suggestions for revision. The resulting product is a fifth edition that addresses specific concerns and suggestions made by users of the fourth edition. Besides general updating, significant changes in the fifth edition include expanding the chapter on concept learning to incorporate higher-level thinking skills, adding additional strategies to the cooperative learning chapter, shortening and simplifying the chapter on classroom management, and adding more material on grading in the evaluation chapter.

We appreciate the assistance offered in the revision of this text by the following reviewers: Christine Walsh, State University of New York — Oswego; Linda Quinn, University of Nevada — Las Vegas; Robert Agostino, Duquesne University; and Ralph Garvelli, University of Pennsylvania — Mansfield.

James M. Cooper

Contents

5 *Questioning Skills*   *115*
Myra Sadker and David Sadker

6 *Concept Learning and Higher-Level Thinking*   *153*
Peter H. Martorella

About the Authors

James M. Cooper is Commonwealth Professor and Dean of the Curry School of Education at the University of Virginia. He received four degrees from Stanford University — two in history and two in education, including his Ph.D. in 1967. He has written or edited nine books, including *Those Who Can, Teach* and *Kaleidoscope: Readings in Education,* coauthored and coedited with Kevin Ryan; and *Developing Skills for Instructional Supervision.* His books and articles address the areas of teacher education, supervision of teachers, microteaching, and teacher education program evaluation. His articles have appeared in such journals as *Phi Delta Kappan, Journal of Teacher Education, Educational Leadership, Elementary School Journal, Elementary English, Journal of Research and Development in Education,* and *Education and Urban Society.* He was Director of one of the USOE Model Elementary Teacher Education Programs at the University of Massachusetts and later was Associate Dean for Graduate Studies in the College of Education at the University of Houston.

Sandra Sokolove Garrett is President of Medifacts, Ltd., a company that provides medical support service to a variety of health-care settings. Dr. Garrett is involved in ongoing research related to physician-patient interpersonal communications and the effects of such interaction on health, blood pressure, and quality of life. She is the author of several articles related to this and other humanistic health care issues. She received her Ed.D. from the University of Massachusetts and has been on the faculties of Lesley College, Wheaton College, University of Texas Health Science Center at Dallas, and Georgetown University School of Medicine.

Mary S. Leighton who earned a Ph.D. at the University of Oregon, is a Research Associate at Policy Studies Associates in Washington, D.C. After graduating from the University of Chicago, she began teaching in first grade and special education in Chicago Public Schools in 1969. Since then, she has also taught in rural elementary schools (including a one-room school), preschool, high school, adult education, preservice teacher education, and graduate school. While employed at the Center for the Study of Effective Schooling for Disadvantaged Students at the Johns Hopkins Univeristy, she worked with Baltimore City elementary teachers implementing the "Success for All" program, which makes extensive use of cooperative learning. In her present position, she conducts research and policy analysis on issues related to compensatory education and teachers' professional development.

Peter H. Martorella is a Professor in the Department of Curriculum and Instruction, North Carolina State University, Raleigh. He received his Ph.D. degree from The Ohio State University and later completed a postdoctoral fellowship at the University of Washington. Additionally, he has studied educational systems in Portugal and Korea under Fulbright fellowships and in Japan under a Japan Foundation grant. The author of two books on concept learning, he also has published extensively in the field of social studies education and computer-based education. His most recent book is *Teaching Social Studies in Middle and Secondary Schools* (Macmillan, 1991). He has been Director of the Education Program of the Rockefeller Family Fund and Head of the Department of Curriculum and Instruction at North Carolina State University. Formerly Professor of Elementary and Secondary Education at Temple University, where he directed the Graduate Program in General Education, Professor Martorella also has taught at the elementary, middle, and senior high levels.

Greta G. Morine-Dershimer is Director of Teacher Education, and a Professor in the Department of Curriculum, Instruction, and Special Education at the Curry School of Education, University of Virginia. She is also a senior researcher in the Curry School's Commonwealth Center for the Education of Teachers. She received her Ed.D. from Teachers College, Columbia University, in 1965 after teaching in elementary and junior high schools for ten years. She has been a teacher educator in New York and California and developed teacher education materials at the Far West Laboratory for Educational Research and Development. Her research has focused on teacher and pupil information processing, and she has recently been involved in studies of student teachers' planning and interactive decision making. In 1988 she was elected to a two-year term as Vice President of the American Educational Research Association, to head Division K (Teaching and Teacher Education). Her publications include five books, and articles in many journals, including *Teachers College Record, Elementary School Journal, Theory into Practice, Social Education, Journal of Teacher Education, Teaching and Teacher Education, Educational Theory,* and *American Educational Research Journal.*

Myra and David Sadker are both professors of education at The American University, where Myra served as Dean for six years. They have coauthored five books, including *Teachers, Schools and Society* (McGraw-Hill, 2nd ed., 1991) and *Sex Equity Handbook for Schools* (Longman, 1982). More than thirty of their articles have appeared in *Phi Delta Kappan, Harvard Educational Review, Educational Leadership,* and other professional journals. Their research interests have focused on educational equity and teacher preparation and curriculum, and they have codirected numerous grants funded by the U.S. Department of Education. They have conducted teaching workshops for principals, teachers, and professors in over forty states. Their research and writing efforts have received distinguished achievement awards from the American Educational Research Association, The Educational Press Association of America, The American University, and The University of Massachusetts. Their degrees are from Boston University, City College of New York, Harvard University, and The University of Massachusetts.

Robert Shostak   is a Professor of Education at Florida International University. He received his bachelor's degree in humanities from Colgate University, an M.S. in teaching English from the State University of New York at Albany, and a Ph.D. in Curriculum and Instruction from the University of Connecticut. He taught high school English for six years before focusing his career on higher education and teacher education. Dr. Shostak has taught general methods and curriculum development courses to both graduate and undergraduate students and supervised student teachers at every grade level. He is now focusing his teaching on the use of computers and multimedia in the classroom. His current publication efforts are being directed at developing multimedia software for the language arts.

Terry D. TenBrink   is Vice President for Institutional Advancement at the Kirksville College of Osteopathic Medicine in Kirksville, Missouri. Formerly on the faculty at the University of Missouri at Columbia, Dr. TenBrink received his Ph.D. in educational psychology from Michigan State University in 1969. His graduate studies emphasized learning theory, evaluation, measurement, and research design. His teaching experience spans elementary, junior high school, high school, and college students, and he has been principal of an elementary school. He stays in touch with the classroom through numerous consulting activities in public schools and in adult education and by teaching seminars and workshops to classroom teachers. While at the University of Missouri, Dr. TenBrink taught courses in evaluation, learning, human development, and general educational psychology. He has published numerous journal articles and is engaged in continuing research on the conditions under which learning occurs efficiently. In 1974 his textbook *Evaluation: A Practical Guide for Teachers* was published by McGraw-Hill.

Wilford A. Weber   is Professor of Education in the Department of Curriculum and Instruction, College of Education, University of Houston. He holds a bachelor's degree in psychology from Muhlenberg College and a doctorate in educational psychology from Temple University. He has taught at Temple University, Villanova University, and Syracuse University and serves as a Visiting Professor at the University of St. Thomas. Dr. Weber has been at the University of Houston since 1971. He presently serves as a member of the Committee of Examiners for the National Teacher Examinations Core Battery Test of Professional Knowledge. Dr. Weber has directed numerous funded research projects and has authored more than one hundred and fifty papers, articles, chapters, monographs, and books concerned with teacher education, teacher effectiveness, classroom management, and school discipline. His major publications include "A Review of the Teacher Education Literature on Classroom Management," a chapter — co-authored with Linda A. Roff — in *Classroom Management: Reviews of the Teacher Education and Research Literature* (a monograph published by Educational Testing Service in 1983). During his career, Dr. Weber has conducted scores of seminars and workshops on the subject of classroom management and school discipline. His audiences have included teachers, administrators, and teacher educators throughout Texas and the United States and in Germany, Italy, and Mexico. Dr. Weber stays in touch with the realities of the classroom and the school through consulting and research activities that take him into the schools, by doing substitute teaching, by teaching graduate courses for classroom teachers, and through his involvement in several professional organizations. His interest in classroom management and school discipline stems from his experience as a teacher of court-committed juvenile delinquents.

The Teacher As a Decision Maker

1

■ James M. Cooper

What Is a Teacher?

At first glance such a question seems obvious. A teacher is a person charged with the responsibility of helping others to learn and to behave in new and different ways. But who is excluded from this definition? Parents? Band directors? Drill sergeants? Boy Scout leaders? At some time or another we all teach and, in turn, are taught.

We generally reserve the term *teacher*, however, for persons whose primary professional or occupational function is to help others learn and develop in new ways. While education, learning, and teaching can, and do, take place in many different settings, most societies realize that education is too important to be left to chance. Consequently, they establish schools to facilitate learning and to help people live better and happier lives. Schools are created to provide a certain type of educational experience, which can be called the *curriculum*. Teachers are trained and hired by societies to help fulfill the purposes of the curriculum. Teachers, in the formal educative process of schooling, are social agents hired by society to help facilitate the intellectual, personal, and social development of those members of society who attend schools.

Until modern times, teachers themselves had little formal schooling; often they knew barely more than their students. As late as 1864 an Illinois teacher described the image of the teacher as "someone who can parse and cypher; has little brains and less money; is feeble minded, unable to grapple with real men and women in the stirring employments of life, but on that account admirably fitted to associate with childish intellects."[1] Needless to say, this image of the teacher has changed considerably for the better. Today teachers are better educated, earn more money, and are more highly respected members of society than their nineteenth-century counterparts. Society requires its teachers to obtain a college education and specific training as teachers. This increase in the educational level of teachers is recognition that, if teachers are to facilitate the intellectual, personal, and social development of their students, then they must be much better educated than ever before.

Effective Teaching

Possession of a college degree does not in any way ensure that teachers will be effective. But what is an effective teacher? What is a good teacher? Are they the same?

Good teaching is difficult to define because the term *good* is so value-laden. What appears to be good teaching to one person may be considered poor teaching by another because each one values different outcomes or methods. One teacher may run the classroom in an organized, highly structured manner, emphasizing the intellectual content of the academic disciplines. Another may run the class in a less structured environment, allowing the students much more freedom to choose subject matter and activities that interest them personally. One observer, because of personal

Class

values, may identify the first teacher as a "good" teacher, while criticizing the second teacher for running "too loose a ship." Another observer may come to the opposite conclusion with respect to which teacher is better, again, because of a different set of values.

Class

While it remains difficult to agree on what "good" teaching is, "effective" teaching can be demonstrated. *The effective teacher is one who is able to bring about intended learning outcomes.* The nature of the learning is still most important, but two different teachers, as in the example above, may strive for and achieve different outcomes and both be judged effective. The two critical dimensions of effective teaching are *intent* and *achievement.*

Without intent, student achievement becomes random and accidental; however, intent is not enough by itself. If students do not achieve their intended learning goals (even if the failure is due to variables beyond the control of their teacher), the teacher cannot truly have been effective.

While effective teachers are defined as teachers who can demonstrate the ability to bring about intended learning outcomes, what enables them to achieve desired results with students? Have you ever stopped to think about what, if anything, makes teachers different from other well-educated adults? What should effective, professional teachers know, believe, or be able to do that distinguishes them from other people? Think about these questions seriously because they are central questions, the answers to which should be at the heart of your teacher education program.

Some people will state that the crucial dimension is the teacher's personality. Teachers, they will say, should be friendly, cheerful, sympathetic, morally virtuous, enthusiastic, and humorous. In a massive study, David Ryans concluded that effective teachers are fair, democratic, responsive, understanding, kindly, stimulating, original, alert, attractive, responsible, steady, poised, and confident. Ineffective teachers were described as partial, autocratic, aloof, restricted, harsh, dull, stereotyped, apathetic, unimpressive, evasive, erratic, excitable, and uncertain.[2] But as two educational researchers once remarked, ". . . what conceivable human interaction is not the better if the people involved are friendly, cheerful, sympathetic, and virtuous rather than the opposite?"[3] These characteristics, then, while desirable in teachers, are not uniquely desirable to that group alone.

It might be difficult to reach a consensus on exactly what knowledge and skills are unique to the teaching profession, but most educators would agree that special skills and knowledge are necessary and do exist. Certainly teachers must be familiar with children and their developmental stages. They must know something about events outside the classroom and school. They must possess enough command of the subject they are going to teach to be able to differentiate what is important and central from what is incidental and peripheral. They must have a philosophy of education to help guide them in their role as teachers. They must know how human beings learn and how to create environments that facilitate learning.

■ *General Areas of Teacher Competence*

Class

B. O. Smith has suggested that a well-trained teacher should be prepared in four areas of teacher competence to be effective in bringing about intended learning outcomes.

1. Command of theoretical knowledge about learning and human behavior

Should already have a base from previous classes. (IDP250

2. Display of attitudes that foster learning and genuine human relationships *difficult to measure.*
3. Command of <u>knowledge in the subject matter</u> to be taught
4. Control of <u>technical skills</u> of teaching that facilitate student learning

variety of teaching skills

1. Command of Theoretical Knowledge About Learning and Human Behavior. For years education has been criticized for its "folkways" practices. Educational recipes and standardized procedures were formally and informally passed on to new teachers to help them survive in classrooms. While this practice still exists, <u>many scientific concepts</u> from psychology, anthropology, sociology, linguistics, cybernetics, and related disciplines <u>are now available to help teachers interpret the complex reality of their classrooms.</u> Those teachers who lack the theoretical background and understanding provided by such scientifically derived concepts can only interpret the events of their classrooms according to popularly held beliefs or common sense. Although common sense often serves us well, there is ample evidence that teachers who habitually rely on it will too often misinterpret the events in their classrooms.

Beginning teachers frequently face the difficult situation of receiving different, contradictory messages from their professors and from the teachers with whom they work. While their professors are apt to focus on theoretical knowledge, the experienced teacher may often advise them, "Forget the fancy theoretical stuff and listen to me. I'll tell you what works in real life." This folkways approach to education may be in conflict with what the new teacher has learned and create a dilemma about how to handle a situation.

The problem confronting new teachers is not that the theories put before them are unworkable, but that they simply haven't internalized those theories to the point where they can be used to interpret and solve practical problems. They have not been provided with sufficient opportunities to apply the knowledge, to translate it from theory into practice, and thereby master it.

An example of a theoretical concept that is derived from psychology and that has enormous implications for teachers is the concept of *reinforcement*. From their educational psychology courses most teachers know that a behavior that is reinforced will be strengthened, and is likely to be repeated. Nevertheless, these same teachers often respond to a disruptive pupil by calling his or her actions to the attention of the class. If the pupil is misbehaving because of a need to be recognized, the teacher, by publicly acknowledging the misbehavior, is reinforcing it. When the pupil continues to act up periodically, the teacher doesn't understand why. Although the teacher may have intellectually grasped a concept such as reinforcement, this understanding is not synonymous with internalizing or mastering the concept. Mastery requires practical application to concrete situations.

Because theoretical knowledge can be used to interpret situations and solve problems, many classroom events that might otherwise go unnoticed or remain inexplicable can be recognized and resolved by applying theories and concepts of human behavior. This is not an easy task. It requires understanding, insight, practice, and feedback from colleagues and professors. Proficiency will not be achieved as a result of formal training alone; it is a lifelong process involving both formal training and an unending program of on-the-job self-improvement.

2. Display of Attitudes That Foster Learning and Genuine Human Relationships.   The second area of competence identified as essential for effective teaching has to do with attitudes. An *attitude* is a predisposition to act in a positive or negative way toward persons, ideas, or events. Most educators are convinced that teacher attitudes are an important dimension in the teaching process. Attitudes have a direct effect on our behavior; they determine how we view ourselves and interact with others.

The major categories of attitudes that affect teaching behavior are: (a) teachers' attitudes toward themselves, (b) teachers' attitudes toward children, (c) teachers' attitudes toward peers and parents, and (d) teachers' attitudes toward the subject matter.

(a) *Teachers' Attitudes Toward Themselves.* There is evidence from psychology that persons who deny or cannot cope with their own emotions are likely to be incapable of respecting and coping with the feelings of others. If teachers are to understand and sympathize with their students' feelings, they must recognize and understand their own feelings. Many colleges are responding to this need by including counseling sessions, reflective thinking, and awareness experiences as part of their teacher education programs. These experiences emphasize introspection, self-evaluation, and feedback from other participants. The goal is to help prospective teachers learn more about themselves, their attitudes, and how others perceive them.

(b) *Teachers' Attitudes Toward Children.* Most teachers occasionally harbor attitudes or feelings toward students that are detrimental to their teaching effectiveness. Strong likes and dislikes of particular pupils, biases toward or against particular ethnic groups, low learning expectations for poverty-level children, and biases toward or against certain kinds of student behavior — all can reduce teaching effectiveness. Self-awareness of such attitudes toward individual pupils or classes of children is necessary if teachers are to cope with their own feelings and beliefs. If teachers possess empathy for their students and value them as unique individuals, they will be more effective and will derive more satisfaction from their teaching.

(c) *Teachers' Attitudes Toward Peers and Parents.* Teachers do not exist in isolated classrooms. They interact with fellow teachers and administrators and often have sensitive dealings with parents. Sometimes they can be effective in dealing with children, but because of negative attitudes toward the adults they encounter, their professional life is unsuccessful. This is a rare instance, however, for most people have similar attitudes toward all persons, adult and child, possessing similar characteristics. Many of the comments already made regarding teachers' attitudes toward themselves and children also apply to their attitudes toward peers and parents.

(d) *Teachers' Attitudes Toward Subject Matter.* The message, in one word, is ENTHUSIASM! Just as students are perceptive in discovering the teacher's attitude toward them, they are also sensitive to the teacher's attitude toward the subject matter. Teachers who are not enthusiastic about what they teach can hardly hope to instill enthusiastic responses in their pupils. After all, if you don't care about the subject matter, how can you ever hope to motivate your students into learning about it?

3. Command of Knowledge in the Subject Matter to Be Taught.   Command of the subject matter to be taught is an obvious necessity for any teacher. But taking courses in biology or history or mathematics is not sufficient. A teacher's subject matter preparation really has two aspects:

(1) a study of the subject matter itself, and (2) a judicious selection of the material that can be transmitted successfully to the student.

College courses taken in disciplines like mathematics or English help teachers acquire an understanding of the disciplines, their basic concepts, and their modes of inquiry; but college courses are not directed toward what should be taught to elementary or secondary school students. What should be taught is obviously much less extensive and advanced than the content of the college courses, and requires that teachers know the school curriculum as well.

Knowledge of the school curriculum is related to another kind — *pedagogical content knowledge.* Lee Shulman of Stanford University coined this phrase to describe knowledge that bridges content knowledge and pedagogy. Pedagogical content knowledge represents the "blending of content and pedagogy into an understanding of how particular topics, problems, or issues are organized, represented, and adapted to the diverse interests and abilities of learners and presented for instruction."[4] Teachers possess pedagogical content knowledge when they can translate the content knowledge they possess into forms that have great teaching power and that meet the needs and abilities of students. Such teachers draw on powerful examples, illustrations, analogies, demonstrations, and explanations to represent and transform the subject so that students can understand it.

Teachers must, therefore, rethink much of the content of a particular discipline as it relates to the lives of their pupils. To be effective communicators, teachers need an understanding of both children and subject matter and, beyond that, special training in linking the two.

As B. O. Smith states:

[T]he teacher should know the content he is to teach as well as that of the disciplines from which his instructional subject matter may be taken. The first is necessary for teaching anything at all. The second applies a depth of knowledge essential to the teacher's feelings of intellectual security and his ability to handle instructional content with greater understanding.[5]

4. Control of Technical Skills of Teaching That Facilitate Student Learning. The fourth area of competence required of effective teachers is possession of a repertoire of teaching skills. Such a repertoire is necessary if teachers are to be effective with students who have varied backgrounds and learning aptitudes. Teacher education programs must, therefore, include a training component focusing on the acquisition of specific teaching skills. No program can afford to concentrate so exclusively on the acquisition of knowledge that it ignores or slights the "practice" dimension of teaching. Whereas the knowledge components involved in teacher preparation focus on the contexts or situations that confront teachers, the skills component focuses directly on the trainees — on the observation, analysis, and modification of their teaching behavior.

The Teacher As Decision Maker

We have examined briefly four general areas of competence in which teachers must develop proficiency to be effective. While this examination is useful for obtaining an overview of the basic components of a well-designed teacher education program, it does not provide any guidelines on what a teacher does when teaching. A model of the teacher and of the instructional process can provide some guidelines to help teachers better understand what they should be doing when they teach. For this purpose, we shall examine the model of the teacher as a decision maker.

First consider the following situation. You are a middle school social studies teacher. You want to teach your students what a protective tariff is. What decisions must you make before this can be accomplished? First, *you have to decide exactly what you want them to know about protective tariffs.* You probably will want them to know how protective tariffs differ from revenue tariffs, why countries impose protective tariffs, how other countries are likely to respond, and who benefits and who suffers when protective tariffs are imposed.

Second, *you must decide what student behavior you will accept as evidence that the students understand protective tariffs and their ramifications.* Will they have to repeat a definition from memory? Will they have to give examples? Will they have to analyze a hypothetical situation and describe the pros and cons of imposing a protective tariff?

Third, *you will have to plan a strategy for obtaining the desired pupil learning.* Will you have the students do some reading? Will you lecture to them? Will you show them some audiovisual materials? How many examples will you need to show them? What provisions will you make for those students who don't understand? How much time will you allot for this learning activity?

Fourth, *as you teach the lesson, you will have to decide, based on student reactions, which parts of your strategy to adjust.* Are the students responding in the manner you thought? Are there any new classroom developments that will force you to change your tactics or the decisions you had previously made?

Fifth, *you will need to evaluate the impact and outcomes of your teaching.* Have the students satisfactorily demonstrated that they understand what protective tariffs are? If not, what is the deficiency in their understanding? What can you do about it? How effective were the strategies you used to teach the concept?

All these questions require decisions from alternative choices. Even the initial decision to teach the concept of protective tariffs required a choice from other social studies concepts. As this example demonstrates, the teacher is constantly making decisions with regard to student learning and appropriate instructional strategies.

What kinds of decisions? In the example of the protective tariff, you would have to decide how the students would best learn the characteristics of protective tariffs, based on their previous learning experiences. If you had decided to lecture, you would be predicting that, given the particular students and the available material, they would learn best through a lecture method.

Suppose that midway through the lecture you pick up cues from the students that they are not really understanding the concept of a protective tariff. It may be that they weren't ready to understand the concept, or it might be that your lecture was ineffective. Now you have to decide whether to continue, try a different strategy, or reintroduce the concept later. The various steps of this decision-making model are depicted in Figure 1.1. Within the instructional role, teachers must make decisions related to the three basic teaching functions shown in Figure 1.1: (1) planning, (2) implementation, and (3) evaluation.

The *planning* function requires that teachers make decisions about their students' needs, the most appropriate goals and objectives to help

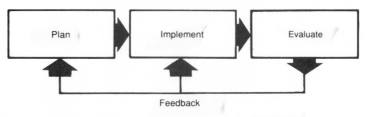

FIGURE 1.1   Model of the teacher as decision maker

meet those needs, the motivation necessary to attain their goals and objectives, and the instructional modes and teaching strategies most suited to the attainment of those goals and objectives. The planning function usually occurs when teachers are alone and have time to consider long- and short-range plans, the students' progress toward achieving objectives, the availability of materials, the time requirements of particular activities, and other such issues. Some teaching skills that support the planning function include observing pupil behavior, diagnosing pupil needs, setting goals and objectives, sequencing goals and objectives, and determining appropriate learning activities related to the objectives.

The *implementation* function requires that teachers implement the decisions that were made in the planning stage, particularly those related to instructional modes, teaching strategies, and learning activities. While much of the planning function is accomplished when teachers are alone, the implementation function occurs when teachers are interacting with students. Teaching skills that support the implementation function include presenting and explaining, listening, introducing, demonstrating, eliciting student responses, and achieving closure.

The *evaluation* function requires decisions about the suitability of chosen objectives as well as the teaching strategies keyed to those objectives and, ultimately, whether or not the students are achieving what the teacher intended. To make the necessary decisions, teachers must determine what kind of information they need and then gather it. Teaching skills that support the evaluation function include specifying the learning objectives to be evaluated; describing the information needed to make such evaluation; obtaining, analyzing, and recording that information; and forming judgments.

The *feedback* dimension of the decision-making model simply means that you examine the results of your teaching and then decide how adequately you handled each of these three teaching functions. On the basis of this examination, you determine whether you have succeeded in attaining your objectives or whether you need to make new plans or try different implementation strategies. Feedback, then, is the new information you process into your decision making to adjust your planning, implementation, or evaluation functions, or to continue on the same basis. It is the decision-making system's way of correcting itself.

The model of the teacher as a decision maker has been introduced as a way of conceptualizing the instructional role of the teacher. Admittedly, this conceptualization is a simplification of what occurs in teaching, but that is why models are useful. They allow us to see the forest without being confused by the trees.

This particular model represents a theory of teaching and makes several basic assumptions. First, the model assumes that teaching is goal directed; that is, some change in the students' thinking or behavior is sought. Second, the model assumes that teachers are active shapers of their own behavior. They make plans, implement them, and continually adjust to new information concerning the effects of their actions. Third, the model assumes that teaching is basically a rational process that can be improved by examining its components in an analytical manner. It assumes teachers can control the feedback process by selecting both the amount and kind of feedback to use. Fourth, the model assumes that teachers, by their actions, can influence students to change their own behavior in desired ways. Stated another way, the model assumes that teaching behavior can affect student behavior and learning.

There are other models that depict the teacher's role differently and are based on different assumptions about effective teaching; however, this model was selected as the organizing rubric of this book because of the model's simplicity and its power to capture the essence of what teachers do in the instructional process. Teachers are professionals who are educated and trained to make and implement decisions.

The four general areas of teacher competence, identified by Smith and discussed earlier, represent the broad categories of preparation that teachers need to make intelligent, effective decisions. Thus, competence in theoretical knowledge about learning, attitudes that foster learning and positive human relationships, knowledge in the subject matter to be taught, and a repertoire of teaching skills provide teachers with the tools necessary to make and implement professional judgments and decisions. Figure 1.2 depicts this relationship.

As you think about Figure 1.2, it should become obvious to you that people may strive toward mastery of the decision-making model without ever achieving it. To achieve mastery would require total command of the four general areas of competence and the ability to apply expertly the knowledge, attitudes, and skills acquired in each instructional decision. Even if decision making cannot be mastered, teachers can become increasingly competent at it and, consequently, become increasingly effective with their students.

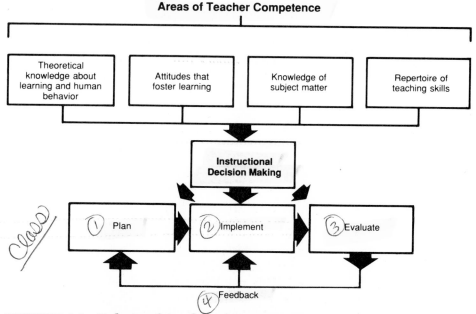

FIGURE 1.2 Relationship of teacher-competence areas to process of instructional decision making

How Are Teaching Skills Acquired?

Classroom Teaching Skills is designed to equip you with a repertoire of teaching skills crucial to the decision-making process. Without such a repertoire of skills, your decision-making alternatives are severely reduced. The skills chosen for this book are skills supported by many teacher educators on the basis of their own teaching experience and their diagnosis of the teacher's role as a decision maker, as well as evidence provided by educational research. These skills are complex, not simple, ones. Their acquisition requires both careful study and diligent practice. This book is designed to start you thinking about the skills; understanding their purposes and how they fit into the instructional act; and practicing their application in analytical, simulated, or classroom situations. It will be up to you and your instructors to provide opportunities where you can practice the skills in more complex and realistic situations, eventually practicing them in a classroom context with students.

How does one go about learning complex teaching skills so that they become part of one's teaching style? Bryce Hudgins has described very well a three-stage process of complex skill acquisition.[6] The first phase is a *cognitive* one. The learner must form a cognitive map of the skill he is to learn. He should know the purpose of the skill and how it will benefit him. Further, this cognitive phase helps the learner to isolate the various skill elements, their sequencing, and the nature of the final performance. As Hudgins says, "[T]his is a time when the learning of the student can be facilitated by assisting him to form a concept of what is contained in the skill, how its elements fit together, and how his present knowledge and experience can contribute (that is, transfer positively) to what he is to learn."[7]

The second phase for complex skill acquisition is *practice.* We have all heard the old saying, "Practice makes perfect." While this statement may not take into account many other requisites, it is certainly true that complex skills cannot be learned without a good deal of practice. The seemingly effortless motion of an Olympic swimmer is not acquired without thousands of miles of practice swimming. Similarly, the skill of driving a car is not learned without a lot of practice. So too, with complex teaching skills.

The third phase for acquiring a complex skill is *knowledge of results.* Practice will not really make perfect unless the persons trying to acquire the skill receive feedback regarding their performance. This point has been repeatedly demonstrated in psychological experiments where subjects are given great amounts of practice in a given skill but are deprived of any feedback regarding their performance. Without such feedback their performance does not improve, while other subjects, whose practice of the same skill includes feedback, do improve upon their initial performance.

Since learning complex teaching skills requires (1) cognitive understanding, (2) practice, and (3) knowledge of performance (feedback), any teacher-training materials aimed at developing such skills should incorporate these three conditions into their design. This book has such a design. *Classroom Teaching Skills* is also self-contained; that is, you can acquire conceptual aspects of a particular skill without reliance on outside instructors, materials, or the availability of a group of students to teach. There will be times, however, when you will be asked to work with some of your peers and provide feedback to one another.

You might be asking yourself, "Can complex teaching skills really be mastered in the absence of pupils to be taught?" Ultimately, no, but there

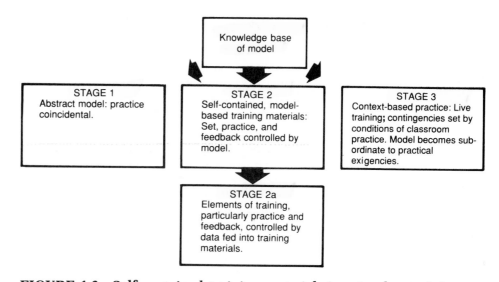

FIGURE 1.3   Self-contained training materials in a teacher-training sequence. Figure shows (1) the dependence of training materials on an adequate knowledge base for the model and (2) the position of the materials as the reality dimension of training is varied.

are various intermediate stages that are helpful to go through as you acquire skills. Hudgins has presented these stages in Figure 1.3.* Stage 1 involves a conceptual understanding of the skill, its elements, their sequence, and the nature of the final performance. Usually this first stage is accomplished by reading about the skill and its elements and/or by seeing the skill demonstrated and having its various elements explained. It does not normally involve practice.

Stage 2 is accomplished through self-contained training materials directed at each of the major elements comprising a model of the skill. Appropriate feedback must also be provided for each of the elements within the model. The training materials should themselves be prepared in accordance with the elements of the model.

Stage 2a requires that the practice exercises contained in the training materials be developed around data obtained from studies of children. In other words, practice situations, drawn from actual data, should be used to make them as realistic as possible and highly transferable to classrooms.

Stage 3 represents classroom situations where the skill can be practiced with students. This is the context where the teacher tries to "put it all together," and receives feedback on his or her performance. The importance of Stages 2 and 2a becomes apparent when one thinks of moving directly from Stage 1 to Stage 3. Reading about the skill and then immediately practicing it in a classroom is analogous to reading a manual on how to operate an automobile and then taking it out into heavy traffic to practice. Obviously, no responsible driver educator would use this proce-

---

*From Bryce B. Hudgins, "Self-Contained Training Materials for Teacher Education: A Derivation from Research on the Learning of Complex Skills," Report 5, National Center for the Development of Training Materials in Teacher Education (Bloomington, Indiana: School of Education, Indiana University), 1974, p. 23. Reprinted by permission.

dure. Instead, the learners would be required to practice various elements in simulated or controlled situations before allowing them to take a car out alone.

Because teacher education has lacked the training materials needed to develop basic teaching skills, beginning teachers have traditionally been asked to move directly from Stage 1 to Stage 3. Sometimes the teacher has succeeded in spite of these circumstances, but in many instances, the results have been disastrous. Although ultimately you must exercise these skills with students in real teaching situations, your probability of success will be greatly increased if you first develop a thorough understanding of the skill and its elements, have controlled practice situations which are reality-based, and receive feedback to adjust your performance in necessary ways.

The Book's Design

The purpose of *Classroom Teaching Skills* is to help you develop competence in selected teaching skills that are basic to implementing the decision-making model. To acquire these complex teaching skills, you will need to follow Hudgins's three-stage model. Accordingly, *Classroom Teaching Skills* incorporates Hudgins's model of complex skill acquisition in its design.

Each chapter in the book focuses on a particular teaching skill. Within each chapter, a cognitive map of the skill you are to acquire is provided. This cognitive map includes the purpose of the skill, its various elements and their sequencing, and the nature of the final performance.

Each chapter consists of self-contained materials that require practice and provide you with feedback on your efforts. If circumstances permit it, your instructor may also provide you with opportunities to practice these skills in classroom contexts.

To develop smoothness and a high level of competence in teaching skills, far more practice is necessary than can be provided in this book. If you are an elementary school teacher, many of these skills must be practiced within the context of different subject matter areas. Your competence in questioning skills, for example, is partially a product of your knowledge of the subject about which you are asking questions. Using our previous example, if you know little about protective tariffs, you are not likely to ask stimulating and provocative questions about that topic.

Format of Each Chapter

Each chapter is written with a common format that contains (1) a set of objectives, (2) a rationale, (3) learning materials and activities, and (4) mastery tests.

1. Objectives.   The objectives, stated in terms of learner outcomes, specify the competency or competencies you will be expected to demonstrate. Wherever it is appropriate, the objectives will be arranged in a learning hierarchy, leading you from relatively simple objectives to more complex ones.

2. Rationale.   The rationale describes the purpose and importance of the objectives within the chapter. It attempts to explain why you should want to spend your time acquiring the competencies the chapter is designed to produce. The rationale is considered important because, if you are not convinced that the particular skill you are being asked to develop is important to effective teaching, then it is unlikely that you will be willing to spend the time and effort needed to acquire competence in that skill.

3. Reading Materials and Activities.   Each objective has an accompanying set of reading materials written specifically for that objective. In addition, some of the authors have provided backup activities for those who want additional work on a particular objective. The nature of the reading materials and activities varies depending on the specific objective for which they were constructed.

4. Mastery Tests.   Each chapter contains mastery tests with answer keys to enable you to assess whether or not you have achieved the objectives. These mastery tests assess your learning after you have completed the reading and backup activities related to each objective. This technique allows you to discover immediately after completing each section whether or not you have met the objective satisfactorily. In addition, at the end of some of the chapters there are final mastery tests that serve as a last check on your achievement.

This format (objectives, rationale, learning activities, and mastery tests) has been successfully tested in hundreds of teacher education programs. It is an efficient design because all the materials are geared to help students achieve the stated objectives. Extraneous and inconsequential materials are eliminated, allowing students to make best use of their time. If used properly, the format increases the probability that you will be able to acquire a beginning level of competency in these basic teaching skills.

Description of the Skills

Skills were included in this book on the basis of their importance in implementing the decision-making model of instruction. While other skills might have been included, those that were selected are among the most crucial to the model.

As you will recall, the three basic elements of the decision-making model are to plan, to implement, and to evaluate. Each skill is important in carrying out at least one of these three functions. Some skills are useful for more than one function. The nine skills that make up this book are:

Plan
- Planning
- Instructional objectives

Implement
- Presentation skills
- Questioning
- Concept learning and higher-level thinking
- Interpersonal communication
- Classroom management
- Cooperative learning

Evaluate
- Evaluation

Planning.   Planning is perhaps the most important function a teacher performs — the whole decision-making model is based on this skill. In Chapter 2, Greta Morine-Dershimer emphasizes the key characteristics of productive planning. On the basis of research studies, Morine-Dershimer examines the differences in how novice and expert teachers plan. Expert teachers establish and effectively use routines such as collecting homework, distributing materials, and calling on students. They also have repertoires of alternative routines and procedures to use for different situations. Instead of having only one way of accomplishing an objective, expert teachers plan for and execute different procedures as needed. Morine-Dershimer also examines characteristics of effective lesson and unit plans by comparing teacher planning to dramatic productions, including the use of scripts, scenes, and improvisation.

Instructional Objectives.   Writing instructional objectives is a basic planning skill. By specifying instructional objectives, teachers define their purposes in terms that are clear and understandable. In Chapter 3, Terry TenBrink makes the distinction between well-written and poorly written objectives. Opportunities are provided within the chapter to (1) write well-defined instructional objectives, (2) write objectives for a specified unit of instruction, (3) use instructional objectives in planning, and (4) use objectives in implementing instruction. Well-written instructional objectives enable teachers to plan and implement their instructional strategies. The success of teachers' implementation skills greatly depends on the thoughtfulness and clarity of their instructional objectives.

Presentation Skills.   In Chapter 4, Robert Shostak presents four basic presentation skills — set induction, explaining, closure, and lectures — which research studies have demonstrated to be important components of effective presentations. Set induction refers to teacher-initiated actions or statements that are designed to establish a communicative link between the experiences of students and the objectives of the lesson. Explaining is planned teacher talk to clarify any idea, procedure, or process not understood by a student. Closure refers to those teacher actions or statements designed to bring a lesson presentation to an appropriate conclusion. Lecturing is, of course, a well-recognized teaching skill, although stimulating and effective lectures are all too infrequent occurrences. The effective use of these four skills will help establish and maintain student interest in the lesson, and will ensure that the main part of the lesson has been learned.

Questioning.   Probably no teaching behavior has been studied as much as questioning. This is not surprising because most educators agree that questioning strategies and techniques are key tools in the teacher's repertoire of interactive teaching skills. In Chapter 5, Myra and David Sadker chose Bloom's *Taxonomy of Educational Objectives: Cognitive Domain* as their system for classifying questions because it is the most widely used cognitive classification system in education. They designed their chapter (1) to classify and construct questions according to the six levels of Bloom's *Taxonomy* and (2) to describe the nature and dynamics of four teaching techniques (wait time, probing questions, rewarding students, and equity in interaction) that can increase the quantity and quality of student responses. If the skills presented in this chapter are utilized in teaching, the net effect will be students who are more active participants in the learning process.

Concept Learning and Higher-level Thinking.   How people learn concepts and how teachers can facilitate student acquisition of concepts and higher-level thinking are the focus of Chapter 6. Concepts, as used in the chapter, are: (1) categories into which our experiences are organized and (2) the larger network of intellectual relationships brought about as a result of the categorization process. As Peter Martorella points out, our view of reality depends on our conceptual network. A primary task of every teacher is to help students gain an understanding of the world both by teaching new concepts and by fitting new phenomena into already existing concepts. Without mutual understanding of concepts and their meanings, communication with one another would be impossible. The organization of concepts into cognitive structures, known as schemata, provides the basis for higher-level thinking. Martorella identifies several instructional strategies that promote higher-level thinking.

Interpersonal Communication.   "He knows his subject matter, but he just can't seem to relate to his students." At one time or another most of us have had a teacher who would fit this description. While much of a teacher's success in relating to students is difficult to explain and even more difficult to teach, some specific behaviors that stimulate personal inquiry can be taught and should contribute positively to the effective climate of the classroom. In Chapter 7, Sandra Sokolove Garrett, Myra Sadker, and David Sadker define interpersonal communication skills as a series of specific behaviors that stimulate personal inquiry — inquiry that leads to greater self-knowledge and eventually to more precise and meaningful communication. Teachers who successfully employ the skills of *attending behavior, active listening, reflection, inventory questioning,* and *encouraging alternative behaviors* will help their students gain greater self-knowledge and become more effective communicators — two vital steps toward better human relations.

Classroom Management.   No problem concerns beginning teachers more than the problem of classroom management. Most new teachers are worried about not being able to control their students and are aware that lack of control will impede effective instruction. Few areas in teacher education curriculums have been neglected as much as classroom management. The major reason for this neglect has been that educators had a poor systematic understanding of classroom dynamics; however, our knowledge in this area has expanded to the point where systematic instruction in classroom management is now possible.

In Chapter 8, Will Weber emphasizes that teachers need to establish and maintain proper learning environments. While the purpose of teaching is to stimulate desired student learning, the purpose of classroom management is to establish the conditions that best promote student learning. Classroom management skills are necessary for effective teaching to occur, but they do not guarantee such behavior. Weber examines several different philosophical positions regarding classroom management, including behavior modification, socioemotional climate, and group processes, and provides numerous opportunities for diagnosing classroom situations according to each of these three viewpoints.

Cooperative Learning.   One of the elements in the hidden curriculum of our schools is the emphasis on competition. Children learn how to compete with each other in numerous ways. Recently, the value of cooperation among learners to increase achievement levels has been recognized by educators. In Chapter 9, Mary Leighton examines various cooperative learning strategies, which research evidence supports, to help students significantly improve their academic achievement, as well as helping them to develop social skills.

Cooperative learning strategies are organized around systematic methods that usually involve presentations of information, student practice and coaching in learning teams, individual assessment of mastery, and public recognition of team success. The three key characteristics of cooperative learning strategies are group goals, individual accountability, and equal opportunities for success. In this chapter, several of the most widely used cooperative learning strategies are described in some detail.

Evaluation.   Evaluation and knowledge of results are essential if teachers are to improve their teaching effectiveness. The critical nature of evaluation is rarely disputed; nevertheless, few teachers receive adequate training in evaluation concepts and procedures. Terry TenBrink's chapter on evaluation focuses on critical components of the evaluation process. His basic position is that educational evaluation is useful only if it helps educators make decisions. (Again, the emphasis is on the teacher as a decision maker.)

TenBrink perceives evaluation as a four-stage process: (1) preparing for evaluation, (2) obtaining needed information, (3) forming judgments, and (4) using judgments in making decisions and preparing evaluation reports. Throughout the chapter, examples of problems and decisions that teachers are likely to face are used. Developing test items, checklists, and rating scales for evaluating student knowledge, products, and performance is a major focus of the chapter. This practical emphasis should make evaluation concepts and procedures for making better instructional decisions easier to understand and apply.

Notes

1. Myron Brenton, *What's Happened to Teacher?* (New York: Coward-McCann, 1970), p. 71.
2. David Ryans, *Characteristics of Teachers* (Washington, D.C.: American Council on Education, 1960).
3. J. W. Getzels and P. W. Jackson, "The Teacher's Personality and Characteristics," in *Handbook of Research on Teaching*, ed. N. L. Gage (Chicago: Rand McNally, 1963), p. 574.
4. Lee S. Shulman, "Knowledge and Teaching: Foundations of the New Reform," *Harvard Educational Review* 57 (February 1987): 8.
5. B. O. Smith, *Teachers for the Real World* (Washington, D.C.: American Association of Colleges for Teacher Education, 1969), p. 122.
6. Bryce B. Hudgins, "Self-Contained Training Materials for Teacher Education: A Derivation from Research on the Learning of Complex Skills," Report 5, National Center for the Development of Training Materials in Teacher Education (Bloomington, IN: School of Education, Indiana University), 1974.
7. *Ibid.*, pp. 5–6.

Additional Readings

Arends, Richard I. *Learning to Teach*, 2nd ed. New York: McGraw-Hill, Inc., 1991.

Fenstermacher, Gary D., and Jonas F. Soltis. *Approaches to Teaching*. New York: Teachers College Press, Columbia University, 1986.

Jackson, Philip W. *The Practice of Teaching*. New York: Teachers College Press, Columbia University, 1986.

Shavelson, Richard J. "What Is *The* Basic Teaching Skill?" *Journal of Teacher Education* 24 (Summer 1973): 144–149.

Shavelson, Richard J. "Review of Research on Teachers' Pedagogical Judgments, Plans, and Decisions." *The Elementary School Journal* 83, No. 4 (1983): 392–413.

Strike, Kenneth A., and Jonas F. Soltis. *The Ethics of Teaching.* New York: Teachers College Press, Columbia University, 1985.

Instructional Planning | 2

■ Greta G. Morine-Dershimer

1 Given a set of directions, to construct a concept map depicting a personal perspective of teacher planning, and to compare this concept map to those constructed by other prospective teachers

2 Given information from studies of the instructional planning of experienced teachers, to identify key characteristics of productive planning

3 Given a description of teacher planning analogous to a dramatic production, to generate additional analogies that highlight important aspects of teacher planning

To Plan Is Human . . .

All people engage in planning on a regular basis. We think in advance about things we want to do, and make preparations that enable us to do them. All planning has a future orientation, and all planning involves some intention for action to fulfill some purpose. According to one theory of planning, there are two important reasons why human beings plan in advance for many of our purposeful actions.[1] First, because humans are, to some extent, rational creatures — we tend to deliberate about what we do. But deliberation takes time, and at the moment when we must act, we rarely have time to deliberate at length about exactly how we want to act. So we deliberate in advance, deciding how we intend to act at some future point, and we call this deliberation *planning*. Second, because we live in groups and must relate to other people, we need to coordinate our own activities with those of others. Also, because we all play more than one role, we frequently need to coordinate these roles, engaging in a series of activities, which we must complete within a short space of time, and determining the best sequence in which to carry out these activities. We manage such coordination by constructing plans for future action.

What kinds of plans have you made for yourself today? Do you have several tasks that ought to be completed before you end your day? Have you thought that perhaps one of these tasks might be postponed until tomorrow? Is there someone that you need or want to see today? Have you arranged a time and place to meet them? Perhaps these types of everyday plans are such an established part of your life that you don't even think of them as planning.

Clearly, you have already had experience in making plans. But how effective are your plans? To what extent are they fully realized? If you are at all typical, many of your plans undergo some change before you put them into action. Because plans involve anticipation of future events, we can never specify fully what we will do at the point that we begin to act on our plan. Usually we begin with partial plans, and fill in more and more details as we get closer and closer to the time for action. This is an efficient way to proceed, for we can rarely predict future events with great accuracy.

Since you have probably been planning important events in your life for several years, you bring a useful experience to one of the most important tasks of teaching. In many ways, instructional planning requires the same skills as the everyday planning you already do. But the planning that a teacher must do is more complex, and this added complexity necessitates some special skills and knowledge. This chapter presents some information about these special skills and knowledge.

OBJECTIVE

1 Given a set of directions, to construct a concept map depicting a personal perspective of teacher planning, and to compare this concept map to those constructed by other prospective teachers

■ *Where Do We Start?*

A good place to start thinking about any relatively new topic is with your own ideas. What do you think is involved in teacher planning? One useful way to clarify and explicate your own ideas is to construct a *concept map.*[2] A concept map is a way of organizing your ideas about a particular topic so that the relationships you see among the various subtopics can be displayed visually.

Here is an example of how to proceed. If you want to construct a concept map on the topic of "leisure activities," you first list all the things related to this topic that come to mind, for example:

Bicycling
Canoeing
Cross-country skiing
Downhill skiing
Dancing
Choral singing
Movies
Reading science fiction
Reading Agatha Christie books
Reading Ngaio Marsh books
Reading P. D. James books
Reading Dick Francis books
Reading John McDonald books
Doing daily newspaper crossword puzzles
Doing the Sunday *Times* crossword puzzle
Hiking
Swimming
Playing cribbage
Playing poker
Playing hearts
Playing Trivial Pursuit
Playing softball
Playing volleyball

The list could be longer, but this is long enough to show what a list might include. Someone else's list of things associated with leisure activities would undoubtedly be different because everyone has different ideas about what's fun.

After making a list of ideas, the next step is to organize those ideas so that similar items are grouped together. For instance, you could group together reading books by Agatha Christie, Ngaio Marsh, and P. D. James, and call this group "reading mystery stories." You could group together playing cribbage, poker, hearts, and Trivial Pursuit, and call the group "playing indoor games." Playing softball and playing volleyball could be combined and called "playing outdoor games," or "team games." There are many alternate ways that the items could be grouped together. For example, reading Dick Francis books could be grouped together with reading John McDonald books, and called "reading adventure books." Or reading Dick Francis books could be grouped with reading books by Agatha Christie, Ngaio Marsh, and P. D. James, and called "reading books by English authors." Since the grouping is done to represent your ideas, there is no one right way to do it.

After some initial groups are formed, they can be combined to form a larger group. For instance, a larger group of "reading books" could be formed to include subgroups of science fiction, mystery, and adventure books. This larger group ("reading books") could be combined with another group of "doing crossword puzzles," to form a still larger group of "sedentary activities."

The final step in constructing a concept map is to place the groups and subgroups in a graphic display around the central topic to show how they are related to each other and to the topic. Your final concept map of "Leisure activities" could look something like the map in Figure 2.1. Mine might have some of the same groups, with different details or subgroups, or some completely different groups. Every concept map on a given topic

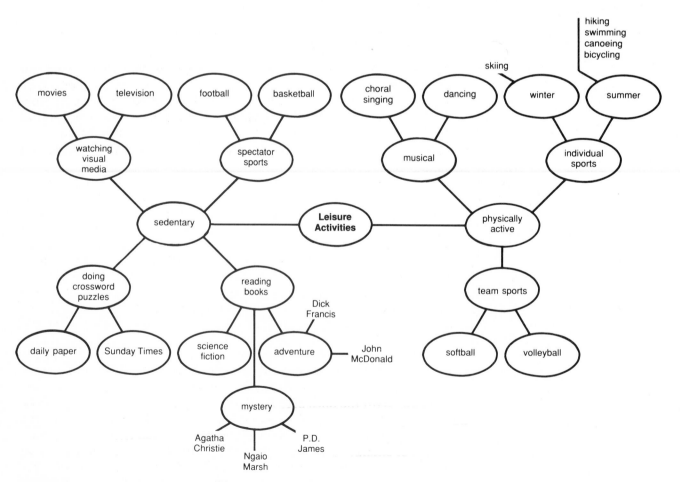

FIGURE 2.1   A concept map of leisure activities

should be somewhat different from others on the same topic because concept maps are designed to display the ideas of individuals.

Learning Activity 1

To construct a concept map of your ideas about teacher planning, follow the same procedures indicated in the above example. First, make a list of all the words and phrases you associate with the topic of teacher planning. Second, group the items in your list together in some way that makes sense to you, and label your groups to indicate what characteristic the items in the group have in common. Third, combine your initial groups to form larger, more inclusive groups. Finally, draw a concept map that shows how your groups and subgroups relate to each other and to the major topic of teacher planning.

Before you read any further in this chapter, you should construct a concept map of your ideas about teacher planning. Then you will have an opportunity to compare your ideas about teacher planning to the ideas of other prospective teachers, to see how typical or unique your thinking might be. Later, as you read further in this chapter and in this book, you can see how the information presented relates to the ideas about instructional planning that you already have.

■ *Concept Mapping: Before and After*

One of the most interesting things about people is that their ideas can change. One of the most interesting things about concept maps is that they can help us trace how our ideas change as a result of education and experience. In this section, you will examine before and after concept maps of elementary and secondary prospective teachers to see what changes occurred in their thinking about teacher planning as a result of planning and teaching a series of lessons.

The students whose ideas are presented were all enrolled in a teacher preparation program at Syracuse University. They constructed their initial concept maps at the beginning of a course on strategies of teaching. During the course, they engaged in peer teaching in addition to reading and discussing information about various important aspects of planning and teaching. Each student planned a series of three or four lessons on a given topic, using different instructional procedures in each lesson.[3] They taught these lessons to small groups of their peers. The students who were elementary education majors also had an opportunity during the semester to plan and teach several lessons to small groups of children in public school settings. At the end of the class, each student constructed a new concept map to show how their concepts of teacher planning had changed. Pre and post (before and after) maps for two of these students are presented in this section. You should find it interesting to compare your own "before map" with the ones presented here, as well as with those of fellow students in your own teacher preparation program. In addition, you will be asked to compare the pre and post maps presented here to determine what kinds of changes you can observe in the thinking of these prospective teachers. These changes occurred as a result of their coursework and practice in planning and carrying out their plans for instruction.

YOUR TURN

Considering Two Cases

Two Cases

Carol was an elementary education major working for dual certification in special education. She had had some prior experience working with children in special education classes. Her pre and post maps of teacher planning are presented in Figures 2.2 and 2.3. During the semester in which she did these maps, she taught a series of language arts lessons to a group of her peers. She also taught reading for two weeks to small groups of pupils in a fourth grade inner-city classroom, and later taught math to small groups of pupils in a second grade suburban classroom.

Ted was a secondary education major working on a masters degree in social studies education. He had done his undergraduate work in business administration. His pre and post maps of teacher planning are presented in Figures 2.4 and 2.5. Between constructing these two maps, he taught four lessons to a group of his peers on the general topic of the free enterprise system. At the end of his peer teaching experience, he began student teaching, teaching social studies to eighth and ninth graders in a suburban middle school.

Comparing and Contrasting. The pre maps of these two prospective teachers have some elements in common. What terms or ideas (an idea that is basically similar may be expressed in different terms) can you identify as common to the two pre maps? Why do you suppose there are so few common elements? Which of the terms or ideas on either of these two pre maps are also included in your own pre map? Can you think of any reasons why these ideas about teacher planning might be shared by some prospective teachers?

What are some differences in the pre maps of these two students? How might their prior experiences have contributed to these differences? You may observe differences in substance (for example, central ideas) or differences in structure (for example, how many "levels" of detail are included, how/whether relationships among subtopics are indicated). How does your own map differ from the two pre maps presented here? Can you identify anything in your own background or experience that might lead you to focus on different features of planning, or to construct a map somewhat differently from other prospective teachers?

Consider the pre and post maps for each of the two students in turn. What changes do you see? What new ideas have emerged? Do these new ideas appear to be common to the two students? What ideas seem to have been eliminated or dropped? How might the teaching experience of each of these students have contributed to the changes you observe? For example, do you observe any differences in the post map of Carol, who had some elementary classroom teaching experience, compared with the post map of Ted, who had only peer teaching experience prior to completing his post map? After studying these post maps, how do you think your own concept map might change, given some practice in planning and teaching lessons in a peer teaching or classroom setting?

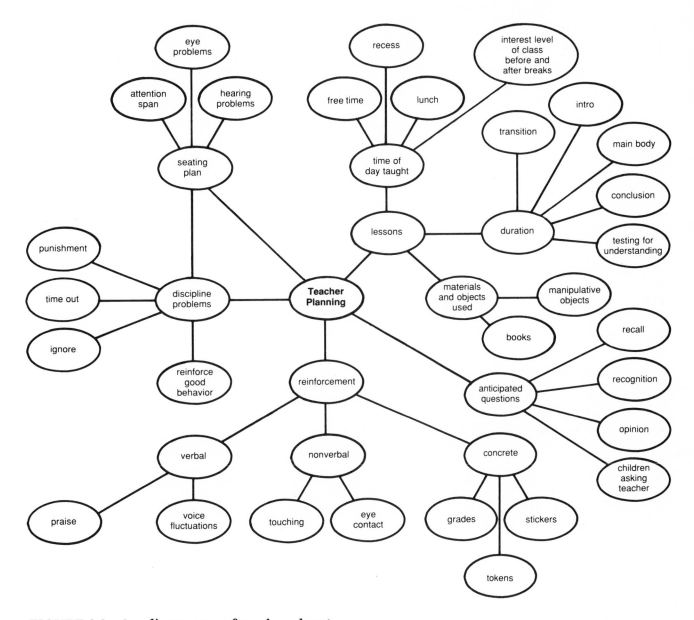

FIGURE 2.2 Carol's pre map of teacher planning

In Their Own Words. The two students whose pre and post concept maps you have been analyzing compared their maps and noted similarities and differences. Here are some of their comments.

Carol: My final map was much more detailed than my first map. Some topics are similar, but the topics that I stated earlier tend to fall under other categories now, rather than being a major category themselves. I have kept the same ideas about problem behaviors [techniques for handling them]. The differences between my two maps [first and final] are very readily apparent. I am now more aware of the strategies behind effective teaching. I realize the different kinds of thinking processes that take place in children. I am more concerned with student involvement and their participation in lessons. I learned a great deal about the makeup of a lesson plan. I know that a teacher has to be thoroughly prepared to successfully teach, with a thorough statement of materials, goals, procedures, and questions to be asked. By consider-

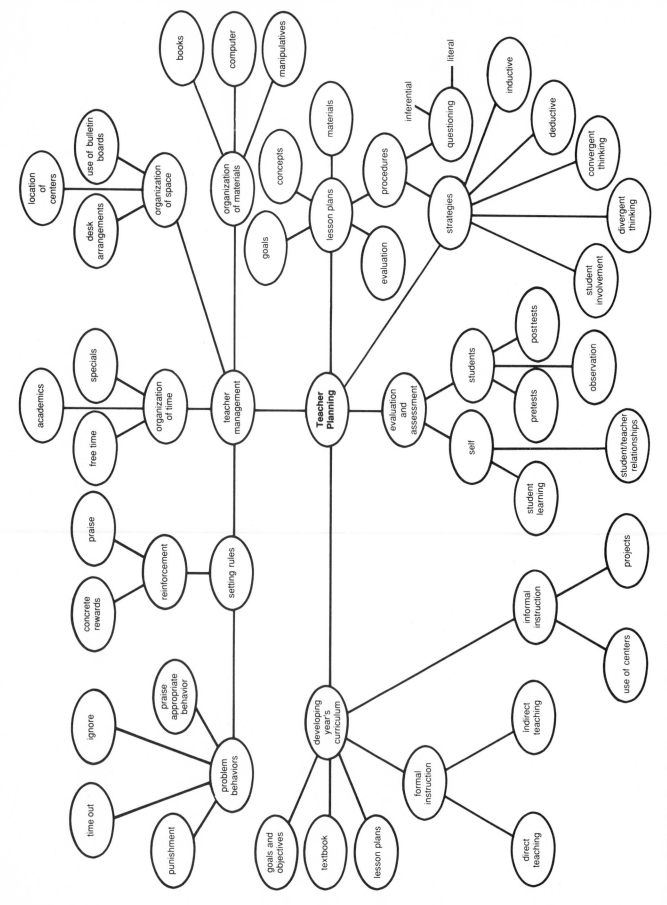

FIGURE 2.3   Carol's post map of teacher planning

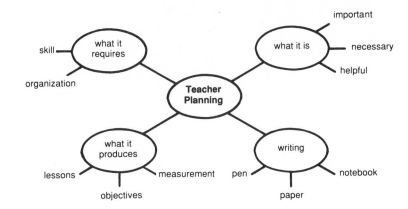

FIGURE 2.4   Ted's pre map of teacher planning

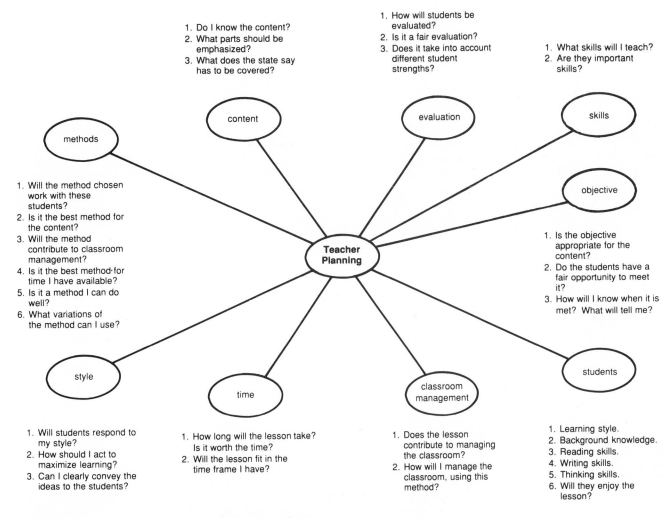

FIGURE 2.5   Ted's post map of teacher planning

ing management techniques within this planning, learning can be facilitated even more. Obviously, due to my field placements and my academic classes, my ideas have changed.

Ted: Two months ago I didn't know what teacher planning was. This showed in my pre concept map with its skeletal nature. My post map focuses on what goes into teacher planning. I thought of all these things and how they are related to each other and affect each other — that any change in one component affects another. These components of teacher planning do not stand independently. Two months ago I thought they did. The peer teaching and the preparation that went into it helped open my eyes to all that is important. I was no longer watching teacher planning, but doing it. If I failed to plan for any of these components, my lesson turned out not to be as good.

Patterns of Change.   Carol's and Ted's experiences are not unique. They illustrate patterns of changes in thinking about teacher planning that have been identified in studies of prospective teachers like yourself. As students engage in planning and teaching lessons, they increase their awareness of the many elements to be considered in conducting a successful lesson, identify the relationships among these various elements, and reorganize their ideas to give priority to different aspects of teaching.

The pre and post concept maps presented here are evidence of *professional development*. A *professional* is a person who possesses some specialized knowledge and skills, can weigh alternatives, and can select from among a number of potentially productive actions one that is particularly appropriate in a given situation. The post concept maps of these soon-to-be-professional teachers show that they have begun to develop specialized knowledge, specialized skills, an awareness of alternatives, and a sense of the situational characteristics to be considered in determining which alternative to choose. For example, the use of terms like *convergent thinking, divergent thinking, inferential questioning,* and *literal questioning* on Carol's post map shows that she is developing a technical vocabulary to represent specialized professional skills and knowledge. The questions raised on Ted's post map ("Is the objective appropriate for the content?," "Will the method chosen work with these students?," "Is it the best method for the content?," "Will the method contribute to classroom management?," "Is it the best method for the time I have available?," "Will the students respond to my teaching style?") show that he has developed an awareness of alternatives, as well as a sense of some situational characteristics to be considered in choosing from among instructional alternatives.

These examples provide evidence that these two prospective teachers are beginning to think and act like professionals. You should be able to observe similar changes in your own knowledge, skills, and awareness of alternatives as you progress through this book. Many of the terms you noted in the concept maps presented here are introduced and discussed in detail later: objectives (Chapter 3), questioning (Chapter 5), concepts (Chapter 6), classroom management (Chapter 8), cooperative learning (Chapter 9), and evaluation (Chapter 10). Lesson presentation skills (Chapter 4) and interpersonal communication skills (Chapter 7) are necessary to carry out your instructional plans successfully.

When you have finished the reading and activities in this book, you should construct another concept map of teacher planning. When you compare your own pre and post maps, you will have solid evidence of your own professional development.

OBJECTIVE   **2** Given information from studies of the instructional planning of experienced teachers, to identify key characteristics of productive planning

Myths and Realities

Many people believe that planning is one of the most important skills a teacher can have, and that teachers who plan better must also teach better. Some people think that planning is something teachers do in the quiet of their classrooms — before pupils arrive for the day or after they leave for the night. Others may suspect that many teachers never really plan at all, except to write down the page numbers of the textbook to be covered each day. The truth, of course, is that none of these views is completely accurate.

The myths about teacher planning are legion. Unfortunately, they are influential in determining what prospective teachers learn about the process of planning. Which of the following statements are myths, and which are probably accurate descriptions of the reality of teacher planning?

Everybody's doing it.
A little goes a long way.
A plan a day keeps disaster away.
Plans are made to be broken.
One size fits all.
Don't look back!
Try it — you'll like it.

Fifteen years ago, it would have been difficult to determine which of these statements were myths and which were realities. Little was known about how teachers went about planning in their classrooms. In recent years, however, a number of researchers have observed and interviewed teachers as they were engaged in instructional planning. While there is still much to be learned, a useful base of knowledge has been established.

Everybody's Doing It — In a Variety of Ways

Teachers do plan, and they plan in a variety of ways. There are four basic types of planning in which teachers regularly engage: yearly, unit, weekly, and daily planning.[4] All are important for effective instruction.

While all teachers plan, they do not all plan in exactly the same way.[5] Some may jot down a few notes in a lesson plan book. Others may write outlines detailing lessons or units they intend to teach. Many teachers write more detailed daily plans for their substitutes than they do for themselves, wanting to ensure that established routines are understood and maintained. Teachers who have embraced the computer age may keep a file of lesson or unit plans stored on disks, and update or revise these each year to fit new circumstances.

Studies have shown that few experienced teachers plan precisely according to the procedures recommended by curriculum experts for many years.[6] Rather than beginning by stating instructional objectives, and then selecting and organizing instructional activities to meet those objectives, many elementary teachers begin by considering the context in which teaching will occur (for example, the instructional materials and time available), then think about activities that will interest and involve their pupils, and finally note the purposes that these activities will serve. Secondary teachers focus almost exclusively on content and preparation of an interesting presentation. This does not mean that teachers have no real goals, but it does suggest that a basic consideration for most teachers is maintaining the interest and involvement of their pupils. Since research has shown that pupil attention and on-task behavior is associated with achievement,[7] pupil involvement is important for teachers to keep in mind when planning for instruction.

A Little Goes a Long Way — Especially at the Beginning

The tricky thing about teacher planning is that one kind of plan is *nested* within another. This means that plans made at the beginning of the year have important effects on the weekly and daily plans that will be made throughout the year. Before the students ever enter the room, most teachers have planned the physical arrangement of the classroom: where and how students will be seated, where materials will be kept, what areas will be set up as centers for particular types of activities, and how bulletin board or wall space will be utilized. Decisions about daily and weekly scheduling of subjects are usually completed by the end of the first week of school. Within the first few weeks, student abilities are assessed and plans are made for instructional grouping. Classroom rules or management procedures are also established during these early weeks. Not all of these plans are made by individual teachers in isolation. A grade level or subject area team may work together to schedule classes or group pupils. General time schedules and rules for student behavior may be determined by school administrators. Wherever these plans originate, however, they will set the framework within which later plans will develop.

Many teachers identify unit planning as their most important type of planning.[8] Weekly and daily plans are nested within unit plans. Since teachers tend to focus on activities in their planning, unit plans serve to organize a flow of activities related to a general topic for an extended period of time (two weeks to a month, typically).

A Plan a Day Keeps Disaster Away — For Novice Teachers

Experienced teachers report that unit, weekly, and daily planning are the most important types of planning that they do during the year.[9] Few of them write out complete lesson plans on a regular basis, though they will make lesson plans when they are dealing with new content or curriculum materials. They do recommend, however, that student teachers and beginning teachers write lesson plans.[10] This suggests that lesson plans are particularly useful tools in less familiar teaching situations, such as working with new students, new subject matter, or new procedures. For novice teachers, all these aspects of teaching are new and unfamiliar, and lesson plans can be helpful.

In their daily planning, as well as in their yearly planning, experienced teachers rely heavily on curriculum guides and textbook materials to determine the content and pace of their lessons.[11] Plans for lessons may consist of selecting and adapting activities suggested in the textbook's teacher's guide so that these are particularly interesting or suitable for the instructional needs of their particular pupils. These teachers have established instructional routines over the years, and they fit these suggested activities into their routines; therefore, extensive planning of procedures does not seem as necessary. Novice teachers are in the process of developing routines, experimenting to see what procedures will work for them. More detailed planning of lessons is an essential activity at this stage of their professional development.

Plans Are Not Made to Be Broken — Just Bent

Lesson plans serve several important functions, and teachers say that one of the most important of these is using the plan as a guide for their interactions with students.[12] A written plan can ensure that directions are structured in exactly the right way when an activity is begun. A plan can operate like a secretary's "tickler file," reminding the teacher about what to do next if the rapid-fire interaction of the lesson causes a sudden lapse of memory. A plan can also provide a framework for later evaluation of a lesson, assisting the teacher in identifying productive learning activities.

Because a lesson plan can be such a useful guide, teachers rarely change their plans drastically in the middle of a lesson.[13] They do make adjustments in their plans as they are teaching, and effective teachers seem to be particularly capable at noting how certain pupils are reacting, and fine-tuning their procedures accordingly.[14] Some teachers seem to have a "steering group" of pupils who are in the low-average range of achievement, and they adjust the pace of their lessons depending on how well these students are doing.[15] Thus, lesson plans are not made to be broken, but flexible enough to bend a little when adjustments are needed.

One Size Fits All — But Not Very Well

Most lesson plans are designed to guide instruction for a whole class of students. Thus, the typical plan aims to motivate and involve the "average" student. But of course it is a rare student who fully exemplifies the profile of the average student, just as there are few people whose measurements exactly duplicate those used to design clothing for the average or medium-sized figure. Even a small group of students is made up of individuals who can exhibit a bewildering array of differences in characteristics that influence instruction, including academic performance, prior knowledge or experience, language acquisition, social skills, cultural background, physical development, intellectual ability, and home and family resources. No general lesson plan will be a perfect fit for every student in the class or group. In fact, it is the rare lesson plan that is a *perfect* fit for *any* individual student.

Most teachers make adaptations to accommodate to individual students as they implement their plans, but sometimes these adaptations are not carefully thought through. Some typical accommodations may have negative consequences for student learning. For example, studies show that many teachers call on boys to participate more frequently than girls,[16] presumably because they anticipate more off-task behavior from boys. Teachers also tend to wait longer for high achievers to answer a question, but provide less time for lower achievers to respond before redirecting the question or answering it themselves,[17] presumably expecting that only the higher achievers will figure out the answer for themselves if given time to think. White teachers have been observed to make negative judgments about the narrative style of black children (topic-associating style, moving from topic to topic rather than focusing on a single theme), and thus to interrupt their stories frequently to ask questions, while permitting white children, using a topic-centered style, to develop their stories without interruption.[18] These types of adaptations lead to unequal opportunities to learn, and unfortunately often provide extra advantages to students who already enjoy a preferred classroom status.

Classroom diversity compels teachers to make adaptations in their lesson plans to accommodate the instructional needs of individual students and thus promote the learning of all students. Such adaptations are more likely to be effective if they are consciously considered in advance. For example, specific activities designed to encourage student expression of personal feelings, experiences, and opinions *related to the subject matter* of the lesson can accommodate individual differences, celebrate diversity, and contribute to effective pupil achievement.[19] Lesson plans that regularly include such activities enable teachers to tailor their lessons to achieve a better fit for all students.

Do Look Back — It Helps in Planning Ahead

Experienced teachers report that, soon after a lesson has been taught, they do rethink it and consider how it might be improved or varied another time.[20] This helps them in planning future lessons. Looking back can be especially helpful in long-term planning, such as unit or yearly planning. Teachers who keep records of their plans from prior years can start by considering what activities or procedures worked well, and what revisions might be made in sequencing or selection of topics and activities. This is more efficient than starting from scratch every year, and it is an effective aid to teachers who want to improve by learning systematically from their own experience.

Try It — You'll Like It

Teachers report that, besides serving as a guide for interactions with students and as an organizational tool (assisting them to organize time, activities, and materials for a lesson), a lesson plan can provide them with a sense of security.[21] Security is a valuable commodity for a beginning teacher. A well-constructed lesson plan or unit plan can provide a strong foundation for a novice teacher, who may be more than a little shaky about those first few days and weeks with a new group of students.

Research has not demonstrated that teachers who write behavioral objectives or detailed lesson plans are more effective than those who state general goals or write sketchy lesson plans. But an early study of teacher planning did show that teachers whose pupils learned more made fewer broad, general statements in their plans than teachers whose pupils learned less.[22]

To summarize, while we still have much to learn about teacher planning, we do know that teachers think ahead; that they consider planning to be an essential activity; and that designing lessons and units is, for many teachers, one of the most interesting parts of teaching, providing them with an opportunity to use their imagination and ingenuity. We know that a great deal of variety exists in the ways different teachers approach planning. We also know that:

- Plans are nested, so that plans made to organize the classroom at the beginning of the year have a strong influence on later plans.
- Lesson plans of experienced teachers rely heavily on textbooks and curriculum guides, and make use of established routines for basic instructional and managerial activities in the classroom.
- Lesson plans of effective teachers are flexible enough to allow for fine tuning of procedures, adjusting to pupil responses to tasks.

Novices and Experts

Recently, research on teaching has begun to build on studies in cognitive psychology that compare the thinking of novices and experts in a given field. For example, some studies have compared beginning chess players with championship chess masters to note differences in the ways they think about the game as they play it. Expert chess players can recall and reproduce a position on a chess board far more accurately than novices,[23] but this superior memory performance operates only for meaningful information.[24] Studies of experts and novices in a variety of fields (for example, medicine, physics) indicate that experts recall meaningful information better than novices, and use different criteria to judge the relevancy or utility of the information that they perceive and remember.[25]

Some studies of teacher planning suggest that expert teachers are similar to experts in other fields in their patterns of thinking. One study compared the responses of novice and expert mathematics and science teachers on a simulated task in which they had to prepare to take on a new class five weeks after school had started. One of the major differences between experts and novices had to do with how they planned to begin. Experts concentrated on learning what students already knew by planning to have them work review problems and answer questions about their understanding of the subject matter covered so far. Novices planned to ask students where they were in the textbook, and then to present a review of important concepts. In other words, experts planned to gather information from students, and novices planned to give information to students. Expert teachers planned to "begin again" by explaining their expectations and classroom routines to students. Novices were more apt to ask students how the former teacher ran the classroom, with the implication that they would follow the same practices.

Expert and novice teachers differed in their judgments of the importance of different types of information. The most important information for experts was what students knew of the subject. The most important information for novices was what management system students were accustomed to following. Expert teachers planned to institute their own routines. Novices planned to adapt to someone else's routines. The expert teachers understood the nested nature of planning. They knew that the classroom management structures they adopted the first few days of class would shape the plans they would be able to make the rest of the year.

The Function of Routines

To some people, *routine* connotes dull, dreary, repetitive, unthinking behavior. Thus, the idea that establishing routines is important for instructional planning may be distasteful. But consider the relationship between routines and plans in your everyday life. What are your established routines as a student? Do you have a seat where you habitually sit in each of your classes? Do you have a time of the day or week when you usually read assignments? Do you have a place in the library or computer lab or in your room where you typically work when you have a paper to write? Do you have some materials that you regularly carry with you when you go to class? If you don't have some established routines for any of these activities, you are a rare person.

Everyday routines such as these are important in relation to planning our daily activities because they free our minds to think about other things. If you had to consider a number of alternatives and choose from among them every time you performed any action, you would soon be worn out from the constant decision making. Setting some patterns for your behavior enables you to concentrate on making the really important decisions. Having some established routines also makes it possible for others to predict your behavior to a certain degree. A friend who knows where you will probably sit in class can take the seat next to you, even if you haven't yet arrived.

Having established routines enables teachers to operate more efficiently for similar reasons. In planning lessons, a teacher who has a routine for collecting homework or distributing materials can concentrate on more important decisions about what information to present, or what questions to ask students. In conducting lessons, a teacher who has routines for calling on students to participate can more readily concentrate on listening to what the student has to say, rather than worrying about whom to call on next. Lesson routines also help to make teacher behavior predictable to students, and when students know what to expect, they are better able to concentrate on content, and are apt to learn more.

Routines can operate at several different levels of teacher planning. For example, at the level of planning for a unit of instruction, routines related to evaluation may include giving a pretest to identify what students already know, scheduling weekly quizzes to assess how well students are mastering concepts presented, and preparing a unit test to determine how much new knowledge students have gained. If students learn that these evaluations are a regular part of the teacher's units of instruction, they will prepare for weekly quizzes by learning material as they go along, rather than waiting and cramming for a final test.

At the level of planning for a daily lesson, routines related to a sequence of activities may include checking homework, presenting new information, conducting group practice with the new information through questioning and discussion, providing for individual supervised practice using new information in assigned seatwork, and providing for independent practice by assigning new homework. This is a pattern of lesson activities followed by many expert teachers of mathematics,[26] and it is a pattern found useful in improving student achievement in many studies of effective teaching.[27] When this sequence of activities is an established pattern for most lessons, the teacher can focus planning decisions on how best to explain and illustrate (with examples) the new information to be presented.

At the level of planning for specific activities within a lesson, management routines become important. When calling on students to participate, a teacher may regularly call only on volunteers when new information is first discussed, believing that volunteers are more apt to be able to answer questions accurately and thus move the lesson along at a lively pace. In the review portion of the lesson, however, the same teacher may use a routine of going up and down rows of students, calling on each in turn, as a way of checking whether all students clearly understand the material previously discussed. A teacher who has such established routines does not need to spend much time planning these specific details of a lesson. Students who become familiar with such routines pay more attention in initial presentations of information, knowing they can expect to be called on in a later review.

The Importance of Repertoire

Routines are an important part of teacher planning for instruction, but expert teachers do not rely on routines alone. Can you imagine an expert chess player who had only one routine way to make an opening move, or to respond to an opponent's opening move, in a chess match? A chess master has a repertoire of alternate ways to open a game, and for each opening move of an opponent, a repertoire of alternate responses. Because different actions are appropriate in different situations, expert teachers also have repertoires that they call on when necessary.

A *repertoire* is a set of alternate routines or procedures, all of which may serve some common, general purpose, and each of which may be particularly appropriate in a different situation. For example, a teacher may have a repertoire of procedures for classroom organization that includes whole class instruction, cooperative group work, individualized seatwork, and peer tutoring. Each of these classroom organizations can be effective in promoting student learning, but cooperative group work can be particularly effective for developing student independence, while supervised, individualized seatwork may be particularly effective for maximizing individual achievement gains. With a repertoire of procedures that are appropriate for different situations, a teacher does not need to spend hours of planning time to devise possible alternate actions. The repertoire provides a range of alternatives to be considered, and knowledge of the specific situation (for example, type of students to be taught, content to be learned, time available) enables the expert teacher to choose an alternative that fits the situation.

The Requirement for Practice

The reason that experts and novices see things differently in any field is that experts have a great deal of experience. With extensive experience in any activity, we learn what types of situations commonly arise, and which of our reactions to those situations work to our advantage and which do not. Experts recognize a new situation as being similar to a type of situation they have faced before, and quickly call on a repertoire of routines that they have used in the past. Novices face a new situation without much prior experience to draw on. They cannot quickly identify a situation as belonging to a familiar category of situations. Even if they could, they would not have an extensive repertoire of developed routines available to use in response to the situation. Novices can become experts with time, however; all experts began as novices. To become an expert requires a great deal of practice and thought.

Novice teachers are different from novices in other fields in one respect: they are already quite experienced in classroom settings. Most novice teachers are expert students. They have had years of practice at recognizing certain types of classroom situations from the student's perspective. They know which of their fellow students have ideas to contribute to class discussions, and they respond by listening carefully to those students. They quickly recognize the student who rambles on at length and says nothing, and will tune him or her out even on the first day of class. On meeting a new teacher, expert students rapidly determine whether assignments must be in on time, and if this is a requirement, they adjust their schedules to ensure that the work gets completed. As expert students, most novice teachers have a ready repertoire of classroom behaviors. To become expert teachers, they must develop a new perspective and a new repertoire of behaviors. And that requires additional practice.

Planning and Practice

Planning is an unusual kind of activity because it can never really be practiced unless a plan is carried out. We learn from practice only if we can get some feedback about the effectiveness of our actions. Can you imagine learning to bowl if there were a curtain across the end of the lane that made it impossible to see where your ball went, or how many pins you knocked down? Hours of practice without any information about the results of your actions would be useless. Practice in making instructional plans that you never try out in any real or simulated setting would be useless in helping you to develop skill or expertise in planning. Unless you carry out a plan, you can never tell how effective it is. Plans must be tested in action.

One study of novice teachers found that they took a great deal of time to plan lessons during their student teaching assignments, and that they mentally rehearsed their lessons before presenting them by practicing what they would say and trying to anticipate what pupils might say.[28] Where possible, these student teachers also received extra practice by using the same lesson plan to teach more than one group or class of pupils. By teaching the same lesson again within a short period of time, they were able to make revisions and improve their plans, and thereby improve their lessons. The students in this study thought that both forms of practice helped to develop their skills in planning.

The novice teachers whose concept maps you studied earlier in this chapter received practice in planning through peer teaching lessons. They also would mentally rehearse their planned lessons frequently before presenting them to their peers. At the end of their lessons, their peers provided feedback about the procedures that worked well, and indicated where they had been confused about procedures or content. These prospective teachers then reviewed their lesson plans to consider how they might improve the lesson if they were to present it again. In a sense, peer teaching is only a simulated setting for instruction, but it provides an opportunity for novice teachers to practice planning skills, try out a variety of routine procedures, and develop a repertoire of routines for instruction.

Throughout this book, you will be presented with ideas about effective instructional procedures for presenting information, teaching concepts, questioning pupils, reacting to pupil responses, managing classroom tasks, using cooperative learning, and evaluating pupil learning. These ideas can make it possible for you to learn useful routines and develop teaching repertoires, but routines and repertoires require practice. As you work through the activities in this book, be prepared to take advantage of every opportunity you have to practice thinking and acting like a teacher. You will not become an expert overnight, but you will get a head start.

YOUR TURN

Choosing Key Characteristics

List six important characteristics of teacher planning that you will want to keep in mind as you begin the transformation from expert student to novice teacher. You may want to review this section as you construct your list. There are more than six characteristics mentioned, so choose the ones that seem most important to you.

OBJECTIVE **3** Given a description of teacher planning analogous to a dramatic production, to generate additional analogies that highlight important aspects of teacher planning

The Play's the Thing

Analogies can be useful in helping us understand new ideas and processes. Researchers engaged in studying the planning and teaching of expert teachers use descriptive terms like *scripts, scenes,* and *improvisation* to describe teacher thinking. These terms suggest that teacher planning may be thought of as being analogous to a dramatic production. This section builds on that analogy to explore important aspects of teacher planning, including lesson plans, unit plans, and classroom organization.

Scripts

The script is a basic feature of a dramatic production. The script provides the dialogue, which carries the message that the play is supposed to convey to the audience. It also frequently indicates specific actions that will convey nonverbal messages to the audience. Actors and actresses follow the script as they perform a play. Before performances, they memorize their lines and rehearse their parts together, so that the play runs smoothly. A script has a fairly standard form, which usually includes some description of the stage arrangements and the props, as well as a careful delineation of who will say what. The scripts of successful writers are performed over and over again, year after year, for many audiences. Frequently, the first draft of a script, even one by a highly successful writer, must be revised during trial runs of the play in out-of-the-way places. This process of polishing a script after seeing the reactions of audiences is an accepted part of the tradition of the theater.

Teachers' lesson plans and unit plans are similar to scripts in many ways. A script is typically organized as a series of acts. Most plays have three acts, and if a change of setting is required, an act may include more than one scene. A lesson plan is analogous to the script for one act of a play. It outlines the procedures to be carried out in a single time segment, and it may include a shift from one type of activity to another, similar to a change of scene within one act of a play. A unit plan is analogous to the full play, in that it covers a larger topic and outlines a series of lessons to be carried out in relation to that topic. Like the acts of a play, the lessons in a unit plan are carefully sequenced to build to a climax. Lessons early in the unit may foreshadow information to be developed more fully at a later point. Units vary in length more than does the typical play, for they are acted out over a period of days or weeks rather than a few hours. Each of these types of plans is written with the intention of conveying an important message to an "audience." The teacher follows the plans as he or she "performs" the lesson or the unit of instruction. Before performance of the plan, the teacher mentally rehearses the procedures to help ensure that the lesson or unit will run smoothly. When a lesson or unit is completed, the teacher frequently makes notes about possible revisions for the next time that lesson or unit is taught.

Of course, there are important differences between teachers' plans and dramatic scripts. A script that is rewritten after a trial run will be performed in its revised form almost immediately. A lesson plan or unit plan that is revised after teaching may not be taught again for a full year. Actors and actresses rarely write their own scripts. Teachers typically write their own plans. A script provides the dialogue for all the roles in a play, and everyone can be counted on to play their role as scripted. Teachers can plan specific activities for students to carry out as part of a lesson or unit plan, but there is no guarantee that students will play their roles exactly as the teacher planned. In mental rehearsals of their plans, teachers may envision student responses to their questions, but students rarely "speak their lines" in a classroom dialogue precisely the way that teachers envision. Students in lessons are part of the "act" at some points, and part of the "audience" at others.

Like scripts, lesson and unit plans have a typical format. Most plans for lessons or units of instruction include five parts. A statement of the *goal or purpose of instruction* (what students are expected to learn, or what message the teacher intends to convey) is an important part of a lesson or unit plan. Expert teachers have a clear goal in mind for any lesson, although they do not always write the goal out explicitly. Similarly, the author of a script has a particular mood in mind that he or she hopes to engender in audiences. Different types of plays engender different moods. Comedies generate laughter, satires produce awareness of social issues; dramas encourage reflection on personal experience. The successful author selects a dramatic form that will produce the desired audience mood. Like plays, lessons can take a variety of forms. Because the goal or purpose of instruction influences the form a lesson or unit may take, novice teachers are advised to begin a lesson or unit with a clear goal statement.

A clear statement of the *central content to be addressed* in the lesson or unit is the second important piece of a lesson or unit plan. Content descriptions may identify concepts or generalizations to be developed, procedures to be implemented, controversial issues to be explored, or a set of facts to be memorized. The expert teacher is thoroughly familiar with his or her curriculum content and can describe it explicitly. Similarly, the author of a script must have a clear idea of the message or theme of his or her play.

Although the theme may not be stated explicitly anywhere in the script, it dictates the dialogue and development of the action. Because the content drives the interaction (questions, answers, explanations) of a lesson, and novice teachers may not be fully conversant with the curriculum being taught, they need to pay particular attention to careful articulation of the content to be learned.

A statement or list of the *instructional materials* to be used in a lesson or unit is the third important part of a lesson or unit plan. A statement about needed materials is similar to a notation about props to be used in a script. It alerts the teacher to the preparations to be made before instruction begins, just as information about props alerts the stage manager to the materials that must be available to the actors. A stage manager cannot wait until the night of the performance to begin gathering the props for the play, and a teacher who is an effective manager does not wait until the last minute to gather or prepare materials for a lesson.

The fourth part of a lesson plan includes a *set of procedures* to be followed in the lesson. These procedures involve a series of activities, and generally some details are included about specific directions to be given, or questions to be asked, in relation to each activity. The fourth part of a unit plan usually includes a series of topics to be dealt with across several lessons in the unit of instruction. Within each topic, specific plans for activities to be used may be included. This part of the lesson or unit plan is similar to the main body of a script. The set of activities or the series of topics are like the separate acts in a play script. The specific plans for directions, questions, or activities are like the specific written dialogue that is provided within each act of the script. The set of procedures in a lesson plan and the series of topics in a unit plan both require skill in devising appropriate sequences of activities. Similarly, sequencing is important in the acts of a play, as some problem is set, developed, and carried to a conclusion.

The fifth part of a typical lesson or unit plan involves a statement about *evaluation procedures*. A teacher may evaluate what students have learned from a lesson or unit in a variety of ways, including tests, written homework, and observation of student responses to oral questions. While many useful means of evaluation exist, teachers do need to plan their evaluation procedures in advance. Lesson and unit plans differ from scripts in this respect. Scripts are evaluated by the audiences and critics who attend the plays. The importance of evaluation in the theater is evident in the opening night tradition, in which the whole company stays up all night to read the critics' reviews in the morning papers to learn whether or not the play is a success. Teachers' lesson and unit plans are rarely required to pass such public scrutiny, but systematic evaluation of student learning by the teacher is a critical aspect of effective teaching. If learning is not taking place, the "script" for the next lesson will need to be revised.

The five basic parts of a lesson or unit plan denote essential aspects of instruction that a teacher needs to consider in preparing for a lesson. Of course, it is possible to develop a lesson or unit plan that does not include all of these basic components, but such incomplete plans will have much less potential for successful student learning. A script that has no indication of which character is to speak which lines, or one that provides no stage directions, will be difficult to follow, and we should not be surprised if such an incomplete script resulted in an unsuccessful production. Similarly, a lesson or unit plan that is lacking one or more of the five basic parts will be an insufficient guide to the teacher during the "performance" of the lesson or unit.

The teacher who simply writes down the page numbers in the textbook that are to be covered in the next lesson has not really planned a lesson. He or she has indicated the materials to be used in the lesson, but has evidently not determined the procedures to be used for involving students in interacting with these materials. The teacher who writes an outline of steps to be followed in a lesson, without any indication of the particular skills or concepts that students are expected to learn as a result of engaging in the activities, has also developed an incomplete plan or script. A set of procedures that are not tied to any particular goal statement or content description provides the teacher with little or no guidance in making the frequent immediate decisions that confront every teacher during a lesson.

Figures 2.6 and 2.7 present examples of lesson plans that include the five basic parts described above. Both of the lessons were designed to teach the general skill of writing "expanded sentences" (sentences that provide more descriptive information to the reader). The first lesson plan was written for use with elementary school children, and the second for secondary school students. Either of these lessons could be part of a unit plan designed to develop skill and interest in expository writing.

Sometimes successful experienced teachers develop plans that seem to be incomplete because not all five basic parts are stated explicitly. In such cases, a few questions to the teacher will usually reveal that the missing part is implicit in some aspect of the stated plan. For example, one group of teachers in England was trying to understand more about how much children were learning as a result of the teachers' instruction.[29] They agreed to include four major pieces of information in their lesson plans: the sequence of key questions to be asked, the main resources to be used, the tasks to be carried out by pupils, and a "content structure diagram" (a specific form of concept map identifying the main ideas associated with the concept they were teaching in the lesson). At first glance, it might seem that these teachers were not including the five basic parts in their lesson plans, but certain apparently missing parts were implicit in their plans. Materials were explicitly noted as "main resources." Procedures were explicitly noted as "sequence of key questions" and "pupil tasks." The content objective of the lesson was clearly delineated in the "content structure diagram." What was implicit was the evaluation procedure. This was not stated in the lesson plans because the teachers had agreed beforehand that they would all use the same method of evaluation. This involved having the pupils form their own concept maps at the end of the lesson and comparing these to the teacher's content structure diagram to determine how well pupils understood the concept being taught. In this instance, the teachers did not state an evaluation procedure as part of each lesson plan because they had developed a routine procedure for evaluation.

This example emphasizes the point that the specific format for a lesson plan can vary widely, but effective lesson plans include the five basic features we have discussed here. Some school districts favor a particular format for lesson plans, and ask all teachers to use the same format. Some education professors may require their students to use a particular format for lesson or unit plans. You may be introduced to new formats and terms for the various parts of a lesson or unit plan as you face new situations in your teacher preparation program and in your later teaching. Whatever the format or terms, look for the five basic parts of a plan, and be sure to consider these critical aspects of instruction as you develop your own "scripts" for the lessons you teach.

Lesson Plan A   (Elementary)

Objective:

Most of the children will be able to add words to a simple two-word sentence, which will change the meaning of the original sentence in at least two ways.

Content (Concept/Generalization/Procedure):

A simple sentence can be expanded by adding adjectives, adverbs, and modifying phrases at the beginning or end of the sentence. Sentence expansion extends the meaning of a simple sentence.

Materials:

1. Wooden chart for sentence strips
2. Sample strips of two-word sentences with companion expanded sentences
3. Two-word sentence suggestions for the children in the group

Procedures:

1. *Introduction.* Place a simple two-word sentence on the chart with the expanded sentence under it. Children will be asked to find *similarities* and *differences*.

   Sample:
    Birds fly.
    The graceful birds fly swiftly in the sky.
   (Have another sample ready if children seem to need it.)

2. *Lesson for Children.* Each child will be provided a two-word sentence to expand. (Option for children — to originate their own if sample doesn't "appeal.") Since these will be prepared in advance, reading levels and interests of the children will be considered.

David C.	Airplanes fly.
Mike D.	Firemen work.
Rebecca F.	Scientists experiment.
Keith E.	Dogs bark.
Chris E.	Cars race.
Larry G.	Planets rotate.
Judith H.	Flowers bloom.
Billy M.	Astronauts prepare.
Anne-Marie M.	Children play.
Guy McC.	Monsters hide.
Decio R.	Doctors help.
Jamie S.	Spring appears.

3. *Summary.* Have children read their sentences aloud. Lead children to discuss which sentences "tell more" and to think about opportunities they have to use expanded sentences.

Evaluation:

Collect written work. How complex are the sentences that the children have written? Have they added single words or phrases? Are they placed at the beginning, end, or middle of the sentence? What forms of expansion need further practice?

FIGURE 2.6

Lesson Plan B   (Secondary)

Objective:

Given a set of simple sentences and a group of logical connectives, students will expand a sentence in at least four different ways while maintaining logical sense.

Content (Concept/Generalization/Procedure):

A simple sentence can be expanded by adding a logical connective followed by a clause at the beginning or end of the sentence. Sentence expansion extends or modifies the meaning of the simple sentence.

Materials:

1. Overhead projector
2. Chalkboard

Procedures:

1. Have each student write a simple sentence on his or her paper by completing the sentence frame, The _____.
2. Have several students read their sentences aloud. Record these sentences on the chalkboard.
3. On the overhead projector write "The helicopter landed *because. . . .*" Have students suggest ways to end the sentence. Write these on transparency.
4. Ask pupils to expand their own simple sentences by adding *because* and an appropriate clause. Have several examples read aloud.
5. Proceed in the same manner for *but, therefore, whenever, since, then,* and *so.*
6. On the overhead projector write "*Although* the helicopter landed, . . ." Have students suggest ways to end the sentence. Write a few on the transparency.
7. Ask students which of the logical connectives already discussed could be used at the beginning of their sentence. Have them write one or two, and have some read aloud.

Evaluation:

Ask each pupil to take any three of the sentences written on the board at the beginning of the lesson and to expand each sentence in four different ways, using the logical connectives listed on the transparency.

FIGURE 2.7

Scenes

While scripts are an important feature of play production, there are other things to be considered as well. Scenery is an important part of any dramatic production. The scenery provides the backdrop against which the play will be performed. The design of the set determines where and how the actors can move around the stage. A change of scene can trigger a change of mood in the audience. There is a great deal of symbolic meaning in the scenery of a dramatic production — some of the message of any play is conveyed to the audience by the way the scene is set.

Similarly, when teachers plan lessons, they communicate a message in the way they set the scene for the lesson, as well as in what they say or ask students to do during the lesson. The teacher's stage is the physical classroom, and the teacher sets the scene by arranging the physical space of the classroom. In addition, the teacher sets the stage for lessons by determining the social organization of the classroom. In a well-designed classroom "scene," the physical and social organizations will complement each other.

It should be noted that, although the two lesson plans in Figures 2.6 and 2.7 have similar "scripts" (both include the same five basic parts of a lesson plan), the teachers who planned these lessons envisioned different classroom "scenes." In Lesson Plan A (Figure 2.6), the teacher envisions a scene (social organization) where children will be working individually at their seats for part of the lesson, and discussing examples of expanded sentences together in a large group for another. There are several "scene changes" required for this lesson. First, students will meet in a large group to discuss sample sentences, then they will work individually at their desks. Next, they will share the sentences they have written, again in a large-group discussion. In planning for these scene changes, the teacher needs to be sure that the physical arrangement of desks in the classroom will facilitate discussion as well as independent seatwork. If children are seated in rows of single desks, they may be able to work alone without being distracted by their neighbors. But this type of seating arrangement is not conducive to a group discussion. Most children will see only the backs of other students' heads. In this type of classroom scene (physical arrangement), students talk to the teacher, not to each other. If this teacher uses these two types of activities as routines in her classroom, she needs to set the scene so that discussion and independent work are both facilitated. Arranging desks in a large semicircle could be one alternative.

In Lesson Plan B (Figure 2.7), the teacher envisions a scene (physical arrangement) where the overhead projector and screen are the focus of attention. The major activity throughout the lesson involves large-group discussion, and the teacher needs to set the scene so that students can see each other as well as the screen at the front of the room. For this activity, a large semicircle of desks might not be appropriate because students at each end of the semicircle might have difficulty seeing the screen.

When planning for lessons, teachers must think in advance about how the physical arrangement of the classroom will help or hinder students as they carry out the instructional activity of the lesson. If the type of activity changes frequently within lessons, or from one lesson to another, the classroom arrangement must be flexible enough to support a variety of activities and social organizations (small-group work, individual work, or large-group discussion). When planning units of instruction, teachers must envision a series of scenes that can encompass these various types of organization. Teachers are the stage managers and set designers, as well as the script writers and the actors.

▓ *Improvisation*

While lesson and unit plans may act like scripts to cue the teacher about what to do next, no plan for instruction is detailed enough to tell a teacher exactly what to say, as a script for a play does. The teacher's guide for a textbook often provides a set of suggested questions to ask as teachers lead discussions based on readings in the text. But even if a teacher used the teacher's guide as a "script," and asked all the questions provided for a given lesson, some improvisation would still be necessary. Students never answer all questions correctly, and a teacher must react to partial or incorrect answers by asking followup questions, or by providing additional information. Furthermore, students ask questions of their own, and neither these questions nor the answers to them are included in a teacher's guide to the textbook.

An actor or actress in a scripted play is not expected to improvise lines, except perhaps in an emergency, when someone misses a cue, and dead silence ensues. But there is a place in the theater for improvisation. In fact, some particularly gifted actors and actresses specialize in improvisation. In improvisational theater, the audience is frequently invited to suggest characters and a situation. The actors then take on the suggested roles, and without any prior rehearsal, act out the situation. The dictionary gives the synonym *unprepared* for the term *improvised*, but it would be a mistake to believe that actors who engage in improvisational performances are unprepared. They have studied a variety of characters and situations, through careful observation of people in everyday encounters and extensive reading of plays and literature. They can call on this rich background of information when they are challenged to react on the spot to requests from the audience. Prior to performing before an audience, they will have practiced improvising skits in response to a variety of possible situations.

Teachers are called on to improvise on a regular basis, just like improvisational actors, but their improvisations may not be as extensive. They may only engage in a brief extemporaneous dialogue with an individual student, rather than carrying out a whole skit. Expert teachers, like actors, are never unprepared for these extemporaneous performances. They also have studied a variety of "characters" (students) and situations, through careful observation over time in their own classrooms. They also have a rich background of information about the subject they are teaching. They can call on this background of experience and knowledge when they are challenged to react on the spot to questions or suggestions from students.

In one sense, a teacher can never plan ahead for the improvisational demands of the classroom. Even experienced teachers cannot predict everything that will happen in a lesson. An effective teacher needs to be flexible enough to respond to the ideas and queries of students. In another sense, it is possible for a teacher to be prepared to deal effectively with situations that are not predictable, and thus require improvisation. This is one way in which routines and repertoires become invaluable. One way to improvise is to call on a familiar routine and use it in a new setting. See Figure 2.8, "The case of Ben," for an example of this use.

Novice teachers do not come into the classroom armed with a set of routines and repertoires. They must develop their routines and repertoires by careful observation and practice, just as expert teachers and improvisational actors have done before them. Early field experiences that include systematic observation in classroom settings and opportunities for practice in working with small groups can be useful to novice teachers who want to become experts. The prospective teachers can observe the routines employed by experienced teachers, and can practice using them. They should also discuss these routines with the teachers from whom they are borrowing them, so that they understand the purposes the routines serve, and the situations in which they are most appropriately used. Eventually, they can adapt these borrowed routines and invent their own; in this way they will develop their own repertoire of routines.

Ben was a secondary education student and a science major. During student teaching in a suburban high school, he conducted a physics lesson, instructing pupils in processes for solving problems that dealt with kinetic and potential energy. In this lesson, Ben demonstrated the problem-solving process to the whole class, working through several problems. He then assigned a seatwork problem for independent practice and reviewed this problem with the whole class after pupils had completed it independently. The lesson concluded with more problems worked in the whole-class setting.

Like many secondary teachers, both novices and experts, Ben had a value conflict that pitted lesson pace against pupil comprehension. He wanted to be sure that pupils understood the processes he was teaching, but he also wanted to cover all the content in the course. Ben had established a routine to help him resolve this conflict. When working a physics problem through with the class, he carefully explained the procedure for setting up the formula to solve the problem, but he did not do the algebraic calculations to obtain the answer. He simply wrote the answer on the board. Ben explained his thinking:

> I don't solve the problems after I set them up algebraically. I did that for a while, but I was getting a lot of questions about the algebra. By now, if they are in physics, they should be able to do basic algebra. But a few of them do have trouble with algebra. So, the last few weeks I didn't do the algebra in class, and if they were having trouble with it, they could see me individually. Most of the pupils don't need that algebra help, so it's kind of boring and wastes the time of the rest of the students to see me go through the algebra again.

Ben's routine for dealing with this issue was to have the few pupils who needed extra help with algebra come in after class to work with him individually. This way he was able to move the lesson along but still be sure that his pupils were learning.

In his lesson on kinetic and potential energy, Ben was faced with a new situation. A pupil questioned the *procedure* that Ben had shown for solving a particular problem. Other pupils did not seem to be confused about the procedure. In this unexpected situation, Ben improvised by calling on his already established routine: he told the pupil, "You can learn to calculate vertical displacement using this method. I'll show you how after class."

FIGURE 2.8   The case of Ben

Alternative Analogies

The analogy of teacher planning as a dramatic production is a useful one because it highlights some important features of teacher planning: the need to consider the "mood" and "message" (goal and content) that the lesson is intended to convey, the need to have the "props" (materials) prepared in advance, the need to have a "script" (sequence of planned procedures) to follow, and the importance of evaluation by "critics" (the thoughtful teacher). The analogy also emphasizes the importance of setting the "scene" (social organization and physical arrangement) for a successful lesson, and indicates that an effective teacher must be skillful at improvising (responding to unpredictable events), drawing on a well-developed repertoire of routines. Like any analogy, this one does not fit completely. No teacher repeats the same script or lesson plan day after day to a series of new audiences, for example.

While the analogy of a dramatic production is a useful one for exploring the concept of instructional planning, it is not the only analogy for teacher planning. Each new analogy tends to highlight different features of a concept, so it can be helpful when clarifying a new concept to consider a variety of possible analogies.

YOUR TURN

Explaining Additional Analogies

One additional analogy for teacher planning is that of a road map. Can you think of some important characteristics of a road map that are also characteristic of teacher planning? Try listing three or four common characteristics now, and then discuss your ideas with your fellow students.

How does the analogy of a road map fail to fit the characteristics of teacher planning? List two ways that a road map is different from a teacher plan.

What new aspects of teacher planning are highlighted by this new analogy? Describe one important characteristic of teacher planning that stands out particularly in relation to the analogy of a road map.

What other analogies can you think of for the concept of teacher planning? Stretch your imagination and invent an analogy of your own. Can you think of a machine or some natural phenomenon that has some characteristics in common with a teacher's plan? Explore your analogy by listing similarities, differences, and highlighted features of teacher planning in relation to the new analogy. Share your analogy with your fellow students.

Only the Beginning

Since all plans are only intentions to act, a plan is only the beginning. And in the beginning, most plans are vague sketches of possible actions. These partial plans are gradually filled out with more and more definite decisions as the time for action approaches. But the phrase *only the beginning* is a deceptive one. Shakespeare wrote that "All's well that ends well," but it is equally true that things are more apt to end well if they begin well. Because a plan is the beginning, planning is one of the most critical skills that a teacher can have.

Instructional planning requires more than information about what is included in a lesson or unit plan. To plan effectively and efficiently, a teacher needs a clear understanding of the subject to be taught, as well as information about alternate goals and objectives, productive use of classroom questions, approaches for teaching concepts, procedures for classroom management, and techniques for evaluation of student learning. To carry out instructional plans, a teacher must have skills in lesson presentation and in interpersonal communication. Just as a plan is only the beginning, so is this chapter only the beginning. To develop real skill in instructional planning, you will need to absorb and apply the information in all the chapters of this book. You will also need to practice making plans for instruction, carrying them out in peer teaching or with small groups in classroom settings, and revising them on the basis of what you learn from the resulting action.

The concept map of teacher planning that you constructed at the beginning of this chapter is a record of your thoughts at this early stage of your development as a professional teacher. It marks a point in your thinking that is "only a beginning." Save it. When you have completed the activities in this book, and have had an opportunity to practice instructional planning by putting your plans into action, construct another concept map of teacher planning. You will see that you are learning to think like a teacher. You already have a sound beginning.

MASTERY TEST

The News About Teacher Planning

The concept hierarchy in Figure 2.9 identifies several of the questions typically answered in news articles, and provides some basic information under each question. Fill in the blanks, then write a newspaper article to inform other students who are not education majors about teacher planning, using this information and other ideas from this chapter. You may want to include what you learned about your own ideas and those of your classmates on the subject of teacher planning. Write a catchy headline for your article.

▓ Answer Keys for Your Turn Exercises

ANSWER KEY

Your Turn: Considering Two Cases

In comparing Ted's and Carol's pre and post maps, make note of changes like:

1. Carol emphasized discipline problems and seating plan as major concepts in relation to teacher planning on her pre map. On her post map, these became third level subconcepts under the major concept teacher management. Carol learned that behavior problems could be minimized by setting rules, and by carefully organizing time, space, and materials. Carol did not mention establishing routines, but that is another important aspect of teacher management.

2. Carol's pre map noted three important aspects of lessons: timing, materials, and the subparts (for example, introduction and conclusion). In her post map, the goals and strategies of instruction were noted as important. Evaluation of student learning was mentioned as a part of lesson plans on both maps. On the post map, however, evaluation was also an important major concept, and it incorporated self-evaluation as well as evaluation of students.

3. Carol's post map emphasized developing the year's curriculum, an important aspect of teacher planning that was omitted entirely from the pre map. Because weekly, daily, and unit lesson plans are nested within the plan for the year, consideration of the year's curriculum, particularly the goals and objectives for the year, is a critical aspect of teacher planning.

4. Ted's pre map is limited and reflects his lack of experience in thinking about teaching when he began his teacher preparation program.

5. The two most striking features of Ted's post map are his use of questions, and the way his questions emphasize relationships among the various aspects of teacher planning he has identified. His questions show that he has learned to think of teacher planning as a series of decisions. His focus on relationships shows he has learned that these decisions are interrelated, not isolated.

6. Ted's map refers to lessons, but the concepts related to teacher planning that he has identified, and the questions he raises, are equally applicable to long-range planning, for example, unit planning or yearly planning.

In comparing your own map to Ted's and Carol's, and to those of your fellow students, you should consider:

1. What terms have I used that others have omitted, and vice versa?

2. In what ways is the structure of my map similar to or different from the maps of others? For example, how many subconcepts have I included? How have I shown relationships among the terms?

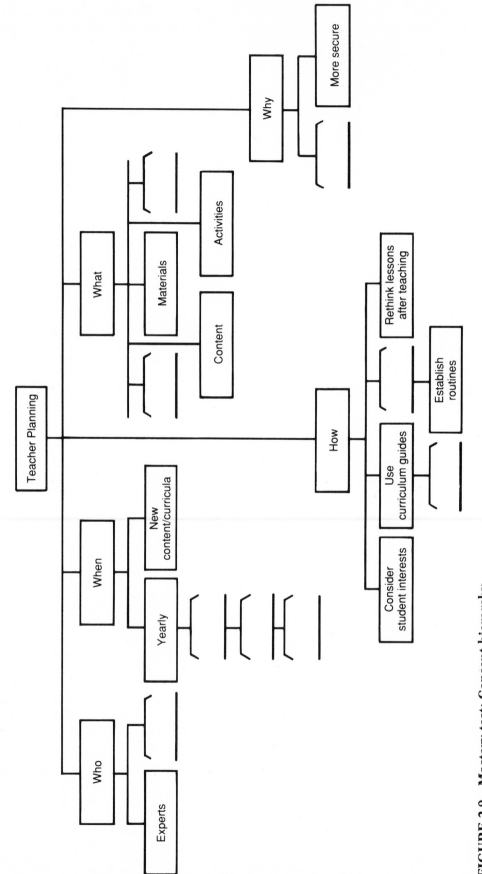

FIGURE 2.9   Mastery test: Concept hierarchy

ANSWER KEY

Your Turn: Choosing Key Characteristics

Here is a list of important characteristics of teacher planning. Which of these did you list? Why do you consider the ones you listed more important than the ones you omitted?

1. The four basic types of teacher planning are yearly, unit, weekly, and daily planning.
2. Few experienced teachers begin planning by stating instructional objectives. A basic goal for most teachers is maintaining the interest and involvement of their students, and they begin planning by considering how to accomplish this.
3. One kind of plan is nested within another. Plans made at the beginning of the year affect the daily and weekly plans for the rest of the year.
4. Many teachers say that unit planning is the most important kind of planning they do. Unit plans organize a flow of activities related to a general topic for a period of two weeks to a month.
5. A lesson plan can serve as an organizational tool, and it also provides teachers with a sense of security.
6. Experienced teachers write out complete lesson plans when they are dealing with new content or new curriculum materials. They recommend that student teachers and beginning teachers write out lesson plans.
7. Experienced teachers rely heavily on curriculum guides and textbook materials to determine the content and pace of their lessons.
8. Teachers rarely change their plans drastically in the middle of a lesson, but they do make adjustments based on pupil reactions to the activity.
9. To deal effectively with student diversity, teachers must make adaptations as they implement their plans. Possible adaptations should be considered in advance.
10. Rethinking a lesson after it has been taught is a useful way to improve planning of future lessons.
11. Experienced teachers have established routines for evaluation of instruction, sequencing lesson activities, and management of classroom interaction. These established procedures free both students and teacher to concentrate on learning and teaching.
12. An effective teacher has a repertoire of alternate routines or procedures, all of which serve some common purpose, and each of which is especially appropriate in a particular situation.
13. It takes a lot of practice to become a successful planner.

ANSWER KEY

Your Turn: Explaining Additional Analogies

There are many ideas you could have mentioned in exploring the analogy, "Teacher planning is like a road map." Here are a few possibilities.

Similarities

1. You use a road map to figure out the best way to reach a certain destination, and teacher planning helps to identify the best way to achieve an instructional goal.
2. A road map shows that there is more than one way to arrive at your destination, and teacher planning helps you to consider alternatives before deciding how to proceed.
3. A road map shows points of interest along the way that you may want to stop and see, and teacher planning can identify special materials that may add interest to a lesson or unit.
4. When you have a routine way to get to a familiar place, you don't use a road map, and when you have a routine procedure that you commonly use in a lesson, you don't need to write it down in your plan.
5. There may be detours along a highway because of road repairs, and road maps don't show these detours. Similarly, there may be interruptions in lessons that are not anticipated in lesson plans.

6. Road maps can show a variety of areas, like a city, state, or region. Teacher planning can address a variety of time periods, like a lesson, week, or unit.
7. It is hard to read a road map and drive at the same time, and it is not effective to read your lesson plan while you are in the middle of teaching a lesson.

Differences

1. Road maps are prepared by someone else to be used by a motorist, but teachers prepare their own plans.
2. Road maps are printed in a variety of colors, but teacher plans are written in black and white.
3. A road map is kept in the glove compartment of the car, to be used again and again, but a lesson plan is usually changed or improved before it is used again.

Key Features

1. The road map analogy emphasizes the idea of trying to reach a goal or destination, and this is an important aspect of teacher planning.
2. The road map emphasizes the idea of alternative routes to the same destination, and this is another important aspect of teacher planning.

■ Answer Key for Mastery Test

ANSWER KEY

Mastery Test, Objective 2

The blanks in the concept hierarchy in Figure 2.9 should be filled in as shown in Figure 2.10. You should be able to fill in all the blanks without difficulty. Did you use an analogy to add interest to your article? If so, you are to be congratulated on applying one of the procedures practiced in this chapter. To check the clarity of your news article, and your ability to present the information in an interesting manner, give your article to a friend who is not in your education class. Ask him or her to read it and raise questions. Do the questions indicate interest in knowing more, or do they suggest confusion about what you wrote? Can you answer the questions without referring back to the chapter? Perhaps some of the questions go beyond information provided in this chapter, but you may find they are answered by the information in later chapters, so keep them in mind as you read on.

This exercise in organizing information that is relatively new to you and presenting it to someone who is unfamiliar with the topic is similar to the task that a teacher engages in when preparing the content of a lesson. To give information to others, we usually have to clarify our own ideas. Did you find that you had to review the chapter and reorganize your ideas to write your article? If so, then this mastery test gave you an opportunity to experience one small aspect of teacher planning — selecting and organizing information to be included in a lesson.

■ Notes

1. Michael E. Bratman, *Intention, Plans, and Practical Reason* (Cambridge, MA: Harvard University Press, 1987).
2. D. Bob Gowin, *Educating* (Ithaca, NY: Cornell University Press, 1981).
3. Bruce R. Joyce and Marsha Weil, *Models of Teaching* (Englewood Cliffs, NJ: Prentice-Hall, 1986).
4. Robert Yinger, *A Study of Teacher Planning: Description and Theory Development Using Ethnographic and Information Processing Methods* (unpublished doctoral dissertation, Michigan State University, 1977).
5. Greta Morine and Elizabeth Vallance, *Teacher Planning*, Beginning Teacher Evaluation Studies Technical Report, Special Study C (San Francisco: Far West Laboratory, 1976).
6. Philip Taylor, *How Teachers Plan Their Courses* (Slough, England: National Foundation for Education Research in England and Wales, 1970). *See also* John Zahorik, "Teacher's Planning Models," *Educational Leadership* 33, no. 2 (1975): 134–139.
7. Charles Fisher, David Berliner, Nicola Filby, Richard Marliave, Leonard Cahen, and Marilyn Dishaw, "Teaching Behaviors, Academic Learning Time, and Student Achievement: An Overview," in Carolyn Denham and Ann Lieberman, eds., *Time to Learn* (Washington, D.C.: National Institute of Education, 1980).
8. Christopher Clark and Robert Yinger, *Three Studies of Teacher Planning*, Research Series No. 55 (East Lansing, MI: Institute for Research on Teaching, Michigan State University, 1979).
9. *Ibid.*
10. Morine and Vallance, *op. cit.*
11. Christopher Clark and Janis Elmore, *Teacher Planning in the First Weeks of School*, Research Series No. 56 (East Lansing, MI: Institute for Research on Teaching, Michigan State University, 1981).
12. Clark and Yinger, *op. cit.*

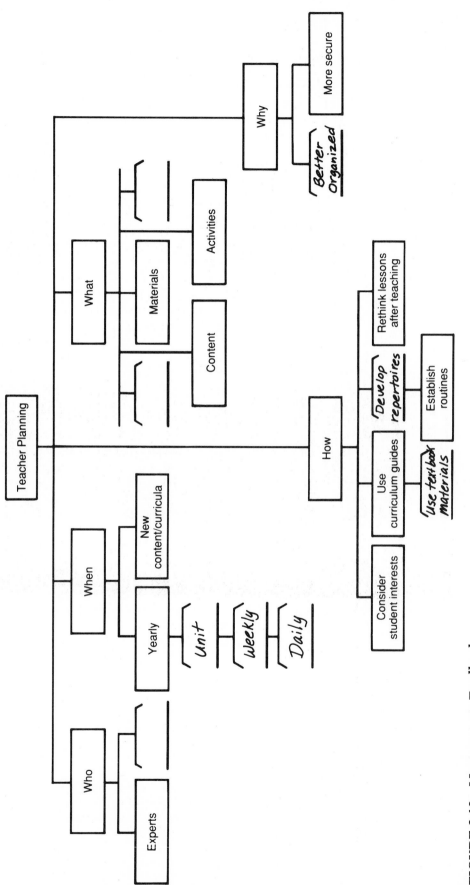

FIGURE 2.10 Mastery test: Feedback

13. Greta Morine-Dershimer, *Teacher Plan and Classroom Reality: The South Bay Study*, Part IV, Research Series No. 60 (East Lansing, MI: Institute for Research on Teaching, Michigan State University, 1979).

14. Bruce Joyce, "Toward a Theory of Information Processing in Teaching," *Educational Research Quarterly* 3, no. 4 (1978–79): 66–77.

15. V. Dahllof and Ulf Lundgren, *Macro- and Micro-Approaches Combined for Curriculum Process Analysis: A Swedish Educational Field Project* (Goteborg, Sweden: Institute of Education, University of Goteborg, 1970).

16. Jere Brophy and Carolyn Evertson, *Learning from Teaching: A Developmental Perspective* (Boston: Allyn and Bacon, 1976). *See also* Greta Morine-Dershimer, *Talking, Listening, and Learning in Elementary Classrooms* (New York: Longman, 1985).

17. Jere Brophy and Tom Good, *Teachers' Communication of Differential Expectations for Children's Classroom Performance: Some Behavioral Data*, Texas Research and Development Center for Teacher Education, Report No. 25 (Austin: University of Texas, 1969).

18. Sara Michaels, "Sharing Time: Children's Narrative Styles and Differential Access to Literacy," *Language in Society* 10 (1981): 423–442.

19. Greta Morine-Dershimer (1985), *op. cit.*

20. Morine and Vallance, *op. cit.*

21. Clark and Yinger, *op. cit.*

22. Morine and Vallance, *op. cit.*

23. A. D. deGroot, *Thought and Choice in Chess* (The Hague, Netherlands: Mouton, 1965).

24. W. G. Chase and Herbert A. Simon, "Perception in Chess," *Cognitive Psychology* 4 (1973): 55–81.

25. Kathy Carter, Donna Sabers, Katherine Cushing, Stefinee Pinnegar, and David Berliner, "Processing and Using Information About Students: A Study of Expert, Novice, and Postulant Teachers," *Teaching and Teacher Education* 3, no. 2 (1987): 147–157.

26. Gaea Leinhardt, "Math Lessons: A Contrast of Novice and Expert Competence" (paper presented at the Psychology of Mathematics Education Conference, East Lansing, MI, 1986).

27. Barak Rosenshine, "Explicit Teaching," in David Berliner and Barak Rosenshine, eds., *Talks to Teachers* (New York: Random House, 1987), pp. 75–92.

28. Hilda Borko and Carol Livingston, "Expert and Novice Teachers' Mathematics Instruction: Planning, Teaching, and Post-Lesson Reflections" (paper presented at the annual meeting of the American Educational Research Association, New Orleans, 1988).

29. Tony Ghaye, "Mapping the Links Between Teacher and Student Thinking in the Classroom" (paper presented at the meeting of the International Study Association on Teacher Thinking [ISATT], Nottingham, England, 1988).

Additional Readings

The following chapters from *Talks to Teachers*, edited by David C. Berliner and Barak V. Rosenshine (New York: Random House, 1987), provide useful additional information about the planning process, and discuss specific important topics to be considered during planning for effective instruction.

Berliner, D. C. Simple Views of Effective Teaching and a Simple Theory of Classroom Instruction (pp. 93–110).

Clark, C. M., and R. J. Yinger. Teacher Planning (pp. 342–365).

Corno, L. Teaching and Self-Regulated Learning (pp. 249–266).

Morine-Dershimer, G. Can We Talk? (pp. 37–53).

Rosenshine, B. V. Explicit Teaching (pp. 75–92).

Instructional Objectives

3

■ **Terry D. TenBrink**

1 To recognize well-defined instructional objectives

2 To write well-defined instructional objectives

3 To use instructional objectives in instructional planning

4 To use objectives in implementing instruction.

Think for a moment about what teachers do. Sit back and try to remember the *one* teacher who you felt had the most influence on you. Write down the characteristics of that teacher as well as you can remember them. Chances are that among the characteristics of your favorite teacher was the fact that the teacher knew you as an individual and knew what he or she wanted for you. This favorite teacher probably had a significant influence on your life, playing a part in the development of your attitudes, the formation of your habits, and the acquisition of information that was new and exciting to you. This teacher may have guided you subtly, or may have directly "pushed" you toward these behavior changes. The teacher may have used a great many visual aids or none at all; or may have given multiple choice tests, essay tests, or no tests at all. What effective teachers have in common is *not* their techniques, their teaching styles, or the kinds of tests they use. It is *what* they accomplish, not how they accomplish it, that makes the difference.

If teachers are going to make a significant difference in the lives of their students, they must know what they want their students to accomplish. Having formulated such goals, teachers can share them with their students so that the students will *also* know where they are going and what is expected of them.

There is considerable evidence to support the contention that when teachers have clearly defined instructional objectives and have shared them with their students, a number of things happen[1]:

1. Better instruction occurs.
2. More efficient learning results.
3. Better evaluation occurs.
4. The students become better self-evaluators.

Teachers need to define instructional objectives, however, so that they will be clear, valid statements of what they want their students to know or be able to do. Then they must learn to use those objectives in ways that will improve their teaching and their testing. The rest of this chapter is designed to help you do just that.

| **OBJECTIVE** | **1** To recognize well-defined instructional objectives |

Learning Activity 1.1

Instructional objectives that are useful in the classroom must meet certain criteria. We have outlined these criteria* below. Look them over carefully, and then we will discuss each of them in turn.

A Useful Instructional Objective Must Be:

1. Student-oriented
2. Descriptive of a learning *outcome*
3. Clear and understandable
4. Observable

1. Good Instructional Objectives Are Student-Oriented. An instructional objective that is student-oriented places the emphasis on what the *student* is expected to do, not on what the teacher will do. Look at the following examples; notice that they all describe student behavior and not teacher behavior.

Examples of Student-Oriented Objectives

1. Students should be able to solve long-division problems using at least two different methods.
2. Students should be able to list the five punctuation rules discussed in the textbook.
3. Students should be able to write down their observations of a simple experiment, stating what was done and what happened.
4. When given the description of a form of government, the student should be able to classify that form of government and list its probable strengths and weaknesses.

Sometimes teachers use instructional goals that emphasize what they are expected to do rather than what they expect of their students. Such teacher-oriented objectives only have value if they direct the teacher to do something that ultimately leads to student learning. A teacher attempting to help his or her students attain the goal of solving long-division problems may work out some of the problems on the blackboard, explaining each of the steps involved. A teacher-oriented objective associated with this behavior might read: "To explain the steps in long division on the blackboard." Notice that this might be a helpful teacher activity, but it is

---

*List taken from *Evaluation: A Practical Guide for Teachers*, by T. D. TenBrink. Copyright © 1974 by McGraw-Hill Book Company. Used with permission.

only *one* of many possible activities that could help the students reach the goal of solving long division.

YOUR TURN

Recognize Student-Oriented Objectives

The following exercise will give you practice in distinguishing between student-oriented and teacher-oriented objectives. Place an *S* before each student-oriented and a *T* before each teacher-oriented objective.

_S_ 1. To read at least 250 words per minute with no less than 80 percent comprehension

_T_ 2. To show students proper eye movements for scanning material

_____ 3. To outline my lecture on the board before class begins

_____ 4. When given the description of a complex machine, to identify the simple machines contained within it

_____ 5. To help the students appreciate classical music

_____ 6. To lecture on the basic steps in the scientific method

_____ 7. To carry out an investigation using the scientific method

_____ 8. To maintain discipline in my class

_____ 9. To write a unified paragraph on a single topic

_____ 10. To evaluate a poem on the basis of the criteria for good poetry as discussed in class

Now check your answers against the Answer Key. If you missed more than three, you may wish to reread this section before going on.

---

2. Good Instructional Objectives Describe Learning Outcomes. The important thing to keep in mind here is that we are interested in what the students will learn to do. In other words, it is the learning *outcome* that is important, not the learning activities that lead to that outcome. To say that students will practice long-division problems using two different methods is not to specify a learning outcome. It specifies an activity designed to help the students reach some outcome. As such, it is a student-oriented activity, *not* an outcome.

It may be valuable for you as a teacher to determine what kind of learning activities you may want your students to carry out. Determining which learning experiences and activities are most appropriate for your students, however, can only be made *after* you have decided what it is you want your students to accomplish. Once learning outcomes are identified and described, then activities that are appropriate for attaining those outcomes can be determined. In the table that follows, you will find a number of learning outcomes listed in the left-hand column, and the corresponding learning activities in the right-hand column. Look these examples over carefully, noting how each learning outcome dictates the kind of learning activity that might help the students reach it. Note, too, that many learning activities may be needed for students to successfully reach a single learning outcome.

Relationship Between Learning Outcomes and Learning Activities

Learning Outcomes	Learning Activities
1. To label the parts of a flower	(a) Read pages 17–22 in your science book.
	(b) Study the diagram of a flower in your book.
	(c) Use the unlabeled diagrams on the study table. Practice filling in the blanks. Check your labels with those in the book.
2. To identify the four main parts of speech in simple and complex sentences	(a) Complete workbook pages 75–78.
	(b) Listen to the teacher's explanation of nouns, verbs, adjectives, and adverbs.
	(c) Play the grammar game (part 5) with some of your classmates.
	(d) Pick a paragraph from your reading book. List the nouns and verbs. Have your teacher check your work.
3. To reduce fractions to the lowest common denominator	(a) Watch the teacher reduce fractions.
	(b) Practice at the blackboard with the teacher's help.
4. To compute the area of a circle	Read page 78 and do Exercise 15.
5. To listen to classical music during free time	Listen to classical music and to the teacher's explanation of it.
6. To make a correct introduction of a friend to your teacher	Listen to the record, "Introducing Friends."

YOUR TURN

Recognize Outcomes, Not Activities

Now it's your turn to practice distinguishing learning activities from learning outcomes. For each statement below, mark an *A* next to each learning activity and an *O* next to each outcome. *Remember:* Activities are necessary for the attainment of outcomes, but outcomes specify what students should ultimately be able to do.

_____ 1. To review the notes taken during yesterday's lecture

_____ 2. To explain the function of the carburetor

_____ 3. To practice multiplication with flash cards

———— 4. To read Chapters 17 and 18

———— 5. To distinguish between learning outcomes and learning activities

———— 6. To identify the parts of speech in a prose passage

———— 7. To identify correctly the types of trees found in this part of the country

———— 8. To locate on a topographical map the most likely place for the development of a large metropolitan area

———— 9. To study the diagram of the structure of an atom

———— 10. To listen to the *Nutcracker Suite*

———— 11. To identify the instruments being played in the *Nutcracker Suite*

———— 12. To identify the instruments being featured in a particular musical performance

———— 13. To practice hearing the difference between a French horn and a trombone

———— 14. To watch the film *How Your Brain Works*

———— 15. To describe briefly the two-party system, listing its strengths and weaknesses

Now compare your answers with those given in the Answer Key that follows. It is possible that you may have misinterpreted one or two statements. If this happened, don't worry about a couple of "wrong" answers. If you missed many of the items in this exercise, however, you may have read this section too rapidly. Go back and reread it, thinking carefully about what is being said. As you read, try to think of additional examples taken from your own school experiences.

---

3. Instructional Objectives Are Clear and Understandable. The first prerequisite for a clear and understandable objective is explicitness. It should contain a clearly stated verb that describes a definite action or behavior and, in most cases, should refer to an object of that action. Examine the examples below. In each case, the verb and its object have been italicized. As you read these examples, try to see if there is more than one possible meaning for any of them. If they are well stated and explicit, only one meaning should be possible.

Examples of Clearly Stated Objectives

1. The student should be able to *label* the *parts of the heart* correctly on a diagram of the heart similar to the one on page 27 of the text.
2. When given words from the list in the back of the spelling book, the student should be able to *identify words that are incorrectly spelled* and make any necessary corrections.
3. The pupils should be able to use a yardstick to *measure* the *length, width, and height* of any piece of furniture in the room. The measurements should be accurate to within half an inch.
4. To be able to *identify* correctly the *ingredients in a mixture of chemicals* prepared in advance by the teacher.
5. When given a *contemporary poem*, the student should be able to *evaluate* it according to the criteria discussed in class.

6. To *list* the *major parts of a friendly letter*, briefly *describing* the *function of each part.*
7. Given several occasions to listen to different types of music, the student will *select* at least *three different types of music* that he or she likes.
8. To *read out loud a prose passage of approximately 300 words*, making no more than three errors. The reading level of the passage will be at the 5.5 grade level.

Notice that in each of the above examples, not only are there a clearly defined verb and its accompanying object, but there is only one possible meaning for each of the statements. It is also important to note that most people observing someone engaged in the behaviors described above, or observing the products of those behaviors, would agree in their judgments about whether the behavior had occurred as stated. In other words, the above objectives are not only explicitly stated, but are also observable. This characteristic (observability) will be described in the next section.

A Word of Caution

Let me digress from the present discussion to caution you against something that occurs frequently when teachers are first learning to write instructional objectives. It is easy to confuse the notion that an objective must be explicit with the idea that it must be highly specific. Objectives should be explicit, that is, unambiguous and understandable. However, being explicit does not mean they have to be highly specific, written down to the minutest of details and the lowest level of a given behavior. Below is an example* of an instructional objective that has been written in general terms and then re-written several times, each time becoming a bit more specific.[2]

1. Students should be able to read with understanding.
2. When given a story to read, the student should be able to answer questions about the content of the story.
3. When given a short story, the student should be able to identify the passages that describe the traits of the main characters.
4. Students should be able to identify the passages that describe the personality traits of the main characters in *Catcher in the Rye.*
5. Students should be able to identify at least five passages from *Catcher in the Rye* that illustrate Holden's confidence in himself.
6. Students should be able to recognize five passages cited in Handout 3 that illustrate Holden's lack of confidence in himself.[3]

Notice that the most useful instructional objectives in the above examples are those that fall somewhere in the middle of the continuum from very general to very specific. When instructional objectives become too specific, they lose much of their value as a guide to study and become little more than test questions to be answered. Instructional objectives that are too specific might very well encourage poor study habits. Students may tend to learn just enough to meet the specific objectives, but not enough to meet the more general end-of-the-course objectives. The value of getting students to identify the passages from *Catcher in the Rye* illustrating descriptions of personality traits is that this ability will transfer to other short stories as well. Transferability makes the objective more valuable than one asking the student to recognize those passages from *Catcher in the Rye* that had previously been discussed and identified (like objective 6).

---

*Examples taken from *Evaluation: A Practical Guide for Teachers*, by T. D. Ten-Brink. Copyright © 1974 by McGraw-Hill Book Company. Used with permission.

YOUR TURN

Clear and Unambiguous Objectives

For each of the following objectives, determine whether it has a single meaning (mark it with a *1*) or two or more meanings (mark it with a *2*). The first three items have been done for you. The first is ambiguous. In fact, it could be interpreted to mean the same thing as items 2 and 3. The problem with item 1, of course, is the fact that the verb is not explicit. Using a more explicit verb (as in item 2 or 3) clears up the ambiguity.

__2__   1. To know the presidents of the United States

__1__   2. To list in writing the presidents of the United States

__1__   3. To recognize and call by name each president of the United States on seeing his picture

_____   4. To see the connection between well-written sentences and well-written stories

_____   5. To identify the vanishing points in a three-point perspective drawing

_____   6. To establish eye contact with at least five different persons during a three-minute persuasive speech

_____   7. To develop a roll of 35 mm, black and white film

_____   8. To run a ten-minute mile

_____   9. To appreciate music

_____   10. To mold a lump of clay into the shape of an animal that can be recognized and correctly named by the rest of the class

_____   11. Not to show favoritism to any given child in the preschool

_____   12. To understand the workings of an atomic energy plant

_____   13. To plan a miniature garden according to the criteria for such a garden as described in the article "Apartment Gardening"

_____   14. To enlarge your concept of realism

---

4. Good Instructional Objectives Are Observable.   The evaluation of learning outcomes hinges on the observability of those outcomes. The key to an observable objective is an observable verb. Consequently, when selecting instructional objectives for use in your teaching, *watch the verbs!* As discussed earlier, an effective objective contains an explicit verb and (usually) a well-defined object of the verb. Both these requirements help make an objective clear and unambiguous. Now we add another requirement: the verb must describe an observable action or an action that results in an observable product.

The verbs in the box* are vague and unobservable. Avoid them.

---

*The verbs in the boxed material on page 60 were taken from *Evaluation: A Practical Guide for Teachers,* by T. D. TenBrink. Copyright © 1974, by McGraw-Hill Book Company. Used with permission.

(handwritten margin notes: "Look over", "Microteach #3!", "Look over")

Vague, unobservable verbs that should be avoided

to know	to enjoy
to understand	to familiarize
to comprehend	to value
to grasp	to realize
to believe	to like
to appreciate	to cope with
to think	to love

The kind of verb you hope to find in instructional objectives is also exemplified below. When you write objectives, use these kinds of verbs.

Verbs describing observable actions or actions that yield observable products*

to identify	to analyze
to speak	to predict
to list	to locate
to select	to explain
to choose	to isolate
to compute	to divide
to add	to separate
to draw	to infer

There are many processes and skills that cannot be directly observed but produce observable products. It is not possible for us to observe the thinking process of a student as he strives to solve an algebraic equation. However, we can examine the solution he arrives at and decide whether or not it is correct. We may be able to look at each of the steps he takes to arrive at that solution if he writes them down for us (displaying his thinking as a product). On the other hand, a well-written prose paragraph, a poem, and an oil painting can all be observed and analyzed. These end products and others like them can serve as "observables," which may help to indicate whether or not an expected learning outcome has occurred.

When selecting or writing instructional objectives, it is helpful to distinguish between those that specify observable behaviors and those that specify end products of behaviors.

The use of strong, active verbs, such as those in the second box, will yield objectives that are either observable or whose end products are observable. If the object of any of these verbs does not describe an observable end product, however, the resulting objective would be vague and nonob-

---

*For a more complete list of these kinds of verbs see Appendix 3 in N. E. Gronlund's *Stating Behavioral Objectives* (London: Collier-Macmillan Ltd., 1970).

servable. For example, examine the following objective: "To explain the Middle East crisis."

What is supposed to be explained? The *causes* of the Middle East crisis? The *positions taken by each side* in the Middle East crisis? The *political ideologies* involved in the Middle East crisis? All of these, and more, are possible explanations. The problem is not in the verb, but in the object of the verb. Make certain that both the verb and its object are clearly defined, pointing to observable actions or observable end products.

YOUR TURN

Observable Objectives

Mark each observable objective with an *O* and each nonobservable object with an *N*. Keep in mind that, to be an observable objective, either the action *or* the end product of that action must be visible, audible, touchable, etc.

_____O_____   1. To reduce fractions to their lowest denominator

_____   2. To locate the fulcrum on a balance beam weighted in a variety of ways

_N___⊘_____   3. To grasp the significance of the Monroe Doctrine

_____   4. To separate the incomplete sentences from the complete ones in a list containing both types

_____   5. To familiarize oneself with the rules of basketball before beginning to play the game

_____   6. When given a limited amount of time, to learn the Morse code

_____   7. To translate a passage from Plato's *Republic*

Learning Activity 1.2

Obtain copies of teacher's manuals for a subject area of interest to you. Find the statements of objectives listed in these manuals and evaluate them. Are they well written, meeting the criteria for objectives specified earlier in this chapter? If not, what is wrong with them? You may wish to keep a tally of the type of error you find most frequently.

Type of Error (If Any)	*Tally*
1. No errors; well defined	_____
2. Not student-oriented	_____
3. Not descriptive of a learning outcome	_____
4. Not clear and understandable	_____
5. Not observable	_____

MASTERY TEST

OBJECTIVE 1   To recognize well-defined instructional objectives

For each of the following pairs, check the objective that best meets the requirements for useful objectives.

1. _____(a) To be able to develop a roll of black and white film

   _____(b) To understand how a developing agent works

2. _____(a) To select useful objectives

   _____(b) To know what makes an objective useful

3. _____(a) To select from a list of definitions the one that best defines the terms provided on Handout 10

   _____(b) To know the meaning of the terms on Handout 10

4. _____(a) To solve math problems requiring an understanding of the place holder

   _____(b) To understand problem-solving techniques

5. _____(a) To recognize the pictures of people in the news

   _____(b) To match the names of people in the news with their pictures

6. _____(a) To select the good poems from good and bad examples

   _____(b) To evaluate a set of poems

7. _____(a) To remember the life cycle of the butterfly

   _____(b) To label, from memory, a diagram of the life cycle of a butterfly

8. _____(a) To hear clearly short and long vowel sounds

   _____(b) To distinguish between short and long vowel sounds

9. _____(a) To know the phonetic rules and their application in reading

   _____(b) To sound out nonsense words

10. _____(a) To punctuate a prose paragraph correctly

    _____(b) To list the punctuation rules

In the space provided, list four criteria for judging the quality of an instructional objective.

11. _____

12. _____

13. _____

14. _____

For each of the following objectives, determine the primary fault.

15. To grasp the meaning of conservation
    (a) affectively oriented
    (b) teacher-oriented
    (c) vague and unobservable

16. To demonstrate to the students the need for cleanliness
    (a) teacher-oriented
    (b) unobservable
    (c) student-oriented

17. To paint
    (a) poorly defined product
    (b) vague
    (c) teacher-oriented

18. To do workbook pages 18–20
    (a) vague
    (b) poorly defined product
    (c) a learning activity

19. To listen to the guest speaker from the narcotics division
    (a) teacher-oriented
    (b) a learning activity
    (c) vague

OBJECTIVE   **2** To write well-defined instructional objectives

Learning Activity 2.1

There are four simple steps for writing effective instructional objectives. Although these steps should normally follow the given order, you may occasionally wish to go back and rework a step before moving on. This constant monitoring of your own work, always checking against the criteria for well-defined objectives, will help you produce a clear list of objectives for your own use.

*Four Steps for Writing Instructional Objectives**

1. Describe the subject matter content.
2. Specify the general goals.
3. Break down the general goals into more specific, observable objectives.
4. Check objectives for clarity and appropriateness.

Although these four steps can be applied to course planning as well as lesson planning, it is important to remember that you will not be able to write a set of objectives for an entire course in a short time. You will find

---

*From *Evaluation: A Practical Guide for Teachers,* by T. D. TenBrink. Copyright © 1974 by McGraw-Hill Book Company. Used with permission.

it useful, therefore, to work on small units of instruction, one at a time. Eventually, you will have a set of objectives that will cover the full course you are teaching; however, your unit objectives and daily objectives should fit into the overall plan for your course. Consequently, the first two steps should be nearly complete before you begin working on the objectives for specific units of instruction or for daily lesson plans.

So that you will be able to see the interrelationship of all four steps, we will now proceed to develop a set of objectives for a complete course. We will develop objectives for a high school psychology course because this is a subject with which all teachers should be familiar. Examples from other subjects at various grade levels will also be used as each step is explained. The four steps discussed here can be used for the development of objectives for any course at any grade level.

Step 1. Describe the Subject Matter Content

Many things have to be considered when describing the content of a given course or unit of instruction. There are the major concepts to be covered, the relationship the material has to a broader base of knowledge, and the value of the content for the student. Perhaps the easiest way to get an effective description of the content of a course is to answer the following questions:

In general, what is the course about?
How does this course fit into the total curriculum?
What would be included in an outline of the course?
What value does this course have for the student?

What is the course all about? The answer should be general. All you need to do is describe what the course will cover in a paragraph or two. Suppose you were writing a friend about what you will be teaching. This friend would probably not be interested in a long, detailed discourse of the subject matter; a general description of the concepts to be covered in the course would be sufficient. Such a summary could serve as the basis for a more detailed course outline. The summary, along with the main topics included in a course outline, will provide the basis for the selection of a textbook and other learning materials.

A summary for a high school psychology course is shown in Exhibit A. Read it carefully. Later you will see how the summary leads to a course outline and to the general goals of the course.

EXHIBIT A   Subject Matter Content of High School Psychology Course

This introductory psychology course is designed to acquaint students with psychology as a science and as a potential area for further study, leading to a specialized career in psychology. Psychology will be discussed both as a research-oriented science, which is in the process of theory building, and as a science of practical application. The content of the course will center on the study of human behavior, seeking answers to questions such as "Why do humans act the way they do, and what causes them to be the kind of beings they are?" and "How do they function as individuals and as group members?"

> The aspects of human behavior that are most important to high school students will be stressed: problems dealing with psychological, physical, and social development; personality; learning; motivation; mental health; and social psychology. The emphasis throughout the course will be on major psychological research findings, and how these findings have been, and can be, applied to the solution of everyday problems.

If you had been asked to write a summary like the one in Exhibit A, what would you have included? Does a summary statement like this one help you to begin thinking about what the students might learn from such a course?

How does this course fit into the total curriculum? Once the general content of the course has been described, the next task is to write a short statement describing how the course fits into the total curriculum. To do this, you must know something about what else is being taught in the school system. You should know what courses your students have had and are likely to have after they finish your own course. Likewise, you will want to know what the other teachers of your course expect of their students. Obviously, what is expected of students at various levels of a curriculum will vary considerably in terms of both skills and attitudes.

Suppose the high school psychology course is the first course of this type the students will be exposed to. It will lead some of them into more advanced courses in college, and eventually to degrees in that field. For others, it will be the only course in psychology they will ever take. Think about what this means to the development of such a course. A "statement of fit" for this course is presented in Exhibit B. Read it carefully. How does it differ from one you might have written? Would such a statement differ considerably from one school system to the next?

EXHIBIT B   Statement of Fit into Curriculum

> This course is to be taught at the senior level and has no prerequisites. The only other area where students might encounter similar information is in home economics or one of the family living courses. While most senior-level courses culminate a series of courses, this one really begins a sequence that will fit into the college curriculum. It is felt, however, that this course not only must serve the needs of students who will continue their studies in psychology, but must also serve the needs of students about to go out into the working world. A greater understanding of what humans are like, how they developed, how they think, what their emotional reactions are like, how they learn, and how they work with other humans may be useful information for maintaining mental health and in learning to live with a variety of personalities.

What instructional goals came to mind as you read Exhibit A? Are there any goals that will not be appropriate because of limitations suggested by the statement in Exhibit B?

What would be included in an outline of the course? This third question involves specifying the major topics to be covered in the course in more detail. It should also determine a logical and defensible sequence for teaching those topics. Given a relatively complete course outline, one should be able to work on the development of instructional objectives for one part of the outline at a time. This will help make the task of writing objectives a manageable one. The outline for the high school psychology course is presented in Exhibit C.

EXHIBIT C   Suggested Course Outline

UNIT I. Psychology As a Science
   A. History of psychology
   B. Psychological theory
   C. Methodology of psychological research
   D. Applicability of psychological concepts and principles

UNIT II. How Humans Develop
   A. General theory
   B. Physical development
   C. Intellectual and emotional development
   D. Social development

UNIT III. Personality
   A. Theory of personality
   B. Measuring personality
   C. Individual differences in personality characteristics

UNIT IV. The Learning Process
   A. Learning theory
   B. Kinds of learning
   C. Measurement of performance
   D. Intelligence
   E. Learning to learn

UNIT V. Motivation
   A. Theories of motivation
   B. Extrinsic motivation
   C. Intrinsic motivation
   D. Motivating yourself and others

UNIT VI. Mental Health
   A. Indicators of mental health
   B. Factors accounting for mental health
   C. Neuroses and psychoses
   D. Maintaining mental health and preventing mental illness
   E. Physiological causes of mental illness

UNIT VII. Social Psychology
   A. Theories of social psychology
   B. Cultures and subcultures
   C. Nationalism
   D. The influence of the group

What value does this course have for the student? Notice that the topics in Exhibit C reflect the general content of the course as summarized in Exhibit A. What is *not* reflected in this course outline are the affective components of the course. Affective objectives are more likely to arise from a statement of the value of the course to the students. Such a statement for the high school psychology course is made in Exhibit D.

EXHIBIT D   List of the Values of This Course to the Students

1. Introduces the students to a new subject
2. Indicates to the students how psychology is a science that is important in all walks of life — in industry, education, business, politics, war, etc.
3. Helps the students to see the relationship between scientific research and the application of research findings to practical situations
4. Gives the students useful information about maintaining their mental health
5. Gives the students the basic tools with which to understand the behavior of people around them
6. May help the students to understand the motives of others, as well as their own motives
7. Gives information about how we learn, which may be helpful in the improvement of their own learning strategies
8. May make students more aware of the needs of others around them
9. May help students understand the social pressures that operate within a society such as ours

Most teachers hope to develop positive attitudes among their students toward the subject they are teaching. That is why the question "What value does this course have for the student?" is so important. A way to answer this question is to imagine yourself having to defend your course to the students who must take it, the parents of those students, and the administrative staff of your school. Pretend, for a moment, that your course has just been introduced into the curriculum, and you have been asked to write a defense of it for the school newspaper. Students, parents, and other people in the community are all interested in finding out why this course should be taught. The better you are able to tell them, the better base you will have for formulating the affective goals that you hope your students will accomplish.

The list of values in Exhibit D not only suggests affective goals, such as "becoming more aware of the needs of others," but also suggests cognitive ones, such as "to understand the social pressures that operate within our society." These goals can be readily translated into clear, observable objectives.

YOUR TURN

Describe the Subject Matter Content

Suppose you were asked to describe the subject matter content of a psychology course similar to the one described in Exhibits A through D. This time, however, the students would be seventh and eighth graders.

1. How would the general course description differ from the one in Exhibit A?

2. How would the course outline differ from the one in Exhibit C?

3. Would the value of such a beginning psychology course for seventh and eighth graders be different from that for high school seniors? How? Why?

4. Would there be differences that would not show up in a course description like the one found in Exhibits A through D? Where would these differences be made apparent?

Compare your answers to these questions with the Answer Key that follows.

■ *Step 2. Specify the General Goals*

In this step you will be determining in a general way what you would expect the students to be able to do. It is usually best to carry out this step in two parts. First, write down the general goals for the entire course. These will be most helpful (along with the course outline) when selecting textbooks, films, and other instructional materials. Second, specify general goals for each unit of instruction. These are intermediate goals and, therefore, should be somewhat more specific.

Look at the general end-of-course goals found in Exhibit E. These are some of the possible goals for the high school psychology course. Compare these goals to the summary of course content (Exhibit A) and the course outline (Exhibit C). The goals represent the first step in defining what the students should be able to do with the subject matter specified. Notice that the goals are not yet observable. At this point, that's not too serious. What is important is getting the general goals down on paper so that they can be rewritten according to our criteria.

EXHIBIT E   General Goals for High School Psychology Course

I.   Terminal Goals
   1. Students should understand what it means when we say that psychology is a science.
   2. Students should know the major facts about the way in which humans develop.
   3. Students should know, in general, how humans interact with their environment, including their interactions with other humans.
   4. Students will be aware of the various theories of personality, motivation, learning and mental health, and social psychology.
   5. Students should be aware of the major research findings in the area of psychology.
   6. Students should be able to apply major findings of psychology to the solutions of specific problems of human behavior and interaction.
   7. Students should be more aware of their own typical behavior and the reasons for that behavior.

YOUR TURN

Specifying General Goals — Parts 1 and 2

Now try writing some general end-of-course goals for the psychology course.
Do not duplicate those found in Exhibit E. You should be able to write at least

five more general goals for this course. Examples of such additional goals are found in the Answer Key for Part 1. Compare what you have written with those examples.

Once the end-of-course goals have been determined, intermediate goals can be written for each unit of instruction. Again, do not worry about whether or not they are observable now. First get them down in a general way, and then they can be rewritten.

Exhibit F presents some possible goals for Unit I: Psychology As a Science. Three cognitive and three affective goals have been written. Read them carefully and then try writing some yourself. *Remember:* Unit-level goals should reflect the broader, end-of-course goals. Compare your work with the further examples of Unit I goals presented in the Answer Key for Part 2.

EXHIBIT F

II. The General Intermediate Goals for Unit I: Psychology As a Science
   A. Cognitive Goals
      1. Students should know the major dates in the history of psychology.
      2. Students should know the major avocations that have made psychology an important applied science.
      3. Students should know the steps that are taken from the development of a theory, to the research and testing of that theory, to the final application of the research findings to practical situations.
   B. Affective Goals
      1. The student should appreciate the value of the science of psychology to a civilized country.
      2. The student should show appreciation for the usefulness of various psychological theories.
      3. The students should be sensitive to the problems of doing psychological research.

■ Step 3. Break Down the General Goals into More Specific, Observable Objectives

In this step, each general goal is broken down into its two major parts: the subject matter content and the expected student response to that content. Look at one of the general goals from Unit I of the psychology course.

Students should know the major founders of psychological theory and the important points in their theories.

First of all, notice that the subject matter content is divided into (1) the major founders of psychological theories and (2) the important points in each of these theories. When we finalize our list of objectives, these two areas should be kept separate, each serving as the basis for at least one objective. It is usually best to deal with only one area of the subject matter in a given objective.

Now we will take these descriptions of subject matter content and answer the following questions about each.

1. Is the subject matter content clearly defined and specific enough?
2. Precisely what response(s) do I want the students to make to that subject matter content?

In the above goal, the subject matter content (the founders of psychological theory and points important to each theory) is fairly well defined. This goal could be made more specific, however, by listing the major founders of theory. The most important concepts for each theory might also be listed. Of course, the real problem with the above goal lies in the use of the vague, unobservable verb "to know." What observable student response could be accepted as evidence that a student "knows"? Would "to list in writing" be acceptable?

The following three objectives were derived from the above general goal. The subject matter content of that goal was clarified, and the expected student response to that content was more precisely specified.

1. Students should be able to list in writing all the founders of psychological theory discussed in the textbook.
2. Students should be able to match each important concept to the theory with which it is associated. (This goal is limited to the theories found in Unit I in the text.)
3. When given the name of an early psychological theorist, students should be able to identify the concept(s) that were central to the theory.

Try breaking down an affective goal:

Students should become interested in finding out more about the specific aspects of human behavior that have been studied by psychologists.

Sometimes teachers fail to plan for the teaching of affective goals because these goals seem difficult to define in observable terms. It is relatively easy, however, if you clearly define the subject matter content and then specify the *behavior(s)* that are likely to accompany the desired attitude toward that content. The following objective was derived from the above goal in just that way.

In an open discussion about the value of psychology, students should ask questions that would help them discover what aspects of human behavior psychologists have studied.

In this objective, the content is "questions that would help them discover what aspects of human behavior psychologists have studied." The behavior expected is "to ask." Notice, however, that something else has been added: "In an open discussion about the value of psychology." This phrase suggests a condition or type of situation under which we expect the desired student behavior to occur.

Although not necessary to the formation of an effective objective, a statement describing the *condition* under which we expect the student to respond is often helpful. Here is another such objective, derived from the above goal (the condition is italicized):

When given the task of formulating questions to be sent to famous living psychologists, the student will include questions like: "What aspects of human behavior have psychologists studied?"

Besides a statement specifying the condition under which the student response is expected to occur, there is one other useful (though not necessary) addition that can be made to most objectives. There are times when it may be useful to specify the *level of performance* expected of the students.[4] For example, we might derive the following objective from the above goal:

> When books and pamphlets describing the aspects of human behavior studied by psychologists are placed in the class library, the students will sign out *two or more* of these resources.

This objective has the criterion for success built in: two or more resources signed out.

Not only is it possible to set a standard (level of performance expected) for each student, but this can also be done for the class as a whole. By determining the level of performance for each student, each student's performance on that objective can be evaluated. By determining how well the class as a whole should learn, you assess your performance as a teacher. Suppose, for example, the above objective is written so it reads:

> When books and pamphlets describing the aspects of human behavior studied by psychologists are placed in the class library, *at least 75 percent of the students* will sign out two or more of these resources.

If less than 75 percent of the students reach the expected level of performance, the goal has not been reached (even though some of our students may have signed out two or more resources).

A review: Breaking down general goals into specific, observable objectives

1. Break the goal into two parts: (1) subject matter content and (2) student response to that content.
2. Clarify the subject matter content and, where necessary, make it more specific.
3. Determine the expected student response(s) to each statement of subject matter content.
4. As needed, identify the conditions under which the student response is expected to occur and/or any useful criteria for judging the level of performance expected.

YOUR TURN

Breaking Down a General Goal into Specific, Observable Objectives

Write observable objectives for the following goal. Make certain you:

1. Identify the subject matter content and decide whether or not it is clearly enough defined. If not, describe what is needed to clarify it.

2. For each aspect of subject matter content identified above, describe at least one *observable* response the students might be expected to make to it.

3. If appropriate, specify the conditions under which the student response is expected to occur, and specify a level of performance that would be acceptable.

Goal: The students should understand the major concepts, terms, and principles used in psychological research.

Step 4. Check Objectives for Clarity and Appropriateness

To some extent, this last step may be unnecessary. If you do a good job in the first three steps, your objectives should be ready to use. A final check on your work, however, may save you the embarrassment of trying to explain to your students what it was that you "really meant to say."

A way to check for the clarity of your objectives is to have a friend (preferably one teaching the subject matter under consideration) review them. If your friend can tell you in his or her own words what each objective means, you can usually tell whether or not the objective is understandable. If it isn't, that objective probably needs clarification.

Not only must an objective be clearly stated in observable terms, but it must also be appropriate for your students. Use the following checklist to help you determine whether or not an objective is appropriate.

Criteria for Appropriate Objectives

_____ 1. Attainable by the students within a reasonable time limit
_____ 2. In proper sequence with other objectives (not to be accomplished prior to a prerequisite objective)
_____ 3. In harmony with the overall goals of the course (and curriculum)
_____ 4. In harmony with the goals and values of the institution

---

If your objectives are clearly stated in observable terms and meet the above criteria, they should be useful to both you and your students. Now take the Mastery Test for this objective on page 72.

The following additional learning activities can be done individually or in small groups. In either case, the results should be shared with the other class members.

Learning Activity 2.2

Select a unit of study from the psychology course outline found in Exhibit C. Develop a list of instructional objectives for one or more of the topics in the unit you selected. You will probably want to write general goals first, and then break them down into more observable objectives.

Learning Activity 2.3

Exchange your set of objectives (from the activity above) for a set that was developed by a classmate (or group of classmates). Analyze the set you received in the exchange. For each objective in the set, identify the following parts:

1. The subject matter content. (Is there only one? Is it clearly defined?)
2. The expected response to that content. (Is it observable? Is it reasonable to expect the students will reach it?)
3. Where appropriate, the conditions under which the response is expected and/or the level of performance expected.

MASTERY TEST

OBJECTIVE 2　To write well-defined instructional objectives

1. List the four steps involved in writing instructional objectives.

2. General, end-of-course goals do not need to be written in observable terms. (True or False)

3. Write at least two observable objectives for each of the following three goals.
    (a) Students should understand how people learn.
    (b) Students should know what motivates people to act.
    (c) Students should understand the value of the metric system.

4. What are the two parts needed in a well-written instructional objective?

5. What are the two useful (although not always needed) parts of a well-written objective?

OBJECTIVE　**3**　To use instructional objectives in instructional planning

Learning Activity 3.1

Despite the fact that there has been considerable controversy over the usefulness of instructional objectives, it is quite clear that they serve an important function in instructional planning.[5] Well-defined instructional objectives can help you:

1. Focus your planning
2. Plan effective instructional events
3. Plan valid evaluation procedures

1. Instructional Objectives Can Help You Focus Your Planning. Teachers often complain that they do not have enough time to cover the material. The process of writing instructional objectives forces you to decide, out of all the material to be covered, what you really want your students to know or be able to do. This helps to focus your planning in two ways. First, it helps you eliminate topics that are of lesser importance and highlight the more important subject matter. Second, it helps you plan for a balance of different levels of learning. By examining your final list of instructional objectives for a course (or unit within a course), you can readily determine if your plans include a balance of memorization, conceptualization, problem solving, etc. Use taxonomies of learning such as those proposed by Bloom[6] or Gagné[7] to help you determine whether or not you have planned for sufficient upper-level learning outcomes.

2. Instructional Objectives Can Help You Plan Instructional Events That Include Appropriate Learner Activities and Appropriate Teacher Activities.   In any given instructional event, the most important thing is what is happening in the minds of the students. Everything the teacher does should be designed to get the students to do the thinking that will produce the expected learning outcome. If an instructional objective calls for the students to memorize information, the learner activities should be designed to get them to repeat that information, to form appropriate associations, etc. If an instructional objective calls for the students to form a new concept, the learner activities should be designed to get students to focus on the criterial attributes of the concepts to be learned, and to compare and contrast positive and negative instances. In each of these cases, the teacher activities should be designed to help the students do the thinking (memorizing, conceptualizing) required to attain the instructional objective.

It is important that you understand the concept of an instructional event. An *instructional event* is any activity or set of activities in which students are engaged (with or without the teacher) for the purpose of learning (for example, attaining an instructional objective). Listening to a teacher's explanation, watching a film, doing an assignment in history, and completing a workbook page are all examples of instructional events.

Each instructional event should be designed to optimize the learning conditions and provide appropriate activities for both the learner and the teacher. Different kinds of learning require different learning conditions.[8] Note, for example, the teacher and learner activities that produce efficient concept learning (see Chapter 6). Note, too, that teachers can use carefully developed questions to help learners reach different levels of learning in Bloom's *Taxonomy*. Sadker and Sadker in their discussion of questioning skills (see Chapter 5) point out the fact that questions can be categorized according to the level of thinking required as defined by Bloom's *Taxonomy*. Objectives can also be classified according to Bloom's *Taxonomy*; and the various lists of words suggested in Chapter 5 by Sadker and Sadker as tools to determine the level of Bloom's *Taxonomy* for questions can also be applied to objectives.

Once you have determined the level of learning required by an objective using either Gagné's or Bloom's *Taxonomy*, for example, you can then plan the kinds of activities that will be most effective in helping students to attain those objectives at those levels.

The first step in planning appropriate learner and teacher activities is to determine, for each instructional objective, the kind of learning involved. If your instructional objectives are well defined, this should be relatively easy. The secret is in the verbs. The verbs should signal the kind of learning. For example, verbs such as *list, recall,* and *describe* suggest memory learning. Verbs such as *distinguish, differentiate,* and *contrast* suggest discrimination learning. *Identify, categorize,* and *recognize* suggest concept learning. *Solve, diagnose, resolve,* and *determine* suggest problem solving. *Like, enjoy, desire,* and *prefer* suggest affective learning. *Manipulate, perform, do,* and *physically control* suggest skill learning.

Once you have determined the kind of learning called for by an objective, your next step is to determine the kind of activities that the students have to do to accomplish that kind of learning. There are a number of books that can help you in this task,[9] and some of the other chapters in this book will also help (see, for example, Chapters 2, 4–6, and 8). You might also wish to read some of the learning research literature to find the latest information on how humans learn particular kinds of learning outcomes. (The Psychological Abstracts are a particularly useful source.)

Now you are finally ready to determine the teacher activities. The key principle to remember is that everything the teacher does should be designed to help the learners do what they need to do to learn. Therefore, you should not only be providing the students with the information they need, but you should also be helping them process that information in appropriate ways. This is why it is so important for teachers to ask the right kinds of questions at the right time (see Chapter 5).

3. Instructional Objectives Can Help You Plan Valid Evaluation Procedures.   Validity and reliability are the two most important considerations when evaluating learning (see Chapter 10). Instructional objectives define the expected learning outcomes and, therefore, are the key to developing valid tests. A test is valid if it measures what it is supposed to. Consequently, whenever teachers want to know how well their students have learned the subject material, they should measure how well those students have attained the outcomes specified in the instructional objectives. Chapter 10 tells you how to use instructional objectives to write tests that are both valid and reliable. For now, remember that, if a test is to be a valid measure of classroom achievement, it must measure as directly as possible each of the instructional objectives taught in that classroom.

Learning Activity 3.2

The education community has accepted the usefulness of instructional objectives in the planning process. An analysis of available instructional plans will help you appreciate more fully the value of instructional objectives in the planning process. Gather together completed copies of several different instructional plans (course syllabi, completed lesson plans, teacher's manuals, etc.). Examine these to determine if objectives are included and, if they are, try to decide how (if at all) the objectives influenced the student activities and/or the teacher activities. Finally, look at the objectives and try to come up with alternate student activities and/or alternate teacher activities that would also be effective in helping the students reach the objectives.

MASTERY TEST

OBJECTIVE 3   To use instructional objectives in instructional planning

1. List three ways in which instructional objectives can help in instructional planning.

2. Which activities should be determined first?
    (a) Teacher activities.
    (b) Learner activities.
    (c) It doesn't matter which is determined first.

3. Which part of an instructional objective is most helpful when trying to determine the kind of learning required by that objective?
   (a) The verb
   (b) The description of the subject matter
   (c) The criteria for performance
   (d) The conditions of performance

4. Why is it important to determine the kind of learning required to accomplish an objective?

5. Which criterion for an effective test is most reinforced by the use of instructional objectives in evaluation planning?
   (a) Usefulness
   (b) Reliability
   (c) Validity

OBJECTIVE   **4** To use objectives in implementing instruction

Learning Activity 4.1

Well-defined instructional objectives can be a big help to you and your students during the teaching process. First, when used correctly, they can help you clarify the expectations for your students, and clarity has been shown to be a critical element in successful teaching.[10] Second, they can serve as a useful guide to the students as they listen, do assignments, and study for tests.[11] Finally, well-defined instructional objectives can help you stay on track as you teach, and can help you deal more effectively with sidetracks. To improve your teaching, you can use instructional objectives:

1. As handouts prior to instruction
2. To prepare students for instruction
3. As a guide throughout instruction

1. Using Objectives As Handouts.   There is some evidence in the literature suggesting that students perform better on tests when they have been provided with handouts of well-defined instructional objectives.[12] There are a number of things you can do, however, to make these handouts as effective as possible. Objectives that are clearly articulated, meeting the criteria specified earlier in this chapter, will contribute most to student achievement.[13] According to Melton,[14] however, objectives should also be of interest to the students, at the correct level of difficulty, and relevant to the content to be mastered.

It has been my experience that if too many objectives are given to students all at once (for example, all the objectives for a six-week period), they are not used effectively and do little to improve achievement. Try handing out a separate set of objectives for each unit of instruction for each subject. Then review those objectives daily as you work with your students.

2. Using Objectives to Prepare Students for Instruction.   Madeline Hunter has been a strong advocate of producing an appropriate learning set in students by telling students what they should be able to expect from any given instructional event.[15] This concept is occasionally criticized by those who advocate a discovery or inquiry approach to learning. The concern is that, if students know the outcome from the beginning, the discovery process will not work effectively. It is my contention, however, that one can adequately prepare students for learning without giving away the answers, and well-written instructional objectives can help you do that. Recall that a well-written objective should not be too specific (though it must be explicit and unambiguous). Therefore, students should be told that they will be expected to be able to solve certain types of problems, or that they should be able to discover things such as relationships or causes and effects. They should not be told, however, which specific finding or answer they are expected to discover. The focus should be on the learning outcome — the skill they are expected to acquire during the discovery process — not the specific outcome of their discovery activities.

Because each instructional activity may require something different of the learner, teachers should prepare students at the beginning of each new instructional event. There are at least four kinds of information that will help prepare students for any given instructional event:

1. Learning outcome
2. Learner activities
3. Teacher activities
4. Evaluation activities

1. Learning Outcome

A well-written objective is the best statement of learning outcome, and is, therefore, especially useful in preparing students for an instructional event. Telling students what they will be expected to know or be able to do on completion of the instructional event will help prepare them for the activities involved.

2. Learner Activities

For many students, knowing just the expected learning outcome may not be enough information to help them get the most out of an instructional event. Some students, for example, when told to "study Chapter 19 (an instructional event) so that they will be able to describe the major causes of the Civil War" (a learning outcome), may not know how to study for such an outcome. Consequently, it is helpful, when preparing students for an instructional event, to tell them what they need to do to get the most out of the activities involved, and to accomplish successfully the expected outcome. When instructional objectives are well defined, it is much easier to determine the kind of learning activities that would be most appropriate.[16]

3. Teacher Activities

In most instructional activities, the teacher has a definite role. The teacher activities may involve providing explanations, giving feedback, observing student performance, etc.; however, they should always involve guiding the learner through the learner activities to the accomplishment of the learning outcome (instructional objective). It is helpful for students to know, from the beginning of an instructional event, exactly what the role of the teacher will be and exactly how much guidance can be expected.

4. Evaluation Activities

How will the students know if they have accomplished an expected learning outcome? How will the teacher judge a student's performance relative to that learning outcome? Providing students with the answers to these two questions helps prepare them for an instructional event and increases the efficiency of their learning. Well-defined objectives are stated in measurable, observable terms, and the type of evaluation is easily determined. Such is not the case when objectives are poorly written.

YOUR TURN

Preparing Students for Instruction

Preparing students to learn is simply a matter of giving them information about the four aspects of an instructional event: expected outcome, learner activities, teacher activities, and evaluation activities. Instructional activities should be designed to help students reach a particular instructional objective. Therefore, as you prepare students to learn, you should begin with the instructional objective, and answer for your students the following four questions:

1. What will the students need to know or be able to do when this instructional activity is over?

2. What do the students need to do to learn that?

3. What are you (as teacher) going to do to help the students learn?

4. How will the students (and the teacher) know if they have learned what was expected of them?

In the following exercise, jot down a single instructional objective, how you would teach that objective, briefly describe an instructional activity (explanation, assignment, etc.) that would help students to reach the objective, and then write answers to the four questions students need answered for them as they begin to learn.

Answers to Student Questions

1. What do I need to know or be able to do on completion of this activity?
2. What do I need to do to learn that?
3. What are you going to do to help me?
4. How will we know when I have learned what was expected?

---

3. Using Objectives As a Guide Throughout Instruction.   Objectives are not only helpful in preparing students to learn, but they can also serve to keep students and teacher alike focused throughout the instructional process. Teachers often talk about ways to handle sidetracks, and students have been known to plot ways to get the teacher off track. Students frequently complain because a test did not measure what they learned. That kind of problem can arise because the students studied the wrong material or studied in the wrong way (for example, memorized when they should have tried to understand or attempted to apply to new situations). By keeping instructional objectives constantly in students' minds throughout the instructional process, teachers can significantly reduce the problems of getting off track or focusing on the wrong topics during instruction. If you make it obvious that you are using instructional objectives to guide what you do as teacher, the things you ask your students to do are designed to help them accomplish the instructional objectives, and your tests do indeed evaluate the instructional objectives, then both you and your students will stay better focused. This is not to say that sidetracks are always bad, or that it is not worth learning if an objective has not been written to cover it. But your instructional objectives should serve as a primary guide for what you teach, what your students learn, and what you test.

Learning Activity 4.2

Here is a simple exercise that can help you understand the value of using objectives as a regular part of the instructional process. You and your classmates should divide into small groups, five to six per group. Each group will develop a handout of four or five objectives for a given unit of instruction (specify the grade level as well as the subject). Using the above guidelines, prepare a brief presentation (it may not take more than a few seconds to present) designed to prepare the students to learn. One member of your group should use the handout and present an overview of the unit, preparing the students for that unit. Each of the other members of your group should make a presentation, preparing the students to begin learning a given objective from those on the handout. Make certain that you tell the students the learning outcome and describe for them the learner activities, teacher activities, and evaluation activities.

MASTERY TEST

OBJECTIVE 4   To use objectives in implementing instruction

1. List three ways that you can use instructional objectives to improve your teaching.

2. Which of the following schedules for handing out objectives to students is most likely to be effective?
   (a) All course objectives provided on a handout as an overview at the beginning of the course.
   (b) Unit objectives provided on a handout as an overview at the beginning of each unit.
   (c) Each objective provided as a handout at the beginning of the class when that objective will be taught.

3. List four things that should be told to students to prepare them for an instructional event.

4. Instructional objectives should guide:
   (a) Teaching
   (b) Evaluating
   (c) Learning
   (d) All of the above

▓ **Answer Keys for Your Turn Exercises**

ANSWER KEY

Your Turn: Recognize Student-Oriented Objectives

1. *S.* A desirable learning outcome.
2. *T.* Students will need to learn proper eye movements, but it is likely that the teacher will have to demonstrate them to the students.
3. *T.* Probably helpful to students, but not an expected student outcome.
4. *S.* A student who can do this has learned well.
5. *T.* How would a teacher do this?
6. *T.* Lecturing is only important if it helps the students reach a desirable learning outcome.
7. *S.* A learning outcome requiring several prerequisite skills.
8. *T.* Of course, maintaining self-discipline may be an important student-oriented objective.
9. *S.* A goal most English teachers hope their students will eventually attain.
10. *S.* A student-oriented objective. The teacher might work through such an evaluation with his or her students, however, as one activity designed to help them reach this goal.

ANSWER KEY

Your Turn: Recognize Outcomes, Not Activities

1. *A*
2. *O*
3. *A*
4. *A*
5. *O*
6. *O*
7. *O*
8. *O*
9. *A*
10. *A*
11. *O (although this could be a practice exercise for the outcome specified in 12)*
12. *O*
13. *A*
14. *A*
15. *O*

Note: Some of the above outcomes (such as 5, 6, 7, and 8) might best be learned by trying to do them and then getting feedback on how successful you were. This kind of practice, using a learning outcome as a learning activity, can be highly successful if (1) the student has reached a high enough level of understanding of the task and (2) feedback is provided.

ANSWER KEY

Your Turn: Clear and Unambiguous Objectives

1. *2*
2. *1*
3. *1*
4. *2*
5. *1*
6. *1*
7. *1*
8. *1*
9. *2*
10. *1*
11. *2*
12. *2*
13. *1*
14. *2*

ANSWER KEY

Your Turn: Observable Objectives

1. *O*
2. *O*
3. *N*
4. *O*
5. *N*
6. *N*
7. *O*

ANSWER KEY

Your Turn: Describe the Subject Matter Content

1. There would probably be little difference. The general topics to be covered could remain the same. The level of understanding expected might be different for seventh and eighth graders, but that would not show up in a general description of course content. Because the course will not serve as a precursor to a college-level course in this case, less emphasis might be placed on research and more on how-to-do-it techniques.
2. Seventh and eighth graders might take a little longer to learn the concepts involved in these topics, so one might shorten the outline slightly. Also, one could replace some of the terms with more commonly used words that would appeal more to seventh and eighth graders.
3. Probably not.
4. Yes, the primary differences would probably be in the level of understanding expected and the learning activities that would be assigned. These differences would only show up in the specific, behavioral objectives at the unit level, and in the assignments designed to help the students reach those objectives.

ANSWER KEY

Your Turn: Specifying General Goals

PART 1

Here are additional general goals for a high school psychology course. Your goals may not be identical to these, but there should be some similarity between these and the ones you have written. If there is not, have your instructor check your work.

1. Students should be aware of their major personality traits, usual learning strategies, the intrinsic and extrinsic motivating factors that influence their decisions and behavior, and the ways in which they respond under social pressure.
2. Students should have an appreciation for the value of psychological research.
3. Students should have an understanding of the importance of specialists in the area of psychology.
4. Students should have an appreciation for the intricacies of personality development.
5. Students should have developed better study habits based on the principles of learning.
6. Students should have a better understanding of why people act the way they do.
7. Students should have developed attitudes of concern and understanding toward the mentally ill.
8. Students should have developed an attitude toward mental illness that is positive.

PART 2

Here are some additional goals for Unit 1: Psychology As a Science. Many other goals could be written. They need not be written in observable terms, but they should be compatible with the end-of-course goals that have been specified.

Cognitive Goals

1. Students should know the major founders of psychological theory and the important points in their theories.
2. Students should be able to describe those aspects of psychology that make it a science.
3. The student should be able to list the methodological steps in psychological research.
4. The student should be able to define the major concepts and terms found in psychological science and research.

Affective Goals

1. The student should be able to accept differences that exist among the ideas of famous psychologists.
2. Students should enjoy doing simple psychological research.
3. Students should become interested in finding out more about specific aspects of psychology.

ANSWER KEY

Your Turn: Breaking Down a General Goal into Specific, Observable Objectives

Below are three objectives that could have been derived from the goal you were given. Compare your objectives to these. Do your objectives contain the necessary elements to make them understandable and observable? Also, compare your objectives with those written by your classmates.

1. When given a major concept or term used in psychological research, the student should be able to select from among a number of alternatives the one definition or example that best illustrates that concept or term.

2. When asked to write a short paper explaining the methodologies of psychological research, the student should be able to use correctly ten out of fifteen major concepts that were presented in class lecture.

3. When given a description of psychological research problems, the student should be able to select from among a number of alternatives the principle(s) that would be most appropriate to the solution of the problem.

ANSWER KEY

Your Turn: Preparing Students for Instruction

The answers to these questions will vary depending on the objective selected. Ask your instructor for feedback on your answers, or compare your answers to that of your classmates. Discussing this exercise with your classmates will help you understand the process of preparing students for an instructional event.

▓ Answer Keys for Mastery Tests

ANSWER KEY

Mastery Test, Objective 1

1. a
2. a
3. a
4. a
5. b
6. a
7. b
8. b
9. b
10. a
11–14. (can be in any order) student-oriented; describes a learning outcome; clear, understandable; observable
15. c
16. a
17. a
18. c
19. b

ANSWER KEY

Mastery Test, Objective 2

1. Describe the subject matter content.
   Specify the general goals.
   Break down the general goals into more specific, observable objectives.
   Check these objectives for clarity and appropriateness.
2. True. When broken down into more specific objectives, the end-of-course goals should be observable; however, the general goals are just a step along the way toward the development of usable, observable objectives.

   Below are suggested answers for items 6–8. Other possibilities exist. Make certain each objective written specifies a clearly defined subject matter content, an observable response to that content, and, where necessary, a statement describing the conditions under which the response is expected to occur and/or the level of performance expected in the response.

3. (a) Given a description of a learning task, students should be able to describe the process utilized by the learner to accomplish that task.
      Describe the major variables affecting the learning process — tell what makes a learning task easier and what makes it more difficult.
   (b) Given several possible "motivators" and a description of a particular human behavior, students should be able to select the "motivator(s)" that would most likely stimulate the behavior.
      To list the major motivators of human behavior.
   (c) To list the advantages and disadvantages of the metric system.
      When given the choice between using the metric system or some other system for solving a given problem, the student should be able to explain why the use of the metric system would be more appropriate.
4. (a) A description of subject matter content.
   (b) An observable, expected response to that content.
5. (a) The conditions under which the student response is expected to occur.
   (b) Level of performance expected, or level of performance that would be acceptable, as evidence that the objective was met satisfactorily.

ANSWER KEY

Mastery Test, Objective 3

1. (a) Focus your planning
    (b) Plan for effective instructional events
    (c) Plan valid evaluation procedure
2. b

3. a
4. Because different kinds of learning require different kinds of thinking and/or different learning conditions
5. c

ANSWER KEY

Mastery Test, Objective 4

1. (a) As handouts prior to instruction
    (b) To prepare students for instruction
    (c) As a guide throughout instruction
2. b
3. (a) Learning outcome

    (b) Learner activities
    (c) Teacher activities
    (d) Evaluation activities
4. d

■ Notes

1. W. J. Popham, "Instructional Objectives 1960–1970," *Performance and Instruction* 26, 2 (1987): 11–14. Also see Additional Readings at the end of this chapter.
2. For additional examples, see Chapter 4 in T. D. TenBrink, *Evaluation: A Practical Guide for Teachers* (New York: McGraw-Hill Book Company, 1974).
3. This list was adapted from T. D. TenBrink, *Evaluation: A Practical Guide for Teachers* (New York: McGraw-Hill Book Company, 1974), p. 102.
4. Some authors use the term *performance* to refer to student outcome, *condition* to refer to conditions under which the performance is expected to occur, and *criteria* to refer to the level of performance expected.
5. S. J. Frudden and S. B. Stow, "Eight Elements of Effective Preinstructional Planning," *Education* 106, 2 (1985): 218–222.
6. B. S. Bloom, et al., *Taxonomy of Educational Objectives, Handbook I: Cognitive Domain* (New York: Longman, Inc., 1984).
7. R. M. Gagné, "Learning Outcomes and Their Effects: Useful categories of Human Performance," *American Psychologist* 39, 4 (1984): 377–385.
8. R. M. Gagné, *Conditions of Learning and Theory of Instruction*, 4th ed. (San Diego: Harcourt Brace Jovanovich, 1992).
9. See R. M. Gagné, et al. (1992) and R. M. Traverse (1982), listed in Additional Readings.
10. C. V. Hines, D. R. Cruickshank, and J. J. Kennedy, "Teacher Clarity and Its Relationship to Student Achievement and Satisfaction," *American Educational Research Journal* 22, 1 (1985): 87–99.
11. J. Hartley and I. Davies, "Preinstructional Strategies: The Role of Pretests, Behavioral Objectives, Overviews and Advance Organizers," *Review of Educational Research* 46 (1976): 239–265.
12. P. C. Duchastel and P. F. Merrill, "The Effects of Behavioral Objectives on Learning: A Review of Empirical Studies," *Review of Educational Research* 45 (1973): 53–69.

13. G. T. Dalis, "Effects of Precise Objectives upon Student Achievement in Health Education," *Journal of Experimental Education* 39 (1970): 20–23.

14. R. F. Melton, "Resolution of Conflicting Claims Concerning the Effects of Behavioral Objectives on Student Learning," *Review of Educational Research* 48 (1978): 291–302.

15. M. Hunter, "Teacher Competency: Problem, Theory, and Practice." *Theory into Practice* 15, 2 (1976): 162–171.

16. R. M. Gagné, "What Should a Performance Improvements Professional Know and Do?" *Performance and Instruction* 24, 27 (1985): 6–7.

Additional Readings

Burns, R. W. *New Approaches to Behavioral Objectives.* Dubuque, IA: Wm. G. Brown Company Publishers, 1972.

Gagné, R. M., et al. *Principles of Instructional Design,* 4th ed. San Diego: Harcourt Brace Jovanovich, 1992.

Gronlund, Norman E. *How to Write Instructional Objectives,* New York: Free Press, 1990.

Kibler, R. J., L. L. Barker, and D. T. Miles. *Behavioral Objectives and Instruction.* Boston: Allyn and Bacon, 1970.

Mager, Robert F. *Preparing Instructional Objectives.* Belmont, CA.: David S. Lake Publishers, 1984.

Popham, W. James. "Probing the Validity Arguments Against Behavioral Goals." In R. C. Anderson, G. W. Faust, M. C. Roderick, D. J. Cunningham, and T. Andre, eds. *Current Research on Instruction,* Englewood Cliffs, NJ: Prentice-Hall, 1969.

Travers, R. M. W. *Essentials of Learning,* 5th ed. New York: Macmillan, 1982.

Lesson Presentation Skills

4

■ **Robert Shostak**

1   To define set induction, explain its purposes, and give examples of when it is used as a lesson presentation skill

2   To plan original sets for use in a series of hypothetical teaching situations

3   To identify the specific, underlying purpose of four different types of explanations frequently used in lesson presentations

4   To plan original explanations, given a series of hypothetical teaching situations

5   To define closure, explain its purposes, and give examples of when it is used as a lesson presentation skill

6   To plan original closures for use in a series of hypothetical teaching situations

7   To identify the instructional purposes for using the lecture and give examples of when it is used in lesson presentations

8   To plan an original lecture, given a series of hypothetical teaching situations

Teaching and learning are two sides of the same coin. It is extremely difficult to talk about one without including the other. However, if you were to examine the nature of professional writing and research dealing with teaching and learning, you would discover an interesting phenomenon. Educators shift their emphasis from teaching to learning in a regular, almost predictable fashion. In the last decade the focus was on the student as learner and on the examination of learning styles. Now this emphasis has shifted, and professional educators have turned their attention to effective teaching performance.

The 1992 yearbook of the Association for Supervision and Curriculum Development is devoted entirely to the subject of supervision in the schools, with one entire section focusing on the improvement of teaching.[1] Researchers from the Educational Testing Service (ETS) in Princeton, New Jersey, have undertaken the task of developing new assessment instruments to measure the complexity of teaching performance, with the goal of being able to isolate and demonstrate the most effective classroom teaching skills.[2] From lists of teaching skills developed recently by several research groups, those pertaining directly to lesson presentation were (1) introducing the lesson, or *set induction;* (2) *explaining;* (3) providing reinforcement through planned summarizing procedures, or *closure;* and (4) verbalizing content to be learned, or *lecture.*

Regardless of the grade level one teaches, the necessity of exposing students to new facts, concepts, and principles; explaining difficult procedures; clarifying conflicting issues; and exploring complicated relationships more frequently than not places the teacher in the position of having to do a great deal of presenting. Consequently, any prospective teacher ought to be interested in mastering those skills needed to become an effective presenter. The purpose of this chapter is to provide you with experiences that will assist you in acquiring the behaviors necessary to make effective classroom presentations.

OBJECTIVE   *1*   To define set induction, explain its purposes, and give examples of when it is used as a lesson presentation skill

Learning Activity 1.1

Set Induction

Set induction refers to those actions and statements by the teacher that are designed to relate the experiences of the students to the objectives of the lesson.[3] Effective teachers use set induction to put students in a receptive frame of mind that will facilitate learning — be it physical, mental, or emotional.

A story is told about a traveler who came upon an old man beating his donkey in an effort to make the animal rise. The animal sat placidly in the middle of the road refusing to get up, and the old man continued to whip the animal until a stranger stepped up and stopped his hand. "Why don't you tell the donkey to rise?" asked the stranger. "I will," replied the old man, "but first I have to get his attention."

The first purpose of set induction is *to focus student attention on the lesson.* DeCecco, after reviewing the relevant theory and research on motivation, says that the first motivational function of the teacher is "to engage the student in learning."[4] The Kelwynn Group, an educational consulting firm that developed a list of twenty criteria for effective teaching performance based on the research of Madeline Hunter, Jane Stallings, Barak Rosenshine, and others, echoes the same notion.[5]

As its second purpose, set induction attempts to *create an organizing framework for the ideas, principles, or information that is to follow.* Gage and Berliner, in discussing the importance of lecture introductions, speak of *advance organizers* — "telling students in advance about the way in which a lecture is organized is likely to improve their comprehension and ability to recall and apply what they hear."[6] DeCecco calls attention to what he terms the *expectancy function of teachers.* He bases this notion on research showing that teachers can best shape student behavior when students have been told in advance what is expected of them.[7]

A dramatic and certainly controversial study that demonstrates the power of set induction was reported by Robert Rosenthal and Lenore Jacobson in their book, *Pygmalion in the Classroom.* The authors conducted an experiment in which they tested all of the pupils from kindergarten through grade six in a particular school. Teachers were told that the test "... will allow us to predict which youngsters are most likely to show an academic spurt."[8] In September following this testing period, each teacher was given a list of students and was told that the students on their lists were the ones most likely to show a marked improvement in their school performance; actually, the student names had been chosen at random. After three successive testing periods, however, the researchers claim that the test performance of these randomly identified students began to rise to meet the erroneous expectations of their teachers. In other words, the teachers, being told that their students were likely to do well academically, worked with the children in such a way that these expectations became a reality. By passing their expectations on to their students, the teachers were practicing a form of set induction that, in this case, had a positive effect on learning.

A third purpose of set induction is *to extend the understanding and the application of abstract ideas through the use of example or analogy.* An idea or principle that is abstractly stated can be difficult for many students to comprehend. Moreover, many students who do understand an idea or principle have difficulty in applying their knowledge to new situations. The clever use of examples and analogies can do much to overcome such limitations. Novelists, dramatists, and poets are particularly good at using analogies to create expanded meaning in their works. For example:

A Patch of Old Snow

There's a patch of old snow in a corner,
    That I should have guessed
Was a blow-away paper the rain
    Had brought to rest.
It is speckled with grime as if
    Small print overspread it,
The news of a day I've forgotten —
    If I ever read it.

— Robert Frost[9]

Literally speaking, the poet is describing a patch of old snow that resembles an old newspaper. By use of metaphor (analogy) the poet creates a literary experience that enables the reader to extend his or her understanding far beyond the simple comparison of a patch of old snow to a discarded newspaper. At one level, the metaphor suggests that the snow, once fallen and now melted, has little meaning in the grand scheme of things. Then, perhaps with tongue in cheek, Frost seems to suggest that what is recorded in the newspaper — today or yesterday — may not really be much more important than the remains of an old snowfall.

The fourth and last purpose of set induction is *to stimulate student interest and involvement in the lesson.* A great deal of research has been carried on over the years on student motivation and the need to increase the student's interest in learning. Maria Montessori observes how strong involvement in play activities can keep a young child motivated and interested in a single game over an extended period of time. The point here is that active involvement at the beginning of a lesson can increase curiosity and stimulate student interest in the lesson.[10] A good example is the teacher who wishes to teach the concept of categorizing and brings a collection of baseball player cards, record jackets, or even a basket of leaves to class. Then the students, divided into groups, are asked to categorize their collections and explain how and why they did what they did.

Learning Activity 1.2

Now that set induction has been defined and its purposes explained, you are ready to focus on when teachers generally use set induction in the course of a lesson. To understand set usage better, think of a classroom lesson as a game. Bellack, in his research on the language used by teachers to direct classroom lessons, talks about "structuring moves [that] *set the context* for the entire classroom *game.*"[11] Furthermore, he views the lesson as containing several "subgames," each of which is identified primarily by the type of activity taking place during a given period of play.

For example, the teacher plans during the course of a lesson to carry on several different activities such as reading, writing, and discussion, each dealing with different subject matter. Each new activity can be seen as a subgame within the context of a larger game, the entire day's lessons. The teacher, then, must structure each situation so that students can participate (play) effectively in the lesson (game).

The kinds of classroom situations (subgames) for which it is necessary to employ a set are innumerable. To assist you in learning when to employ set induction in your own lessons, study carefully the following list.

Examples of When to Use Set Induction

To begin a long unit of work in which the class might be studying plants, rockets, or local government

To introduce a new concept or principle

To initiate a discussion

To begin a skill-building activity such as reading comprehension or visual discrimination

To introduce a film, TV program, record, or tape

To initiate a question-and-answer session

To prepare for a field trip

To present a guest speaker

To introduce a homework assignment

To begin a laboratory exercise

To redirect a presentation when you see that students do not understand the content

MASTERY TEST

OBJECTIVE 1   To define set induction, explain its purposes, and give examples of when it is used as a lesson presentation skill

Questions 1 and 2 are designed to determine your knowledge and comprehension level. Successful completion of these questions meets the objective of the learning activity. Question 3 is designed to test a more advanced level of learning — analysis and application. It is a bonus, and tests your ability to identify and analyze a set when it is being used in a teaching situation.

1. Define set induction as a teaching skill, and explain three specific purposes it serves in lesson presentations.

2. Describe briefly three different situations in which you would use set induction in making a classroom presentation.

3. Identify and explain how set induction has been employed in the presentation of this chapter.

 **OBJECTIVE**   **2** To plan original sets for use in a series of hypothetical teaching situations

Learning Activity 2

Now that you know what set induction is and the general purposes for which it is used, you are ready to begin practicing how to plan your own sets. Before you begin doing this, you should take time to familiarize yourself with some examples of how experienced teachers might use set induction in their lessons.

Uses of Set Induction

Study carefully the following list of specific uses of set induction employed by experienced teachers. Then read each of the sample lessons that follow and the accompanying analysis. You should then be ready to plan your own sets for a given teaching situation.

1. To focus the student's attention on the presentation the teacher is about to make by employing an activity, event, object, or person that relates directly to student interest or previous experience
2. To provide a structure or framework that enables the student to visualize the content or activities of the presentation
3. To aid in clarifying the goals of the lesson presentation
4. To provide a smooth transition from known or already covered material to new or unknown material by capitalizing on the use of examples (either verbal or nonverbal), analogies, and student activities that students have interest in or experience with
5. To evaluate previously learned material, before moving on to new material or skill-building activities, by employing student-centered activities or student-developed examples and analogies that demonstrate understanding of previously learned content

Sample Lesson Number 1

The teacher has planned to start the topic of percent and is aware of students' interest in local baseball. The teacher decides to introduce the unit with a brief discussion of the previous day's game. Talk is directed to batting averages, and the teacher demonstrates how they are calculated. Students are permitted to work out one or two of the averages for favorite players.

Analysis.   This set is most appropriately used for introducing a unit on percent or the concept of percent itself. Referring to the list of uses for set induction mentioned above, note:

1. The set focuses students' attention on the concept of percent, which is the unit or topic being initiated by the teacher in this lesson.
2. It uses an event (like yesterday's baseball game) and an activity that is familiar to the students, and in which they have considerable interest.
3. It provides a ready frame of reference (batting averages) for application of the percent concept to other situations.
4. Through teacher comment, the concept of batting averages and percent can be easily connected to help clarify the goals of the new unit or topic.

Sample Lesson Number 2

The students working in a science unit have already demonstrated in the first part of their lesson some basic understanding of mixtures. The teacher has planned to conduct an experiment to demonstrate visually the concept of mixtures. She brings to class several bottles of different kinds of popular salad dressings. The students are directed to experiment with the various bottles and to observe differences in their appearance before and after they are vigorously mixed.

Analysis.   This set is most appropriately used to begin a laboratory exercise. Referring to the list of uses for set induction mentioned above, note:

1. It is used specifically to provide a smooth transition from what the students already know (knowledge of mixtures) to the new material to be covered in the lesson.
2. It relies on the use of an activity (experiment) that is familiar to all the students.

Sample Lesson Number 3

The students have been reading short stories and examining the techniques authors use to create a mood through setting. The teacher begins the lesson by providing the class with a list of words that suggest different moods. Each student is asked to select one word and tell how he or she, as an author, might create a setting appropriate to the suggested mood.

Analysis.   This set is most appropriately used to initiate a discussion or question-and-answer session. Referring to the list of uses for set induction mentioned above, note:

1. It is being used to determine how well students understand the relationship of setting to mood.
2. It relies on student-developed examples that demonstrate their understanding of the relationship of setting to mood.

MASTERY TEST

OBJECTIVE 2   To plan original sets for use in a series of hypothetical teaching situations

Following these directions are five hypothetical teaching situations. Read each one carefully and plan a set of your own that you feel would work effectively in that particular situation. You may refer to the list of uses for set induction on page 94, and the sample lessons that follow to help you generate ideas for your own sets.

Situation 1.   The class has been working on a unit in government. During the first part of the period, the students saw a short filmstrip on the three branches of government. The filmstrip is not an in-depth experience, but gives an overview. The teacher wishes to use the remainder of the period to promote a more thorough understanding of the role or function of each branch of the government, using a different kind of activity.

Situation 2.   You are introducing the study of pollution and the environment to your class. It is important that you get off on the right foot.

Situation 3.   You are exploring the world of work with your class and have an excellent film you wish to show.

Situation 4.   Your class has been studying the letters of the alphabet. You wish to use part of the day to take up this subject again, and to determine how far your students have come in being able to place the letters in order.

Situation 5.   Your class has been working on different techniques to put life into their writing. In this lesson, you wish to present the idea of using descriptive words to paint verbal pictures.

OBJECTIVE

3 To identify the specific, underlying purpose of four different types of explanations frequently used in lesson presentations

Learning Activity 3

Explaining Behavior

One cold, dark night a fire broke out in a small, European, medieval town. After the townspeople had fought the destructive blaze for hours and successfully extinguished the flames, the mayor brought the people together for a few words. "Citizens," he began, "this fire was truly a blessing from God." Noting the hostile glances from the crowd, the mayor hastily explained: "You must understand. If it were not for the light provided by the flames, how would we have been able to see how to fight the fire?" The story never tells how the people accepted this explanation, but the lesson presentation skill that follows reveals a great deal about explaining behavior.

Explaining refers to planned teacher talk designed to clarify any idea, procedure, or process not understood by a student. Every teacher, as well as every student, knows the importance of being able to give clear explanations. Teachers rely heavily on this skill in lesson presentation; students know only too well the difficulty of learning from the teacher who lacks this critical skill.

The use and importance of explaining behavior extend far beyond the classroom. You encounter the use of explanations, both oral and written, in every aspect of your personal life. You open cans, put furniture together, operate all kinds of devices that require simple training through directions, and frequently listen to experts explain what lies behind every contemporary problem imaginable. Unfortunately, the explanations you hear in these varied situations are frequently not satisfying. Some time ago I bought a pair of snow chains for my automobile. I carefully unpacked them and read with great interest the simple, brief directions for putting on the chains:

> Lay out the chains as illustrated in the diagram, and proceed to hook up in the usual manner.

You can imagine my frustration trying to follow a faded diagram that didn't really tell me anything, and guessing wildly at what was meant by "the usual manner" — never having put on a set of tire chains in my life.

The importance of explaining in lesson presentation is well documented. Miltz cites a number of research studies that support the importance of explaining and its effect on student learning.[12] And in *The Praxis Series: Professional Assessments for Beginning Teachers*, the researchers include making clear explanations in domain C of their assessment criteria.[13]

An efficient way to begin acquiring skill in explaining is first to understand the underlying purpose of an explanation. Generally speaking, an explanation may have any of four different, underlying purposes.

1. To show a direct cause-and-effect relationship
2. To show that a particular action is governed by a general rule or law
3. To illustrate a procedure or process
4. To show the intent of an action or process

YOUR TURN

Examples of ideas, procedures, and processes frequently requiring careful explanation follow. Note that, although a wide range of subjects is covered, the explanation of each idea, procedure, or process will have a particular underlying purpose. Study each group one at a time. Then complete the exercise and compare your results with other students.

1. Examples that require explanations whose underlying purpose is to show a cause-and-effect relationship:
   (a) The effect of heat in changing a liquid to gas
   (b) The result of inaccurate measurement in constructing a woodworking project, baking a cake, etc.
   (c) The effect of an unclear communication
   (d) The effect of pollutants in the air

Now that you have had a chance to study the examples, write three of your own examples that require an explanation whose underlying purpose is to show a direct cause-and-effect relationship.

2. Examples that require explanations whose underlying purpose is to show that a particular action is governed by a general rule or law:
   (a) The reason for sterilization procedures in a hospital operating room
   (b) The need for a particular kind of clothing in varied weather conditions
   (c) The need for protective glasses when using power tools

Now that you have had a chance to study the examples, write three of your own examples that require an explanation whose underlying purpose is to show that a particular action is governed by a general rule or law.

3. Examples that require explanations whose underlying purpose is to illustrate a procedure or process:
   (a) Preparing vegetables for a salad
   (b) Developing an outline for an essay
   (c) The appropriate way to clean up after an art activity
   (d) The proper care of a musical instrument

Now that you have had a chance to study the examples, write three of your own examples that require an explanation whose underlying purpose is to illustrate a procedure or process.

4. Examples that require explanations whose underlying purpose is to show the intent of an action or process:
   (a) The motivation for a character's behavior in a story
   (b) Why we fire pottery
   (c) The use of a particular defense in football, basketball, baseball, etc.
   (d) The function of a custom in a particular ethnic group

Now that you have had a chance to study the examples, write three of your own examples that require an explanation whose underlying purpose is to show the intent of an action or process.

MASTERY TEST

OBJECTIVE 3   To identify the specific, underlying purpose of four different types of explanations frequently used in lesson presentations

Identify what the underlying purpose would be for each of the following ideas, procedures, or processes that require an explanation. Use the letter preceding the definition of the underlying purpose to indicate your answer and write it in the space provided.

Underlying Purpose

A. To show a direct cause-and-effect relationship
B. To show that a particular action is governed by a general rule or law
C. To illustrate a procedure or process
D. To show the intent of an action or process

Idea, Procedure, or Process to Be Explained

( ) a. Internal combustion

( ) b. The purpose of a bat's radar system for flying

( ) c. The entrance of the United States into World War II

( ) d. The use of the question mark in written English

( ) e. The motivation for a character's behavior in a novel

( ) f. The ill effects of an improper diet

( ) g. How a bill is introduced in Congress

( ) h. The use of a sign or symbol, for example, a red light to stop

---

OBJECTIVE   **4** To plan original explanations, given a series of hypothetical teaching situations

Learning Activity 4

Now that you understand the importance of explaining behavior and the underlying purposes for which it is used, you need to know how to plan or structure an effective explanation. Explaining behavior is a teaching skill that depends a great deal on a teacher's knowledge and creativity. No two teachers utilize their skill in exactly the same way. Beginning teachers can follow a simple procedure to help develop effective explaining behavior. Once you have made a decision about what needs to be explained, the following four procedural steps will help you plan an effective explanation:

1. Identify the purpose of the explanation for yourself.
2. Prepare a definition for students of the key ideas (process or procedure) in the simplest terms possible.
3. Illustrate for students with examples or demonstrations.
4. Summarize for or with students.

Examples of how the procedure can be used to help structure an effective explanation — each with a different underlying purpose — follow. The material to be explained was chosen from the lists presented in the previous learning activity. Study them carefully. Then you should be ready to plan explanations in your particular teaching situation.

EXAMPLE 1: *You wish to explain to a general science class that the property of a liquid may be changed by raising its temperature.*

Step 1: *Identify purpose for yourself.* The purpose of this explanation is to show the *direct cause-and-effect relationship* between the application of heat to a liquid and the consequent change of its property.

Step 2: *Define key ideas.* Changing the property of a liquid in this instance simply means changing water from a liquid to a gas.

Step 3: *Illustrate.* The simplest illustration of this change is to heat a tea kettle full of water until steam begins to come out of the spout.

Step 4: *Summarize.* An oral or written summary of what occurred in the demonstration should be made by the teacher or a student.

EXAMPLE 2: *You need to explain the use of a question mark in written English to a group of elementary school children who have not yet been formally introduced to this punctuation mark.*

Step 1:   *Identify purpose for yourself.* The purpose of this explanation is to indicate that there is a rule governing the use of the question mark (?) in written English.

Step 2:   *Define key ideas.* A question mark (?) is a mark of punctuation used in writing in the English language to indicate that a question is being asked.

Step 3:   *Illustrate.* One of the simplest ways to illustrate this rule is to prepare handwritten examples of sentences, some of which are simple direct statements and others questions. Distribute the examples to the students and have them read the material aloud. The same procedure can be followed using examples from textbooks, newspapers, and magazines.

Step 4:   *Summarize.* An oral or written summary of the rule for the use of the question mark should be given by either the teacher or a student.

EXAMPLE 3:   *You need to explain the process known as internal combustion to a group of students beginning to study auto mechanics.*

Step 1:   *Identify purpose for yourself.* The purpose of this explanation is *to illustrate the process* of internal combustion as it takes place in a gasoline engine.

Step 2:   *Define key ideas.* Internal combustion is a process in which a mixture of gasoline vapor and air is burned inside a cylinder.

Step 3:   *Illustrate.* Depending on materials available, you may wish to demonstrate the process with a simple experiment, or the use of photographs, slides, film, or a cut-away model.

Step 4:   *Summarize.* An oral restatement of the process itself, including the individual steps necessary for internal combustion to take place, should be made by the teacher or a student.

EXAMPLE 4:   *You are teaching a pottery unit, and in the course of explaining each of the steps necessary to produce a finished product, you need to indicate the intent of the firing process.*

Step 1:   *Identify purpose for yourself.* The purpose of this explanation is *to show the intent* of the firing process in producing a finished piece of pottery.

Step 2:   *Define key ideas.* Firing is a drying process that removes water or moisture from clay to make the clay hard.

Step 3:   *Illustrate.* Allowing students to compare, by seeing, touching, and smelling samples of pottery that have not been fired with pottery that has been fired, is a way to illustrate the intent of the firing process.

Step 4:   *Summarize.* An oral restatement of the process, focusing on the intent of firing the unfinished pottery, should be made by the teacher or a student.

MASTERY TEST

OBJECTIVE 4   To plan original explanations, given a series of hypothetical teaching situations

Following these directions are four hypothetical teaching situations. Read each carefully and plan an explanation of your own, using the step procedure outlined in the previous learning activity. If you are unfamiliar with any of these teaching situations, you may select one you are more familiar with to complete this exercise.

Situation 1.   You need to explain to a group of elementary school pupils what causes day and night.

Situation 2.   You are teaching a course or unit in economics and must explain why we pay federal income taxes.

Situation 3.   You are teaching in a woodworking shop and must instruct your students in the proper procedure for setting up the wood lathe.

Situation 4.   You are reading a story and wish to explain the reason why the main character behaved as he or she did.

OBJECTIVE   **5** To define closure, explain its purposes, and give examples of when it is used as a lesson presentation skill

Learning Activity 5.1

Closure

Anyone familiar with weekly television shows will find it easy to understand the meaning of the term *closure* when it refers to a lesson presentation skill. Television script writers use closure when, each week, they faithfully bring their shows to a satisfying close — that is, the audience has the comfortable feeling that all the loose ends have been tied up, the conflict has been resolved, and things are as they should be with the main characters. Is there any reason that students should feel any different following a well-delivered lesson? Remember that a lesson primarily directed at delivering new material must be carefully planned and structured, much in the same way the television writer prepares a weekly script. If a teacher wishes to create for students the same sense of satisfaction or completion achieved by the television writer, then that teacher must learn how to use closure skillfully. *Closure* refers to those actions or statements by teachers that are designed to bring a lesson presentation to an appropriate conclusion. Teachers use closure to help students bring things together in their own minds, to make sense out of what has been going on during the course of the presentation.

Consider closure the complement of set induction. If set induction is an initiating activity of the teacher, then closure is a culminating activity. Research into the psychology of learning indicates that learning increases when teachers make a conscious effort to help students organize the information presented to them, and to perceive relationships based on that information.

Another way to view closure is to compare it to the paper-and-pencil process of lesson planning. An effective lesson plan will usually indicate where the students will be going, how they will get there, and how they will know when they have arrived. Making certain that students know *when they have arrived* is the result of the skillful teacher's use of closure. In their discussion of the results of research on cognitive learning strategies, Rosenshine and Meister suggest that *summarizing* serves "a comprehension-fostering function" that leads to "deeper processing."[14]

Closure, then, has as its first purpose *to draw attention to the end of a lesson or lesson segment*. Unfortunately, many teachers have neglected the development of this important skill. Your own experience will tell you that a typical closure procedure goes something like this:

Teacher A: "Okay. There's the bell! Get going — you'll be late for your next class!"
Teacher B: "Enough of this! Let's close our books and line up for recess."
Teacher C: "The bell? All right, we'll stop here and pick up at the same point tomorrow."
Teacher D: "Any questions? No? Good. Let's move on to the next chapter."

The students are certainly aware that something has concluded in each case, but that is about all. These unsophisticated forms of closure completely ignore the fact that effective learning depends on the proper sequencing of lesson presentations. And one of the most important events in effective sequencing is providing opportunity for feedback and review.

The teacher who uses closure effectively understands the importance of cueing students to the fact that they have reached an important point in the presentation and that the time has come to wrap it up. This activity must be planned just as carefully as its counterpart, set induction, and timing is critical. The teacher must be aware of the clock and must begin to initiate closure proceedings well before the activity is due to end.

Consequently, a second major purpose of closure is *to help organize student learning*. Simply calling attention to the lesson's conclusion is not enough. A great deal of information and a great many activities may have been covered, and it is the teacher's responsibility to tie it all together into a meaningful whole. The learner, just like the television viewer, should not be left with a feeling of incompleteness and frustration. Like the TV detective who explains to the audience how the various pieces of the puzzle finally formed a coherent picture, so the skillful teacher should recapitulate the various bits and pieces of his or her lesson, and place them into a coherent picture for the learner.

Finally, closure has as its third purpose *to consolidate or reinforce the major points to be learned*. Having signaled the end of the lesson and made an effort to organize what has occurred, the teacher should briefly refocus on the key ideas or processes presented in the lesson. The ultimate objective here is to help the student retain the important information presented in the lesson, and thus increase the probability that he or she will be able to recall and use the information at a later time. Gagné and Briggs, in discussing information storage and retrieval, say: "When information or knowledge is to be recalled, . . . the *network of relationships* in which the newly learned material has been embedded provides a number of different possibilities as cues for its retrieval."[15] Closure, then, is the skill of reviewing the key points of a lesson, tying them together into a coherent whole, and finally, ensuring their use by anchoring them in the student's larger conceptual network.

Learning Activity 5.2

Now that closure has been defined and its purposes explained, you are ready to focus specifically on when the teacher uses closure in the course of the lesson. You should be able to understand more easily when closure is used if you completed the section on set induction. In that section, a lesson was compared to a game containing several "subgames." In the classroom situation, such subgames might involve a lesson introducing some new concept or skills, or an activity with some combination of reading, writing, viewing, or discussing. Each of these activities can be viewed as a subgame within the context of a larger game — an entire class period for a particular subject or an entire day of nondepartmentalized instruction.

The role of the teacher is to structure each situation (subgame) so that it begins and ends in such a way as to promote student learning. This is the function of both set induction and closure technique. To assist you in learning when to use closure in a lesson presentation, study carefully the following list of situations.

Examples of When to Use Closure

To end a long unit of work in which the class might be studying animals, the family, or a country
To consolidate learning of a new concept or principle
To close a discussion
To end a skill-building activity such as locating words in the dictionary or practicing basic functions in arithmetic
To follow up a film, television program, record, or tape
To close a question-and-answer session
To consolidate learning experiences on a field trip
To reinforce the presentation of a guest speaker
To follow up a homework assignment reviewed in class
To end a laboratory exercise
To organize thinking around a new concept or principle (for example, all languages are not written, or different cultures reflect different values)

MASTERY TEST

OBJECTIVE 5   To define closure, explain its purposes, and give examples of when it is used as a lesson presentation skill

1. Define closure as a teaching skill and explain three specific purposes it serves in lesson presentations.

2. Try responding to the following statements by placing the letter *T* next to those that are true and the letter *F* next to those that are false.

_____ a. Closure as a lesson presentation skill is a natural complement to set induction.

_____ b. Closure is less important than set induction because students can tell by the clock when the class period ends.

_____ c. Closure helps students know when they have achieved lesson objectives.

_____ d. One of the purposes of closure is to draw attention to the end of a presentation.

_____ e. Closure opens the opportunity for students to review what they are supposed to have learned.

_____ f. Closure is a natural phenomenon and does not require planning.

_____ g. One of the purposes of closure is to help organize student learning.

_____ h. Timing is critical in using closure.

_____ i. Closure helps to get your lesson off on the right foot.

_____ j. One of the purposes of closure is to consolidate or reinforce the major points to be learned in a presentation.

3. Describe briefly ten different situations in which you could use closure in your lesson presentations.

 **OBJECTIVE**   *6* To plan original closures for use in a series of hypothetical teaching situations

Learning Activity 6

Now that you know what closure is and the general purposes for which it is used, you are ready to begin practicing how to plan your own closures. Before you begin doing this, you should take time to familiarize yourself with some examples of how experienced teachers might use closure in their lessons.

Uses of Closure

A list of specific uses of closure employed by experienced teachers follows. Study them carefully. Then read each of the sample lessons and the accompanying analysis. You should be ready then to plan your own closures for a given teaching situation.

1. Attempts to draw students' attention to a closing point in the lesson
2. Reviews major points of teacher-centered presentation
3. Reviews sequence used in learning material during the presentation
4. Provides summary of important student-oriented discussion
5. Relates lesson to original organizing principle or concept
6. Attempts to lead students to extend or develop new knowledge from previously learned concepts
7. Allows students to practice what they have learned

Sample Lesson Number 1

The lesson is in geography, and the teacher has planned to introduce two basic concepts: (1) humans as the active shapers of their environment, and (2) environment as a limiting context within which humans must live. The teacher has reached the critical point in the lesson where it is time to call students' attention to the fact that the presentation of the first concept is ready for closure.

> *Teacher closure:* "Before moving to the next important idea, the restrictions that environment places on humans, let's review the main points I've already covered on how humans can play a critical role in shaping the environment." The teacher then proceeds to review the major points of the presentation, using either a prepared outline or one developed on the chalkboard during the lesson.

This type of closure is appropriate to use when you wish to help students organize their thinking around a new concept before moving on to a new idea. Referring to the list of uses for closure, note:

1. The closure draws attention to the end of the lesson with a verbal cue —"before moving to the next important idea."
2. It reviews important points of the teacher's presentation.
3. It helps organize student thinking around the first concept presented by utilizing an outline on the chalkboard.

Sample Lesson Number 2

The lesson is in language arts, social studies, science, etc., and the teacher is conducting a discussion around some specific issue that is important in the lesson plan for that particular day. The time has come to bring the discussion to a close.

> *Teacher closure:* Teacher calls on specific student and says, "Elena, would you please summarize what has been said thus far and point out what you felt were the major points covered?"

This type of closure is appropriate to use when you wish to bring a classroom discussion to a close. Referring to the list of uses for closure, note:

1. The closure draws attention to the fact that the teacher is calling for a temporary end to the discussion by requesting a student summary.
2. It summarizes what students have been discussing.
3. It helps students organize or rearrange their own ideas by specifically asking students to list major points made in the discussion.

Sample Lesson Number 3

The lesson is in American history. The class has been given the homework assignment of recording the reactions in 1939–1941 of private citizens, the president, members of Congress, and the press to the idea of going to war. After reading student responses to that assignment, the teacher senses that the students have the idea and wishes to close.

> *Teacher closure:* "Your responses to this homework assignment have been very good. Now let's turn to the present day and compare the responses of private citizens, the president, members of Congress, and the press to the current situation. How are they alike and how do they differ?"

This closure technique is appropriate to use when following up on a homework assignment being reviewed in class, before moving on to application of ideas newly learned. Referring to the general characteristics for this closure, note:

1. It draws attention to the close of the assignment through the teacher's comment or approval, "Your responses to this homework assignment have been very good!"
2. It reviews material covered in the assignment by having students extend their knowledge of what they have already learned about the past to what is happening in the present.

Sample Lesson Number 4

The lesson is in mathematics and the teacher is presenting a general reading skills approach to problem solving: (1) preview, (2) identify details or relationships, (3) restate problem in own words, and (4) list computational steps to be taken. The time has come to see how well the students have understood the use of the new procedure.

> *Teacher closure:* "Before you try to use this new approach to problem solving by yourselves, let's list the steps on the chalkboard and try to apply them to the first problem in your textbooks on page 27. When you finish, I will ask some of you to share with the class your experience using this new technique."

This closure technique is effective when ending a skill-building activity, and you wish to help students consolidate what they have learned. You will have to refer to the characteristics for *both review and transfer* in the analysis that follows:

1. It draws attention to the close of the presentation by the teacher's verbal signal, "Before you try to use this approach . . . let's list the steps. . . ."
2. It reviews the sequence used in learning new reading skills during the presentation.
3. It permits students to practice immediately what they have learned.

MASTERY TEST

OBJECTIVE 6   To plan original closures for use in a series of hypothetical teaching situations

Following these directions are five hypothetical teaching situations. Read each one carefully and plan a closure of your own that you feel would work effectively in that particular situation. You may refer to the list of uses for closure on page 100 to help you generate ideas for your own closures.

1. You have just completed a presentation on the steps one takes in preparing a green salad.

2. You have just completed a demonstration of parallel bar exercises.

3. You have reached a point in a class discussion at which it would be appropriate to close.

4. The teacher begins a lesson on theme in literature by comparing it to the threads running through a colorful tapestry, and now wishes to close.

5. You have presented an important concept to the class, and asked the students how the idea might be used in other situations.

OBJECTIVE   **7** To identify the instructional purposes for using the lecture, and give examples of when it is used in lesson presentations

Learning Activity 7.1

Lecture

Gage and Berliner found that teachers do a considerable amount of verbal structuring and directing of the lesson.[16] Other research on teachers' verbal classroom behavior further supports the view that teachers tend to do most of the talking in their classrooms. Flanders states that almost 70 percent of the talk in the average classroom is teacher talk.[17] What this research reflects is the fact that teachers, of necessity, spend considerable time presenting material to their students; and in many instances the teacher will choose the lecture as the preferred means of presentation. Alice Sims-Gunzenhauser, a senior ETS examiner, commenting on the "Teaching for Student Learning" assessment criteria now being used by ETS, indicates the necessity for the teacher to be able "... to convey information in ways that students can learn ...," and help "... students in the class to extend their thinking and assimilate new knowledge."[18] The lecture can be an extremely effective way to convey information and extend student thinking, if the teacher knows how to plan properly and execute effectively.

The traditional lecture used as a means of presenting information had its beginning in the medieval university. At that time in the history of education, the principal objective of instruction was the acquisition of knowledge. In universities, the lecture was deemed the most effective means of achieving this objective, particularly given the limited number of books that were available to students. Today the lecture is still the predominant mode of lesson presentation in many modern colleges and universities around the world.

Teachers in elementary, middle, junior high, and senior high schools seldom use the lecture as their predominant mode of lesson presentation. There are some situations where schools are experimenting with different types of scheduling arrangements, and large-group instruction is part of the school's total delivery system. The lecture there is a necessary choice for lesson presentation.

It is not difficult to understand why teachers view the lecture as a dependable and effective means for particular kinds of lesson presentations. To begin with, the teacher has complete control over time in a lecture. The lecture can be as brief or as long as the instructional situation dictates. The lecture can focus directly on the particular message the teacher wishes to communicate, and this message reaches all students at the same time. In addition, the lecture is easy to prepare and requires little time for gathering materials. The instructional purposes of the lecture, when used as a means of lesson presentation, are to

1. Present information that the student does not already have
2. Arouse interest
3. Stimulate thinking
4. Organize thoughts
5. Help students understand and recall important facts or ideas
6. Review

Learning Activity 7.2

Now that you understand the instructional purposes of the lecture in lesson presentations, you need to know when to use the lecture most effectively in the course of instruction. To assist you in learning this, study carefully the following list.

Examples of When to Use the Lecture

1. To provide students with specific information not readily available from other sources
2. To create interest in specific subject matter, a real or imagined problem, or an issue of historical or contemporary importance
3. To introduce a new instructional unit or topic of study
4. To assist students in organizing facts, ideas, and relationships so that they may be brought into sharper focus and understood more clearly
5. To summarize key concepts, important facts, or a procedure that needs to be reviewed at the end of a unit or assignment
6. To present a set of facts or an important idea quickly

MASTERY TEST

OBJECTIVE 7   To identify the instructional purposes for using the lecture, and give examples of when it is used in lesson presentations

1. Explain four instructional purposes for using the lecture in lesson presentations.

2. Describe briefly two different situations in which you would choose to use the lecture as the preferred means of presenting your lesson. For each situation, give three reasons to justify your choice.

   **8** To plan an original lecture, given a series of hypothetical teaching situations

Learning Activity 8

Now that you know the instructional purposes for which the lecture is used and the appropriate times to select this mode of instruction for a lesson presentation, you are ready to learn how to prepare your own lectures. As indicated earlier, teachers in elementary, middle, junior high, and senior high schools seldom use the lecture as their preferred mode of lesson presentation. When they do lecture, however, they must be certain to take into consideration the class's attention span and ability level. Planning a lecture is like preparing an outline for writing an expository essay. The objective of both activities is primarily to inform. Consequently, the teacher doing the informing needs to be well versed in the material being presented, and well acquainted with the audience being addressed. Whatever the nature of the presentation, it must be carefully planned.

Assuming you have the knowledge of both the subject and the nature of the students in your class, you now need to consider how to plan what you are going to say. First, study the list of procedural steps. Then examine the model outline that follows. When you have finished this task, you should be ready to develop your own lecture plan for a given teaching situation.

1. Develop a clearly stated purpose, objective, or theme.
2. Create a motivational *set*.
3. Summarize briefly, in logical order, your main points.
4. Develop each main point separately with supporting evidence.
5. Create an appropriate *closure*.

Model Lecture Plan

This lecture plan is to be used for part of a lesson in a unit on the power of language.

1. *Purpose:* To demonstrate how the use of language can influence how we feel, and, consequently, how we act.
2. *Set:* Prepare two or three hypothetical questions designed to make a student feel uncomfortable, for example, "If I told you that your new haircut looked stupid, how would you feel?" Pose one of your questions to a student, and follow it up by asking what feelings were aroused in that student or other students in the class. Then ask the class how their feelings could affect their future behavior.
3. *Summary:* Today you are going to learn something about the power of language. You are going to see how words can cause people to have emotional reactions, which can lead them to think and behave in frequently predictable ways. We will discuss both the *denotative*, or dictionary, meaning of words, and the *connotative*, or emotional, meaning of words. And we will see how the ability to use both denotative and connotative words can help you communicate more effectively with others.
4. *Main Points:*
   1. Arousing feelings in people can cause them to react favorably or unfavorably.
   2. The dictionary meaning of a word is its denotative meaning.
   3. The emotional meaning of a word is its connotative meaning.
   4. Connotative words are really double-duty words.
5. *Closure:* To bring closure to this lecture, students will be given an opportunity to apply the concepts presented to a series of practice problems, for example, "Rewrite the following sentence so that it retains the same meaning, but gives a different impression — The Dolphins clobbered the Bears 27 to 24."

MASTERY TEST

OBJECTIVE 8   To plan an original lecture, given a series of hypothetical teaching situations

Following these directions are five general ideas that could be developed as lectures for a lesson presentation. Study them carefully. Then select one of these themes, or one of your own, and develop a lecture plan for it, using the model on page 109 as your guide.

1. Many students ride their bicycles to school. The principal has asked all the teachers at your grade level to present a lesson on bicycle safety.

2. You are beginning a unit in history on the American Revolutionary War. You decide to introduce the unit with a lecture that describes the circumstances leading up to, and the consequences of, that war. (You may substitute other content for this situation, while keeping the same basic structure of the lecture.)

3. Because your school has adopted a special physical fitness program for the year, each teacher has been asked to prepare several special lessons on some aspect of fitness. You decide to present a lecture on the importance of diet in keeping fit.

4. Your unit in shop calls for several lessons dealing with the safe use of power tools. You decide to introduce a mini-unit with a lecture on safety in the shop.

5. You are an art teacher, or you have decided to use paintings to illustrate a particular theme in a social studies or English lesson. You need to illustrate how artists use color to express feelings, create a mood, or symbolize an idea. You decide to use the lecture for this lesson presentation. (You may use this same basic format to illustrate how a composer uses music or the writer uses words to create these same effects.)

■ Answer Keys for Mastery Tests

ANSWER KEY

Mastery Test, Objective 1

1. *General definition:* Should include the idea that a set is something a teacher does or says to relate the experiences of students to the objectives of the lesson.

   Any three of the following four purposes could be listed: (1) to focus student attention on the lesson, (2) to create an organizing framework for the information to be learned, (3) to extend understanding and applications of the lesson content, and (4) to stimulate student interest in the lesson.

2. You may use any of the situations described in the examples, or include situations of your own.

3. The author used previous television viewing experiences of the reader, and drew an extended analogy of what the television director does in the presentation of a drama to what the teacher must do in the presentation of a classroom lesson.

ANSWER KEY

Mastery Test, Objective 2

Of course, no single response to any of the five situations will be the same. If you have read carefully each of the situations, however, each suggests a general direction that you might follow.

Situation 1. A set to determine how well the students understood the filmstrip, or could apply what they learned to some new activity, seems appropriate here.

Situation 2.   A set to orient students or focus their attention on the significance of pollution and its effect on the environment would be helpful in this case.

Situation 3.   As in the previous lesson, student attention needs to be focused on the important concepts or ideas about to be presented in the film.

Situation 4.   The set in this situation should incorporate some kind of evaluation activity so that students are actively engaged in using previously learned knowledge, and the teacher has an opportunity to see how much students have learned.

Situation 5.   The set should be transitional so that students have an opportunity to integrate previously learned material with new techniques.

ANSWER KEY

Mastery Test, Objective 3

(C) a. The underlying purpose is to illustrate the internal combustion process.

(D) b. The underlying purpose is to show the intent or purpose of the bat's radar system — to enable it to fly.

(A) c. The underlying purpose would be to show the causes that precipitated the entry of the United States into World War II.

(B) d. The underlying purpose is to indicate that the use of a question mark is governed by certain linguistic rules.

(D) e. The underlying purpose is to clarify the meaning behind a character's behavior.

(A) f. The underlying purpose is to indicate how poor nutrition leads to poor health.

(C) g. The underlying purpose is to illustrate the process that brings legislation before Congress.

(B) h. The underlying purpose is to illustrate the general rule that a sign or symbol requires a particular kind of action.

ANSWER KEY

Mastery Test, Objective 4

Of course, no single response to any of the four situations will be the same; however, each plan you develop should follow the procedural steps listed in Learning Activity 6: identify purpose, define, illustrate, and summarize.

Situation 1 was intended to show a direct cause-and-effect relationship.

Situation 2 was intended to indicate that there is a law requiring the payment of income taxes.

Situation 3 was intended to illustrate the procedure for setting up a wood lathe.

Situation 4 was intended to show the motivation for a character's behavior in a story.

ANSWER KEY

Mastery Test, Objective 5

1. *General definition:* Should include the idea that closure is something a teacher says or does to bring a presentation to an appropriate close.
   Purposes:
   (1) To draw attention to the end of a lesson
   (2) To help organize student learning
   (3) To consolidate or reinforce major points to be learned

2. (a) T. Whereas set induction *initiates* instruction, closure *terminates* it.
   (b) F. Clocks tell time, but only teachers can close a lesson.
   (c) T. Appropriate use of closure enables students to evaluate their own understanding of a lesson.
   (d) T. Closure signals the natural conclusion of a presentation sequence.
   (e) T. One purpose of closure is to recapitulate the important points in a lesson presentation.
   (f) F. Effective closure does not occur naturally, but requires conscious control by the teacher.
   (g) T. Closure helps provide a coherence to learning through review.
   (h) T. Since closure is part of a planned sequence of instructional events, it requires careful timing.
   (i) F. Closure *terminates* a lesson, whereas set induction *initiates* it.
   (j) T. Closure helps students organize and retain learning through review.

3. You may use any of the situations described in the examples, or include situations of your own.

ANSWER KEY

Mastery Test, Objective 6

Of course, no single response to any of the five situations will be the same as another. If you have read carefully each of the situations, however, each suggests a general direction you might follow.

Situation 1. A closure that reviewed the sequence demonstrated in the presentation would seem most appropriate in this lesson.

Situation 2. A closure activity that would give students an opportunity to practice what they have observed seems appropriate in this instance.

Situation 3. A review of the points, ideas, or concepts developed in the discussion would seem to be the most appropriate closure at this point in the lesson.

Situation 4. As in the previous lesson, a review closure in which the teacher relates what has gone on to the organizing principle introduced at the beginning of class seems most appropriate.

Situation 5. A closure activity in which students can apply what they have learned in the lesson to a new situation seems most appropriate in this instance.

ANSWER KEY

Mastery Test, Objective 7

1. Any four of the following six purposes could be listed: (1) to present information the student does not already have, (2) to arouse interest, (3) to stimulate thinking, (4) to organize thoughts, (5) to help students understand and recall important facts or ideas, and (6) to review.

2. You may use any of the situations described in the examples, or include situations of your own. Your justifications should come from the six instructional purposes stated in number 1.

ANSWER KEY

Mastery Test, Objective 8

Of course, no single response to this question will be the same as another. Your answer should include, however, the five basic steps necessary to develop a well-organized lecture plan: (1) develop a clearly stated purpose, objective, or theme; (2) create a motivational set; (3) summarize briefly, in logical order, your main points; (4) develop each main point separately with supporting evidence; and (5) create an appropriate closure.

■ Notes

1. Glickman, Carl D., ed. *Supervision in Transition: The 1992 ASCD Yearbook* (Alexandria, VA: Association for Supervision and Curriculum Development, 1992).
2. "Classroom Performance Assessment: Creating a Portrait of the Beginning Teacher," Educational Testing Service, Princeton, NJ, *ETS Developments* 38 Number 1 (Fall 1992): 2.
3. Set induction as a lesson presentation skill was developed for use in teacher training by Dr. J. C. Fortune and Dr. V. B. Rosenshine for the School of Education, Stanford University, Stanford, CA.
4. John P. DeCecco, *The Psychology of Learning and Instruction: Educational Psychology* (Englewood Cliffs, NJ: Prentice-Hall, 1968), p. 159.
5. "Criteria For Effective Teaching Performance," Educational Services, Inc., Jackson, MS, *The Effective School Report*, February 1991, pp. 6, 7.
6. N. L. Gage and David C. Berliner, *Educational Psychology*, 4th ed., (Boston: Houghton Mifflin Co., 1988), p. 405.

7. DeCecco, *op. cit.*, p. 162.
8. Robert Rosenthal and Lenore Jacobson, *Pygmalion in the Classroom* (New York: Holt, Rinehart & Winston, 1968), p. 7.
9. From *The Poetry of Robert Frost*, ed. Edward Connery Lathem. Copyright 1916, © 1969 by Holt, Rinehart & Winston. Copyright 1944 by Robert Frost. Reprinted by permission of Holt, Rinehart & Winston, Publishers.
10. Maria Montessori, *The Montessori Method* (New York: Schocken Books, 1964), p. 170.
11. Arno A. Bellack et al., *The Language of the Classroom* (New York: Teachers College Press, Columbia University, 1966), p. 134.
12. Robert J. Miltz, *Development and Evaluation of a Manual for Improving Teachers' Explanations* (Stanford, CA.: Stanford Center for Research and Development in Teaching, Stanford University, 1972).
13. *ETS Developments, op. cit.*, p. 3.
14. Barak Rosenshine and Carla Meister, "Reciprocal Teaching: A Review of Nineteen Experimental Studies" (paper presented to the American Educational Research Association, Chicago, April 1991).
15. Gagné and Briggs, *op. cit.*, p. 132.
16. Gage and Berliner, *op. cit.*, p. 505.
17. Ned A. Flanders, *Teacher Influence, Pupil Attitudes, and Achievement*, U.S. Department of Health, Education, and Welfare, Office of Education, Cooperative Research Monograph no. 12 (Washington, D.C.: U.S. Government Printing Office, 1965), p. 1.
18. *ETS Developments, op. cit.*, pp. 3, 4.

Additional Readings

Berliner, David C., and Barak V. Rosenshine, eds. *Talks to Teachers.* New York: Random House, 1988.
Dunkin, M. J., ed. *International Encyclopedia of Teaching and Teacher Education.* Oxford: Pergamon Press, 1987.
Gage, N. L., and David C. Berliner. *Educational Psychology.* Boston: Houghton Mifflin Company, 1992.
Glickman, C. D. *Supervision of Instruction: A Developmental Approach.* Boston: Allyn and Bacon, 1990.
Kennedy, M. M. "NCRTL Special Report: An Agenda for Research on Teacher Learning." East Lansing, MI: National Center for Research on Teacher Learning, 1990.
Resnick, L. B., and L. E. Klopfer. *Toward the Thinking Curriculum: Current Cognitive Research.* Alexandria, VA: ASCD, 1989.
Schlechty, P. C. *Schools for the 21st Century.* San Francisco: Jossey-Bass, 1990.

Questioning Skills

5

- Myra Sadker
- David Sadker

OBJECTIVES

1 To classify classroom questions according to Bloom's *Taxonomy of Educational Objectives: Cognitive Domain*

2 To construct classroom questions on all six levels of Bloom's *Taxonomy of Educational Objectives*

3 To describe additional teaching strategies for increasing the quantity and quality of student response

The student teacher was composed. She quickly dispatched with the administrative details of classroom organization — attendance records and homework assignments. The classroom chatter about the Saturday night dance and the upcoming football game subsided as the tenth grade students settled into their seats. The students liked this teacher, for she had the knack of mixing businesslike attention to academic content with a genuine interest in her students. As the principal of Madison High walked by her room, he paused to watch the students settle into a discussion about *Hamlet*. Classroom operation appeared to be running smoothly, and he made a mental note to offer Ms. Ames a contract when her eight weeks of student teaching were over. Had he stayed a little longer to hear the discussion, and had he been somewhat sophisticated in the quality of verbal interaction, he would not have been so satisfied.

Ms. Ames: I would like to discuss your reading assignment with you. As the scene begins, two clowns are on stage. What are they doing? Cheryl?

Cheryl: They are digging a grave.

Ms. Ames: Right. Who is about to be buried? Jim?

Jim: Ophelia.

Ms. Ames: Yes. One of the grave diggers uncovers the skull of Yorick. What occupation did Yorick once have? Donna?

Donna: He was the king's jester.

Ms. Ames: Good. A scuffle occurs by Ophelia's graveside. Who is fighting? Bill?

Bill: Laertes and Hamlet.

Ms. Ames: That's right. In what act and scene does Ophelia's burial occur? Tom?

Tom: Act V, Scene 1.

Throughout the forty-five minute English class, Ms. Ames asked a series of factual questions, received a series of one- and two-word replies — and

Shakespeare's play was transformed into a bad caricature of a television quiz show.

It is extremely important that teachers avoid ineffective questioning patterns such as the one just described because the questioning process has always been crucial to classroom instruction. The crucial role that questions play in the educational process has been stated by a number of educators.

> To question well is to teach well. In the skillful use of the question more than anything else lies the fine art of teaching; for in it we have the guide to clear and vivid ideas, and the quick spur to imagination, the stimulus to thought, the incentive to action.[1]
>
> What's in a question, you ask? Everything. It is the way of evoking stimulating response or stultifying inquiry. It is, in essence, the very core of teaching.[2]
>
> The art of questioning is . . . the art of guiding learning.[3]

It was John Dewey who pointed out that thinking itself is questioning. Unfortunately, research indicates that most student teachers, as well as experienced teachers, do not use effective questioning techniques. Think back to your own days in elementary and secondary school. You probably read your text and your class notes, studied (or, more accurately, memorized), and then waited in class for the teacher to call on you with a quick question, usually requiring only a brief reply. It did not seem to matter much whether the subject was language arts or social studies or science; questions revealed whether or not you remembered the material. But questions need not be used only in this way, and the appropriate use of questions can create an effective and powerful learning environment. Consider the following description of Mark Van Doren's use of questions:

> Mark would come into the room, and, without any fuss, would start talking about whatever was to be talked about. Most of the time he asked questions. His questions were very good, and if you tried to answer them intelligently, you found yourself saying excellent things that you did not know you knew, and that you had not, in fact, known before. He had "educed" them from you by his questions. His classes were literally "education" — they brought things out of you, they made your mind produce its own explicit ideas. . . . What he did have was the gift of communicating to [students] something of his own vital interest in things, something of his manner of approach; but the results were sometimes quite unexpected — and by that I mean good in a way that he had not anticipated, casting lights that he had not himself foreseen.[4]

It is all too easy to describe Van Doren as a gifted teacher, and to dismiss his technique of questioning as an art to which most teachers can never aspire. It is our strong belief that the teacher's effective use of questions is far too important to dismiss in this way. Unfortunately, research concerning the use of questions in the classroom suggests that most teachers do *not* use effective questioning techniques. If one were to review the research on questioning, the results would reveal both the importance of questioning in school and the need for teachers to improve their questioning technique. For example, did you know about any of the following facts or research that had been done about questioning techniques?

1. The first major study of classroom behavior was performed in 1912. The findings showed that 80 percent of classroom talk was devoted to asking, answering, or reacting to questions. Most of these questions were strictly memory, calling for only a superficial understanding of the material.[5]

2. Since 1912, the United States has seen two world wars; a depression; a dozen presidents; the cure for several major diseases; the conquest of space; and tremendous social, economic, and political upheavals, but the state of questioning techniques in the classroom has remained basically unchanged. Studies into the 1970s show that most teachers still use questions as a major tool of learning, but the vast majority of these questions depend only on rote memory for a correct response.[6]

3. Teachers ask a tremendous number of questions. One study reveals that primary school teachers ask 3½ to 6½ questions per minute! Elementary school teachers average 348 questions a day. A recent study of student teachers found them asking 70 to 90 questions in several twenty-minute science lessons. Both at the elementary and secondary levels, there are an enormous number of questions asked by the typical teacher.[7]

4. Although teachers ask a large number of questions, they generally show little tolerance in waiting for student replies. Typically, only *one second* passes between the end of a question and the next verbal interaction! After the answer is given, only 9/10 second passes before the teacher reacts to the answer. The tremendous number of questions asked and the brief amount of time provided before an answer is expected reinforce the finding that most questions do not require any substantive thought. Classroom questions simply call for the rapid recall of information.[8]

5. Although the research on the effect of questions on student achievement has accumulated slowly and at times is contradictory, findings generally suggest that higher order questions (questions that require thought rather than memory) increase student achievement. In classes where higher order, thought-provoking questions are asked, students perform better on achievement tests.[9]

6. Studies also reveal that the quality and quantity of student answers increase when teachers provide students with time to think. If teachers can increase the one second of silence that usually follows a question to three seconds or more, student answers will reflect more thought, and more students will actively participate in the classroom.[10]

7. Although learning is designed to help students receive answers for their questions, become independent citizens, and understand their world, little provision is made in schools for student questions. The typical student asks approximately one question per month.[11]

The significant number of research findings related to classroom questions indicates that questions play a crucial role in the classroom and that teachers need to improve their questioning strategies. Other studies reveal that programs designed to improve this crucial skill have been effective.[12] A variety of self-instructional booklets have been published with the purpose of providing teachers with questioning skills. One that we have found to be particularly helpful as we developed this chapter was *Minicourse 9: Higher Cognitive Questioning* by Gall, Dunning, and Weathersby.[13] The activities in this chapter are designed to increase your mastery of questioning skills.

OBJECTIVE   **1** To classify classroom questions according to Bloom's *Taxonomy of Educational Objectives: Cognitive Domain*[14]

Learning Activity 1.1

As the research in the introductory section reveals, questioning plays an important role in the classroom. Ever since Socrates, teaching and questioning have been viewed as integrally related activities. To be an effective teacher, one must be an effective questioner. The first step in effective questioning is to recognize that questions have distinct characteristics, serve various functions, and create different levels of thinking. Some questions require only factual recall; others cause students to go beyond memory and to use other thought processes in forming an answer. Both kinds of questions are useful, but the heavy reliance teachers place on the factual type of question does not provide the most effective learning environment. Learning the different kinds of questions and the different functions they serve is a crucial step in being able to use all types of questions effectively.

There are many terms and classifications for describing the different kinds of questions. Most of these classification systems are useful because they provide a conceptual framework, a way of looking at questions. We have selected only one system, however, to simplify the process and eliminate repetitive terms. Bloom's *Taxonomy* is probably the best-known system for classifying educational objectives as well as classroom questions. There are six levels of Bloom's *Taxonomy*, and questions at each level require the person responding to use a different kind of thought process. Teachers should be able to formulate questions on each of these six levels to encourage their students to engage in a variety of cognitive processes. Before teachers are able to formulate questions on each of these levels, they must first understand the definitions of the six categories, and they must be able to recognize questions written on each of these six levels. The six levels are:

1. Knowledge
2. Comprehension
3. Application
4. Analysis
5. Synthesis
6. Evaluation

The following definitions, examples, and exercises are designed to help you recognize and classify questions on the six cognitive levels of Bloom's *Taxonomy*. (By the way, *taxonomy* is another word for *classification*.)

Level 1. Knowledge

The first level of the *Taxonomy*, knowledge, requires the student to recognize or recall information. The student is not asked to manipulate information, but merely to remember it just as it was learned. To answer a question on the knowledge level, the student must simply remember facts, observations, and definitions that have been learned previously.

Examples of Knowledge Questions

What is the capital of Maine?
What color did the solution become when we added the second chemical?
Who is the secretary of state?
Who wrote *Hamlet?*

It has become fashionable to scoff at questions that ask the student to rely only on memory. For example, a common complaint about some college exams is that they ask students to "spit back" the information they have memorized from their text and class notes. Memorization of material, however, is important for several reasons. The knowledge, or memory, category is critical to all other levels of thinking. We cannot ask students to think at higher levels if they lack fundamental information. Some memorization of information is also required to perform a variety of tasks in our society, ranging from being an effective citizen to being a good parent. Our society expects that many things be memorized.

Although important, the knowledge category does have severe drawbacks, the main one being that teachers tend to overuse it. Most questions that teachers ask both in class discussions and on tests would be classified in the knowledge category. Another drawback to questions on this level is that much of what is memorized is rapidly forgotten. And a third drawback to memory questions is that they assess only a superficial and shallow understanding of an area. Parroting someone else's thoughts does not, in itself, demonstrate any real understanding. Further, use of knowledge questions promotes classroom participation and high success experiences for students. Students from lower socioeconomic backgrounds achieve more in classrooms characterized by a high frequency of knowledge questions. Studies show that effective teachers provide both low ability and high ability students with high success opportunities, and that in these successful classrooms, students are responding correctly at least 70 to 80 percent of the time.[15] The use of knowledge questions plays a key role in establishing this high success rate. Some words frequently found in knowledge questions are listed in the following box.

Words often found in knowledge questions

define	who
recall	what
recognize	where
remember	when

YOUR TURN

Knowledge

The following questions will test your understanding of knowledge level questions, and your ability to classify questions at the knowledge level of Bloom's

Taxonomy correctly. Your answers will also provide you with a useful study guide when preparing for the Mastery Test.

In questions 1–5, mark a *T* for true and an *F* for false statements.

_____ 1. The first level of Bloom's *Taxonomy* requires higher order thinking.

_____ 2. Most classroom and test questions that teachers ask are memory questions.

_____ 3. A drawback to knowledge, or memory, questions is that they are unimportant.

_____ 4. Knowledge, or memory, questions are important because they are necessary steps on the way to more complex, higher order questions.

_____ 5. All the questions asked so far in this activity (questions 1–4) are on the first level of the *Taxonomy* — knowledge and memory.

Mark a *K* in the space in front of those questions that are at the knowledge level and a "—" for those that are not.

_____ 6. Who discovered a cure for yellow fever?

_____ 7. Can you analyze the causes of World War I?

_____ 8. Where does the United States get most of its tin from?

_____ 9. What does this poem mean to you?

_____ 10. Who was the eighth president of the United States?

_____ 11. Define *antediluvian.* (The class has previously been given the definition of this word.)

_____ 12. Can you think of a title for this poem?

_____ 13. What do you predict will happen to teachers if this recession were to continue over the next several years?

_____ 14. When did the Spanish-American War end?

Check your answers with the answers and comments included in the Answer Key that follows. If you answered all correctly — terrific! One wrong is pretty good also. Two wrong suggests that you should check your answers again. If you got three or more wrong, perhaps you should reread this section to make sure that you understand it before you proceed to the next level.

■ *Level 2. Comprehension*

Questions on the second level, comprehension, require the student to demonstrate that he or she has sufficient understanding to organize and arrange material mentally. The student must select those facts that are pertinent to answering the question. To answer a comprehension level question, the student must go beyond recall of information. The student must demonstrate a personal grasp of the material by being able to rephrase it, give a description in his or her own words, and use it in making comparisons.

For example, suppose a teacher asks, "What is the famous quote of Hamlet's that we memorized yesterday, the quotation in which he puzzles over the meaning and worth of existence?" By asking students to recall information, in this case a quotation, the teacher is asking a question on the knowledge level. If the teacher had asked instead, "What do you think Hamlet means when he asks, 'To be or not to be: that is the question'?," the teacher's question would have been on the comprehension level. With the second question, the student is required to rephrase information in his or her own words.

Frequently, comprehension questions ask students to interpret and translate material that is presented on charts, graphs, tables, and cartoons. For example, the following are comprehension questions.

Examples of Comprehension Questions

What is the main idea that this chart presents?
Describe in your own words what Herblock is saying in this cartoon.

This use of the comprehension question requires the student to translate ideas from one medium to another.

It is important to remember that *the information necessary to answer comprehension questions should have been provided to the student.* For example, if a student has previously read or listened to material that discusses the causes of the Revolutionary War, and then the student is asked to explain these causes in his or her own words, the student is being asked a comprehension question. If the student has *not* been given material explaining the causes of the Revolutionary War and is asked to explain why the war started, he or she is *not* being asked a comprehension question, but, rather, a question on a different level of the *Taxonomy*.

Words often found in comprehension questions

describe	rephrase
compare	put in your own words
contrast	explain the main idea

YOUR TURN

Comprehension

In questions 1–4, mark a *T* for true and an *F* for false statements.

_____   1. A comprehension question may require the student to use new information not previously provided.

_____   2. Comprehension questions may require students to rephrase information.

_____   3. It is possible to remember a definition without being able to put the definition in your own words.

_____   4. A comprehension question asks students to recall information exactly as they have learned it.

Some of the following questions are at the knowledge level and others are at the comprehension level. Write a *C* next to those questions on the comprehension level, and a *K* next to those questions on the knowledge level.

_____   5. When did the American Revolution begin?

_____   6. Compare socialism and capitalism.

_____   7. How do whales differ from sharks?

_____   8. What is the meaning of this cartoon?

_____   9. Who is the author of *Stopping by Woods on a Snowy Evening*?

_____   10. What is the main idea of this poem?

_____   11. Describe what we saw on our visit to the planetarium.

_____   12. Compare Hemingway's style with that of Steinbeck.

_____   13. Where was the Declaration of Independence signed?

_____   14. Explain in your own words what the author suggests were the main reasons for the Civil War.

Check your answers with those in the Answer Key that follows. If you missed two or more, you should reread the description of comprehension questions before going on to the next section.

■ *Level 3. Application*

It is not enough for students to be able to memorize information, or even to rephrase and interpret what they have memorized. Students must also be able to apply information. A question that asks a student to apply previously learned information to reach an answer to a problem is at the application level of the *Taxonomy*.

Application questions require students to apply a rule or process to a problem, and thereby determine the single right answer to that problem. In mathematics, application questions are quite common. For example,

$$\text{If } x = 2 \text{ and } y = 5,$$
$$\text{then } x^2 + 2y \quad = ?$$

But application questions are important in other subjects as well. For example, in social studies, a teacher can provide the definitions of *latitude* and *longitude*, and ask the student to repeat these definitions (knowledge). The teacher can then ask the student to compare the definitions of latitude and longitude (comprehension). At the application level, the teacher would ask the student to locate a point on a map by applying the definitions of latitude and longitude.

To ask a question at the application level in language arts, the following procedure might be used. After providing students with the definition of a *haiku* (a type of poem), a teacher would hand out a sheet with several different types of poems, then ask the students to select the poem that is a haiku, that is, the one that fits the definition of a haiku poem. To do this, the students must apply the definition to the various poems and select the poem that fits the definition.

In all the examples given, the student must apply knowledge to determine the single correct answer. Here are some other examples of questions at the application level.

Examples of Application Questions

In each of the following cases, which of Newton's laws is being demonstrated?

According to our definition of socialism, which of the following nations would be considered socialist?

Write an example of the rule we have just discussed.

According to our criteria, which answer is correct?

If John works three hours to mow the lawn, and it takes Alice only two hours, how many hours would it take for them to mow the lawn together?

What is the rule that is appropriate in case 2?

Words often found in application questions

apply	write an example
classify	solve
use	how many
choose	which
employ	what is

YOUR TURN

Application

Indicate the level of the *Taxonomy* that each of the following questions represents. Use a *K* for those at the knowledge level, *C* for those at the comprehension level, and *Ap* for those at the application level.

_____   1. What did I say we would do today?

_____   2. What does *freedom* mean to you?

_____   3. Using the rules we discussed, solve the following problems.

_____   4. How are these two solutions similar?

_____   5. Using the scientific method, solve this problem.

_____   6. Who was the author of *The Great Gatsby?*

_____   7. If these figures are correct, will the manager make a profit or suffer a loss?

_____   8. Applying the rules of supply and demand, solve the following problem.

_____   9. Classify the following plants according to the ten categories we reviewed.

Check your answers with those provided in the Answer Key that follows. If you missed two or more, reread this section and do the additional questions. If you would like extra practice, the additional questions will provide you with that opportunity. When you feel ready, go on to the next level of the *Taxonomy*. At this point, you're halfway through with the first learning activity.

Additional Questions

_____   10. We have learned the definition of a noun. What are three examples of nouns?

_____   11. Rephrase the definition of a noun in your own words.

_____   12. Which of the following sentences has an error in punctuation?

_____   13. State the three steps we have learned that must be followed before starting on a hike in the forest.

_____   14. Solve this problem by using the procedure we discussed for quadratic equations.

_____   15. According to our definition of a mammal, which of the five animals listed would be considered a mammal?

Check your answers in the Answer Key. If you still need help, you may want to check with your instructor, with some other students who are getting the exercises correct, or the references listed at the end of the chapter. If you understand the application level, move on to the analysis level.

■ *Level 4. Analysis*

Analysis questions are a higher order of questions that require students to think critically and in depth. Analysis questions ask students to engage in three kinds of cognitive processes.

1. To identify the motives, reasons, and/or causes for a specific occurrence.
2. To consider and analyze available information to reach a conclusion, inference, or generalization based on this information.
3. To analyze a conclusion, inference, or generalization to find evidence to support or refute it.

Following are examples of three kinds of analysis questions.

1. To identify the motives, reasons, and/or causes for a specific occurrence.

   What factors influenced the writings of Robert Frost?
   Why did Senator Robert F. Kennedy decide to run for the presidency?
   Why was Israel selected as the site for the Jewish nation?
   Why does our economy suffer from economic upswings and downturns?

   In all these questions, students are asked to discover the causes or reasons for certain events through analysis.

2. To consider and analyze available information to reach a conclusion, inference, or generalization based on this information.

   After reading this textbook, how would you characterize the author's background, attitudes, and points of view?
   Look at the diagram of this new invention. What do you think the purpose of this new invention is?

After studying the French, American, and Russian revolutions, what can you conclude about the causes of revolution?

Now that your experiments are completed, what is the name of the gas in the sample test tube?

This type of analysis question calls on the learner to draw a conclusion, inference, or generalization based on evidence.

3. To analyze a conclusion, inference, or generalization to find evidence to support or refute it.

What information could you use to support the proposition that President Nixon was not a successful president?

What evidence can you cite to support the statement that Emily Dickinson was a more effective poet than Robert Frost?

Now that we have finished playing the simulation game, what did you experience to support the idea of peaceful coexistence among nations?

These questions require students to analyze information to support a particular conclusion, inference, or generalization.

If you tried to answer any of these questions, you probably realized that several answers are possible. Because it takes time to think and analyze, these questions cannot be answered quickly or without careful thought. The fact that several answers are possible and that sufficient time is needed to answer them is an indication that analysis questions are higher order ones. Unfortunately, teachers too often avoid higher order questions in favor of lower order ones, especially memory questions. But analysis questions are important because they foster critical thinking in students. Analysis questions not only help students learn what happened, but also help them search for the reasons behind what happened.

A student cannot answer an analysis question by repeating information or by reorganizing material to put it into his or her own words. Students cannot rely directly on instructional materials when answering an analysis question. Once again, analysis questions require students to analyze information to identify causes, reach conclusions, or find supporting evidence.

Words frequently found in analysis questions

identify motives or causes	support
draw conclusions	analyze
determine evidence	why

Review of the First Four Levels

1. *Knowledge*   Requires memory only, repeating information exactly as memorized (define, recall, recognize, remember, who, what, where, when).

2. *Comprehension*   Requires rephrasing and comparing information (describe, compare, contrast, rephrase, put in your own words, explain the main idea).

3. *Application*	Requires application of knowledge to determine a single correct answer (apply, classify, use, choose, employ, write an example, solve, how many, which, what is).
4. *Analysis*	Requires student to go beyond direct reliance on instructional materials to analyze a problem or situation. 1. Identify motives or causes 2. Draw conclusions 3. Determine evidence (support, analyze, conclude, why)

YOUR TURN

Analysis

_____ 1. Analysis questions call for higher order thinking. (true or false)

_____ 2. Which of the following processes is *not* required by analysis questions? (a) identifying evidence to support a statement, (b) making a statement based on evidence, (c) explaining motives or causes, (d) making evaluations.

_____ 3. "Why" questions are often on the analysis level. (true or false)

_____ 4. Analysis questions require students only to rephrase information, to state it in their own words. (true or false)

_____ 5. Analysis questions require students to use or locate evidence in formulating their answers. (true or false)

Identify the levels of the following questions (*K* = knowledge, *C* = comprehension, *Ap* = application, *An* = analysis).

_____ 6. Why didn't Hamlet act when he first learned of the treachery? (The student has not previously been given these reasons.)

_____ 7. What did Hamlet say?

_____ 8. What evidence can you find to support your statement that Hamlet was a coward? (The student has not previously been given this evidence.)

_____ 9. What was Hamlet's position or title in Denmark?

_____ 10. In your own words, how did we characterize Hamlet in yesterday's discussion?

_____ 11. After reading *Hamlet, Macbeth*, and *King Lear*, what can you conclude about Shakespeare's writing style? (These conclusions have not been given in previous reading or discussion.)

_____ 12. Using the definition of *climax*, what part of *Hamlet* would you consider to be the climax?

Check your answers with the Answer Key that follows. Two or more wrong answers suggest you should review this section and answer the additional questions. If you made fewer than two errors, you may wish to solidify your expertise by answering the additional questions, anyway. If not, move on to the fifth level of the *Taxonomy*, Synthesis.

Additional Questions

_____ 13. When did Robert Kennedy campaign for the Democratic nomination for the presidency?

_____ 14. Why did R. F. Kennedy lose the Oregon primary? (The causes have not been given previously in reading or discussion.)

_____ 15. What can you conclude about the narrow victory for R. F. Kennedy over Eugene McCarthy in California? (The conclusions have not been given previously in reading or discussion.)

_____ 16. Can you analyze Kennedy's campaign strategy?

_____ 17. What evidence can you cite to support the contention that had Robert Kennedy lived, he would have won the presidency?

_____ 18. How would you describe Kennedy's campaign style?

The answers are in the Answer Key. If you missed more than one of these additional questions, find out why. If the reading and examples aren't working for you, check with the references at the end of the chapter, with another student, or with your teacher. It is important that you understand the analysis level before you move on to the last two levels.

Level 5. Synthesis

Synthesis questions are higher order questions that ask students to perform original and creative thinking. These kinds of questions require students (1) to produce original communications, (2) to make predictions, or (3) to solve problems. Although application questions also require students to solve problems, synthesis questions differ because they do not require a single correct answer but, instead, allow a variety of creative answers. Here are some examples of the different kinds of synthesis questions.

1. To produce original communications.

   Construct a collage of pictures and words that represent your values and feelings.
   What's a good name for this machine?
   Write a letter to the editor on a social issue of concern to you.

2. To make predictions.

   What would the United States be like if the South had won the Civil War?
   How would life be different if school were not mandatory?
   How would life be different if the courts did not exist?

3. To solve problems.

   How can we measure the height of a building without being able to go into it?
   How can we raise money for our ecology project?

Teachers can use synthesis questions to help develop the creative abilities of students. Unfortunately, as in the case of analysis questions, teachers too often avoid synthesis questions in favor of lower order questions, particularly knowledge questions. Synthesis questions rely on a thorough understanding of material. Students should not make wild guesses to answer synthesis questions. For example, one synthesis question that we suggested, "What would the United States be like if the South had won the Civil War?," requires the student to have a firm grasp of information before being able to offer a sound prediction. To review, synthesis questions require predictions, original communications, or problem solving in which a number of answers are possible.

Words often found in synthesis questions

predict	construct
produce	how can we improve
write	what would happen if
design	can you devise
develop	how can we solve
synthesize	

YOUR TURN

Synthesis

In questions 1–10, identify the level of the question by using the code provided (*K* = knowledge, *C* = comprehension, *Ap* = application, *An* = analysis, and *S* = synthesis).

_____   1. What is the state capital?

_____   2. Where is it located?

_____   3. Point it out on the map.

_____   4. If you could decide on a location for a new state capital, what location would you choose?

_____   5. Why?

_____   6. What would happen if we had two state capitals?

_____   7. Draw a simple blueprint of your ideal state capital.

_____   8. Quote what your textbook says about the primary function of a state capital.

_____   9. Describe this primary function.

_____   10. Given the categories of different kinds of state capitals, how would you classify the capital of Maine?

_____   11. Synthesis questions require students to do all the following *except*
(a) Make predictions
(b) Solve problems
(c) Rely primarily on memory
(d) Construct original communication

_____   12. Synthesis questions require original and creative thought from students. (true or false)

The Answer Key that follows will provide you with feedback on your progress in this section. If you want additional practice, then tackle these questions.

Additional Questions

—————— 13. How would you describe your school?

—————— 14. What would your ideal school be like?

—————— 15. Write a letter describing your ideal school.

—————— 16. What name would you give to this school?

—————— 17. Why?

▪ *Level 6. Evaluation*

The last level of the *Taxonomy* is evaluation. Evaluation, like synthesis and analysis, is a higher order mental process. Evaluation questions do not have a single correct answer. They require the student to judge the merit of an idea, a solution to a problem, or an aesthetic work. They may also ask the student to offer an opinion on an issue. Following are some examples of different kinds of evaluation questions.

Examples of Evaluation Questions

Do you think schools are too hard?
Should young children be allowed to read any book they want, no matter what it is about?
Which picture do you like best?
Which song do you prefer?
Is busing an appropriate remedy for desegregating schools?
Which approach offers the best method for attacking this problem?
Do you think that the statement "Americans never had it so good" is true?
Which U.S. senator is the most effective?

To express your opinion on an issue or to make a judgment on the merit of an idea, solution, or aesthetic work, you must use some criteria. You must use either objective standards or a personal set of values to make an evaluation. For example, if you answer the last question in the list of examples using a personal set of values, you might decide that the senator whose voting record is most congruent with your own political philosophy is the most effective senator. If you are strongly against defense spending or strongly in favor of civil rights legislation, these personal values would be reflected in your evaluation of the most effective senator.

Another way of evaluating senators would be through the use of objective criteria. Such criteria might include attendance records, campaign financing practices, influence on other senators, the number of sponsored bills that became law, etc. By comparing each senator to these criteria, a judgment can be made in relation to "the most effective senator."

Of course, many individuals use a combination of objective criteria and personal values when making an evaluation. The important thing to remember about evaluation questions is that some standard must be used. Differing standards are quite acceptable, and they naturally result in different answers. Evaluation questions are higher order questions, and different answers are expected.

Words often used in evaluation questions

judge	give your opinion
argue	which is the better picture,
decide	solution, etc.
evaluate	do you agree
assess	would it be better

Review of the Taxonomy

1. *Knowledge*   Requires memory only, repeating information exactly as memorized (define, recall, recognize, remember, who, what, where, when).

2. *Comprehension*   Requires rephrasing, rewording, and comparing information (describe, compare, contrast, rephrase, put in your own words, explain the main idea).

3. *Application*   Requires application of knowledge to determine a single correct answer (apply, classify, choose, employ, write an example, solve, how many, which, what is).

4. *Analysis*
   1. identify motives or causes
   2. draw conclusions
   3. determine evidence
   (support, analyze, conclude, why)

5. *Synthesis*
   1. make predictions
   2. produce original communications
   3. solve problems (more than one possible answer)
   (predict, produce, write, design, develop, synthesize, construct, how can we improve, what happens if, how can we solve, can you devise)

6. *Evaluation*
   1. make judgments
   2. offer opinions
   (judge, argue, decide, evaluate, assess, give your opinion, which is better, do you agree, would it be better)

YOUR TURN

Evaluation

Using all levels of the *Taxonomy,* classify the following questions (*K* = knowledge, *C* = comprehension, *Ap* = application, *An* = analysis, *S* = synthesis, and *E* = evaluation).

_____   1. Who was the founder of the school of abstract art?

_____   2. Describe the first attempts of the pioneers of abstract art.

_____   3. What were some of the factors that motivated Picasso to join this new school?

_____   4. We have read about the techniques of Picasso and Miro. Compare and contrast Picasso's techniques to those of Miro.

_____   5. Which artist do you prefer, Miro or Picasso?

_____ 6. Paint your own abstract piece.

_____ 7. We have learned about the principle of balance. How is it used in this work?

_____ 8. Considering the different kinds of abstract paintings we have studied, what generalizations can you make about abstract art?

_____ 9. What do you predict is the future of abstract art?

_____ 10. What is your opinion of abstract art?

___

At this point, we have reviewed all levels of the *Taxonomy,* and you should know whether or not you are ready for the Mastery Test. In the Mastery Test, you will be asked to identify the levels of a number of questions; all six levels of the *Taxonomy* will be represented. If, before taking the Mastery Test, you would like to have some more practice and also to compare your responses with those of another student, you might want to try Learning Activity 1.2, "The Question Master Game." You will find it in the perforated section at the back of the book. Two to six people can play at a time. The game should provide you with more practice in understanding the *Taxonomy* and in classifying questions. As an additional benefit, you might enjoy it and, undoubtedly, you will be victorious over siblings, friends, relatives, and strangers who probably will not be able to use the *Taxonomy* with your facile abandon.

Learning Activity 1.2

The Question Master Game

The Question Master Game is designed to help you achieve competence in the first objective: "To classify questions on all six levels of Bloom's *Taxonomy.*" In addition, we hope that you will enjoy playing the game. To play, you must be able to recall specific information about the characteristics of questions on the different levels of the *Taxonomy,* classify questions on the various levels of the *Taxonomy,* and you should try to maintain your sense of humor. Having read Learning Activity 1.1 should help you to achieve the first two requirements. (Turn to Appendix A at back of the book to play.)

MASTERY TEST

OBJECTIVE 1

To classify classroom questions according to Bloom's *Taxonomy of Educational Objectives: Cognitive Domain*

Read the paragraph below and then classify the following questions according to their appropriate level on Bloom's *Taxonomy.* Use the following abbreviations: (*K* = knowledge, *C* = comprehension, *Ap* = application, *An* = analysis, *S* = synthesis, and *E* = evaluation).

To pass the Mastery Test, you should classify 10 of the 11 questions accurately. Good luck!

> School reading texts were also studied. It was found that the major reading series used in almost all public and private schools across the country teach that being a girl means being inferior. In these texts, boys are portrayed as being able to do so many things: they play with bats and balls, they work with chemistry sets, they do magic tricks that amaze their sisters, and they show initiative and independence as they go on trips by themselves and get part-time jobs. Girls do things too: they help with the housework, bake cookies and sit and watch their brothers — that is assuming they are present. In 144 texts studied, there were 881 stories in which the main characters are boys and only 344 in which a girl is the central figure.*

> *Nancy Frazier and Myra Sadker, *Sexism in School and Society.* New York: Harper and Row, 1973, pp. 103–104.

_____ 1. In your own words, compare the portrayal of males and females in school texts.

_____ 2. Why do you think feminists are concerned with the passive way in which girls are portrayed in textbooks?

_____ 3. What do boys do in the school reading texts that were studied?

_____ 4. What is the main idea of this paragraph?

_____ 5. Considering the category descriptions of sexist and nonsexist books that we have studied, how would you classify *Miracles on Maple Hill?*

_____ 6. What would your ideal nonsexist book be like?

_____ 7. How many texts were analyzed for sexism?

_____ 8. If all books became nonsexist during the next five years, what do you predict would be the effects on children?

_____ 9. Why do you think that girls have been portrayed in such a stereotyped manner in school texts?

_____ 10. What is your opinion on the issue of sexism in books?

_____ 11. Do you think that sexist books should be banned from children's libraries?

 **OBJECTIVE**   **2**   To construct classroom questions on all six levels of Bloom's *Taxonomy of Educational Objectives*

Learning Activity 2.1

The first, and perhaps the most difficult, step in learning to ask effective classroom questions is that of gaining a thorough understanding of Bloom's *Taxonomy.* Now that you have demonstrated your ability to classify questions, you are ready to begin constructing them. Effective classroom questions make provision for student thinking on all levels of the *Taxonomy.* Although during a short period of time only one or two levels of the *Taxonomy* may be reflected in a teacher's questions, over the course of an entire semester, students should have ample opportunity to answer questions phrased at all levels. The sample questions and the information in Learning Activity 1.1 provide you with useful information for constructing questions. The following review should provide you with a reference as you construct questions on the various levels of the *Taxonomy.*

Suggestions for Constructing Questions

In the next few pages, we will review the nature of the cognitive processes, verbs, and key phrases that are frequently associated with specific levels of the *Taxonomy.* As you go over this review, remember that it is important to analyze each question you write because inclusion of key phrases is not an unconditional guarantee of the taxonomic level of a particular question. After a brief review, you will get a chance to practice constructing questions that pertain to a specific reading selection.

1. *Knowledge:*   recall   who
                      define   what
                      recognize   where
                      identify   when

A knowledge question requires students to recall or recognize information.

2. *Comprehension:* describe   in your own words compare similarities and differences
                      compare
                      illustrate
                      interpret   derive main idea
                      rephrase
                      reorder
                      contrast
                      differentiate
                      explain

To answer a comprehension level question, the student must be able to organize previously learned material so that he or she can rephrase it, describe it in his or her own words, and use it for making comparisons.

3. *Application:*   apply   select
                      solve (one answer only is   use
                        correct)   employ
                      classify
                      choose

An application question asks students to use previously learned information to solve a problem.

4. *Analysis:*   analyze   why
                      identify motive, cause, or   determine the evidence
                      reason   determine a conclusion
                      conclude
                      infer
                      distinguish
                      deduce
                      detect

Analysis questions ask students (1) to identify reasons, causes, and motives; (2) to consider available evidence to reach a conclusion, inference, or generalization; and (3) to analyze a conclusion, inference, or generalization to find supporting evidence.

5. *Synthesis:*   solve (more than one answer correct)
                      predict
                      write

        draw
        construct
        produce
        originate
        propose
        plan
        design
        synthesize
        combine
        develop

Synthesis questions require students (1) to produce original communications, (2) to make predictions, or (3) to solve problems.

6. *Evaluation:*   judge   what is your opinion
                     argue   do you agree
                     decide   which is better
                     appraise
                     evaluate

Evaluation questions ask students to judge the merit of an idea, a solution to a problem, or an aesthetic work.

Before proceeding to the exercises in this learning activity, you may find it helpful to keep in mind the following general comments about question construction. It is important to phrase your questions carefully. You have probably been a student in more than one class where the teacher's questions were so cumbersome or wordy that you lost the meaning of the question. In fact, one study indicates that 40 percent of teacher questions are ambiguous and poorly phrased. You should be explicit enough to ensure understanding of your questions, but, at the same time, you should avoid using too many words. When a question is too wordy, students become confused and unable to respond; frequently, the result is that the question has to be rephrased.

Now you are ready to construct questions at each of the six levels of Bloom's *Taxonomy*. Read the paragraph in the test that follows. Then construct at least twelve questions relating to it. When you are done, you should have two questions on each of the six levels of the *Taxonomy*. As you construct your questions, keep the following in mind. What facts are in the paragraph that you might want students to recognize or recall (knowledge level)? What are the main points in the reading selection that you would want students to comprehend and be able to rephrase in their own words (comprehension level)? What information is there in the paragraph that students could apply to solving problems, classifying, or giving examples (application level)? What questions can you ask about the reading selection that require students to consider reasons and motives, examine the validity of a conclusion, or seek evidence to support a conclusion (analysis level)? Using this paragraph as a springboard, how can you stimulate original student thought — creative problem solving, the making of predictions, and the production of original communication — in writing, music, dance, art, etc. (synthesis level)? Finally, what issues can you raise from the material in this paragraph that will cause students to judge the merit of an idea, the solution to a problem, or an aesthetic work (evaluation level)? As you develop your questions, it may be helpful to review the information in Learning Activities 1.1, 1.2, and 2.1.

After you have finished writing your questions, compare them with the sample questions in the Answer Key that follows. Obviously, a wide variety of questions could be written pertaining to this particular selection. The sample questions are simply meant to give you a basis for comparison, and to indicate the kinds of questions that can be asked on each of the six levels of the *Taxonomy.*

Compare your questions with the information and examples in Learning Activities 1.1 and 2.1. Discuss the questions you develop with your instructor and with other members of your class. If eleven or twelve of your questions accurately reflect the appropriate level of the *Taxonomy,* you are doing well. If you miss two or three, you will probably want to review the information in Learning Activity 2.1 and study the sample questions carefully, particularly those on the levels where you did not construct the questions accurately. If you missed more than three, a careful review of Learning Activity 1.1 and additional practice in constructing questions may be necessary before you take the Mastery Test.

YOUR TURN

Constructing Questions on the Six Levels of Bloom's *Taxonomy*

In Des Moines, Iowa, two high school students and a junior high student, in defiance of a ban by school authorities, wore black armbands to class as a protest against the Vietnam War. As a result, they were suspended from school. But the U.S. Supreme Court later ruled the suspensions were illegal, holding that the first amendment to the Constitution protects the rights of public school children to express their political and social views during school hours.

This case illustrates a significant new trend in American life. Young people, particularly those under twenty-one, are demanding that they be granted rights long denied them as a matter of course. And, with increasing frequency, they are winning those rights.

Michael Dorman, *Under 21* (New York: Delacorte, 1970) pp. 3 and 5.

Write two questions at each level of the *Taxonomy* based on the above material: 1) knowledge level, 2) comprehension level, 3) application level, 4) analysis level, 5) synthesis level, and 6) evaluation level.

Learning Activity 2.2

If you feel that you need additional practice in constructing questions or if you would like to improve your question construction skills, Learning Activity 2.2 provides that opportunity. This learning activity involves another way of playing the Question Master Game. All you need do is make one rule change. Instead of using the "Classification Cards" that have already been developed, you must construct a question of your own whenever you land on a square marked with a *C*. The question must be at the same level of the *Taxonomy* as the number of spaces you move. Avoid using the same question more than once, and try to vary your question stems.

Example

The die (or cards or spinner) indicates *6*, and you move your piece six spaces. If you land on a *C* space, you must construct a question at level six of the *Taxonomy* (Evaluation). If you fail to do this, you must go back three spaces from your original space. If you are successful, you can remain on that space until your next turn.

The *C* spaces now represent *Construct* a question rather than *Classify* a question. All other rules remain the same. Any missed questions result in going backward three spaces.

If the die shows:	Question must be at:
1	Knowledge
2	Comprehension
3	Application
4	Analysis
5	Synthesis
6	Evaluation

Any disputes that cannot be resolved by referring to the explanations and examples in Learning Activity 1.1 will have to be arbitrated by your instructor.

Good luck!

MASTERY TEST

OBJECTIVE 2   To construct classroom questions on all six levels of Bloom's *Taxonomy of Educational Objectives*

Read the following paragraphs and then construct twelve questions based on this reading selection. Two of your questions must be at the knowledge level, two at the comprehension level, two at the application level, two at the analysis level, two at the synthesis level, and two at the evaluation level. To pass this Mastery Test successfully, nine of the twelve questions should accurately reflect the level of the *Taxonomy* at which they are constructed.

> Death may be an unwelcome terrifying enemy, a skeleton with an evil grin who clutches an ugly scythe in his bony hand. Or death may be a long awaited friend who waits quietly, invisibly, beside the bed of a dying patient to ease his pain, his loneliness, his weariness, his hopelessness.
>
> Man alone among the things that live knows that death will come. Mice and trees and microbes do not. And man, knowing that he has to die, fears death, the great unknown, as a child fears the dark. "We fear to be we know not what, we know not where," said John Dryden. But what man dreads more is the dying, the relentless process in which he passes into extinction alone and helpless and despairing. So he puts death and dying out of his mind, denying that they exist, refusing to discuss them openly, trying desperately to control them. He coins phrases like "never say die," and somehow, when he says something is "good for life," he means forever. Unable to bear the thought of ceasing to be, he

comforts himself with thoughts of a pleasant afterlife in which he is rewarded for his trials on earth, or he builds monuments to himself to perpetuate at least his memory, if not his body.

John Langone, *Death Is a Noun* (Boston: Little, Brown, 1972) pp. 3–4.

Now that you have read the paragraphs, construct twelve questions, two at each level of the *Taxonomy.* When you write the application level questions, you may find it helpful to consider that the following information has previously been given to the class: (1) definitions of various literary images including metaphor, simile, and personification; (2) a list of terms and definitions that characterize various psychological states; and (3) several novels that portray death as a central or minor theme.

1. Two knowledge questions:

2. Two comprehension questions:

3. Two application questions:

4. Two analysis questions:

5. Two synthesis questions:

6. Two evaluation questions:

OBJECTIVE

3 To describe additional teaching strategies for increasing the quantity and quality of student response

Learning Activity 3

Much of this chapter has emphasized the need to ask questions on all levels of Bloom's *Taxonomy.* This is an important step in encouraging many levels of student thought and discussion. But just asking thought-provoking questions isn't enough; in fact, one research study found that there was only a limited correspondence between the cognitive level of teachers' questions and the cognitive level of students' answers. When teachers asked application, analysis, or synthesis level questions, there was only a 50-50 chance that students would answer on the appropriate application, analysis, or synthesis level.[16]

So besides asking higher order questions, you will need to determine whether the student's response adequately matches the question you have asked. If the student's response is not accurate — or if it is inadequate in matching the level of your question — it's time to employ some new teaching strategies.

Recently a noted educator, John Goodlad, along with a team of researchers, conducted an in-depth observation study of over a thousand classrooms. As a result of this research, he observed:

> [T]here is a paucity of praise and correction of students' performance as well as of teacher guidance, in how to do better next time. Teachers tend not to respond in overtly positive or negative ways to the work students do. And our

impression is that classes generally tend not to be strongly positive or strongly negative places to be. Enthusiasm and joy and anger are kept under control.[17]

Goodlad concluded that the emotional tone of schools is neither punitive nor joyful. Rather, he says, the school environment can best be characterized as "flat." Part of the reason for this bland quality may lie in the way teachers deal with student answers to questions. Trained observers visited more than a hundred classrooms along the East Coast, and analyzed teacher reactions to student answers and comments. They found:

- Teachers don't often praise students. Approximately 10 percent of teacher reactions praise students. In approximately 25 percent of the classrooms observed, teachers never praised students.
- Teacher criticism is even more rare. (In this study, criticism was defined as an explicit statement that a student's behavior or work was wrong.) Approximately two-thirds of the one hundred classrooms observed contained no criticism. In the approximately thirty-five classrooms where teachers did criticize students, it constituted only 5 percent of teacher interaction.
- Teacher remediation of student answers was quite frequent. It occurred in all classrooms and constituted approximately 30 percent of all teacher reactions. (Teacher remediation was defined as teacher comments or questions that would help students reach a more accurate or higher level response.)
- But neither praise, criticism, nor remediation is the most frequent teacher response. Teachers most often simply *accept* student answers. Accept means that they say "uh-huh," or "okay," or that they don't say anything at all. Acceptance occurred in all of the classrooms and it constituted over 50 percent of teacher reactions. There was more acceptance than praise, remediation, and criticism combined.[18]

The way the classroom question cycle most often goes is:

- Teacher asks a question.
- Student gives an answer.
- Teacher says, "Okay."

The "okay" classroom is probably a bland, flat place in which to learn. Further, the okay classroom may not be okay in terms of encouraging student achievement. Research on teaching effectiveness indicates that students need specific feedback to understand what is expected of them, correct errors, and get help in improving their performance. If a student answers or questions, and the teacher reacts by saying "uh-huh" or "okay," the student is not getting the specific feedback he or she needs. Also these flat "acceptance" reactions to student comments are not likely to encourage high quality of student thought and discussion.

There are specific strategies you can use in reacting to student answers and avoiding the trap of the "okay" classroom. The remainder of this learning activity is composed of four brief sections. Each discusses a teaching technique that can help you increase the quantity and quality of student responses in your classroom.

Wait Time[19]

If we were to stop and listen outside a classroom door, we might hear classroom interaction similar to this.

Teacher: Who wrote the poem *Stopping by Woods on a Snowy Evening?* Tom?

Tom: Robert Frost.

Teacher: Good. What action takes place in the poem? Sally?

Sally: A man stops his sleigh to watch the woods get filled with snow.

Teacher: Yes. Emma, what thoughts go through the man's mind?

Emma: He thinks how beautiful the woods are.... (She pauses for a second)

Teacher: What else does he think about? Joe?

Joe: He thinks how he would like to stay and watch. (Pauses for a second)

Teacher: Yes — and what else? Rita? (Waits half a second) Come on, Rita, you can get the answer to this. (Waits half a second) Well, why does he feel he can't stay there indefinitely and watch the woods and the snow?

Rita: He knows he's too busy. He's got too many things to do to stay there for so long.

Teacher: Good. In the poem's last line, the man says that he has miles to go before he sleeps. What might sleep be a symbol for? Sarah?

Sarah: Well, I think it might be — (Pauses a second)

Teacher: Think, Sarah. (Teacher waits for half a second) All right then — Mike? (She waits again for half a second) John? (Waits half a second) What's the matter with everyone today? Didn't you do the reading?

There are a number of comments we could make about this slice of classroom interaction. We could note the teacher's development from primarily lower order questions to those of a somewhat higher order. We could comment on the inability of the students to answer her later questions, and on the teacher's increasing frustration. But perhaps the most devastating thing we could say about this interaction segment is that it lasts for less than a single minute.

In less than one minute of dialogue, this teacher manages to construct and ask six questions, some of them, at least, requiring a fairly high cognitive level of response. As discussed earlier, a rapid questioning rate is not at all atypical of many classrooms across the country. The mean number of questions a teacher asks averages between two and three per minute, and it is not unusual to find as many as seven to ten questions asked by a teacher during a single minute of classroom instruction.

The effect of this rapid "bombing rate" is that students have little time to think. In fact, research shows that the mean amount of time a teacher waits after asking a question (wait time 1) is approximately *one second!* If the students are not able to think quickly enough to come up with a response at this pace, the teacher repeats the question, rephrases it, asks a different question, or calls on another student. If a student manages to get a response in, the teacher reacts or asks another question within an average time of nine-tenths of a second (wait time 2). It is little wonder that high rates of teacher questioning tend to be associated with low rates of student questions and student declarations. In classrooms where questions are asked at this bombing rate, students have little time or desire to think or to express themselves in an atmosphere so charged with a sense of verbal evaluation and testing.

When teachers break out of the bombing rate pattern and learn to increase wait time 1 (after asking a question) and wait time 2 (after a student responds) from one second to three or five seconds, many significant changes occur in their classrooms. For example:

1. Students give longer answers.
2. Students volunteer more appropriate answers, and failures to respond are less frequent.
3. Student comments on the analysis and synthesis levels increase. They make more evidence-inference responses and more speculative responses.
4. Students ask more questions.
5. Students exhibit more confidence in their comments, and those students whom teachers rate as relatively slow learners offer more questions and more responses.
6. Student achievement is higher.

Simply by increasing his or her ability to wait longer after asking a question, especially a higher level question, a teacher can effect some striking changes in the quantity and quality of student response and achievement. It is not as easy as you might think to learn to wait three to five seconds after asking a question. If a teacher does not get an immediate response to a question, the natural reaction seems to be one of panic — an assumption that the question is not an effective one and that the student does not know the answer. Indeed, teachers who have experimented with trying to increase their wait time find that they become frustrated at about the second or third week of practice. They go through a period of indecision about how long exactly they should wait after asking a question. If they receive encouragement during this difficult time, however, most teachers are able to increase wait time from one second to three or five seconds. Some teachers have found the following suggestions helpful as they try to increase their wait time.

1. Avoid repeating portions of student response to a question (teacher echo).
2. Avoid the command "think" without giving the students clues to aid their thinking, or sufficient time in which to get their thoughts together.
3. Avoid dependency on comments such as "uh-huh" and "okay."
4. Avoid the "yes . . . but" reaction to a student response. This construction signals teacher rejection of the student's idea.

Currently, too many classrooms are characterized by a rapid rate of interaction, as teachers fire one question after another at students without giving them sufficient time to think, formulate their answers, and respond. If teachers can master the skill of increasing wait time from one second to three or five seconds, particularly after questions at a higher cognitive level, they will probably find some positive changes in both classroom discussion and student achievement.

Rewarding Students

Encouraging desired student performance through the use of rewards has been a long-recognized teaching skill; however, it is used with surprising infrequency. Rewards fall into two broad categories: verbal and nonverbal. Probably the most common verbal reward is the one-word or brief-phrase response: "Good," "Nice job," "That's right," "Excellent," and the like. But there are a number of other comments that are not used as extensively, yet they can provide students with other powerful rewards. An important type of verbal praise occurs when teachers use student ideas in developing their lessons. Applying, comparing, and building on the contributions of students are important reward techniques, and research shows that they provide students with a voice in directing their own learning. In classes where such reward techniques are applied, students have more positive attitudes and higher achievement than in classrooms where student ideas are not incorporated into the development of the lessons. Such verbal praise can be an important motive for increasing the student's desire to participate.

Nonverbal rewards may, in fact, be even more powerful than verbal praise. Nonverbal reward refers to the physical messages sent by teachers through cues such as eye contact, facial expression, and body position. Does the teacher smile, frown, or remain impassive as a student comments in class? Is the teacher looking at or away from the student? Where is the teacher standing? Does the instructor appear relaxed or tense? All these physical messages indicate to the student whether the teacher is interested or bored, involved or passive, pleased or displeased with a student's comment. In various subtle ways, nonverbal rewards can be used to encourage student participation or to inhibit it.

Several studies comparing the relative effect of nonverbal and verbal rewards on students have been undertaken. One study had teachers send out conflicting messages to determine which message students accepted as the more powerful. In one group, the teacher displayed positive nonverbal rewards (smiled, maintained eye contact, indicated positive attitude to student answers with facial and body cues), but, at the same time, sent out negative verbal messages. In the second case, the process was reversed, and negative nonverbal disapproval was coupled with positive verbal praise (frowns, poor eye contact, and the like, coupled with "good," "nice job," etc.).

Although no evidence was accumulated as to whether the teacher was perceived as schizophrenic, the results of the study were nonetheless interesting. In both cases, the nonverbal message was perceived as the stronger message by the majority of students. Whether the nonverbal message was positive or negative, most students responded to the nonverbal rather than to the verbal comments. This study provides fascinating support for the notion of "silent language," or of "body language," and it emphasizes the importance of teachers' attending to what they do not say as well as to what they do say when they reinforce student participation.

For many years educators have assumed that rewards, verbal and nonverbal, were a positive tool in promoting student learning, and, certainly, this is frequently the case. But reward is not always an effective teaching skill. In some cases reward is ineffectual and, on occasion, it is detrimental to learning.[20]

When a teacher relies totally on one or two favorite types of reward and uses these repeatedly, the eventual result may be that the reward becomes ineffectual. The teacher, for example, who continually says "Good" after each student response is not reinforcing, but simply verbalizing a comment that has lost its power to reward. Overusing a word or phrase is a pattern that many teachers, both new and experienced, fall into. Continual repetition of a word like *good* seems only to ease teacher anxiety, and to provide the teacher with a second or two to conceptualize his or her next comment or question.

In other cases, rewards can detract from educational objectives and student learning. Praise given too quickly and too frequently may interfere with or block the complete development of student ideas and interactions.

When students are engaged in problem-solving activities, continual praise can be an interruption to their thought processes, and may terminate the problem solving altogether. Rewards can also interfere with pupil-to-pupil interactions. Teachers who react to each student comment refocus the discussion on themselves, inhibiting the possibility of student-to-student interactions.

Another misuse of reward is exemplified by those teachers who are unable to differentiate the student's comment from the student's ego and, as a result, praise almost every student response, regardless of its appropriateness. To these teachers, fearful of alienating or discouraging students, every student comment is automatically rewarded, and critical thinking and accuracy are sacrificed for the sake of goodwill. It is possible, however, for teachers to reward student participation ("Thanks for that answer") and still indicate that the student response is not appropriate ("Remember now, we are focusing on American civilization before the introduction of the railroad. Can someone tackle the question again, keeping this in mind?"). In other words, it is possible to separate a student's ego from the answer. Rewarding all answers indiscriminately is an example of a poor use of praise, but rewarding the student's participation is possible, even when the answer itself may be incorrect.

Finally, it should be pointed out that different individuals respond to different kinds of rewards. Teachers should learn to recognize that, while some students find intensive eye contact rewarding, others find it uncomfortable; some students respond favorably to a teacher referring to their contributions by name, but others find it embarrassing. Although it is unrealistic to expect that a teacher will be able to learn the various rewards to which each individual student responds, it is possible for teachers to try, in general, to be sensitive to the effects of different rewards on students.

Researchers who have studied teacher praise conclude that it must have the following characteristics to be effective: (1) praise must be contingent on the student's answer, (2) praise should indicate the specific student performance to be reinforced, and (3) praise should be honest and sincere.[21]

In summary, rewarding students is a traditional but infrequently used skill. Although a positive prod for learning that can increase student participation, it is sometimes misused, and can result in decreasing student participation and learning. Praise should be contingent on student behavior, specific, and honest. It should be planned with care, so that such rewards encourage, rather than inhibit, the quantity and quality of student response.

Probing Questions

Rewarding students and increased wait time are two means whereby teachers can increase student participation in classroom discussion. A third technique designed to increase the quantity, and particularly the quality, of student participation is the probing question. Probing questions follow student responses and attempt to stimulate students to think through their answers more thoroughly. They cause students to develop the quality of their answers and to expand on their initial responses. Probing questions require students to provide more support, be clearer or more accurate, and offer greater specificity or originality.

Probing questions may be used to prompt student thinking on any level of the *Taxonomy*, but they are probably most effective at the analysis, synthesis, and evaluation levels. Here are some examples of probing questions as they might appear in a classroom discussion.

Teacher: How is a president elected?
Student: By the people.
Teacher: How? Be more specific. (probe)
Student: They vote.
Teacher: Explain how the votes determine who is president. (probe)
Student: I think that an electoral college — state representatives — do the voting. The people's votes decide which representatives will be chosen. The representatives actually choose the president.
Teacher: How are the people certain that these representatives, these electors, wouldn't vote for someone else? (probe)
Student: They give their word. They promise to vote for a certain candidate.
Teacher: Was there ever a case when an elector did not keep this promise? (probe)
Student: Yes. I remember that one elector in the 1960 election decided not to vote for Kennedy, even though most of the people in his state voted for Kennedy. I think he voted for Senator Byrd, who wasn't even running.

In this brief dialogue, the teacher asks a series of probing questions at various levels of the *Taxonomy*. The teacher does not accept the student's initial response, "By the people," but probes for more specificity as to how the electoral system works, and eventually moves the student to the higher cognitive response. Without probing the student's initial answer, the teacher would have been left with a superficial answer, and the student would not have had the opportunity to consider her response more carefully. Probing questions increase the level of student thinking, as well as the quality of student response.

Here is another sample classroom dialogue, with some more examples of probing questions.

Teacher: How can we convince auto manufacturers to build smaller cars, cars that burn less gasoline?
Student: Pass a law.
Teacher: Can you be more specific? (probe)
Student: Sure. Put a limit on the size of cars.
Teacher: Why do you think that would work? (probe)
Student: Well, smaller cars burn less gas. If you just ask them to make smaller cars, they wouldn't do it. So pass a law requiring it.
Teacher: Wouldn't car manufacturers rebel at being forced to make smaller cars? (probe)
Student: I guess. But they would do it.
Teacher: What effect might such a law have on businesspeople in other industries? How would they perceive such a law? (probe).

Equity in Interaction

If you ask teachers if they treat male and female students differently, most would be surprised — maybe even offended. "Of course not," they might respond, "I treat all my students the same." If you probed a little more, teachers might acknowledge that they discipline boys more often and more harshly than they do girls. And, in fact, research shows that boys received from three to ten times as many reprimands as do their female counterparts.[22] Researchers who have observed classroom interaction closely have discovered another difference in the way teachers tend to talk with girls and boys in classrooms. Analyze the following discussion that took place in a sixth grade accelerated English class. See if you can detect any differences in the way the teacher talks to male and female students.

Teacher: Class, the poem I have put up on the board is called *Stopping by Woods on a Snowy Evening.* It's one of the poems that you had for your assignment last night. Can you remember who wrote the poem? Marsha?

Marsha: Robert Frost.

Teacher: Yes, he's a poet from New England who writes a lot about nature. What is the setting for this particular poem, Alice?

Alice: There's someone in a sleigh, and he's watching the woods get covered with snow. I think he says that there aren't any farm houses nearby, so it must be far away from people.

Teacher: That's right. Describe in more detail what this scene is like. How does the man feel about it? Put it in your own words. Arthur?

Arthur: It's night. The man is all alone. There're no people and no noise — except for the sounds of the horse. The woods are turning all white in the dark, and it's beautiful. The man feels very peaceful. It's almost as if he wants to walk right into the woods and stay there. But at the end of the poem he says he can't because he's promised things to people and he has responsibilities.

Teacher: Arthur, you've captured the mood exactly. Arthur says that the man feels so drawn to the scene before him that he almost wants to walk into the woods and stay there. Why do you think he feels this way? Jim?

Jim: It seems as though there are two reasons. He says that the woods are "lovely, dark and deep." They're so beautiful and peaceful, they're pulling him to become part of them. It also sounds as if he's got some hassles on his mind because he's got these promises he's made to people. Maybe he'd just like to stay in the woods and forget about these problems.

Teacher: That's an excellent analysis, Jim. In the last line of the poem the man says that he has miles to go before he sleeps. I want you to think carefully about this line. Is there another meaning sleep could have besides just resting for the night? Tony?

Tony: It's probably way-out, but when a man talks about "miles to go before I sleep," could he mean before he dies? It's as though he's saying that he has a lot to do during his life before he can rest at peace in the woods forever.

Teacher: Tony, that's not way-out at all. You've done a wonderful job interpreting this poem. It's one of those poems that can be read on more than one level. And, on a deeper level, it may be a poem about death and how this man feels about it.[23]

If you read this vignette carefully, you might have noticed that the teacher directs more questions to boys than to girls. Also, boys receive more of the questions that call for higher-order thinking and more creative responses. Several studies indicate that boys, particularly high-achieving boys, are likely to receive most of the teacher's active attention.[24] They receive more praise on the quality of their academic work,[25] and they are asked more complex and abstract questions.[26] Other research has shown that teachers in mathematics classrooms give significantly more wait time to boys than to girls. The researchers conclude that "this difference could possibly have a negative effect on girls' achievement in mathematics."[27]

When teachers realize that they are distributing their attention and their questions in an unfair manner, they can change their teaching behavior. It is important to check yourself for equity in interaction and questioning so that you actively involve all your students in classroom discussions. The four techniques discussed in this section — wait time, rewarding students, probing questions, and equity in interaction — provide teachers with classroom approaches designed to make the student a more active participant in the learning process. When you feel that you understand these skills, go directly to the Mastery Test. To pass the Mastery Test, you need to demonstrate a knowledge and comprehension level understanding of the major points contained in the preceding four sections.

MASTERY TEST

OBJECTIVE 3 To describe additional teaching strategies for increasing the quantity and quality of student response

Discuss how wait time, rewarding students, probing questions, and equity in interaction can increase the quantity and/or quality of student response in the classroom. You should include the following in your discussion:

(a) A description of typical teacher reactions to student comments.
(b) A description of the bombing rate and the amount of wait time characteristic of most classrooms today.
(c) A description of four positive effects that increased wait time has on student participation.
(d) A description of how rewards can promote, as well as how they may inhibit, if used ineffectively, student response.
(e) A description of how probing questions can increase the quality of student response.
(f) A description of how patterns of inequity may characterize the interaction and questioning process.

■ Answer Keys for Your Turn Exercises

ANSWER KEY

Your Turn: Knowledge

1. F. Knowledge, or memory, requires recall, a lower level activity.
2. T. Unfortunately.
3. F. Memory, or knowledge, questions are important. Learners must have mastery of a wide variety of information. Other levels of thought are not possible without such a base.
4. T.
5. T.
6. K.
7. —. Unless the student has just learned this material, and is remembering it, this is *not* a knowledge level question. It calls for analysis, a higher level thought process.

8. K.
9. —. Calls for higher order thinking.
10. K.
11. K.
12. —. Calls for a more creative thought process than recall or recognition.
13. —. Unless the student has been told what will happen if the recession continues, he or she must use a thought process at a higher level than memory to answer this question.
14. K.

ANSWER KEY

Your Turn: Comprehension

1. F. Although the student would use original phrasing, only previously provided information could be used.
2. T.
3. T. That's one reason why comprehension questions are important.
4. F. A comprehension question asks students to reorganize information and to phrase it in their own words.
5. K. Calls for recall of a fact.
6. C. Calls for a comparison.
7. C. Calls for a comparison.
8. C. Asks the student to translate from one medium to another.
9. K. Asks for the recall of a fact.
10. C. Asks students to reorganize information so that they can put the main idea in their own words.
11. C. Asks students to describe something in their own words.
12. C. Asks for a comparison.
13. K. Asks for the recall of a fact.
14. C. Again, placing information in one's own words is the key.

ANSWER KEY

Your Turn: Application

1. K. Calls for recall of teacher's words.
2. C. Interpret in your own words.
3. Ap. Learner must apply the rules to solve a problem.
4. C. Calls for a comparison.
5. Ap. Learner must apply the scientific method to solve the problem.
6. K. Recall of a name is needed.
7. Ap. Must apply information about profit and loss to determine if there will be a profit or a loss.
8. Ap. In this case, the rules of supply and demand must be applied. The verb *apply* is a giveaway.
9. Ap. To classify the plants, the definitions of the categories must be applied to each case.

Additional Questions

10. Ap. To write examples of the definition, the rules of the definition must be applied.
11. C. "In your own words" is the clue.
12. Ap. Applying the rules of punctuation to a specific example.
13. K. Recalling previous information.
14. Ap. To solve the problem, a certain procedure must be applied.
15. Ap. To choose the correct answer, the rules of the definition must be applied.

ANSWER KEY

Your Turn: Analysis

1. True.
2. (d) Making evaluations belongs at another level of the *Taxonomy.*
3. True. "Why" questions usually require the analysis of data to locate evidence or to determine causes, reasons, or motives.
4. False. Rephrasing information is required when a student answers a comprehension question.
5. True.
6. An. The student must analyze Hamlet's actions to identify a motivation.
7. K. Memory only is required.
8. An. Evidence to support a statement is sought.
9. K. Only memory is required.
10. C. Rephrasing a previous discussion.
11. An. A conclusion is called for.
12. Ap. Applying a definition to *Hamlet* to determine an answer.

Additional Questions

13. K. Memory needed.
14. An. Identification of causes.
15. An. Conclusion or generalization based on evidence called for.
16. An. Analysis verb is a giveaway. Analysis of elements of campaign style needed.
17. An. Evidence to support a statement. (If the student had been given evidence in a previous lecture, discussion, or reading, this could be considered a knowledge or comprehension question.)
18. C. Description in student's own words required. (If the student had not previously read or talked about Kennedy's campaign style, this could be considered an analysis question.)

ANSWER KEY

Your Turn: Synthesis

1. K.
2. K, C, or Ap. Depending on the student response, it could be at any of these levels. Pure repetition would be the knowledge level. Rephrasing the description of the location would place the answer at the comprehension level. Going to a map to point it out would place the response on the application level.
3. Ap. Calls for the student to demonstrate or apply the information.
4. S. Calls for problem solving with more than one answer possible.
5. An. Calls for evidence to support decision.
6. S. Calls for a prediction.
7. S. Original communication required.
8. K. Memorization of author's comments.
9. C. Rephrasing and description needed.
10. Ap. The student needs to apply rules to solve a problem.
11. (c). Synthesis is a higher order activity that calls for much more than memorizing.
12. True.

Additional Questions
13. C. Description is all that is necessary to answer this question. If the student responds to this question with a creative essay, however, it could be considered synthesis.
14. S. Response to this question calls for prediction, an original statement, and some problem solving.
15. S. Original communication.
16. S. Problem solving. Whenever an original name, title, or main idea is called for, we are at the synthesis level.
17. An. Supporting evidence needed to explain the reason(s) for the name that was selected. To explain "why."

ANSWER KEY

Your Turn: Evaluation

1. K. Recall required.
2. C. Description in one's own words needed.
3. K or An. Knowledge if the material was already learned. Analysis if the causes must be thought out.
4. C. Calls for comparison.
5. E. Calls for a judgment.
6. S. Original communication.
7. Ap. Calls for the application of a principle or rule to a given work.
8. An. Asks student to consider evidence and make a generalization.
9. S. Prediction called for.
10. E. Calls for a judgment.

ANSWER KEY

Your Turn: Constructing Questions on the Six Levels of Bloom's *Taxonomy*

Here are some questions on the six levels of the *Taxonomy* that you might have asked about the paragraphs. They are *not* the only questions that could have been asked but are simply meant to provide examples.

1. *Knowledge level questions*
   1. What action did the three students in Des Moines, Iowa, take that caused their suspension?
   2. What was the ruling of the Supreme Court on their case?
   3. What part of the Constitution did the Supreme Court refer to as a basis for its decision?
2. *Comprehension level questions*
   1. What is the main idea in this paragraph?
   2. In your own words, explain why the Supreme Court declared the suspensions illegal.
3. *Application level questions*
   1. Considering the ruling in the Des Moines case, what would the legal ruling be on a student who, despite a ban by school authorities, wore a yellow cloth star sewn on her jacket as a protest against the United Nations policy toward Israel?
   2. Considering the Supreme Court ruling in the Des Moines case, what do you think the legal ruling would be on a group of students who blockaded the entrance to a classroom as a protest against race discrimination?
4. *Analysis level questions*
   1. Why did the Supreme Court support the rights of students to express their political and social beliefs during school hours?

2. What evidence, other than the specific case described in this paragraph, can you cite to support the conclusion that young people are now gaining long denied rights?

5. *Synthesis level questions*
   1. Develop a short story that portrays a young person seeking to attain a legal right denied to those under twenty-one.
   2. If children gained the full legal rights enjoyed by adults in America, what implications would it have for family life?

6. *Evaluation level questions*
   1. What is your opinion on the issue of minors enjoying the full legal rights of adults?
   2. If you had been a judge on the court in the case of the Des Moines students who protested the Vietnam War with black armbands despite a school ban, how would you have ruled?

■ Answer Keys for Mastery Tests

ANSWER KEY

Mastery Test, Objective 1

1. C
2. An
3. K
4. C
5. Ap
6. S
7. K
8. S
9. An
10. E
11. E

ANSWER KEY

Mastery Test, Objective 2

To pass the Mastery Test for objective 2, you must have constructed twelve questions relating to the given reading selection. There should be two questions on each level of the *Taxonomy;* at least nine of the twelve questions you develop should be well constructed and should accurately reflect the appropriate taxonomic level.

Obviously there is a wide variety of questions that could be constructed on the given paragraphs. Below are three sample questions for each of the six levels of the *Taxonomy.*

1. *Knowledge questions*
   1. What are two somewhat contradictory images that man holds of death?
   2. Who alone, among all things that live, realizes the eventual coming of death?
   3. Who was the author who said, "We fear to be we know not what, we know not where"?

2. *Comprehension questions*
   1. In your own words, what did Dryden mean by his sentence "We fear to be we know not what, we know not where"?
   2. People often hold different images of death. Compare two different conceptions of death that people hold.
   3. What is the main idea of the second paragraph?

3. *Application questions*
   1. Considering our previous study of metaphor and simile, which of these two literary devices applies to the statement in the first paragraph: "Death may be an unwelcome, terrifying enemy, a skeleton with an evil grin who clutches an ugly scythe in his bony hand"?
   2. You have previously been given a list of terms and definitions that characterize various psychological states. Which of these terms best applies to people's tendency to push the reality of death and dying out of their minds?
   3. Give an example of a character from one of the novels we have read this semester who clearly exhibits this tendency to deny the reality of death.

4. *Analysis questions*
   1. Why do you think people push the reality of death and dying out of their minds?
   2. The author suggests that people are unable to face the notion of death. What evidence can you find to support this contention?
   3. Considering the information you have in these paragraphs, how do you think the author feels people should react to death?

5. *Synthesis questions*
   1. Write a poem or short story in which the main character must face his own or another's impending death.
   2. What do you predict life would be like if there were no death?
   3. What ideas can you propose to help people become more accepting of their own mortality?

6. *Evaluation questions*
   1. Do you think it would be better for people to ignore death, as many do now, or to be more aware and accepting of death in their daily living patterns?

2. What do you judge to be the finest literary or artistic expression that has the inevitability of death as its central theme?

3. In your opinion, is it a good idea for children to read books about death?

ANSWER KEY

Mastery Test, Objective 3

(a) Teachers most frequently react to student responses with acceptance comments such as "uh-huh" or "okay." Acceptance is used so frequently that it may lead to a flat classroom environment. The second most used reaction is remediation — comments and probing questions that will help students reach the best possible response. Teacher praise and criticism are reactions that teachers do not use frequently.

(b) *Bombing rate:* Teachers ask questions at an extremely rapid rate, on the average of two or three per minute. It is not unusual to find as many as seven to ten questions asked during a single minute of classroom instruction.

Wait time: The mean amount of time a teacher waits after asking a question is only one second.

(c) Increased wait time has these positive effects on student participation (you may have chosen any four):

1. Students give longer answers.
2. They volunteer more appropriate answers.
3. Failures to respond are less frequent.
4. Student comments on the analysis and synthesis levels increase.
5. Students ask more questions.
6. Slower students offer more questions and responses.

7. Students exhibit more confidence in their comments.

(d) Rewards, both verbal and nonverbal, promote student participation, thus encouraging further participation.

Rewards can hinder student participation when (1) teacher comments interfere with student thinking, (2) teacher eye contact is so strong that it detracts from student-to-student interaction, (3) a particular praise statement is overused and loses its power, (4) rewards are given too frequently or too quickly, without a thorough analysis of the quality of student response.

(e) Probing questions increase the quantity and quality of student participation by requiring the student to go beyond the initial answer and extend his or her thinking.

(f) Boys receive not only more teacher reprimands, but also more teacher attention in general. They are praised more often and are asked more higher-order questions. It is important that teachers recognize this potential inequity so that they will involve all students as active participants in the learning process.

■ Notes

1. Charles DeGarmo, *Interest and Education* (New York: Macmillan Co., 1902), p. 179.
2. John Dewey, *How We Think*, rev. ed. (Boston: D. C. Heath, 1933), p. 266.
3. Joseph Green, "Editor's Note," *Clearing House* 40 (1966): 397.
4. Thomas Merton, *The Seven Storey Mountain* (Garden City, NY: Doubleday Co., 1948), p. 139.
5. Romiett Stevens, "The Question As a Measure of Classroom Practice," *Teachers College Contributions to Education*, no. 48 (New York: Teachers College Press, Columbia University, 1912).
6. O. L. Davis and Drew Tinsley, "Cognitive Objectives Revealed by Classroom Questions Asked by Social Studies Teachers and Their Pupils," *Peabody Journal of Education* 44 (July 1967): 21–26. Also see O. L. Davis and Francis P. Hunkins, "Textbook Questions: What Thinking Processes Do They Foster?," *Peabody Journal of Education* 43 (March 1966): 285–292; P. E. Blosser, "Review of Research: Teacher Questioning Behavior in Science Classrooms," *ERIC Clearinghouse for Science, Mathematics, and Environmental Education*, ED 18418 (Columbus,

OH: December 1979); D. Trachtenberg, "Student Tasks in Text Material; What Cognitive Skills Do They Tap?," *Peabody Journal of Education* 52 (1974): 54–57.

7. Stevens, *op. cit.* See also E. Dale and L. Raths, "Discussion in the Secondary School," *Educational Research Bulletin* 24 (1945): 1–6; Davis and Hunkins, *op. cit.*; W. D. Floyd, "An Analysis of the Oral Questioning Activity in Selected Colorado Primary Classrooms" (Ph.D. diss., Colorado State College, 1960); Roger T. Cunningham, "A Descriptive Study Determining the Effects of a Method of Instruction Designed to Improve the Question-Phrasing Practices of Prospective Elementary Teachers" (Ph.D. diss., Indiana University, 1968), p. 156.

8. Mary Budd Rowe, "Wait-Time and Rewards As Instructional Variables: Their Influence on Language, Logic and Fate Control" (paper presented at the National Association for Research in Science Teaching, Chicago, April 1972).

9. Hilda Taba, Samuel Levine, and Freeman Elzey, *Thinking Elementary School Children*, Cooperative Research Project No. 1574, San Francisco State College, San Francisco, CA, April 1964, p. 177; see also Francis P. Hunkins, *Questioning Strategies and Techniques* (Boston: Allyn and Bacon, 1972); D. L. Redfield and E. W. Rousseau, "A Meta-Analysis of Experimental Research on Teacher Questioning Behavior," *Review of Educational Research* 51 (1981): 237–245; William Wilen, *Questioning Skills for Teachers* (Washington, D.C.: National Education Association, 1982); Paul Otto and Robert Schuck, "The Effect of a Teacher Questioning Strategy Training Program on Teaching Behavior, Student Achievement, and Retention," *Journal of Research in Science Teaching* 20 (1983): 521–528.

10. Rowe, *op. cit.*

11. G. L. Fahey, "The Questioning Activity of Children," *Journal of Genetic Psychology* 60 (1942): 337–357. See also V. M. Houston, "Improving the Quality of Classroom Questions and Questioning," *Educational Administration and Supervision* 24 (1938): 17–28; and W. D. Floyd, *op. cit.*

12. Virginia Rogers, "Varying the Cognitive Levels of Classroom Questions in Elementary Social Studies: An Analysis of the Use of Questions by Student Teachers" (Ph.D. diss., University of Texas at Austin, 1968). See also Hilda Taba, *Teaching Strategies and Cognitive Functioning in Elementary School Children*, Cooperative Research Project No. 2404 (Washington, D.C.: U.S. Office of Education, 1966).

13. Meredith D. Gall, Barbara Dunning, and Rita Weatherby, *Minicourse 9: Higher Cognitive Questioning, Teacher's Handbook*, Far West Laboratory for Educational Research and Development (Beverly Hills, CA: Macmillan Education Services, 1971).

14. Benjamin Bloom, ed. *Taxonomy of Educational Objectives, Handbook I: Cognitive Domain* (New York: David McKay, 1956).

15. J. Brophy and C. Evertson, *Learning from Teaching: A Developmental Perspective* (Boston: Allyn and Bacon, 1976).

16. S. R. Mills, C. T. Rice, D. C. Berliner, and E. W. Rousseau, "The Correspondence Between Teacher Questions and Student Answers in Classroom Discourse," *Journal of Experimental Education* 48 (1980): 194–209.

17. John Goodlad, *A Place Called School* (New York: McGraw-Hill, 1984), p. 124.

18. David Sadker and Myra Sadker, *Promoting Effectiveness in Classroom Instruction, Final Report*, Contract No. 400-80-0033 (Washington, D.C.: Department of Education, 1984). See also K. Watson and B. Young,

"Discourse for Learning in the Classroom," *Language Arts* 63, no. 2 (1986): 126–141.

19. The findings in this section are based on work by Mary Budd Rowe, *op. cit.* See also K. Tobin, "The Role of Wait Time in Higher Cognitive Level Learning," *Review of Educational Research* 57, no. 1 (1987): 69–95.

20. Jere Brophy, "Teacher Praise: A Functional Analysis, Occasional Paper no. 2" (East Lansing, MI: Michigan State University, The Institute for Research on Teaching, 1979).

21. *Ibid.*

22. Jere Brophy and Thomas Good, *Teacher-Student Relationships: Causes and Consequences* (New York: Holt, Rinehart & Winston, 1974).

23. Myra Sadker and David Sadker, *Sex Equity Handbook for Schools* (New York: Longman, 1982).

24. Brophy and Good, *op. cit.*

25. Carol Dweck, William Davidson, Sharon Nelson, and Bradley Enna, "Sex Differences in Learned Helplessness: II. The Contingencies of Evaluative Feedback in the Classroom, and III. An Experimental Analysis," *Developmental Psychology* 14, no. 3 (1978), 268–276.

26. Sadker and Sadker, *Promoting Effectiveness in Classroom Instruction, Final Report*, Contract No. 400-80-0033 (Washington, D.C.: Department of Education, 1984).

27. Delores Gore and Daniel Roumagoux, "Wait Time As a Variable in Sex Related Differences During Fourth-Grade Mathematics Instruction," *Journal of Educational Research* 76 (1983): 273–275.

Additional Readings

Berliner, David. "The Half-Full Glass: A Review of Research on Teaching," in *Using What We Know About Teaching*, Philip Hosford, ed. Alexandria, VA: Association for Supervision and Curriculum Development, 1984.

Bloom, Benjamin, ed. *Taxonomy of Educational Objectives, Handbook I: Cognitive Domain*. New York: David McKay, 1956.

Cunningham, Roger T. "Developing Question-Asking Skills," in *Developing Teacher Competencies*, James Wiegand, ed. Englewood Cliffs, NJ: Prentice-Hall, 1971.

Dillon, J. T., *The Practice of Questioning*. New York: Routledge, 1990.

Gall, Meredith, Barbara Dunning, and Rita Weatherby. *Minicourse 9: Higher Cognitive Questioning, Teachers Handbook*. Far West Laboratory for Educational Research and Development. Beverly Hills, CA: Macmillan Educational Services, 1971.

Gillin, Caroline, Marcella Kysilka, Virginia Rogers, and Lewis Smith. *Questioneze: Individual or Group Game Involvement for Developing Questioning Skills*. Columbus, OH: Merrill, 1972.

Hyman, Ronald T. *Strategic Questioning*. Englewood Cliffs, NJ: Prentice-Hall, 1979.

Sadker, David, and Myra Sadker. *The Intellectual Exchange: Equity and Excellence in College Teaching*. McCrel, 1988.

Sander, Norris. *Classroom Questions: What Kinds*. New York: Harper and Row, 1966.

Strother, Deborah Burnett. "Developing Thinking Skills Through Questioning," *Phi Delta Kappan* 71 (1989): 324–372.

Wilen, William. *Questioning Skills for Teachers*. Washington, D.C.: National Education Association, 1991.

Concept Learning and Higher-Level Thinking

6

■ Peter H. Martorella

1 (a) To identify five different ways in which the term *concept* is used in educational literature, (b) to identify the basic characteristics of concepts, and (c) to distinguish between essential and nonessential characteristics of a concept

2 (a) To classify concepts according to types, using four classification systems; and (b) to identify developmental differences that occur among students in concept learning

3 (a) To distinguish between the personal and public dimensions of concept learning, and (b) to identify and briefly describe the seven key steps in the *Basic Model for Concept Instruction*

4 (a) To identify five dimensions of concept learning that can be assessed and to arrange them according to their level of complexity, and (b) to identify and briefly describe three procedures for assessing the private dimensions of students' concepts

5 (a) To analyze the relationship among concepts, schemata, and higher-level thinking; and (b) to identify three instructional strategies that promote concept enrichment and higher level thinking

It began like any other day. Ginny Peters awoke at approximately 7 o'clock, stretched, and rolled out of bed. She put on her clothes that were neatly folded on the chair where she had placed them the night before, rolled her pajamas into a ball, and stuffed them under her pillow. Unaware of what was happening downstairs, she brushed her hair the usual 100 times and then washed her face and hands and brushed her teeth.

As she descended the stairs, she greeted her dog Missy and bounded into the kitchen. "Mornin', mom, dad," she said with her usual good cheer. The worried looks on her parents' faces called her up short, and signaled to her that something was amiss. "Sh-h, we're trying to hear the latest report," her mother said gently.

The radio on the kitchen table continued blaring out a news bulletin in excited tones. "Last night while most of Dublin City slept, an unprecedented robbery took place. Striking swiftly and quietly, the thieves moved with unusual efficiency. Informed sources report that law enforcement officials are completely baffled by the case. No clues have been uncovered, nor have any eye witnesses come forth. A night watchman working in the 1700 block of Highland Avenue, however, reported that a speeding blue car was observed at approximately 3:00 A.M. No one in Dublin City recalls such a theft occurring where. . . ." Ginny's patience gave out. "What's going on? What happened?" she interrupted.

Her father switched off the radio. Glancing nervously at his wife, he said in solemn tones, "I guess we better tell her, Martha. She's sure to find out about it from someone else, if we don't." Martha began with slow and measured phrases. "Ginny, I don't want you to be upset by what I am about to tell you. Things may be difficult at first, but you — we all — will learn to adjust to it. After a while, our lives will go on just as before."

"Mother, please tell me *what* has happened. I can't stand the suspense," Ginny implored.

Her father leaned across the table and picked up the conversation. Ginny thought she saw a tear in his eye. "Ginny, someone has stolen *happiness*. From now on, no one will ever be able to know about, feel, or share happiness." Just then Ginny awoke with a start. "Wow," she shuddered, "that was a terrible dream."

Fortunately for all of us, as well as our hypothetical Ginny, we still have the concept of happiness among us. The above melodrama was contrived to draw attention to the importance of concepts. The loss of even one of our most precious concepts would be a significant personal, as well as a social, loss.

The Importance of Concepts

We build our world on concepts. They come in all types, and some are much more significant than others. Throughout any day, hundreds, perhaps thousands, will be pressed into service. Ginny's concepts of "tooth brushing," "politeness," "news," "radio," and "sadness" — to name just a few — were employed in her brief dream. Countless other concepts were at work also, just as they are for each of us every conscious moment of our lives. As we learn and experience new things, we both draw upon and increase our conceptual banks. We constantly put old concepts to use and, in the process, frequently extend them and acquire new, related ones.

Where does it all end? The chain of concept acquisition, usage, enlargement, and revision is continuous for as long as we are able to think. For some of us, the conceptual juices flow faster or slower, depending on factors such as our current and past experiences and the formal instruction we receive.

Everyone learns concepts, whether they like to or not. Most of us enjoy learning them — at least, some of the time. Concepts enrich, as well as extend and order, our psychological worlds. Many concepts, such as *chair*, are acquired because they have functional value; they are useful for something we need or want to do. Others, such as *cowboy*, are learned just because they are fun, or because they make our lives more interesting and pleasant. Still others, such as *square root, balance of trade, verb*, and the like, are learned on a "good faith" basis. They are not immediately functional nor are they much fun, so we must simply take it on faith that some day they will be useful or entertaining. Much of our concept learning in school is on such a good faith basis. When a teacher appears to tax or violate our good faith, we may balk at learning. We begin to suspect that we are "being had." In addition to their ability to entertain us and to help satisfy our immediate needs, concepts serve us in three additional ways.

1. They simplify our learning tasks.
2. They expedite communication.
3. They help us distinguish between reality and imagery.

Our intellectual world is composed of millions of bits and pieces of knowledge. If each of these items required a separate category in our knowledge network, information retrieval would be extremely unwieldy. Concepts allow us to organize and store similar pieces of information efficiently. Once formed, they eliminate our need to treat each new piece of knowledge as a separate category. In a sense, concepts are "hooks" on which we can hang new experiences. When we confront a sufficiently novel situation for which we have no hooks, we either force the information onto an incompatible hook or else we create a new one. In short, concepts organize our knowledge structure and keep it from becoming unwieldy and dysfunctional.

Perhaps the most useful aspect of concepts lies in their ability to speed up and simplify communication among people. Because you and I share similar concepts, we can easily communicate without any need on my part to explain in great detail every idea, event, or object. Each new concept builds on preceding ones; their cumulative pattern and sequencing make extended descriptions of each one unnecessary. When communication between two people breaks down, it is often because one member has not learned concepts that are basic to the conversation. Frequently, this problem occurs in textbooks when the author incorrectly assumes knowledge of certain concepts on the part of the readers. On the other hand, communication proceeds efficiently between individuals who are at a similar stage of conceptual learning. We frequently refer to such people as "being on the same wavelength." For communication to proceed at all, mutual knowledge of some concepts is essential.

One of the more subtle functions of concepts is their ability to help us distinguish between illusion and reality. One who has acquired the concept of *cow* has no trouble distinguishing between a picture or a three-dimensional model of a cow and a real Holstein. Similarly, knowledge of other concepts allows one, without much conscious analysis, to recognize that various pictures and models are only representations. Confusion between real examples of concepts and their secondhand representation can occasionally be detected in children, as with a little girl who believed that chickens were an inch and a half high.

What is the nature of concepts? How are they different from one another? How are they learned? What role do they play in higher-level thinking? The remainder of this chapter will discuss these four fundamental questions.

YOUR TURN

What Do You Know About Concepts?

Let's see what you already know about concepts. Mark a *T* for true and an *F* for false statements.

___T___   1. This page is filled with concepts.

_____   2. Down deep, all concepts are alike.

___T___   3. Every subject area is built around concepts.

___T___   4. It is the subject area from which a concept is drawn that makes it easy or difficult to learn.

_____ 5. Another name for a concept is *generalization.*

_____ 6. No matter what your age, concept learning occurs in the same way.

_____ 7. Learning a concept occurs in the same way that everything else does.

_____ 8. The more information we have about a concept, the easier it is to learn.

_____ 9. You teach for concept learning in the same way that you teach for other objectives.

_____ 10. Unless you can tell what a concept is in your own words, you have not really learned it.

Compare your answers to these questions with the Answer Key that follows.

OBJECTIVE **1** (a) To identify five different ways in which the term *concept* is used in educational literature, (b) to identify the basic characteristics of concepts, and (c) to distinguish between essential and nonessential characteristics of a concept

Learning Activity 1

The Nature of Concepts

People's concepts of a concept vary considerably. Some use the term *concept* synonymously with *idea:* "That's my concept of how a house should be designed." Others use the term to mean a *theme* or *topic:* "These are the concepts we will study in history: 'the Great Depression,' 'the New Deal'. . . ." A third way to use *concept* is to express a *general, all-encompassing statement:* "All men are mortal." And a fourth way is to refer to the most fundamental *elements* or *structures of disciplines,* such as in the sciences and social sciences: "The concept of culture underlies all of anthropology."

In psychology, and specifically in areas where different types of learning outcomes are being considered, concepts have a distinct fifth meaning with which the remainder of this chapter will be concerned. Concepts in this last sense refer to the *categories* into which we group our knowledge and experiences. Once formed, these categories act as intellectual magnets that attract and order related thoughts and experiences. The categories we create generally have single or multiword *labels* or *names* that serve to identify them, such as *tree* or *balance of trade.* As we experience objects or events, we sort them into the various categories we have created; once sorted, we begin relating them to other items in the same category. This relating process may be brief and simple, or it may evolve into an extended analysis of multiconcept interrelationships.

Concepts Defined

Thus, we may simultaneously speak of concepts as being (1) *categories* into which our experiences are organized and (2) *the related web of ideas brought about through categorization.* We do not merely sort out and label the objects and events we encounter; we actively reflect on them to greater or lesser degrees. As we are faced with new or old phenomena, we must relate them, sometimes quickly, to what we already know to make much sense of them.

Our concepts not only organize our experience but also affect *how* we attend to or reflect on that experience. Suppose that each day we pass a hole in the ground partially filled with dirt and water. We may label it a "hazardous mud hole," thereby ensuring that we carefully avoid it. On the other hand, a passing biologist, using a different set of conceptual glasses, might experience the hole as a scientific gold mine filled with interesting organisms. His or her conceptual glasses, developed through specialized training, produce a different set of categories that, in turn, lead to different reflections concerning the same object.

Conceptual categories and related reflections may be limited or extensive, simplistic or complex, depending on one's interests and experiences. Occasionally, concepts may lack labels or precise referents. When this is so, communication with others may be difficult. We say things such as "I can't exactly describe it; you sort of have to *feel* it," "I don't know what you call it, but all of these paintings have it," "They don't have any names. I just call them 'squiggles' because they are sort of squiggly."

Objects or events are sorted into concept categories through a check of their basic characteristics. We may check these characteristics against our memories of past examples and mental models or *prototypes* that represent our notion of a typical case of the concept. The interrelated collection of characteristics comprises the *criterial* (or *critical*) *attributes* of the concept. If an item of information meets the criteria for a concept category we hold, we connect the concept *name* with the phenomenon. Then we begin to relate it to other associated information we hold in memory, thus forming a network or web of ideas.

The particular sequence, pattern, or relationship of attributes is significant in determining whether they comprise an example of a particular concept. This specific ordering of attributes is known as a *concept definition or rule.* Consider, for example, the attributes *land*, *water*, and *a surrounding body.* Without the rule or way in which each of the three critical attributes is related, we cannot be sure whether the concept under consideration is *island* or *lake*. The rule tells us that "land surrounded by water" is an island, whereas "water surrounded by land" is a lake.

Essentially then, concepts consist of (1) names such as "island," (2) criterial attributes such as "body of land," and (3) rules such as "body of land surrounded by water." Cases or illustrations of a concept are referred to as *examples*; *nonexamples* of a concept are any cases or illustrations that lack one or more of the criterial attributes of the concept, or else have a different rule. Each concept is a nonexample for every other one; for instance, island is a nonexample of the concept of *isthmus*. The closer the resemblance of the concept (their sets of related criterial attributes), the greater the difficulty in discriminating among them.

As with examples and nonexamples, criterial attributes also have a negative counterpart — *noncriterial* (or *noncritical*) *attributes*. These are features that frequently are present in concept illustrations, though they are *not* an essential part of the concept. They are analogous to accessories on a car. Almost always, some accessories come with an automobile, although they are unnecessary for the vehicle to function. Noncriterial attributes are present under many forms, as seen in the following table. They may appear as *length* in examples of the concept "sentence," as *color* when dealing with the concept "chair," as *size* in examples of "triangle" or "island," and so on.

Concept	Noncriterial Attribute
sentence	length
chair	color
triangle	size
island	size

The list of possibilities for noncriterial attributes is endless.

Stereotypes and Misconceptions

When we attend too closely to noncriterial attributes and begin to treat them as criterial ones, we often create *stereotypes* and *misconceptions*. For example, on the basis of three dates with three different Italian men, a woman might conclude that all Italian men are great lovers. A child being introduced to geometric shapes notes that, in all examples of the concept *triangle*, there are two equal sides and that the third side is always parallel to the plane of the floor. He or she overgeneralizes these conditions as essential for all triangles. A high school boy observes that every poem he has ever heard or read has rhymed. He mistakenly concludes that verse must rhyme to be classified as poetry. Children in a family grow up in a neighborhood where most of the blacks they encounter are physically aggressive, poor, and boisterous. From these limited and isolated cases, they begin to form their concepts of all blacks.

Much of the instruction we give and receive inadvertently confuses noncriterial and criterial attributes. To correct this error and sharpen our discrimination capabilities, we must periodically be called up short and be made to analyze carefully the similarities and differences in diverse cases of concept examples and nonexamples.

Almost never, except perhaps with certain abstract concepts, are examples completely free of any noncriterial distractors. Inevitably, there are some details in nearly all illustrations that may serve to mislead us concerning the concept's essential properties. For one whose grasp of a concept is shaky, noncriterial properties may be a source of great perplexity. On the other hand, for one who has a clear understanding of the concept, noncriterial features often provide enrichment. They enhance our already formed concept and enlarge our range of examples. Having already learned to sort out cases on the basis of defining characteristics, we can appreciate and even seek out new, subtle variations on old themes.

MASTERY TEST

OBJECTIVE 1   (a) To identify five different ways in which the term *concept* is used in educational literature, (b) to identify the basic characteristics of concepts, and (c) to distinguish between essential and nonessential characteristics of a concept

1. In brief, what are five different ways in which the term *concept* is used in educational literature?

2. List the basic characteristics of concepts.

3. Take a moment to examine this list of concepts. What are some of the more common noncriterial attributes that might be present in examples of these concepts?

mammal	mountain
tree	state
river	death
winter	cloud
prime number	comb

Now compare your answers with those that follow in the Answer Key.

OBJECTIVE   **2**   (a) To classify concepts according to types, using four classification systems; and (b) to identify developmental differences that occur among students in concept learning

Learning Activity 2

Types of Concepts

What makes a concept easy or hard to learn? Let's try an experiment to find out. Detach (along the dotted lines) the various cards shown at the back of the book in Appendix B. Sort them into two piles: those you consider *easy* to learn into the first pile, and those you consider *hard* into the second. Arrange these two piles into nine new piles, ranging from easiest to hardest. You may sort as many cards as you wish into each pile, but each pile must have *at least one* card in it. When you finish your sorting, take some time to compare your results and the rationale you used with someone else.

What were the similarities and differences in the two sets of piles and in the two rationales? Note the criteria you used in judging the concept's level of difficulty. After reading the remainder of the section, you may wish to refer back to your conclusions.

▪ Classifying Concepts

There are many different bases by which to classify concepts as easier or harder to learn. A frequently cited criterion of difficulty is the extent to which concepts are perceived to be *concrete* or *abstract*. For purposes of simplification, let us use the rough definition that concreteness refers to what we can perceive directly through one of the five senses: taste, smell, touch, sound, sight. In contrast, abstractness refers to what we acquire only indirectly through the senses, or cannot perceive directly through the senses. There are some problems with these distinctions in practice, but they will suffice to illustrate one type of classification system. Clearly, in this system, *chair, tree, glass,* and similar objects are concrete concepts and presumably easier to learn. Similarly, *beauty, freedom, justice, empathy,* and similar terms are abstract and presumably harder to learn. In between are a wide range of concepts that defy simple classification in this system.

Another way to view concepts is to examine whether they are most frequently learned in *formal* or *informal* contexts. Many of the concepts we acquire come through informal channels of experience (car, house, television, fire), while others come through systematic channels of instruction such as schools, job-training programs, or parents (legislature, hydrogen, preposition, square). Not all abstract concepts are acquired formally, however; beauty and truth, for example, result from a complex blend of formal and informal instruction. It would be difficult to assess which type of instruction is generally dominant for such concepts.

A third perspective on concept types divides them into three classes: *conjunctive, disjunctive,* and *relational.* According to this frame of reference, a conjunctive concept is less difficult to learn because it has only a single set of qualities or characteristics. A little girl might say to herself, "If it has this and that and those things, it must be a whatchamacallit." *Chair* is a conjunctive concept, as the dictionary definition testifies: "A piece of furniture consisting of a seat, legs and back, and often arms, designed for one person." There are many kinds or examples of chairs, but the easy part of learning the concept is that the basic set of defining characteristics is always essentially the same.

A disjunctive concept is slightly more complicated. To learn this type of concept, one must learn two or more sets of alternative conditions under which the concept appears. *Citizen* is such a concept. The dictionary states that a citizen is "a native *or* naturalized member of a state or nation who owes allegiance to its government and who is entitled to its protection." Either being born in a country or fulfilling some test of citizenship can lead to the status of citizen. In short, disjunctive concepts can have more than one set of criterial attributes.

The most complex type of concept to learn is a relational one. *Waste, resource, pollution, a little, a lot, parallel,* and *symmetry* are all relational concepts. Their meaning stems from a comparison or a relationship between objects or events. A line segment or an object cannot be assessed "parallel" unless something specific about its relationship to another line or object is known. Similarly, one cannot tell if something is "a lot" unless it is compared to something else — another item, an average or norm, or the whole of which it is a part.

So it is with all relational concepts; they describe *relationships* between items. A line segment that is parallel on some occasions can be perpendicular on other occasions. Only its particular relationship to another line segment makes it perpendicular or parallel. Five apples are a lot of apples for a small child's snack, but they are only a little for a troop of Boy Scouts. Learners of relational concepts must focus on the characteristics of the items being compared, and also on the basis being used for comparison. In observing a line segment, for example, a student must also note another line segment, as well as the relationship between the two.

Determining whether a concept is one of the three preceding types allows a teacher to anticipate learning difficulties and to prepare corresponding instruction. One investigator discovered, for example, that preschoolers have a tendency to treat relational concepts as if they were conjunctive ones.

> When the four-year-old first learns the concept dark, he regards it as descriptive of an absolute class of color — black and related dark hues. The phrase "dark yellow" makes no sense to him, for dark signifies dark colors, not relative darkness.[1]

Older students who have misconceptions of *resource* and *waste* reflect similar problems when they fail to understand that oil, water, wood, and the like may be examples of resources and waste simultaneously.

A fourth system for classifying concepts has a developmental basis. It concentrates on the dominant medium through which our concepts are represented as we develop chronologically. According to Jerome Bruner, three representational media for acquiring concepts exist: *enactive* — "knowing something through doing it," *iconic* — "through a picture or image of it," and *symbolic* — "through symbols such as language."[2] Thus, one might learn the concept of *swimming* through doing it (enactive), through viewing a filmstrip on swimming techniques (iconic), or through reading a book on the topic (symbolic). Bruner also notes of these three representational forms: "Their appearance in the life of the child is in that order, each depending upon the previous one for its development, yet all of them remaining more or less intact throughout life — barring such early accidents as blindness or deafness or cortical injury."[3] Enactive representation is dominant during infancy and early childhood; iconic representation becomes the norm through preadolescence; thereafter, symbolic representation dominates. From a teacher's perspective, concepts may be analyzed with respect to which one of the three representational forms — enactive, iconic, or symbolic — seems most appropriate for teaching that concept.

As noted earlier, the process of examining and categorizing concepts may take many forms. The four perspectives, summarized in the following table, suggest only some of the possibilities. From an instructional viewpoint, the important issue is that we, as teachers, try to: (1) determine which concepts are most likely to present learning difficulties, (2) identify what the potential problems are likely to be, and (3) use such data to build systematic assistance into learning activities. All concepts are not alike with respect to how they are learned and, to the extent that our instruction reflects this fact, it will be more or less effective.

Classification System for Concepts

Basis for Classification	Types of Concepts
Degrees of concreteness	1. Concrete (chair) 2. Abstract (lonely, hot)
Context in which learned	1. Formal (school, training program) 2. Informal (socializing, casual observation)
Nature of criterial attributes	1. Conjunctive (lake) 2. Disjunctive (citizen) 3. Relational (dark)
Form or manner in which learned	1. Enactive (play tennis) 2. Iconic (watch tennis match on TV) 3. Symbolic (read book on tennis)

YOUR TURN

Subject Matter Concepts

You may wish to try a simple activity to help you identify the sorts of concepts students typically are asked to learn in subject matter areas. For the focus of your investigation, pick a grade level range in which to explore a particular subject matter.

1. A subject matter area (mathematics, social studies, etc.) for grades 1–6

2. A subject matter area for grades 4–9

3. A subject matter area for grades 7–12

Within that subject matter area and for each of those six grade levels, identify a popular related textbook. Examine each of the six texts and locate twenty concepts that seem to occur with some frequency. List your concepts and note five conclusions that you have drawn based on your analysis of the texts.

Share your results with others who are working in similar areas. If possible, arrange to examine alternative textbooks so that you will have sampled collectively a wide range of texts. Compare similarities and differences in your lists, as well as your individual conclusions. Note what overall conclusions seem warranted based on the collective set of tabulations.

MASTERY TEST

OBJECTIVE 2 (a) To classify concepts according to types, using four classification systems; and (b) to identify developmental differences that occur among students in concept learning

1. Give a brief definition of the following types of concepts, each of which was used in one of the concept classification systems: (a) concrete, (b) abstract, (c) formal, (d) informal, (e) conjunctive, (f) disjunctive, (g) relational, (h) enactive, (i) iconic, and (j) symbolic.

2. Which of the concept types you have just defined are most closely related to developmental differences among children?

 **3** (a) To distinguish between the personal and public dimensions of concept learning, and (b) to identify and briefly describe the seven key steps in the *Basic Model for Concept Instruction*

Learning Activity 3

Learning and Teaching Concepts

No matter what the subject area or particular concept, each of us has a unique personal history that influences how we use concepts. My concepts of *primate, rhombus,* or *whiskers* are slightly different from anyone else's, the unique product of specific percepts being processed through my total conceptual network. Compared to the biologist, mathematician, and dermatologist, I may appear to be a conceptual dunce if the conversation deals solely with primates, rhombi, or whiskers. Still we can communicate at a basic level because we share a minimal level of concept learning.

Personal and Public Dimensions of Concepts

We may label the unique, personalized side of concepts their *personal dimension.* This idiosyncratic aspect is not really teachable, although traces may sometimes be acquired through formal instruction. For concepts to function as shared experiences, they must also possess a *public dimension* that each of us holds in common. These are the shared attributes or properties that serve as the basis of communication, and must be understood by anyone claiming to have learned the concept. When we move beyond that basic public level of understanding, we generally need to explain in some detail our personal associations with the concept. Two individuals who find they "have a lot in common" often mean they have discovered their personal associations with concepts are surprisingly similar.

Try an experiment to discover your own personal associations with a concept that you share with most other people in our culture. Refer to the object shown in Figure 6.1. Give it a name and write that name in the circle at the center of the diagram in Figure 6.2. Next jot down your immediate associations following the first set of arrows in the spaces marked 1. Now consider what the words in these spaces remind you of and record these new associations in the spaces marked 2. Repeat the process for the spaces marked 3. Take no more than two minutes to complete the diagram.

Compare your results with those of others. First examine the names used to categorize the object, then the associations found in the spaces marked 1, 2, and 3. In what ways were all of the associations similar? In what ways did they differ? At what points, if any, did some of the concepts' criterial attributes get listed? At what points were noncriterial attributes listed? What did you learn about your own personal concept from Figure 6.2?

Whatever the character of the personal network each of us generates, it would seem that the *criterial* attributes are the common or *public* aspects of concepts that provide the basis of communication. While formal instruction, such as that occurring in classrooms, always makes some contribution to the personal dimensions of concept learning, its primary focus initially should be on the *public* dimensions. Such basic, culturally shared elements of concepts generally can be derived from dictionaries, encyclopedias, scholarly works, tradition, authoritative experience, or the mass media. While the vast majority of concepts are learned informally, with highly personal and public elements intertwined, many are so specialized that they can only be acquired through formal instruction. Also, a person's

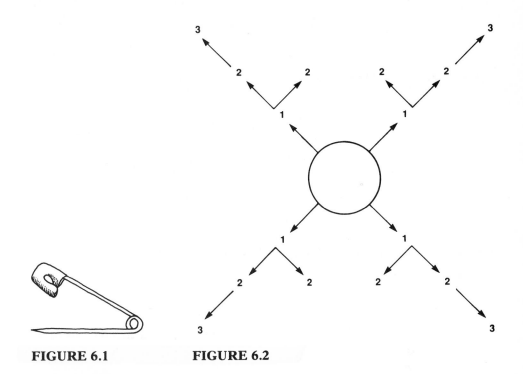

FIGURE 6.1   **FIGURE 6.2**

lifestyle may be so limited or different from the lifestyles of others that he or she requires assistance in learning the public elements of concepts.

What Is It Like to Learn a Concept?

Everyone learns hundreds of new concepts without ever giving much thought to the matter. Trial-and-error, question-and-answer, and chance observations bring us a wealth of concepts that we are not even aware we are learning. As time passes and we mature, many of these concepts are reinforced, refined, and amplified. This process continues naturally throughout our lives.

Let us try to capture the sensation of someone who is trying to learn a new concept. What strategies are employed? What feelings do we have? What successes and failures do we encounter, and what led to them?

YOUR TURN

Compare Four Concept Examples

Shown here in Figures 6.3–6.6 are some materials taken from the elementary science study unit of *Teacher's Guide for Attribute Games and Problems.*[4] We can treat each of the four sets of figures as a concept to be learned. Examine the first two rows of each set, looking for the criterial attributes (defining properties) of that concept, then select the examples of that concept from the third row. Below each of the four sets, write as specifically and clearly as possible what you consider to be the definition or criterial attributes of the concepts. Compare your conclusions with others who have examined the four sets. If your choices and definitions differ, consider whose results seem most accurate and why. Then turn to the Answer Key that follows.

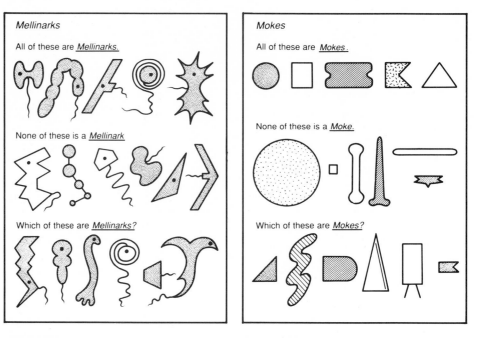

FIGURE 6.3   **FIGURE 6.4**

Figures 6.3, 6.4, 6.5, and 6.6 were originally published in *Teacher's Guide for Attribute Games and Problems* (New York: McGraw-Hill, 1968), pp. 75 and 77.

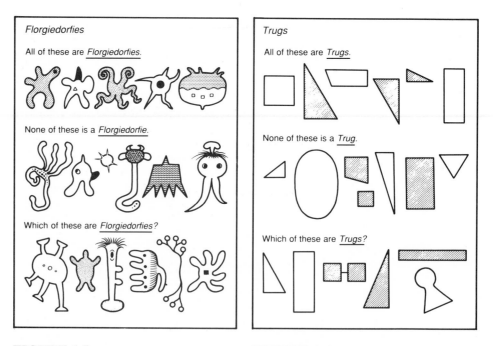

FIGURE 6.5   **FIGURE 6.6**

Consider the following questions.

1. In what ways are the four sets alike?

2. What makes some of the concepts easier to learn than others? (In other words, what is the meaning of the term *easier* in these cases?)

3. If you or anyone else was unable to identify or define one or more of the concepts correctly, what were the problems you encountered?

4. In what ways is the learning of these artificial concepts similar to the learning of other reality-based new concepts?

5. Were any of you able to *identify* concept examples correctly but not *define* them accurately? If so, what are the implications of this fact for school learning?

6. What were the feelings you experienced in the various stages of trying to learn the concepts?

The phenomenon of confusing noncriterial attributes with criterial properties, while deliberately introduced into this demonstration, occurs naturally in the learning of academic concepts. On these occasions, unless a teacher is willing to reexamine his or her instruction rather than fault the learner's capabilities, little progress toward the learning of concepts will occur. An instructor *must resist* the easy defensive position, "Most of the class got the correct answer when I explained the concept. If you didn't, then I guess you are just not trying hard enough!"

Let's reflect a moment on some of the instructional assistance given to you about the preceding concepts, Mellinarks, Mokes, Florgiedorflies, and Trugs. Most of the conditions provided for your instruction are not available in a typical concept learning situation.

Condition 1.   Little irrelevant material — material that might have diverted your attention from the essential characteristics of the concept — was included in your instruction.

Condition 2.   All the cases you needed, examples and nonexamples, were put before you *simultaneously*. This allowed you to recheck conclusions and to compare cases easily.

Condition 3.   The characteristics of the concepts were relatively simple ones. Mellinarks were *conjunctive* concepts, the least difficult type to learn, while the fourth concept, Trugs, was *disjunctive* and the second and third, Mokes and Florgiedorflies, were *relational*.

Condition 4.   All our concepts had concise graphic referents that required little or no verbal ability to understand.

Those readers who experienced difficulty with the pronunciation of concept names or who could not now correctly spell some of them should be able to empathize with students' linguistic burden. Similarly, some readers may have discovered it is possible to identify *instances* of a concept correctly without being able to explain accurately or define the concept in one's own words. Students frequently exhibit this phenomenon, and it often leads to a misinterpretation of their learning level. Persons who can consistently discriminate examples of a concept from nonexamples may be said to have "learned" that concept, whether or not they can articulate a definition of it.

How Do You Teach a Concept?

To initiate the process of teaching a concept, you need to ask yourself several basic questions: Do educators and subject matter specialists suggest that the concept is an important one for students to acquire? Should a student receive systematic instruction in the concept, or is it more appropriately acquired through informal means? Is there sufficient agreement on the criterial attributes and the concept rule to have a basis for designing instruction?

Assuming the answers are yes to these three questions, you are ready to move on to the next phase of instructional planning.

Planning Inventory

1. What name is most commonly applied to the concept? (*Example:* lake)
2. What is a statement of the concept's rule or definition (the arrangement of its criterial attributes)? (*Example:* body of water surrounded by land) *Self awareness allows you to learn who you are.*
3. What are the essential characteristics or *criterial attributes* of the concept, based on your readings and reference sources? (*Example:* land, water, surrounding) *Know physical & personal characteristics*
4. What are some *noncriterial attributes* typically associated with the concept? (*Example:* size, location, depth) *friends, family*
5. What is an example that best or most clearly represents the most typical case of the concept? (*Example:* aerial photo clearly showing all the features of a lake) *Recognizing your unique characteristics*
6. What are some other <u>interesting</u> and <u>learner-relevant *examples*</u> or cases of the concept that you can use in its explanation? (*Example:* local lakes, mountain lakes, desert lakes) *School behavior, your behavior with + without friends getting along with others*
7. What are some contrasting *nonexamples* of the concept that will help clarify and illustrate the concept? (*Examples:* ocean, stream) *Self-centered Selfish*
8. What are some <u>cues, questions,</u> or <u>*directions*</u> that you can employ to call attention to criterial attributes and noncriterial attributes in the concept examples? (*Example:* "Look at all the points where the water meets the land.") *Recognizing your char. doesn't mean your Self centered or selfish*
9. What is the most efficient, interesting, and thought-provoking *medium* (or media) by which to present examples and nonexamples? (*Example:* slides, air photos) *By doing individual ditto sheets require Self-Reflection + by group discussion*
10. What level of *concept mastery* do you expect of students, and how will you assess it? (*Example:* Be able to define *lake* and state the similarities and differences this body of water has with other major bodies of water through a project.) *Be able to define Self awareness and state the benefits of being self-aware.*

As noted earlier, there are many types of concepts, and the process of learning them differs from that used for other kinds of knowledge such as generalizations. Among concept types, there are also differences that require alternative methods of instruction. Detailed discussions of these variations exist elsewhere. In this chapter, we shall limit ourselves to a single basic model for organizing concept learning instruction. It emphasizes essential phases of instruction underlying the approach to all types of concepts.

Outlined here is a system for analyzing concepts in some detail. It was developed at the University of Wisconsin Research and Development Center in Cognitive Learning. It uncovers some of the data on concepts that a teacher would need to know to organize an instructional activity. The example, using the concept *mammal,* is adapted from a publication by the Center.[5]

Example of a Concept Analysis

Subject area: Biological science
Concept name: Mammal
Criterial attributes: Mammals
    1. Feed their young on mother's milk
    2. Have hair
    3. Are warm blooded
Noncriterial attributes: Color, habitat, pattern in coat, eating habits
Concept rule: A mammal is a warm blooded animal that has hair and
    feeds its young on the mother's milk.
Some concept examples: Cow, dog, cat, pig, goat, rabbit, camel
Some concept nonexamples: Chicken, toad, spider, fish, duck, alligator,
    snake
Relationship with another concept: Mammals use lungs for breathing.

    Select a concept from the list you compiled from textbooks in the earlier exercise or identify one that interests you and seems suitable for an analysis. Then locate information to complete the Concept Analysis Form that follows. Where a simple word or two will not suffice to indicate examples and nonexamples, briefly outline the nature of the appropriate illustrations. In the set of examples, be sure to include one that clearly or best illustrates the concept.

Concept Analysis Form

Subject area: _____

Concept name: _____

Criterial attributes: _____

Noncriterial attributes: _____

Concept rule: _____

Some concept examples, including a clear or best example: _____

_____

Some concept nonexamples: _____

_____

Relationship with another concept: _____

_____

▪ *Basic Model for Concept Instruction*

A flexible basic model that may be used for teaching concepts consists of seven key steps.
1. Develop an introduction to your concept lesson. The introduction should orient the learner to the task and arouse his or her curiosity. It

might be a short story, anecdote, relating of experiences, or brief sequence of questions that focus attention on the concept.

2. Prepare the set of examples and nonexamples identified, and place them in some logical order for presentation. (There are no hard and fast rules on how many, but you can consider seven as a rule of thumb.) Include at least one example that best or most clearly illustrates an ideal type of the concept. Direct students to compare all examples with the best or clearest one, and provide feedback.

3. Develop a set of cues, directions, questions, and student activities for the instructional materials, drawing attention to the criterial attributes and to similarities and differences in the examples and nonexamples. In written materials, cues may be arrows, marginal notes, underlining, and the like. Where criterial attributes cannot be clearly identified or are ambiguous, focus attention on a few best examples of the concept, and help students remember their salient features.

4. Where a clear definition of a concept exists, elicit it from students or state it in meaningful terms at some point in the instruction.

5. Through discussion, place the concept in context with other related concepts that are part of students' prior knowledge.

6. Assess concept mastery at a minimal level, namely, determine whether students can correctly discriminate between new examples and nonexamples.

7. Assess concept mastery at more advanced levels, consistent with the developmental capabilities of the students and with your own objectives.

Organizing Instructional Materials for Concept Learning

The organization of instructional materials for concept learning may take many forms. Suppose we wish to teach the concept of *island* to a class of third graders. We have concluded that the concept is considered by social studies educators to be an important one for children to learn, should be taught formally, and its essential characteristics can be spelled out. The Planning Inventory described earlier then is completed as a way to analyze the concept. The concept rule is "a body of land surrounded by water," and the criterial attributes are "land," "water," and "surrounding" (all-aroundness). After a brief introduction and a short question-and-answer session, the students are shown a series of slides like those following, accompanied by related questions and commentary. At various points in the discussion the teacher defines the concept and compares the different examples with slide 1 (best example).

Slide 1:	Best or clearest example	Aerial shot of large uninhabited island with vegetation, clearly showing all attributes.
Slide 2:	Example	Shot of small uninhabited island with no vegetation. Arrows on slide are pointing to the surrounding water.
Slide 3:	Nonexample	Shot of peninsula.
Slide 4:	Example	Shot of large island with buildings, etc.
Slide 5:	Example	Shot of small island with inhabitants.

Slide 6:	Nonexample	Shot of bay with inhabitants adjacent.
Slide 7:	Example	Shot of uninhabited island with unusual shape.
Slide 8:	Nonexample	Shot of an isthmus.
Slide 9:	Example	Shot of an island with a lake within.
Slide 10:	Nonexample	Shot of a lake with arrows pointing to the land all around.
Slide 11:	Example	Shot of an uninhabited island with mountains.
Slide 12:	Example	Shot of an inhabited island with mountains.
Slide 13:	Example	Shot of an island with an unusual shape.

After the slide presentation, a series of simple charts with hand-drawn and/or pasted pictures may be used to assess learning in conjunction with the following basic set of questions. After presenting the charts, the teacher asks the students to state in their own words what an island is.

Chart 1:	Which of these pictures is a picture of an island?
Chart 2:	Which of these pictures is not a picture of an island?
Chart 3:	Which of these pictures shows something that all islands have? (illustrates one attribute)
Chart 4:	Which of these pictures shows something that all islands have? (illustrates another attribute)

Let us now consider an older group of students about to learn the concept of *nonverbal communication*. We might follow a similar format, using pictures and/or role-played episodes as examples and nonexamples. Scenes from printed advertisements, as well as commercially made photographs and pictures, could be used. Three-dimensional models also can be employed effectively as examples and nonexamples, particularly in the areas of science and mathematics, for demonstrating concepts like molecules and sets. Three-dimensional models have the additional advantage of providing hands-on experience with the concept. Simple hand-prepared charts and posters are another medium that lends itself to all subject matter areas. In mathematics, for example, the concept of *mode* can be cleanly and quickly illustrated through a series of charts or through a single one, as shown here.

Examples of Mode

5, 6, 7, _8, 8,_ 9, 10

9, 10, _12,_ 13, 10, _12,_ 8, _12, 12,_ 6

_97,_ 94, 32, _97,_ 75, 63, 29, 85, _97_

1, 13, _22, 22,_ 12, 14, 27, 83, 15, _22_

_72, 72, 72, 72, 72, 72_

_65,_ 64, _65,_ 63, 71, 62, 63, _65_

_1,_ 0, 9, 6, 5, 7, 7, 8, _1,_ 3, _1, 1_

An alternate format for the instruction would be to use the chalkboard or the overhead projector. A simple mastery test could consist of a series of new number examples and nonexamples for correct identification, or else a sequence of open-ended questions such as: "What do all the examples have in common?" "How would you define a mode in your own words?" Materials for concept learning also may be designed as self-instructional units.

Several dimensions of concept mastery are measured in this test, as well as some characteristics of the instructional materials.

Item 1 measures whether, given the name of a concept, the student can select an example of the concept.

Item 2 measures whether, given the name of a concept, the student can select a nonexample of the concept.

Item 3 measures whether, given an example of a concept, the student can identify its name.

Items 4 and 5 measure whether, given the name of the concept, the student can select the names of criterial attributes of the concept.

Item 6 measures whether, given the name of the concept, the student can select the names of noncriterial attributes of the concept.

Item 7 measures whether, given the name of the concept, the student can select the correct definition of the concept.

Item 8 measures whether, given the name of a concept, the student can select a broader concept to which it is closely related.

Audio recordings also are a useful medium for concept instruction, particularly for the areas of language arts, foreign language, and music. Playing contrasting examples and nonexamples of concepts, such as *polyphony* and *counterpoint*, offers learners concrete and structured experiences with the concept. Similarly, certain concepts from other subject areas, such as *soliloquy, feedback,* and *idiomatic expression,* are effectively presented through audio formats.

Case studies are a general vehicle for concept instruction. They may be drawn from commercially prepared materials, constructed by a teacher, or adapted from a variety of sources (including commercial materials). Such materials contain carefully structured vignettes with as many noncriterial attributes as possible removed and with focusing instructions and questions included. Where case studies are used in conjunction with teacher directions, the questions and focusing may occur in the context of general discussion. Case studies are suitable for all areas of the curriculum, especially social studies, science, language arts, music, and health education.

A concept learning activity that can take many forms, and can be used at all grade levels for a variety of subject areas, involves students in the construction of *concept folders.* Older students can use 8½ × 11 folders, and young children boxes, to store data on particular concepts. A concept is identified, and after its attributes and rule have been identified and clarified, and some examples provided, students are asked to collect data — pictures and/or cases, etc. — that are examples of the concept. When the projects are completed, the various folders may be exchanged and shared. Where required, students may be asked to explain the meaning and content of their collections. Several different concepts may be assigned simultaneously.

A bulletin board prepared by either the teacher or students can be used to highlight examples and nonexamples of a concept. As with concept folders, bulletin boards can contain pictorial or written materials. Examples and nonexamples should be close to each other and should be appropriately labeled. Once the initial bulletin board is developed, students can be encouraged to look for additional examples and similar nonexamples, and to add to the display. Here is a sample of a bulletin board display for *transportation:*[6]

These Are Transportation	These Are Not Transportation
(Attach pictures of the following items under the appropriate columns.)	
Bus full of people	Room full of people
Subway	
Airplanes	Kite
Train	
Golfcart	Ferris wheel
Ships	
Submarine	Fish in water
Raft	
Rocket	Telegraph wires
Truck	
Bicycle	Stationary exercise bicycle
Hovercraft	
Balloon	Cloud
Car	
Blimp	Park bench
Motorcycle	
Horse	Cat
Wagon	
Stagecoach	Rocking horse
Tractor	
Oxen and cart	Windmill
Rickshaw	
Dog sled	Arrow being shot

MASTERY TEST

OBJECTIVE 3 (a) To distinguish between the personal and public dimensions of concept learning, and (b) to identify and briefly describe the seven key steps in the *Basic Model for Concept Instruction*

1. What is meant by the personal and public dimensions of concepts?

2. Identify and briefly describe the seven key steps in the *Basic Model for Concept Instruction.*

 4 (a) To identify five dimensions of concept learning that can be assessed and to arrange them according to their level of complexity, and (b) to identify and briefly describe three procedures for assessing the private dimensions of students' concepts

Learning Activity 4

Assessing Concept Learning

Several approaches to measuring concept learning already have been suggested through the illustrations in the preceding section. A basic measure of whether a concept has been learned involves the ability to discriminate correctly between new examples of the concept and nonexamples. Unless a student can perform satisfactorily on this fundamental test, learning may not be inferred. Ability to verbalize the concept rule is a more complex dimension of concept learning. Young children particularly have great difficulty with this task, even though they perform satisfactorily on discrimination tasks.

Essentially, measurement of concept learning may be viewed as dealing with the following increasingly complex dimensions:

1. Identification of criterial and noncriterial attributes
2. Discrimination of examples from nonexamples
3. Identification of the concept rule
4. Ability to relate the concept to other concepts
5. Use of the concept in a novel way

Depending on the significance of the concept and a teacher's objectives, mastery may be assessed over one or all of these dimensions. For many simple instructional activities, identification of criterial attributes can be presumed and a discrimination test will suffice. Other situations will call for measurement of all five dimensions.

Assessing Personal Dimensions of Concept Learning

Often a teacher wishes to tap the personal dimensions of concept learning, either prior to or following related instruction. Such an assessment can proceed informally through open-ended discussions, simple paper-and-pencil questionnaires, or inventories. Figures 6.1 and 6.2 are one such approach. Three alternative diagnostic activities are outlined here. The first is borrowed from the studies of Michael Wallach and Nathan Kogan on thinking in young children, the second is based on research in thinking strategies conducted by Hilda Taba, and the third employs a technique known as *concept mapping*, in which concept relationships are diagrammed.

Concept Games

The Wallach and Kogan activity, although developed for young children, is applicable to all grade levels and subject areas. We will call it the *Like-Things Game*. Concepts from any curricular area may be substituted for the ones used in the example here. Instructions similar to those provided here are used with the students. The instructions may be modified as necessary for different age levels or concepts.

"In this game I am going to name two objects, and I will want you to think of all the ways that these two objects are alike. I might name any two objects —

like door and chair. But whatever I say, it will be your job to think of all the ways that the two objects are alike. For example, tell me all the ways that an apple and an orange are alike." (The child then responds.) "That's very good. You've already said a lot of the things I was thinking of. I guess you could also say that they are both round, and they are both sweet, they both have seeds, they both are fruits, they both have skins, they both grow on trees — things like that. Yours were fine, too."[7]

Sets of similar objects, events, or people, like those listed, might be used with some basic instructions.

Tell me all the ways in which squares and quadrilaterals are alike.
Tell me all the ways in which sharps and flats are alike.
Tell me all the ways in which a lithograph and a print are alike.
Tell me all the ways in which a river and a stream are alike.
Tell me all the ways in which rockets and planes are alike.
Tell me all the ways in which love and hate are alike.
Tell me all the ways in which density and cubic feet are alike.
Tell me all the ways in which wind and water currents are alike.
Tell me all the ways in which churches and banks are alike.
Tell me all the ways in which architects and engineers are alike.

Assume you are dealing with a high school government class. You might wish to use the game activity to compare the students' concepts of

Electoral college and legislature
Primary and election
City and state
Norm and law
Executive privilege and judicial review

The list of concepts can be as long or as short as desired.

The Taba Strategy

Several years ago, Hilda Taba developed, and later her associates refined, a systematic strategy that allows a teacher to diagnose student concept states easily. Her strategy consists of three key steps to be carried out in exactly the sequence indicated, with as much time spent on each point as is required. The three basic steps are:

1. Enumerate and list students' responses to an opening question.
2. Have the students group the responses.
3. Have the students label the groups.

Within each of these three key activities, there is a structured role that the teacher must play. The Northwest Regional Educational Laboratory has developed some appropriate questions and statements for a teacher to use in carrying out this role. The following sequence is drawn and adapted from their analysis of the teacher's role.[8]

1. *Enumeration and Listing*

Opening question.   Raise an open-ended question that calls for re-membered information concerning the concept to be analyzed and expanded.

"What comes to mind when you hear the word *heredity?*"
"What do you know about triangles?"
"What do you think of when you hear the word *poetry?*"

Refocusing statement.   When the responses indicate that students have begun to stray from the topic, call attention to the opening question.

> "Let me repeat the original question."

Clarifying question.   Frequently students use a term that is unclear or that has many meanings. Ask for clarification.

> "What sort of modern paintings?"
> "Can you give me an example of a 'way out' person?"
> "Can you help me out? I'm not sure I understand what you mean by *getting snookered.*"

Summarizing question.   Frequently a student will respond to your opening question with a paragraph or two. Request that he or she abstract the main idea.

> "How could we put that on the board?"
> "How could we write that in one sentence?"
> "Can you help me out? How could we state that to get it in this little space on the board?"

Mapping-the-field question.   Try to get as much information as possible.

> "Are there any areas that we have missed?"
> "Can you think of any other things?"

2. *Grouping the Responses*

Grouping questions.   The initial question in the grouping process requests students to group their responses in any fashion they wish.

> "Let's look over our list. Can you find any items that could be grouped together?"
> "Are there any items on the board that could be grouped together?"

Grouping rationale question.   A key element in the grouping process is focusing attention on the rationale used to categorize items. When students do not provide it automatically, request a reason.

> "Why did you put _____, _____, and _____together?"

3. *Labeling the Groups*
   Labeling question.   The basic question for the labeling process asks the students to analyze a group of items and state a name or label for the grouping.

> "Let's look at the first group. What title could we give to this list?"

Unlike the preceding model, Taba's schema should be followed in *exactly* the order specified. It is also crucial that the teacher accept *all* student responses without judging them as correct or incorrect. While, to be sure, students are likely to offer factually incorrect statements or offer apparently illogical groupings and labels, the teacher's role in this model is *not* to challenge or correct, but to accept and list all responses. Keep in mind that the objective is to analyze and expand conceptual associations. In this vein, when students disagree on classmates' groupings, *they have to be reminded that each individual's conceptual organization is unique, and that the rules of discussion in this case require the freedom of self-expression.*

At this point, refer back to the earlier discussion indicated and reread the procedures before attempting the following response form. You will need to have the Taba procedures clearly in mind to complete this activity successfully. Complete the response form by yourself. You are about to discover how well you have internalized one dimension of the Taba procedure for concept diagnosis — handling student responses — by engaging in a role-playing activity with a series of hypothetical students.

Response Form

You have the role of teacher, and you have just asked a group of high school students the question "What comes to mind when you hear the word *drama*?" Some of the students have answered as indicated below. You are poised by the chalkboard, chalk in hand, ready to record responses. After each of their answers, note how you would handle their statements or exactly how you would respond to them. Remember to stay in your role and to answer just as if you were talking to each student. Be as specific in your answers as you would be when you ask for clarification, etc.

1. *Paula:* "I think of lots of action and fine acting."

2. *Perry:* "It reminds me of when I was a kid and my grandfather took me to see a Shakespeare play. I didn't know what was coming off. There were all these people in funny costumes, and I couldn't understand most of what they were saying."

3. *Tito:* "It reminds me of life, how things really are."

4. *Wally:* "When you have a drama, you always have a big cast of characters."

5. *Pam:* "That's not true, Wally. I remember reading about a drama that only had two characters."

6. *Mary:* "Dramas always seem to deal with basic emotions that all people have."

7. *Dorothy:* "I guess for me what comes to mind is Saturday nights and my family."

8. *Jack:* "But drama as I think of it is a bunch of clever lines and speeches."

9. *Taffy:* "It makes me think of how much I like musical plays!"

After you have completed your role playing, check with others who have also completed the exercise to see how they responded to the students. Analyze all the sets of responses against the Taba procedures specified. How closely did your treatments of the responses follow the suggested format? Finally, consider the following analyses in evaluating your own.

1. *Paula:* Her response can simply be acknowledged and recorded as some variation of "Lots of action and fine acting." A minor alternative re-

sponse would be to ask, "Would you like me to list 'lots of action' and 'fine acting' as separate items?"

2. *Perry:* He is just a little verbose. You need to ask him to summarize. Any way to accomplish this without rejecting his original comment is satisfactory. For example, "How could I summarize that to get it in this little space?"

3. *Tito:* You might just accept this response as is, or, to be sure that everyone understands the point, you might ask, "Could you give us an example of what you mean?"

4. *Wally:* Record "Always have a big cast of characters," *even though the association is incorrect.* You are *diagnosing* the level of knowledge the students have, whatever it may be. To get an honest assessment, you must establish the discussion ground rule by explaining, "We just want to find out what people think of when they hear the word *drama.* Later on we can examine whether things are right or wrong."

5. *Pam:* Tell her to remember the discussion ground rules, and verbalize the ground rule just cited.

6. *Mary:* Just record "Always seem to deal with basic emotions that all people have."

7. *Dorothy:* Clarification is in order. Ask, "Can you help us out? What is meant by your reference to 'Saturday nights and my family'?"

8. *Jack:* Just record "A bunch of clever lines and speeches."

9. *Taffy:* Just record "How much I like musical plays." Taffy's negative or indirect association is clear and to the point.

Your final listing on the board would appear in some fashion similar to the following:

Lots of action and fine acting
(Perry's summary statement)
Life, how things really are (possibly followed by an example, if you requested one)
Always have a big cast of characters
(Pam's response after being reminded of the ground rule)
Always seem to deal with basic emotions that all people have
Saturday nights and my family (followed by a clarification of the meaning of the terms)
A bunch of clever lines and speeches
How much I like musical plays

Once you have internalized some of the basic responding procedures related to the first phase of the Taba strategy, you should be prepared to try all *three* steps with a live audience. If you wish to test your competency, organize a group of seven to ten students for a microteaching lesson. (Fewer than seven students will restrict considerably the amount of interaction, though the activity is still possible.) Select any concept you feel is both appropriate and potentially interesting for the group. Take three minutes or so to introduce the situation, and then begin the strategy.

■ *Concept Mapping*

Concept mapping[9] may be used to demonstrate understanding of meaningful relationships among concepts. The maps are diagrams that represent the ways in which an individual links the concepts in a cognitive web. For

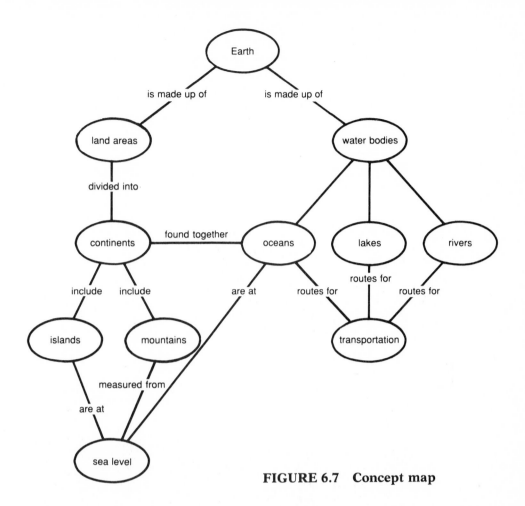

FIGURE 6.7   Concept map

example, after studying a geography unit, students might be given the following list of concepts:

Transportation
Water bodies
Earth
Lakes
Oceans
Rivers
Sea level
Land areas
Continents
Mountains
Islands

They first might be asked to sort the concepts in rank order, from the most general to the least general. Then they would be directed to complete a map to demonstrate their understanding of concept relationships. They would be told that *earth* was the most inclusive concept, or the one to be used as a starting point in the map. The maps should consist of diagrams and linking statements similar to the one drawn in Figure 6.7. The linking words help clarify the concept relationships.

MASTERY TEST

OBJECTIVE 4   (a) To identify five dimensions of concept learning that can be assessed and to arrange them according to their level of complexity, and (b) to identify and briefly describe three procedures for assessing the private dimensions of students' concepts

1. List five different dimensions of concept learning that may be assessed, and arrange them in order of decreasing complexity by starting with the most complex process and working down to the least complex process.

2. Identify and briefly describe three procedures for assessing the personal dimensions of students' concepts.

OBJECTIVE   **5**   (a) To analyze the relationship among concepts, schemata, and higher-level thinking, and (b) to identify three instructional strategies that promote concept enrichment and higher-level thinking

Learning Activity 5

Concepts, Schemata, and Higher-Level Thinking

The concepts we have constructed are organized into cognitive structures known as *schemata* (or schemas). Schemata provide the basis for higher-level thinking, such as comprehending and learning information. Schemata theory postulates that the form and content of all new knowledge are in some way shaped by our *prior knowledge*. Our individual collections of existing schemata comprise the store of prior knowledge that we bring to each learning task. Students, for example, bring their plants schemata to the study of biology. They have certain beliefs about the nature and types of plants that exist, which teachers may draw upon in developing lessons.

Schemata are activated as our experiences elicit them. When we acquire new experiences in relation to our concepts, we enrich and clarify them. Old schemata are modified and new ones emerge from what we learn. New ones are shaped as we acquire concepts that are novel to us, such as onomatopoeia, osmosis, square root, presentism, or measure (in music).

When our prior knowledge conflicts with new data, as, for example, when our prior information about plants is contradicted by a biology text, restructuring of existing schemata may occur. On the other hand, firmly embedded prior knowledge may be resistant to transformation and require skillful challenging by a teacher. In such cases, students may even make cognitive accommodations by creating parallel schemata, one for "plants-in-real-life" and one for "plants-on-the-test."

In addition to myriad concepts, schemata hold other forms of knowledge, such as facts, generalizations, and hypotheses. Thus, when we engage in activities that reflect higher level thinking, such as problem solving, decision making, or comprehending and interpreting text, we are drawing upon a network of schemata that include interwoven concepts, facts, generalizations, and hypotheses.

Higher-level thinking requires a rich store of well-stocked knowledge, including well-formed concepts, within our schemata. If our existing concepts are ill shaped or incomplete, so will the ideas we build from them be improperly formed. Thus, an important part of the teacher's instructional task is correcting *mis*conceptions that students hold and guiding them in fleshing out fragmentary knowledge.

Instructional Strategies that Promote Concept Enrichment and Higher-Level Thinking

Educators have identified a number of strategies that help students employ and enrich concepts in higher-level thinking tasks. These strategies activate students' prior knowledge relevant to a learning task and provide a scaffold (i.e., form of support) to assist them in moving from the known to the unknown.[10] Concept mapping, described and illustrated earlier, is an example of such a strategy. Three others that have wide utility across grade levels and subject areas are *data retrieval charts*, *discussion webs*, and *semantic webs*.

Data Retrieval Charts

Data retrieval charts encourage students to organize data they have gathered from research or text examination in a way that synthesizes, makes comparisons, highlights important relationships, and draws conclusions. Such charts offer students a structure for gaining insights from data that might otherwise appear fragmented and without meaning.

A "shell" of a data retrieval chart is provided in Figure 6.8. It deals with an analysis of subject matter relating to cities. The teacher has created the shell, and students through their research and reading will fill the chart cells with information. Once they have completed this task, the teacher will guide them in a discussion of the implications of their findings.

Quality of Life Indicators in Selected Asian Cities

	Size (km²)	Population	Per Capita Income	Quality of Water	Degree of Air Pollution
Cities					
Beijing					
Calcutta					
Seoul					

FIGURE 6.8   Data retrieval chart

Discussion Webs

Like a data retrieval chart, a discussion web may be used to help students organize arguments or evidence in relation to some issue. It is suitable for questions that are not resolved, or for which there are balanced pro and con arguments. An example of a discussion web appears in Figure 6.9. As illustrated, a web begins with a teacher question related to information that students have gathered or are in the process of collecting.

The format for a discussion web is flexible, but students, individually or in small groups, work to locate information that supports both positions in an argument. For example, in Figure 6.9, under the "Yes" column, a student might write, "The sun will be our primary source of energy." After completing the web, students, under the teacher's guidance, discuss the arguments presented on both sides of the issue. Thereafter, they take an individual position on the issue, for example, "Overall, life will not be that different."

Semantic Webs

Semantic webs are similar to concept maps and brainstorming activities. They represent an easy way for students, with teacher guidance, to draw relationships among ideas and gather ideas for discussions or written projects. Their essential features are a focus concept or theme, several supporting concepts or ideas, related items of information, and a set of lines that link items.

Semantic webs can take many different forms, one of which is illustrated in Figure 6.10. The teacher provides the initial scaffold to help students focus on the issue and guides them through the process of constructing networks of information. Students then contribute ideas and related themes and make connections.

In the example the teacher applied the semantic web technique after engaging her students in a brainstorming session concerning problems of freed slaves. She began by providing a focus topic, *freed slaves* on the board.

She then drew a line to the upper right-hand of the chalk board and connected the key word to the word *problems*. She connected some of the words generated by students during brainstorming to the cluster. The teacher then asked what

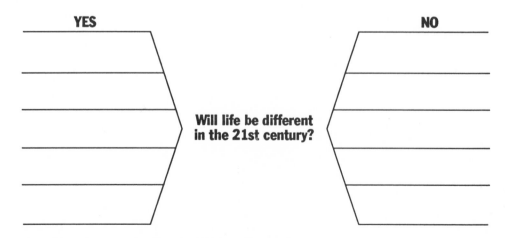

FIGURE 6.9   Example of a discussion web

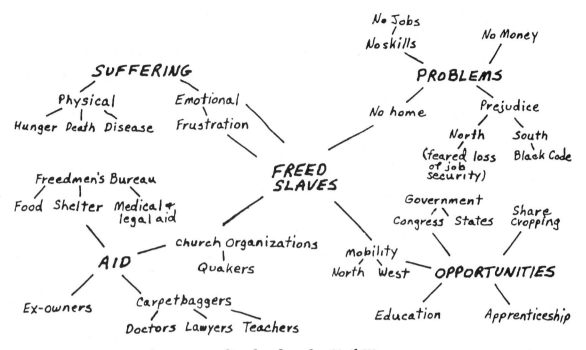

FIGURE 6.10   Free slaves immediately after the Civil War

From Richard T. Vacca and JoAnne L. Vacca, *Content Area Reading*, 2nd ed. (Boston: Little, Brown & Company, 1986), p. 235. Reprinted by permission of HarperCollins.

some of the results of the freed slave's problems would be. One student volunteered the word *suffering*. The teacher wrote *suffering* in the upper left-hand corner of the cluster and asked students to brainstorm some examples. These examples were then connected to the cluster.

The remainder of the prewriting experience centered on discussion related to the *aid* freed slaves received and the *opportunities* that resulted from the Reconstruction years. . . .

With the cluster [Figure 6.10] as a frame of reference, students were assigned to write about what it would have been like to be a freed slave in the 1860s and '70s.[11]

Since you have now completed this chapter, try your hand at applying the semantic web technique. Your focus will be the information you have been processing relating to concepts and higher-level thinking. Study the example in Figure 6.10, and then create your own web using the key word *concept* as your focal point.

The web can serve as a summary of the knowledge you have constructed from reading the chapter. It can also represent the linkages between your new and prior knowledge. You may wish to compare your representation with that of a classmate or broaden the scope of the analysis by forming a small discussion group.

MASTERY TEST

OBJECTIVE 5

(a) To analyze the relationship among concepts, schemata, and higher-level thinking, and (b) to identify three instructional strategies that promote concept enrichment and higher-level thinking

1. How are concepts, schemata, and higher-level thinking related?

2. Identify and describe three instructional strategies for promoting concept enrichment and higher-level thinking.

FINAL MASTERY TEST

At the outset, you were asked to assess what you knew about concepts through a basic true/false test. Reexamine your responses in that first test to determine how much information you have mastered in this chapter. To test your mastery of various objectives established for the chapter, see how many of the following questions you can answer.

1. What are at least four different ways in which the term *concept* is used in educational literature?

2. What basic information is required to teach a concept?

3. How do criterial and noncriterial attributes differ?

4. Identify at least two basic reasons why concepts are important.

5. Identify at least three systems for classifying concepts, and explain their meaning.

6. Which concept classification system takes into account developmental differences? In what way?

7. How do the personal and public dimensions of concepts differ?

8. Summarize the seven steps in the *Basic Model for Concept Instruction.*

9. What are three different levels of concept learning that may be assessed?

10. How are concepts, schemata, and higher-level thinking related?

11. Identify and describe three instructional strategies for promoting concept enrichment and higher-level thinking.

■ Answer Keys for Your Turn Exercises

ANSWER KEY

Your Turn: What Do You Know About Concepts?

1. T	6. F
2. F	7. F
3. T	8. F
4. F	9. F
5. F	10. F

ANSWER KEY

Your Turn: Compare Four Concept Examples

These four examples should have sensitized you to what it's like to confront a concept for the first time. To qualify as a Mellinark, examples must have spots, a black dot, and a tail. Moke examples have only one defining attri- bute, the fact that they are of the same height. The criterial attributes of Florgiedorfies are their height and number of arms, while Trugs may be *either* shaded tri- angles *or* unshaded quadrilaterals.

■ Answer Keys for Mastery Tests

ANSWER KEY

Mastery Test, Objective 1

1. (a) To mean the same thing as an "idea"; (b) to mean a "theme" or "topic"; (c) as a general, all-encompassing, or broad statement; (d) to mean the basic structure or elements of a discipline; (e) as categories into which we group our knowledge and experience.
2. Names, criterial attributes, rules.

3. There are a number of possible noncriterial attributes that you might have listed. Consider the following ones for comparisons:
   mammal — color; tree — size; river — length; winter — temperature; prime number — size; mountain — location; state — size; death — age; cloud — shape; comb — color.

ANSWER KEY

Mastery Test, Objective 2

1. Answers should be similar to the following definitions:
   (a) *Concrete.* Those concepts we can perceive directly through one of the five senses.
   (b) *Abstract.* Those that cannot be directly perceived through one of the senses.
   (c) *Formal.* Concepts acquired through systematic channels of instruction.
   (d) *Informal.* Concepts acquired through undirected and unorganized means.
   (e) *Conjunctive.* Concepts defined by a single set of qualities or characteristics.

   (f) *Disjunctive.* Concepts defined by two or more alternative sets of qualities or characteristics.
   (g) *Relational.* Concepts defined by the relationships among objects or events.
   (h) *Enactive.* Concepts acquired through doing or acting.
   (i) *Iconic.* Concepts acquired through imagery or pictures.
   (j) *Symbolic.* Concepts acquired through verbal or symbolic forms (such as reading or speaking).
2. Enactive, iconic, and symbolic; concrete and abstract.

ANSWER KEY

Mastery Test, Objective 3

1. The personal dimensions of concepts are all the personal, noncriterial associations, correct or incorrect, that an individual identifies with the concept name. The public dimensions of concepts are the essential or criterial properties that are agreed upon and shared by those who can correctly identify examples and nonexamples of the concept.
2. The seven-step process should proceed as follows:
   (a) Develop an introduction to the instruction sequence. The introduction should orient the learner to the task and arouse his or her curiosity.
   (b) Prepare the set of examples and nonexamples identified, and place them in some logical order for presentation. (There are no hard and fast rules on how many, but you can consider seven as a rule of thumb.) Include at least one example that best or most clearly illustrates an ideal type of the concept. Direct students to compare all examples with the best or clearest one, and provide feedback.
   (c) Develop a set of cues, directions, questions, and student activities for the instructional materials,

   drawing attention to the criterial attributes, and to similarities and differences in the examples and nonexamples. In written materials, cues may be arrows, marginal notes, underlining, and the like. Where criterial attributes cannot be clearly identified or are ambiguous, focus attention on a few clear or best-example cases of the concept, and help students remember their salient features.
   (d) Where a clear definition of a concept exists, elicit or state it in functional terms at some point in the instruction.
   (e) Through discussion, place the concept in context with other related concepts that are part of students' prior knowledge.
   (f) Assess concept mastery at a minimal level, namely, determine whether students can correctly discriminate between new examples and nonexamples.
   (g) Assess concept mastery at more advanced levels, consistent with the developmental capabilities of the students and with your own objectives.

ANSWER KEY

Mastery Test, Objective 4

1. The correct arrangement of the items in order of decreasing complexity is

   Use of the concept in a novel way
   Ability to relate the concept to other concepts
   Identification of the concept rule
   Discrimination of examples from nonexamples
   Identification of criterial attributes and nonattributes

2. One approach is the *Like-Things Game.* It calls for students to describe how sets of objects, events, or people are similar by answering a series of open-ended questions. A second approach is a three-step strategy devised by Hilda Taba to assess what associations a group of students attach to a particular concept. The steps involve enumerating and listing associations, grouping them, and finally labeling them. Still a third approach involves each student completing a concept map similar to Figure 6.7.

ANSWER KEY

Mastery Test, Objective 5

1. The concepts we have constructed are organized into cognitive structures known as *schemata* (or schemas). Individual schemata are the store of prior knowledge and experiences that we bring to each new knowledge acquisition task. Higher-level thinking draws upon a network of schemata that include interwoven concepts, facts, generalizations, and hypotheses.
2. Besides concept mapping, discussed under Objective 4, three other instructional strategies are data retrieval charts, discussion webs, and semantic webs. Data retrieval charts are matrices that teachers create for students to help them to organize and analyze information they have collected through research and reading. Discussion webs are activities that are used to help students organize arguments or evidence, pro and con, in relation to some issue. They are structured around a teacher question. Semantic webs are similar to concept maps and brainstorming activities. With teacher guidance, students draw relationships among ideas and gather ideas for discussions or written projects. The essential features of a semantic web are a focus concept or theme, several supporting concepts or ideas, related items of information, and a set of lines that link items.

ANSWER KEY

Final Mastery Test

Your answers should be similar to the following.

1. As ideas; as themes or topics; as a general, all-encompassing statement; as elements or structures of a discipline; or as categories into which we organize and relate our knowledge and experiences.
2. Name, criterial attributes, noncriterial attributes, rule, examples, and nonexamples.
3. Criterial attributes are the essential, defining characteristics of concepts. Noncriterial attributes are those that are frequently present in concept examples, but are not essential.
4. Concepts simplify our environment; they simplify our learning task; they make communication easier; they help us distinguish between reality and imagery; they enrich our lives.
5. Concrete and abstract; conjunctive, disjunctive, and relational; formal and informal; enactive, iconic, and symbolic. (Check pages 160–162 for the meanings.)
6. Enactive, iconic, and symbolic. (See page 162 for the meanings.)
7. Personal dimensions are the personal associations that each of us has with concepts; public dimensions are the basic or criterial characteristics of concepts that people share in common.
8. (a) Develop an introduction to the instruction sequence. The introduction should orient the learner to the task and arouse his or her curiosity.
   (b) Prepare the set of examples and nonexamples identified, and place them in some logical order for presentation. (There are no hard and fast rules on how many, but you can consider seven as a rule of thumb.) Include at least one example that best or most clearly illustrates an ideal type of the concept. Direct students to compare all examples with the best or clearest one, and provide feedback.
   (c) Develop a set of cues, directions, questions, and student activities for the instructional materials, drawing attention to the criterial attributes, and to similarities and differences in the examples and nonexamples. In written materials, cues may

be arrows, marginal notes, underlining, and the like. Where criterial attributes cannot be clearly identified or are ambiguous, focus attention on a few clear or best-example cases of the concept, and help students remember their salient features.

(d) Where a clear definition of a concept exists, elicit or state it in functional terms at some point in the instruction.

(e) Through discussion, place the concept in context with other related concepts that are part of students' prior knowledge.

(f) Assess concept mastery at a minimal level, namely, determine whether students can correctly discriminate between new examples and nonexamples.

(g) Assess concept mastery at more advanced levels, consistent with the developmental capabilities of the students and with your own objectives.

9. Identification of criterial attributes and nonattributes; discrimination of examples from nonexamples; identification of the concept rule; ability to relate the concept to other concepts; use of the concept in a novel way.

10. The concepts we have constructed are organized into cognitive structures known as *schemata* (or schemas). Individual schemata are the store of prior knowledge and experiences that we bring to each new knowledge acquisition task. When we engage in activities that reflect higher-level thinking, such as problem solving, we are drawing upon a network of schemata that includes interwoven concepts, facts, generalizations, and hypotheses.

11. Besides concept mapping, discussed under Objective 4, three instructional strategies are data retrieval charts, discussion webs, and semantic webs. Data retrieval charts are matrices that teachers create for students to help them to organize and analyze information they have collected through research and reading. Discussion webs are activities that are used to help students organize arguments or evidence, pro and con, in relation to some issue. They are structured around a teacher question. Semantic webs are similar to concept maps and brainstorming activities. With teacher guidance, students draw relationships among ideas and gather ideas for discussions or written projects. The following are essential features of a semantic web: a focus concept or theme, several supporting concepts or ideas, related items of information, and a set of lines that link items.

Notes

1. Jerome Kagan, "Preschool Enrichment and Learning," *Interchange* II (1971): 17.
2. Jerome S. Bruner, *Beyond the Information Given: Studies in the Psychology of Knowing* (New York: W. W. Norton, 1973), p. 316.
3. *Ibid.*, pp. 327–328.
4. *Teacher's Guide for Attribute Games and Problems* (New York: McGraw-Hill, 1968), pp. 74–77.
5. Adapted from A. M. Voelker and J. S. Sorenson, *An Analysis of Selected Classificatory Science Concepts in Preparation for Writing Tests of Concept Attainment*, Working paper No. 57 (Madison, WI: Research and Development Center for Cognitive Learning, University of Wisconsin, 1971).
6. Peter H. Martorella, *Social Studies for Elementary School Children* (New York: Macmillan, 1994).
7. Michael Wallach and Nathan Kogan, *Modes of Thinking in Young Children* (New York: Holt, Rinehart & Winston, 1965), p. 32.
8. John A. McCollum and Rose Marie Davis, *Trainer's Manual: Development of Higher Level Thinking Abilities*, rev. ed. (Portland, OR: Northwest Regional Educational Laboratory, 1969), pp. 160–161.
9. Joseph D. Novak and D. Bob Gowin, *Learning How to Learn* (Cambridge, England: Cambridge University Press, 1984).
10. Barak Rosenshine and Carla Meister, "The Use of Scaffolds for Teaching Higher-Level Cognitive Strategies," *Educational Leadership* (April, 1992): 24.

11. Richard T. Vacca and JoAnne L. Vacca, *Content Area Reading*, 2nd ed. (Boston: Little, Brown & Company, 1986), p. 234.

▦ Additional Readings

Brown, Roger. *Words and Things*. New York: Free Press, 1968.

Bruner, Jerome S., et al. *A Study of Thinking*. New York: John Wiley & Sons, 1956.

Carroll, John B. "Words, Meanings and Concepts," *Harvard Educational Review XXIV* (Spring 1964): 178–202.

Costa, Arthur L. *Developing Minds: A Resource Book for Teaching Thinking*. Vols. 1 and 2. Alexandria, VA: Association for Supervision and Curriculum Development, 1991.

Eisner, Elliot W. *Cognition and Curriculum: A Basis for Deciding What to Teach*. New York: Longman, 1982, pp. 27–46.

Heimlich, Joan E., and Susan D. Pittleman. *Semantic Mapping: Classroom Applications*. Newark, DE: International Reading Association, 1986.

Howard, R. W. *Concepts and Schemata: An Introduction*. Philadelphia: Cassell, 1987.

Marzano, Robert J., et al. *Dimensions of Thinking: A Framework for Curriculum and Instruction*. Alexandria, VA: Association for Supervision and Curriculum Development, 1988.

Pressley, Michael, et al. *Cognitive Strategy Instruction*. Cambridge, MA: Brookline Books, 1990.

Taba, Hilda. *Teaching Strategies and Cognitive Functioning in Elementary School Children*. Cooperative Research Project no. 2404. Washington, D.C.: U.S. Office of Education, 1966.

Tennyson, R. D., and M. J. Cocchiarella. "An Empirically Based Instructional Design Theory for Teaching Concepts," *Review of Educational Research* 56 (1986): 40–71.

Vygotsky, L. S. *Thought and Language*. Eugenia Hanfmann and Gertrude Vakar, ed. and trans. Cambridge, MA: M.I.T. Press, 1962.

Interpersonal Communication Skills

7

- Sandra Sokolove Garrett
- Myra Sadker
- David Sadker

OBJECTIVES

1 To describe the characteristics of attending behavior

2 To differentiate between the intellectual and the emotional content of messages (active listening)

3 To differentiate among the three types of reflecting — word messages, behaviors, inferences

4 To differentiate among inventory questions that (a) stimulate communication, (b) clarify information, (c) identify discrepancies, and (d) seek alternatives or solutions

In times of rapid change, when there are few beliefs to hold on to, there is one maxim that has withstood the test of time: "Know thyself." Socrates' message to his disciples thousands of years ago still has a great deal of relevance for today's teachers and their students. Yet knowing oneself is rarely a topic discussed in the classroom. Further, in these times of education reform, with emphasis so heavy on the cognitive domain, developing teaching strategies to facilitate such inquiry is rarely included in the curriculum of most teacher-education programs.

In this chapter, you will have the opportunity to master positive interpersonal communication skills — communication that leads to self-inquiry and greater self-knowledge. While the emphasis in this chapter is on interaction with students, these skills have important implications for effective communication with parents and colleagues as well.

The quest for self-knowledge, as a critical dimension of healthy growth and development, finds its roots in the literature of humanistic psychology. This branch of psychology portrays a dynamic and positive picture of the nature of human beings. Among its basic tenets is a belief that people are free and unique creatures, who, when given a choice, will intuitively choose effective paths of action. Humanistic psychologists also believe that, to function in the most effective manner and to maximize individual potential, people must first become aware of their internal thoughts and feelings about both themselves and the world at large. By consciously describing these thoughts and feelings, people may gain an awareness of how such states influence their behavior. The interrelationships among thoughts, feelings, and behaviors thus form a blueprint for living. Yet how the individual pieces are shaped within this blueprint need not remain static. Human beings are responsible for and in control of their own actions.

Weinstein and Fantini (1970)[1] propose that often the thoughts and feelings people have about themselves focus around three broad areas of concern that they have termed *identity, connectedness,* and *power.* For example, they state that most persons have deep concerns about themselves and their sense of identity. They ask questions such as, "Who am I? Where am I going? What do I want out of life?" Most people are also concerned about their relationships with others. They may ask: "How do I fit or connect with other people? Do people like me? Do they want to be with me?" All people need to define their own limits, to develop a sense of empowerment that will enable them to take some measure of control over their lives.

Although a variety of psychologists have defined other areas of concern [McClelland (1961), achievement, affiliation, power; Schutz (1967), inclusion, control, and affection; Glasser (1965), relatedness, respect; Horney (1942), sense of competence and approval], most of them can be included in the Weinstein and Fantini model. Regardless of the labels presented, healthy development depends on people's conscious ability to define behavior; a critical part of the learning process is the ability to judge whether or not one's thoughts and feelings are productive, and then make whatever modifications that seem necessary. The ultimate goal of this search for self-knowledge is greater self-control and more productive living.

Alschuler and his colleagues (1975) present the following working definition of self-knowledge: "A verbal description of one's characteristics or habitual internal and external responses (thoughts, feelings, and actions) to a set of similar stimuli and the consequences of those specified responses."[2] Further, they state that self-knowledge "increases one's options for going beyond unsatisfying habitual responses."[3] In other words, once human beings gain an increased awareness of how they respond to various situations and what the consequences of these responses are, they can then proceed to choose more satisfying options — options that can lead to more directed, purposeful, and productive lives.

The process of gaining self-knowledge is a continuous and complicated one that depends on people's interactions with one another. "How we interact, relate and transact with others, and the reciprocal impact of this phenomenon form the single most important aspect of our existence. Through interaction with others we become more aware of our own identity."[4]

Within the context of public education, teachers are an integral part of this interactive process. They are the ones who can create a classroom environment that will stimulate and reinforce personal inquiry and help students gain insight into their own identities. Research (Combs, 1965) has shown that students' attitudes about themselves are often influenced by how they imagine their teachers perceive them. When teachers project a positive regard for their students, students in return often begin to see themselves and their abilities in more positive ways. Still further, students' attitudes and values are often greatly influenced by their perceptions of their teachers' behaviors (Sokolove, 1975). Students consciously and unconsciously imitate their teachers' styles of behavior, and often accept the attitudes and values projected by their teachers as their own. Therefore, if teachers are to create an environment that is conducive to personal growth, they must first explore their own feelings about themselves and their students. Next, they must consider the effects these emotions have on their actions and, finally, they must deliberately model interpersonal communications that facilitate teacher-student interaction.

Interpersonal communication skills may be defined as a series of specific verbal and nonverbal behaviors that stimulate personal inquiry between two or more persons — inquiry that leads to greater self-knowledge. By employing these behavioral skills, a teacher can help students express and clarify their thoughts and feelings, and understand how these internal states affect their behavior. The modeling of such behaviors by the teacher helps initiate this interactive process and provides guidance to students as they too learn to employ these skills.

Before providing a brief overview of these skills, let's look at the dynamics of effective interpersonal communications. As previously mentioned, the personal growth process is interactive in nature; that is, the assistance of other trusted persons is needed before interpersonal sharing can begin. Speakers must be willing to receive both verbal and nonverbal feedback from listeners, and listeners must feel secure enough to provide such feedback.

The following diagram, called the "Johari Window," will help to clarify how self-knowledge is gained through the process of interpersonal communication.

JOHARI WINDOW*

	(A) Known to Self	(B) Not Known to Self
(C) Known to Others	Area I (A, C) Public Self (common knowledge)	Area III (B, C) Blind Area
(D) Not Known to Others	Area II (A, D) Private Self (secrets, private thoughts)	Area IV (B, D) Unconscious Self (undeveloped potential)

There is specific information that is known both to yourself and to others (Area I, Public Self). It may be information received from visual cues such as "You are wearing a red dress today," or it may be information that you are willing to disclose to others, such as a fear of snakes or a vote you cast for a particular candidate in the last election. The content may be thoughts (cognitive) or emotions (affective) and/or behaviors.

At the same time, you may have personal concerns such as "I need money," "I am afraid of speaking in front of others," or "I'm confused" that you may not wish to share with others. This represents the Private Self (Area II).

Still other information may be known to others but unknown to you: your face gets red when you are angry, you cut off speakers in the middle of their sentences, or your body is fidgeting when you speak. This information is known as the Blind Area (Area III).

Finally, there exists an area of information that is unknown both to yourself and to others: the Unconscious Self (Area IV). The goal of the personal growth process is to continue gaining more information about yourself and, ultimately, to open up areas of unknown potential (Area IV). Consider the following dynamics. As you develop a helping relationship with others and begin disclosing information about yourself, Area I (the Public Self) gradually becomes larger, and Area II (the Private Self) becomes smaller. Remember, this is a reciprocal process. Your disclosures prompt

---

*From *Of Human Interaction* by Joseph Luft, by permission of Mayfield Publishing Co., copyright © 1969 by the National Press.

feedback from others concerning their perceptions of you. Consequently, Area I becomes still larger, while Area III (the Blind Area) becomes smaller. Through the combined interaction of disclosure and feedback, you can also begin opening up Area IV (the Unconscious Self), an area of unexplored thoughts, feelings, and behavior.

This disclosure and feedback process does not denote telling everything to everybody. Rather, it involves the sharing of information that is relevant to a helping relationship. For example, you may have feelings of shyness or incompetence that can affect your ability to perform well in social situations. By sharing those feelings and receiving feedback from an empathetic listener, you can gain an awareness of how another person sees you and the effects of your actions on that person. You and your friend have not only shared valuable information and clarified possible misperceptions, but the entire process, if honest and sincere, may have built a more satisfying relationship. The process of verbalizing internal thoughts and feelings also helps you to hear yourself, and to determine if what you say really reflects what you are feeling inside — that is, if you are sending congruent messages.

Interpersonal communication skills include behaviors such as *attending behavior, active listening, reflection, inventory questioning,* and *encouraging alternative behaviors.* These skills will encourage students (1) to express their thoughts and feelings; (2) to analyze and clarify their thoughts, feelings, and behaviors; (3) to note potential discrepancies between their actual response patterns and their desired response patterns; and (4) to choose, from among alternatives, new behaviors more in keeping with their desired behavior pattern.

These interpersonal communication skills are hierarchical in nature, with each successive skill including elements of the preceding ones. Together they comprise a taxonomy, with the skills on the lower levels requiring mastery before the skills on the higher levels can be attained. By gaining proficiency in each of the skills of this taxonomy, a teacher can aid students in the process of gaining greater self-knowledge. Such knowledge will help sensitize students to any discrepancies that might exist between their actual and desired behaviors and, thereby, set the stage for eliminating these discrepancies. Ineffective behavior need not remain static; it can be changed. Once teachers and students become aware of their actions, and realize that not only do they have other choices, but they can also make such changes occur, they are in control. The following table gives a further explanation of the interpersonal communication skills taxonomy.

Taxonomy of Interpersonal Communication Skills

Student Process	Teaching Skill	
Cluster III Encouraging alternative behaviors	Practicing alternative behaviors	
Cluster II Clarifying students' expressions of feelings	Reflection	Inventory questioning

Taxonomy of Interpersonal Communication Skills, continued

Student Process	Teaching Skill	
Cluster I Eliciting students' expressions of feelings	Attending behavior	Active listening

Adapted from Sadker and Sadker, *Interpersonal Skills of Teaching* (University of Wisconsin-Parkside, 1972).

Cluster I. Eliciting Students' Expressions of Feelings.   The two skills or behaviors that initiate interpersonal communication and provide the foundation of this taxonomy are (a) attending behavior and (b) active listening behaviors. They stimulate personal disclosure on the part of teachers, students, or parents. People will not risk sharing their feelings and attitudes if they feel threatened or manipulated. Consequently, an environment that is conducive to sharing is supportive rather than antagonistic, questioning rather than judgmental, flexible and somewhat permissive rather than highly structured and controlled. Students need to feel that their personal disclosures are being listened to seriously and will not lead to ridicule and rejection.

(a) *Attending.* Through various nonverbal and verbal cues such as eye contact, facial and body gestures, and brief verbal acknowledgments, teachers can demonstrate that they are listening with care and empathy to what is being said. Consequently, they can encourage students and others to share their thoughts and feelings, and know that they are being heard.

(b) *Active listening.* One of the key steps in active listening is being able to differentiate between intellectual content and emotional content. Most messages contain both, and teachers must be able to differentiate between them to help their students gain awareness of their own internal thoughts and feelings and ensuing behaviors. Active listening helps the listener make inferences privately about these two types of content by attending to the speaker's verbal and nonverbal cues.

Cluster II. Clarifying Students' Expressions of Feelings.   Once students feel comfortable enough to disclose information about themselves, teachers can then help them clarify that information. To do this teachers must be skilled at (a) reflecting and (b) inventory questioning.

(a) *Reflecting.* The skill of reflecting holds a mirror up to the speaker. Teachers can give students direct feedback about the way their verbal and nonverbal messages are being received. They may choose to reflect verbal communication, nonverbal communication, or even to make some inferences regarding the feelings that underlie these verbal and nonverbal messages. Carl Rogers says, "The student, seeing his own attitudes, confusions, ambivalences, feelings and perceptions accurately expressed by another, but stripped of the complication of emotion with which he himself invests them, paves the way for acceptance into the self of all those elements which are now clearly perceived."[5]

(b) *Inventory questions.** By asking inventory questions, teachers can help students describe their thoughts, feelings, and actions. Questions like these help students identify specific patterns of behavior, or ways in which they characteristically respond to events. From that point, students can assess the effectiveness of their behavior patterns. If this assessment shows a discrepancy between their actual and desired behavior, they may begin to consider other options that are more congruent with their personal goals.

Cluster III. Encouraging Alternative Behaviors.*   The final level of the taxonomy involves the exploration of alternative behaviors. This process includes (a) generating alternative behaviors, (b) practicing them and sensing how they feel, (c) receiving feedback from others regarding their effectiveness, (d) predicting their short-term and long-term consequences, and (e) choosing which pattern of behavior seems most congruent with personal needs.

Only the first two clusters of skills, eliciting and clarifying, will be presented in this chapter. Once you have mastered the skills of attending, active listening, reflecting, and inventory questioning, the transition to the third cluster — encouraging alternative behaviors — will be a logical next step.

Several notes of caution are in order before you begin mastering the Taxonomy of Interpersonal Communication Skills. First, the word *skill* may be misleading; it often connotes a series of techniques or actions, such as technical skills in typing, computers, and the like. There is a great danger in the erroneous assumption that interpersonal communication is composed of a series of skills divorced from attitudes and feelings. It is not enough for teachers to model these skills. Behind teachers' actions there must be a sincere concern for the personal growth of their students, a genuine respect for the inherent good in each human being, and a real commitment to the actualization of human potential.

In addition, interpersonal communication often takes place in a private situation. Whatever information is shared between you and others must not be discussed publicly without prior consent of the students or parents involved. It takes a long time to establish a sense of trust; it can be destroyed in an instant if private information is discussed publicly, even in an innocent fashion.

Many of the attending cues discussed in the following section must be adapted to the needs and styles of the different individuals with whom you interact. For example, for some students, physical touch may be an uncomfortable form of exchange. This type of contact may have multiple connotations for different cultures and ethnic groups. Although, in general, touch evokes a sense of emotional closeness, some students may find it threatening. The same message also relates to the use of eye contact and physical space during communication.

Finally, behaviors used to stimulate interpersonal communication can be powerful. When used inappropriately, they can be both manipulative and destructive; however, when used effectively, the taxonomy of interpersonal communication skills may stimulate within the student the greatest level of knowledge — self-knowledge.

---

*Adapted from the Trumpet Model of Weinstein and Fantini. In *Towards Humanistic Education: A Curriculum of Affect* (New York: Praeger, 1970).

OBJECTIVE   *1* To describe the characteristics of attending behavior

Learning Activity 1.1

One of the factors that makes interpersonal communication so complicated is that both participants, the speaker and the listener, are sending and receiving messages simultaneously. For example, when you are involved in a conversation with another person, what cues are you looking at, reacting to, or being affected by? What nonverbal messages are being sent through the speaker's body language? What verbal message is the speaker conveying through his or her words? What environmental stimuli distract your attention? To create an environment that is conducive to disclosure and inquiry, you must first identify and then seek to control any stimuli that influence the interpersonal communication process. Among the more important stimuli are those labeled *attending behaviors*.

We are all aware of what nonattending behavior looks like, and the frustration that occurs when the listener is occupied with personal thoughts, or suddenly interjects, "I know exactly what you mean. Let me tell what happened to me. . . ." Such nonattending behaviors detract measurably from effective interpersonal communication. Conversely, attending behaviors are those that put the speaker at ease. The speaker is not interrupted; rather, he or she receives brief verbal or nonverbal acknowledgments during the conversation.

Since communication is both verbal and nonverbal, people's actions often speak louder than their words. In fact, through his research, Mehrabian (1966)[6] determined that over 90 percent of the messages teachers send to their students are nonverbal. Teachers can often say more with the wink of an eye than they can with several sentences. Students are often keenly aware of the power of nonverbal cues, which can be seen in the following comments by an elementary school student.

Professor: How do you know when your teacher really means what she says?
Third grader: Well, her eyes get big and round and she looks right at us. . . . Sometimes she stands over us and looks down at us.
Professor: What happens then?
Third grader: The class does what she wants.[7]

Several suggestions follow for developing your own attending behavior. They have been divided into both verbal and nonverbal components.

Nonverbal Cues

1. *Eye Contact.*   Look directly at the speaker, but be sensitive to the effect such eye contact may have. Many people feel uncomfortable with direct or prolonged eye contact, and tend to shy away from it. Nonverbal cues also vary according to racial and ethnic differences. For example, African-American students may be less likely than white students to look directly at the teacher while she or he is speaking.[8]

2. *Facial Expressions.*   Your expression provides feedback to the speaker, prompting him or her to say more, slow down, clarify. More important, let your face tell the speaker that you empathize. Smiles, frowns, expressions of surprise or disappointment don't cost much. In fact, they are priceless, so share them! A word of caution though. Too much expression, particularly negative expression, can be distracting. Be aware of your own facial expressions and the effect that they have on the speaker. Simultaneously, attend to the facial expressions of the speaker. What nonverbal messages are being conveyed?

3. *Body Posture.* You can help the speaker relax by relaxing your own body. Body gestures also communicate meaning. Think how you feel when a listener points a finger at you, or stands straight with arms folded across the chest. What nonverbal message does that body position communicate to you? Does it stimulate you to say more? Probably not. In fact, Mehrabian (1969)[9] noted that an arms akimbo position most often occurs in conversation with a disliked person. In contrast, when the listener leans toward or touches the speaker, a high level of interest and involvement is communicated. Attend to the body language of the speaker — it also sends messages.

4. *Physical Space.* Edward T. Hall (1966)[10] notes that the distance people create between themselves has an inherent communication value. He describes an eighteen-inch distance between speakers as "intimate space," the eighteen-inch to four-foot distance as "social distance," and beyond twelve feet as "public distance." Each of these distances communicates distinct nonverbal messages — from those of intimacy or emotional closeness where physical touching is possible, to the space where physical touch is impossible, and fine verbal and nonverbal details are imperceptible. Research shows that both black and white children need more personal space as they grow older. Young children interact at the closest distances, adolescents at intermediate distances, and adults at greatest distances.[11] Females tend to use less personal space than males at all age levels.[12] Keep these guidelines in mind as you select a comfortable space between you and your students, one that communicates the message, "I want to make closer contact with you." If you are standing far away, walk across the room toward the student. Don't place physical or psychological obstacles in your path.

■ *Verbal Cues*

1. *Silence.* When used appropriately, silence can, indeed, "be golden." It can give both parties a chance to stop and reflect on what has been said. It may also encourage the speaker to say more if he or she doesn't have to anticipate an instant response. Too often, listeners feel compelled to make an immediate response and, consequently, they begin searching for a reply before the speaker has concluded. Wait a few seconds to be sure that the speaker has completed his or her thoughts. Be careful not to interrupt the speaker. Research shows that women are more often interrupted than men, so you may need to be particularly sensitive to this potential pattern.[13]

2. *Brief Verbal Acknowledgments.* On the other hand, nothing is more deadly than a "void silence," so you will do well to occasionally interject brief verbal acknowledgments, such as "I see," "Wow," "Oh," "That's too bad." The goal is to express interest and concern, without interrupting or interjecting personal comments. Keep the reactions brief, and quickly refocus on the speaker.

3. *Subsummaries.*   When appropriate, summarize the essence of what the speaker has said in a sentence or two. By feeding back to the speaker the gist of his or her message, you validate the communication, and this often encourages further conversation.

Summary of effective attending behavior

Nonverbal cues

1. Eye contact.
2. Facial expressions that reflect empathy.
3. Relaxed body posture and body gestures.
4. Close spatial proximity.

Verbal Cues

1. Effective use of silence.
2. Minimal verbal acknowledgments.
3. Brief subsummaries.

MASTERY TEST

OBJECTIVE 1   To describe the characteristics of attending behavior

Below are three classroom vignettes that contain both effective and ineffective examples of attending behavior. Read each vignette and answer the accompanying questions. You must answer all questions correctly to pass this Mastery Test.

VIGNETTE 1

Mr. Donaldson has had a long day, a typical Monday when everything seems disorganized. As he sits at his desk, preparing the chemistry quiz, Matthew walks in.

    Matthew: "Hi, Mr. Donaldson. Do you have a few minutes to talk?"
Mr. Donaldson: (looks up briefly, then back down at his work and continues writing).
    Matthew: (rather sheepishly) "I don't understand the equation that you presented today. Can you go over it again?"
Mr. Donaldson: (continues writing) "Go find the equation in the lab manual and read it while I finish this."

Mr. Donaldson finally looks up and sees Matthew huddled in a chair and with a forlorn expression on his face. Remaining seated behind his desk and with an impassive expression, Mr. Donaldson asks: "Well, did you find it yet?"

---

1. Indicate two ways Mr. Donaldson demonstrated nonattending behavior.

2. What were Matthew's nonverbal cues? List two.

VIGNETTE 2

Mr. Donaldson repeats his question: "Well, did you find it? The formula is on page 66."

> *Matthew:* (looking rather frustrated) "I must be dense or something. I read the description three times but it doesn't make any sense to me. Could you . . .?"
>
> *Mr. Donaldson:* (facing the board, interrupts Matthew) "How do you calculate the square root?"

3. Describe at least three attending behaviors (verbal and nonverbal) that Mr. Donaldson could have used to increase effective communication.

VIGNETTE 3

When Matthew doesn't respond, Mr. Donaldson turns around, and walks over to Matthew: "These formulas can be confusing in the beginning. Come over to the board with me and we will write them out, step by step."

Mr. Donaldson waits a few seconds, looks at Matthew, puts his hand on Matthew's shoulder and smiles. "Okay?"

Matthew: "Okay."

4. Describe at least four attending behaviors that Mr. Donaldson used to facilitate more effective communication.

On Your Own: From Theory to Practice

You have now mastered the first objective in the interpersonal communication skills hierarchy: describing the characteristics of attending behavior. Effective instruction, though, goes beyond the mere knowing or describing of skills. Effectiveness is measured by performance — demonstrating the skills in the classroom with your students. The following exercise, entitled "Practicing Attending Behavior," has been designed as an enrichment activity. Similar activities follow the mastery tests in each section of this chapter. You will notice that there are no objectives for these enrichment activities, nor are there any mastery tests to complete. Rather, these activities enable you to practice the interpersonal communication skills on your own.

Learning Activity 1.2

▨ *Practicing Attending Behavior*

Now that you have reviewed the basic components of effective attending behavior, you are ready to try the behavior and assess your own effectiveness. You may choose to practice attending in your classroom, at home, or anywhere that seems comfortable to you. Several suggestions follow for setting up a practice experience. (A word of caution, however, may be helpful. Remember that you are acquiring a series of minibehaviors, one step at a time. Ultimately, these minibehaviors will be synthesized into a fluid pattern of action — looking, listening, and responding. As you begin practicing the skills, accept the fact that trying a single skill, such as attending, may feel awkward and even unnatural.)

1. Field Placement.   If you are presently teaching or student teaching, you may choose to practice attending behavior directly with your students. You may also choose to practice such a skill with your peers in the teachers' room, at the next staff meeting, or with a visiting parent.

2. Microteaching.   If you have access to videotape equipment, teach a ten- or fifteen-minute lesson to your peers or to a small group of students. Have this practice session videotaped, and replay it as soon as possible. The content that you choose to transmit in this situation is secondary. Your primary concern is to demonstrate the characteristics of attending behavior.

3. Informal Conversation.   The ultimate goal is to use interpersonal communication skills naturally and spontaneously. They form a critical component of your entire style of communicating. Therefore, it need not be necessary to restrict yourself to a classroom situation. The next time you are involved in any one-to-one or small-group conversation, make a deliberate attempt to attend to the speaker. With continual practice, you will begin to internalize these skills and use them spontaneously. This can be reinforcing and satisfying. Don't be surprised if other people also begin to notice the positive effects of such behavior.

You now have a basic understanding of attending behavior. The following checklists will help you assess your effectiveness as you practice this skill.

Checklists

Included in this learning activity are two checklists that will help you assess your ability to demonstrate attending behavior: (1) an Observer's Assessment and (2) a Self-Assessment checklist. A series of steps that may be helpful in using these checklists follows.

Step 1.   Read each of the behavior characteristics described in the Observer's Assessment. Then, within any of the situations already described, observe someone else involved in a conversation. Practice identifying and evaluating these behaviors as an observer. Try tallying the number of times each specific behavior occurs. Jot down specific examples of the behaviors. Observing attending behavior in others may help you incorporate it into your own communication.

Step 2.   Now try demonstrating the skills yourself. If you choose to practice these skills in a classroom, seek the assistance of a peer, a friend, or your supervisor. Have this person observe your interaction over a ten- or fifteen-minute period and keep a careful tally of those characteristics described on the Observer's Assessment. The three categories used to rate the frequency with which you demonstrate these characteristics are: frequently, occasionally, and never. The first two categories are somewhat subjective, and will require you to discuss the checklist with the observer. It will be helpful to you if your observer keeps brief notes describing the specific instances in which you displayed the behaviors.

If you are involved in a microteaching situation, you can assess your own performance by using the checklist during the video playback. You may also have a friend assess your demonstration and compare notes.

Step 3.   After either a live presentation or a videotape laboratory experience, complete the Self-Assessment checklist. You may then choose to compare your own assessment with that of an impartial observer. How similar were your perceptions?

After completing these three steps, you will have received multiple feedback from a variety of sources — an observer, perhaps videotape, and your own self-assessment. Relax your body, maintain appropriate eye contact, and let your facial expressions reflect the emotions experienced by the speaker. Be aware of the space between yourself and the speaker, and avoid interruptions. By using subsummaries and brief acknowledgments, let the speaker know that you are listening.

Attending Behavior Checklist: Observer's Assessment

	Frequently	*Occasionally*	*Never*
1. The teacher had direct eye contact with the speaker.	_____	_____	_____
2. The teacher seemed distracted by other actions. Examples of distractions:	_____	_____	_____
(a) _____			
(b) _____			
3. The teacher's facial expressions reflected involvement in the conversation. Examples:	_____	_____	_____
(a) _____			
(b) _____			
4. The teacher stood close enough to the speaker so that physical contact was possible.	_____	_____	_____
5. The teacher did not interrupt the speaker while he or she was talking.	_____	_____	_____
6. The teacher used brief acknowledgments and subsummaries that indicated understanding. Examples:	_____	_____	_____
(a) _____			
(b) _____			

Attending Behavior Checklist: Self-Assessment

	Frequently	*Occasionally*	*Never*
1. I was aware of the comfort level of the speaker and modified my eye contact accordingly.	_____	_____	_____
2. My body posture was relaxed.	_____	_____	_____
3. I attempted to reflect the speaker's messages through appropriate facial expressions. Example:	_____	_____	_____
4. I established a physical space that seemed comfortable for both the speaker and for me. Example:	_____	_____	_____
5. I used and felt comfortable with periods of silence.	_____	_____	_____
6. I used brief comments to acknowledge the speaker during the conversation. Examples of such brief comments were:	_____	_____	_____
7. I used subsummaries to indicate understanding. Examples of such subsummaries were:	_____	_____	_____
8. I observed the speaker's nonverbal cues. These included:	_____	_____	_____

OBJECTIVE   **2** To differentiate between the intellectual and the emotional content of messages

Learning Activity 2.1

Unlike the reflecting and inventory questioning skills that follow, active listening is difficult to assess through overtly demonstrated behaviors. It is an internal state that can be known only to the listener. Although the listener can demonstrate nonverbally most of the characteristics of attending, he or she may still not be listening to the speaker.

As with all the skills described in this chapter, active listening behavior cannot be developed unless specific motivation is present. What motivates you to be engaged in conversation — necessity or choice? Do you feel obligated to listen, or do you have a genuine concern for the speaker? Are you listening to the *person*, his or her thoughts and feelings? Or are you listening to the words to act as a judge, a problem solver, an analyzer, or a critic? Are you entering into the conversation with preconceived expectations of what the speaker is feeling and/or thinking? Do you have any bias or prejudice toward the speaker that may turn you off or distort what you hear?

When listeners concentrate on the words being expressed, or on their preconceived impressions of the speaker, they are thinking about the speaker. By trying to find solutions to problems before the speaker has concluded, they are thinking for the speaker. By summarizing or drawing conclusions before the speaker has concluded, they are thinking ahead of the speaker. By being empathetic listeners, they are thinking with the speaker. They are not anticipating, judging, analyzing — they are just listening.

To demonstrate active listening, you must first be an empathetic listener. You must be motivated to listen because you have a genuine concern for what the speaker is feeling as well as saying. You must temporarily eliminate old impressions and momentarily suspend judgment. Only then can you begin to fully concentrate your energies on looking, listening, and recording the verbal and nonverbal messages of the speaker.

Active listening includes:

1. Blocking out external stimuli
2. Attending carefully to both verbal and nonverbal messages
3. Differentiating between intellectual and emotional content
4. Making inferences about the speaker's feelings

The critical steps involved in developing the skill of active listening follow. The three basic components include (1) personal inventory, (2) attending skills, and (3) identifying feelings.

Step 1. Personal Inventory. Effective listening requires you to be aware of your own feelings, prejudices, and expectations about the speaker. Ask yourself:

1. How do I feel about the speaker and the topic being discussed?
2. Do I really want to hear what that person is saying? What is my role? Am I here to act as critic? As problem solver?
3. If there is a problem, do I really want to help?
4. Can I accept the feelings and attitudes of the speaker even if they are different from my own?

Even though the spontaneous nature of most conversations makes these self-inventory questions difficult, try to ask one or two of them at the outset of any interpersonal communication. This initial assessment will help you concentrate on the intellectual and emotional content of the conversation. Dealing with people's feelings is a sensitive matter. It requires not only highly specialized skills like active listening, but also personal honesty about your motivation and commitment to the communication process.

Step 2. Attending Skills. At this point, your attending skills become important. Establish eye contact, relax, and listen. Attend directly to both the verbal and nonverbal cues of the speaker. What is the tone and pitch of the speaker's voice? Is she or he speaking loudly or softly; rapidly or slowly? What messages do the hand and body movements convey?

Specialists involved in the study of interpersonal communication often differentiate between the words used in conversation and the manner in which those words are delivered. They apply the term *verbal* in describing the words being spoken, and the term *vocal* in describing the volume, note, tone, pitch, and inflection of the words being expressed.[14] Usually, a speaker's emotions have a direct bearing on both the verbal and vocal messages. For example, Joel Davitz[15] concludes that when someone is feeling angry, he or she may communicate through blaring timbre, fast rate, high pitch, and loud delivery. Conversely, when someone is feeling bored, he or she may speak at a slower rate, lower pitch, and with less amplitude. If you wish to attend to the speaker's affect, you will need to listen for these vocal cues.

Step 3. Identifying the Speaker's Feelings.   As the conversation proceeds, try to listen not only to what the speaker is saying, but also to what the speaker is feeling. Are the verbal and nonverbal messages consistent with each other? An incongruent message is easy to spot. It is like looking at a child whose body is rigid, whose hands are clenched, and who says to you with stuttering words, "Everything is t-t-terrific." Try to answer the questions "What is the speaker saying" and "How does this person feel toward the topic being discussed?"

You will also need to be aware of sex differences in both verbal and nonverbal communication. For example, females tend to speak in a more tentative style than do males. They are more likely to use qualifiers such as "kind of" or "I guess." They also use more tag questions at the end of declarative sentences ("This is a good restaurant, 'isn't it?'").

Although their speech is often tentative, girls and women are more likely to disclose personal information. They are also more animated in their use of nonverbal cues, including intensity and amount of gestures, and body movement. They are far more likely to smile than males, even when they are not happy or amused. Knowledge of differences in how males and females communicate will help you become a more sensitive listener, one who is skilled in interpreting both the intellectual and emotional content of a speaker's message.[16]

The following vignettes offer you the chance to test your knowledge of active listening.

SCENE I

You are seated at your desk, after school, organizing your materials. It is the end of a busy day and you are getting ready to leave. Suddenly you look up and see Bruce, one of your fifth grade students, seated at his desk. He's been moody all day, and you sense that he has something on his mind. As he approaches you, you quickly check your own feelings about the potential conversation.

These are several questions you might ask yourself. Do you really want to stay and listen to Bruce? How have you felt about any previous after school conversations that you have had with him? What are the different issues that he might want to talk about with you? If as a result of the inventory, you decide that you really don't want to talk with Bruce (don't have the energy, don't have the time, etc.), what could you say? Perhaps, "Bruce, I'm so tired that I am not sure that I could listen to you in a way that you deserve. Could it wait until tomorrow?" There are times when this may be the wisest response for a caring educator. If you do not have time, or are not in a frame of mind that will facilitate effective interpersonal communication, then it is appropriate to set another time. Remember, however, to hold your discussion with Bruce tomorrow. Also, before putting the discussion off for a day, check with Bruce to see how pressing his needs and concerns appear to be.

SCENE II

Bruce says, "Do you have a couple of seconds?" Slowly, he begins to talk about the upcoming math test. He drops his eyes to the floor and quietly says, "You know, this stuff is really silly." You may consider Bruce's past performance in math and think to yourself, "Now, he is usually an excellent student. I wonder what he is trying to say."

Based on both Bruce's verbal cues ("this stuff is silly") and his nonverbal cues (head and voice drop), what do you imagine he is feeling? There are several inferences you can make. Perhaps he is saying, "I feel scared about the test," "I'm not prepared," or "I don't understand it." He could be leading up to: "I'm feeling bored with this material. It's too easy," or "If I get 100 on the test tomorrow, everyone will make fun of me."

Remember, not every message may have an emotional overtone, so don't exhaust yourself trying to find one. If a student does respond with such emotions, attend to them. The absence of emotional reaction from a student when circumstances would warrant one (for example, a fight or some other highly emotional experience) could alert you to listen more actively and intently.

Summary of active listening

1. Think about your personal motivation for listening. Put aside preconceived expectations. Suspend judgment.
2. Attend to the speaker's (a) verbal cues and vocal cues, and (b) nonverbal cues.
3. Begin making private inferences concerning the speaker's feelings. Be aware of potential gender or racial differences in communication. Tune into incongruent messages, if any are apparent.

MASTERY TEST

OBJECTIVE 2 To differentiate between the intellectual and the emotional content of messages (active listening)

Read each statement and try to differentiate between the intellectual content and the emotional content being transmitted. Sometimes it helps to read the statements aloud. Each time you read one, put the accent on a different word. Does it communicate a different emotional message? In the right-hand columns, record both the intellectual message and the emotional message. Some of the statements may contain several different emotions. List them all. When you have finished, compare your list with those in the Answer Key. To pass this test, you must receive a total score of at least 85. If you disagree with any of the answers listed, ask friends for their reactions. What messages do they receive?

Statements	Intellectual (Cognitive) (I'm Saying)	Emotional (Affective) (I'm Feeling)
1. "I don't need any help. I'm old enough to do it myself."		
2. "Just go away and leave me alone. I don't want to talk to you or anyone else."		
3. "I couldn't believe it. Imagine me, getting an A on that paper."		
4. "I tried to do it three times and I still don't understand it."		
5. "No matter what I do, I can't seem to please him."		
6. "I don't feel that I have to answer that. It's none of your business."		
7. Every place I turn, you are always there, standing over me."		
8. "Just trust me."		
9. "Cool it, I'll do it when I'm good and ready."		
10. "Just give me a chance. I know I can do it."		

On Your Own: From Theory to Practice

You have now mastered the second objective in the interpersonal communication skills hierarchy: differentiating between the intellectual and the emotional content of messages. As described in Learning Activity 1.1, effective teaching goes beyond knowledge. It demands using the skill and incorporating it into your own interpersonal communication. So, practice active listening on your own.

Learning Activity 2.2

▓ *Practicing Active Listening*

All the situations described in Learning Activity 1.1 — classroom teaching, microteaching, and informal conversations — are also appropriate for practicing your active listening skills. Within any of these contexts, participate in a conversation with another person. If you have the opportunity to initiate the conversation, you may wish to select a topic that has some emotional overtones. For example, if you are reading a short story, you may ask your student, "How did you feel about the ending of the story?" At a party, you may ask, "What were your reactions to last night's debate?" Then look, listen, and make private inferences about the speaker's affective messages.

Although active listening skills are important in all forms of communication, they are especially critical when there are emotional overtones in the speaker's messages. When you demonstrate the skills of active listening, you are performing several tasks simultaneously. You are looking at the nonverbal cues of the speaker, listening to the verbal cues, and making private inferences about the emotions the speaker may be experiencing. All these actions are happening privately. Other than the overt demonstration of attending behavior, the effectiveness of your listening ability is often known only to yourself. The only checklist used in assessing your ability to listen actively is a self-inventory.

Active Listening Checklist: Self-Assessment

1. I analyzed my personal feelings about the speaker. Two specific questions I asked myself were:

    (a) _____

    (b) _____

2. I focused my attention directly on the speaker. I showed the speaker I was listening by:

    (a) _____

    (b) _____

3. Nonverbal cues that gave me information about the speaker's feelings were:

    (a) _____

    (b) _____

    (c) _____

    Inferences I made regarding these cues were:

    (a) _____

    (b) _____

    (c) _____

4. I listened to the speaker's words as well as to the tone, pitch, and rate of speech. I was able to differentiate between the intellectual and emotional content.

(a) The intellectual content was:

_____

_____

(b) The emotional content appeared to be:

_____

_____

3 To differentiate among the three types of reflecting — word messages, behaviors, inferences

Learning Activity 3.1

Take a few moments to review objectives 1 and 2. These eliciting behaviors should help provide an environment that is conducive to sharing and self-disclosure. By first attending to your students' nonverbal and verbal cues, and then differentiating between the intellectual and the emotional content of their messages, you say to them, "I see you, and I am listening carefully to what you are saying and doing."

Suppose a student expresses an emotional reaction that you wish to respond to. What do you do? What do you say? Consider the following situation and then write down your responses to the students' comments.

Attending to Students

You notice that a student is seated at her desk, with her math book opened. She has been staring into space for several minutes and can't seem to concentrate on her work. She is playing with the pages of the book. You go over to her desk and she suddenly says:

Actively Listening to Students

"Math is dumb. I don't want to do any of this stuff."

Depending on your past information regarding this student, you may decode the message as:

Content: Math is hard, dumb, boring, etc.

Affect: 1. "I'm frustrated. I need help."
(or)   2. "I'm feeling tired, and I don't want to work."
(or)   3. "I'm dumb. I can't do it."
(or)   4. "I'm feeling bored. This stuff is too easy."

There are many approaches a teacher could take in responding to this student. One appropriate way would be to use the skill of *reflecting*. You could reflect at any one of three levels: (1) you might choose to pick up on the student's words and try to capture and reflect back the gist of the verbal message, (2) you could respond to the student's nonverbal or body cues by describing his or her actions, or (3) you could make an inference about the emotions being transmitted and share this inference with the student. The effective use of reflecting behavior by the teacher can communicate to the student, "I have listened carefully to what you have said, and I would like to share my observations with you." Following are sentence stems that often begin reflections on each of these three levels.

"I heard you say . . .	(reflecting the student's words, the verbal content of the message)
"I saw you do . . .	(reflecting the student's actions, the nonverbal behavior)
"I imagine you're feeling . . .	(reflecting the student's feelings that may underlie the verbal and non-verbal behavior)

The teacher's response, in effect, serves as a mirror for the student's words, feelings, and behaviors, thus providing direct feedback about the success of the student's communication. Effective reflecting behavior often facilitates self-exploration because it provides speakers with an opportunity to ponder their listeners' feedback before reorganizing and clarifying their messages. Reflection can also provide an opportunity for teachers and students to clarify any misinterpretations that may block the process of communication.

The skill of reflecting is composed of successive behaviors, ranging from simply paraphrasing the speaker's words, to describing the speaker's body cues or behaviors, to reflecting the speaker's affective or feeling messages to make inferences or interpretations.

Reflecting Word Messages (Paraphrasing)

To reflect word messages, a teacher repeats or paraphrases the essence of the words just communicated. No attempt is made to reflect the feelings being conveyed or the nonverbal cues or behaviors being displayed. Sometimes hearing an exact repetition or paraphrase of what was just said can be a clarifying experience for both the speaker and the listener.

Look again at the dialogue at the beginning of Learning Activity 3.1. To reflect the student's word message, the teacher could respond to the student by saying, "So you think that the math is dumb" or "You don't want to do your math today." Even though such a response may sound trite and mechanical, practice using it for a while — it will not only help to develop your own listening skills, but it will also serve as a means for clarifying the speaker's messages. A teacher may choose to use this type of response before deciding whether to continue the interaction by reflecting the emotional messages that appear to underlie the verbal content. Reflecting word messages thus serves several purposes: (1) it initiates dialogue between the teacher and students, (2) it provides some "lead time" for the teacher to decide whether to continue the discussion, and (3) it may motivate the student to provide additional information about his or her thoughts and feelings.

Such a response is reflecting rather than confrontative; it does not force the student to respond. Simply letting a student know that you are listening may be all that is needed to stimulate further dialogue.

Reflecting Nonverbal Messages (Behavior Description)

The second component of reflecting requires you to describe the physical behaviors of the speaker. When reflecting nonverbal messages, use only the visible behavioral evidence.

Refer again to the interaction at the beginning of Learning Activity 3.1. If the teacher had chosen to reflect the student's nonverbal message, he or she might have said, "I see you sitting here, staring into space, and playing with your math book. What's up?" Usually the behavior description is followed by a question that will open up some dialogue. You observe, give feedback by describing the behavior, and then ask a question. By describing specific, observed behaviors, you provide insight to the speaker about how he or she is being perceived. Such responses are descriptive and nonevaluative. They do *not* include accusations or inferences about the other person's motives, attitudes, or personality traits. Telling a child that he or she is rude is offering an accusation rather than a description of specific behavior. Young children often have a difficult time differentiating between themselves and their actions. Are they, as human beings, rude people, or are their actions inappropriate to the situation? Remember, describe specific *actions* only.

Reflecting to Make Inferences or Interpretations

This third level of reflecting incorporates the skills described in the two preceding behaviors; however, it goes beyond both the paraphrasing of words and the reflection of nonverbal cues. It represents an attempt on the part of the teacher to summarize what he or she saw and heard, and to check out those observations by sharing some inferences about the speaker's feelings. Did the listener's perceptions match the original intentions of the speaker? Was the speaker really "in touch" with his or her own messages? In the earlier interaction with the student who seemed to have problems with his math, the teacher might have responded at this level: "I see you sitting there, playing with the math book (reflecting behavior), saying that math is dumb (reflecting the word messages). Are you feeling frustrated by the problems?" (interpretation of the student's feelings).

Effective reflecting behavior is not a semantic game or a way of putting the person's ideas in new terms. It comes from a genuine desire to understand exactly what the student is expressing and feeling both verbally and nonverbally. You are never expected to play the role of a mind reader. You do not have to try to guess what the speaker is thinking or feeling. After summarizing what you saw (behavior description) and what you heard (reflection of content), you share your inference about whatever thoughts or feelings you associate with such a response. In short, check your interpretations with a question. How accurate were your inferences? Did they match the speaker's intentions?

Both the *timing* and the *number* of reflected statements are critical elements in practicing this skill. It can be just as ineffective to reflect too much as too little. It becomes annoying to the speaker to have verbal or nonverbal communications reflected and interpreted constantly. It can often cause students to doubt that you really are seeking clarification. They may suspect that you are trying to manipulate them by putting your own thoughts and values in their mouths. Communication then becomes unbalanced and strained.

Frequent reflecting seems especially appropriate when mistakes could be costly and, consequently, accuracy becomes vital; and when strong feelings in either the sender or the receiver increase the probability of misunderstanding. In such cases, reflecting becomes crucial as a way of ensuring that the message comes through undistorted. The next time you are having a disagreement with someone, try reflecting what has been said until he or she corroborates your understanding. Note what effect this has on the other person's feelings and also on your own.

When used effectively, reflecting enhances the development of a non-threatening environment in which learners can feel free to express themselves. Reflections should never be judgmental, advisory, challenging, or sarcastic. Rather, they should be descriptive, questioning, and exploratory.

Summary of effective reflecting behavior

1. Become aware of any preconceived thoughts or feelings you may have about the speaker and/or the topic being discussed. Will they hinder communication? If so, how?
2. Attend carefully to both the verbal and nonverbal messages of the speaker. *Observe.*
3. Make a mental note of the exact words being spoken and the specific behaviors being demonstrated. *Look, listen, and record.*
4. Differentiate between the verbal messages and the emotional messages being delivered. What is the speaker saying? What feelings are associated with the words? *Look, listen, record, and infer.*
5. Respond to the student by:
   (a) Paraphrasing the words. *Reflect words.*
   (b) Describing the specific observed behaviors of the speaker. *Describe behavior.*
   (c) Share your inferences concerning the student's thoughts and feelings that may underlie verbal and nonverbal behavior. *Interpret.*
6. Be aware of the tone of voice you use. Avoid sarcasm, judgment, reprimand.
7. Ask for clarification to assess the accuracy of your perceptions. *Clarify.*

MASTERY TEST

OBJECTIVE 3   To differentiate among the three types of reflecting — word messages, behaviors, inferences

Code each of the following responses to determine which of the three types of reflecting behavior is being exhibited. Use the following abbreviations: *WM* = reflecting word messages, *B* = reflecting behavior, *I* = interpretive reflections. To pass this test successfully, you must accurately code at least 9 of the 10 responses.

_____   1. *Student:* (twisting in seat, biting pencil) "I don't like creative writing. I'm no good at writing."

Teacher: "You don't care for the writing assignments, and you don't feel you have much talent as a writer. What do you find the most difficult about writing?"

_____ 2. Student: (smiling broadly and displaying a medal) "Look at the medal I just won. I took first prize in the swimming competition."

Teacher: "It looks to me as though you're really proud and happy to have done so well."

_____ 3. Student: (frowning and slumped in chair) "I don't want to go to the school dance. I hate standing in a line hoping some dumb boy will ask me to dance."

Teacher: "It sounds like you feel awkward or maybe left out, and as if you're standing alone while your friends are dancing. Is that true?"

_____ 4. Student: (with his hands in his pockets and shrugging his shoulders) "You know my father. He is really big on sports. He played football, so I have to play football."

Teacher: "It sounds as if you feel resentful. Is that true?"

_____ 5. Student: "That was a stupid thing for him to do. I told him he'd probably get caught."

Teacher: "So you warned him."

_____ 6. Student: "I can do that as well as any boy can. Why can't I try it?"

Teacher: "Are you saying that you feel like you're being discriminated against?"

_____ 7. Student: (running across the room, almost knocking over the fish tanks)

Teacher: "When you run across the room like that, you could easily knock over the tanks."

_____ 8. Student: (seated under a tree, reading a book while the rest of the class is playing kickball)

Teacher: "Are you sitting here because you would rather read or because you didn't get picked for the team?"

_____ 9. Student: (seated under a tree, reading a book while the rest of the class is playing kickball)

Teacher: "I see you sitting here reading instead of playing with the class. What's happening?"

_____ 10. Student: (seated under a tree, reading a book while the rest of the class is playing kickball) "I'd rather read than play kickball. I have to finish this book by fourth period."

Teacher: "Oh, you didn't finish your assignment?"

On Your Own: From Theory to Practice

You have now completed the third objective, differentiating among the three types of reflecting behaviors. It is difficult to make the transition from knowing the three types of reflecting to demonstrating these behaviors in your own interpersonal communication. To help you make this transition, we have included an additional enrichment activity, Constructing Responses. Because of the complexity of this skill, we encourage you to try your hand at writing the three types of reflecting responses before you practice this new behavior. When you feel confident constructing the messages, move from theory to practice on your own.

Learning Activity 3.2

Constructing Responses

Directions: Working alone or with a partner, read each of the brief vignettes and dialogues that follow. Then write a statement incorporating the reflecting response indicated in the parentheses. When you have completed the activity, compare your responses with the sample answers that follow.

VIGNETTE 1

Teri, at the age of eight, still has difficulty sharing her materials with other children. She often begins fighting with them when they borrow her materials, even when she is not working with them. Alice innocently picks up one of her games, which is lying on the table. Teri immediately runs up to her and grabs it away.

(a) The teacher walks over to the table and says to Teri:

_____

(reflect behavior)

(b) Teri is screaming: "It's my game and she can't play with it. Tell her to give it back to me."

Teacher: _____

(reflect word message)

(c) Teri, red in the face, seems angry. She says: "It's mine. She just came over and took it!"

Teacher: _____

(interpretive reflection)

(d) *Teri:* "She'll probably just break it anyway."

Teacher: _____

(reflect word message)

(e) Alice, getting flustered, her eyes filling with tears, says, "I didn't know it was yours. Stop pulling at my arm."

Teacher: _____

(reflect behavior)

(f) Alice pulls the game away from Teri and puts it back on the table. She looks at the teacher and says, "Can I play with it?"

Teacher: _____

(open response)

VIGNETTE 2

For the big history fair, the class has decided to re-create the landing on the moon by the first astronaut. The students are to decide among themselves who will play the astronaut. The selection process has turned into a popularity contest between two students, Mike and Frank. They both seem to be battling with each other.

(a) Frank hits his fist on the desk and shouts, "I even look like the guy. I should be it."

Teacher: _____

(reflect behavior)

(b) *Frank* (still demanding): "So what's the big deal? I just want to play this role."

Teacher: _____

(reflect word message)

(c) Mike, equally agitated, shouts: "Just wait one big minute — let me say something."

Teacher: _____

(interpretive reflection)

(d) *Mike:* "You bet I'm angry. What happened to the big democratic thing we were supposed to have here?"

Teacher: _____

(reflect word message)

(e) *Frank:* "Why don't we both read the part and let the kids decide?"

Teacher: _____

(interpretive reflection)

(f) *Mike:* "That will probably turn out to be one big game . . . a popularity contest."

Teacher: _____

(reflect word message)

VIGNETTE 3

Half the class is gathered for a class meeting. There have been several incidents of stealing from the lockers lately, and the teacher thinks it is necessary to discuss it openly.

(a) *Judy:* "What difference does it make who's taking all the stuff? Let's just put guards out in the hall and keep a lookout for the thief."

Teacher: _____

(reflect word message)

(b) *Kenny:* "That doesn't make sense to me. Let's just set a reward system. Give money to anyone who knows anything about it."

Teacher: _____

(reflect word message)

(c) *Dorie:* (seated quietly in her chair, suddenly blurts out): "That's *crazy.*"

Teacher: _____

(interpretive reflection)

(d) Donald opens his eyes wide and nods his head.

Teacher: _____

(reflect behavior)

(e) *Donald:* "Boy, we are assuming a lot. How do we know there's just one thief?

    Teacher: _____

                                       (reflect word message)

(f) *Melissa:* "Wait a minute. Why don't we just give the thief a chance to return everything before we start a big hunt team?"

    Teacher: _____

                                       (interpretive reflection)

VIGNETTE 4

Annette's mother, Mrs. Simpson, has made an appointment to see her child's teacher. She wants to discuss Annette's report card.

(a) *Mrs. Simpson:* "I'm glad we were able to arrange this meeting. As you can imagine, I was shocked by Annette's report card."

    Teacher: _____

                                       (reflect word message)

(b) *Mrs. Simpson:* (leaning forward and frowning) "I have never been so disappointed."

    Teacher: _____

                                       (reflect behavior)

(c) *Mrs. Simpson:* "I'm really puzzled. Whenever I ask Annette how things are going at school, she says they're great. I ask how her grades are, and she says all As. But her report card is mainly Cs and even Ds."

    Teacher: _____

                                       (interpretive reflection)

(d) *Mrs. Simpson:* "I don't know what to make of this situation."

    Teacher: _____

                                       (reflect word message)

(e) *Mrs. Simpson:* "Is there something she hasn't told me?"

    Teacher: _____

                                       (open response)

▧ *Potential Responses*

Take a look at the following responses to each vignette. Obviously, you will not have written the identical statements. The critical issue is to determine if your statements follow the basic guidelines of effective reflecting behavior. Ask yourself if you have successfully captured the intent of the speaker.

VIGNETTE 1

(a) "You're pulling that box away from Alice. What's happening?" (Reflect behavior)

(b) "It's yours and no one else can play with it." (Reflect word message)

(c) "Your face is getting red. I think that you are angry because Alice didn't ask you if she could borrow it. Is that true?" (Reflect behavior and interpret)

(d) "You're worried Alice will break it?" (Interpretive reflection)

(e) "I can see that you are about to cry. Calm down." (Reflect behavior)

(f) (Open response)

VIGNETTE 2

(a) "You're so upset, you're shouting and hitting the desk." (Reflecting behavior)

(b) "You really want this part." (Reflect word message)

(c) "You look angry. Do you feel like you haven't had a chance to speak?" (Interpretive reflection)

(d) "You don't think that the selection process is fair? democratic?" (Reflect word message)

(e) "You think the kids will be fair judges? Is it because you think they will vote for you?" (Interpretive reflection)

(f) "You think the kids will vote for the most popular? Do you have any other suggestions?" (Reflect word message)

VIGNETTE 3

(a) "You think a guard system is a way to deal with the problem?" (Reflect word message)

(b) "So are you suggesting a reward system?" (Reflect word message)

(c) "You obviously disagree with those two ideas. Is it because they seem unfair to you?" (Interpretive reflection)

(d) "I see you nodding your head. Is it because you think they are unfair?" (Reflect behavior)

(e) "You think we are assuming a lot . . . that maybe there is more than one thief?" (Reflect word message)

(f) "When you used the term 'hunt team,' I imagine you thought that there was something inhuman or scary about the process of finding the thief. Is that true?" (Interpretive reflection)

VIGNETTE 4

(a) "You were surprised by Annette's grades." (Reflect word message)

(b) "You look concerned." (Reflect behavior)

(c) "Your daughter has given you one evaluation, but the report card paints an entirely different picture. Do you think Annette's been giving you a full report?" (Interpretive reflection)

(d) "It seems confusing." (Reflect word message)

(e) (Open response)

Learning Activity 3.3

Practicing Reflecting Behavior

Now that you have refined your skill in constructing responses, you are ready to try the three types of reflecting behaviors. As the skill becomes more complicated, so does the checklist. Take a few moments to analyze the checklists before using them to assess your own performance. Note that both the effective and the ineffective characteristics of this skill are listed. Both types of characteristics are included to focus on some of the common errors that may occur as you begin practicing this new behavior.

When setting the scene to practice this skill with your friends or students, keep the situation simple. Limit the number of people and distracting variables. Start with reflecting word messages. You may also choose to tell the people you are working with that you are practicing new skills and would like some feedback from them. How did they react when they heard their statements being reflected? How accurately did you reflect their messages?

Reflecting Behavior Checklist: Observer's Assessment

	Frequently	*Occasionally*	*Never*
1. The teacher reflected the speaker's messages.	———	———	———
Examples:			
2. The teacher reflected the speaker's behavior.	———	———	———
Examples:			
3. The teacher used interpretive reflection.	———	———	———
Examples:			
4. The teacher's inferences appeared to be inaccurate.	———	———	———
Examples:			

5. At the end of the reflections (verbal, nonverbal, and/or inferential), the teacher asked a question for clarification. ("What's happening?," "Is that true?")

   Examples:

   _____

   _____

6. The teacher responded with a judgment instead of a reflection. ("That's wrong," "You're rude.")

   Examples:

   _____

   _____

7. The teacher's tone seemed to communicate a sense of acceptance.

   Examples:

   _____

   _____

8. The teacher paraphrased the speaker's messages so often during the conversation that it was distracting.

   Examples:

   _____

   _____

Reflecting Behavior Checklist: Self-Assessment

1. I described the speaker's nonverbal behavior.

   I specifically said: _____

2. I summarized the speaker's verbal messages.

   I specifically said: _____

3. I added personal inferences and/or interpretations to my observations.

   I specifically said: _____

4. I checked my perceptions of the speaker's verbal and/or nonverbal messages by asking direct questions for clarification.

   The specific questions I asked were: _____

5. My responses were/were not well timed, and I did/did not interrupt the speaker. The specific cues that told me it was an appropriate time to speak were: _____

_____

_____

6. When I misinterpreted the message, I asked for clarification.

(a) The misinterpretation was: _____

_____

(b) The way I asked for clarification was: _____

_____

(c) The clarified message was: _____

_____

7. The most comfortable type of reflecting for me was (check one):

(a) Reflecting verbal messages   _____

(b) Reflecting nonverbal messages   _____

(c) Reflecting with an attempt to make inferences or interpretations   _____

OBJECTIVE   **4** To differentiate among inventory questions that (a) stimulate communication, (b) clarify information, (c) identify discrepancies, and (d) seek alternatives or solutions

Learning Activity 4.1

Let's take a few moments to review the development of the interpersonal communication skills taxonomy thus far. The skills involved in the first cluster, entitled Eliciting Students' Expressions of Feelings, are mood behaviors that stimulate interaction and enhance the potential for effective interpersonal communication. When you model attending and active listening behaviors, you are communicating to students, parents, and colleagues that you have put aside other business and are ready to listen and interact with them.

By attending effectively, you communicate your interest in others. Your body posture reflects a comfort level that puts others at ease. By observing their facial expressions and body postures and by listening to the pitch and tone of their voices, as well as to their words, you are listening actively and differentiating between feeling and word messages. The Cluster II skills, Clarifying Students' Expressions of Feelings, teach you how to respond to students in specific ways. By paraphrasing your students' verbal messages, you allow them to hear their own words, and in doing so, you help clarify any misinterpretations. By describing their behaviors, you help them become more aware of the physical reactions that accompany their verbal dialogue. By adding interpretation to these descriptions, you share your perceptions of why they may be speaking or acting in a certain manner. Such interpretations can provide additional insights regarding the connection between their thoughts, feelings, and behaviors.

At any of these three levels of reflecting, your students are given the opportunity to accept or reject your reactions and perceptions. Mutual feedback will enable both of you to gain valuable information about one another. Such interpersonal interactions will help students become more aware of their own thoughts, feelings, and resulting behaviors. At this point, they may begin to see the effects of their actions on other persons.

Inventory questions may now be appropriate. Such questions will help your students clarify specific aspects of their behavior. Too often, people simply take their style of behavior for granted and give little thought about whether it serves them productively. Taking inventory of one's behavior pattern is a necessary condition for growth.

■ *Inventory Questions*

Questioning behavior has been an integral part of the interpersonal communication hierarchy from the outset. As you were attending to your students' or parents' verbal and nonverbal messages, you may have been asking yourself questions such as: "What is he/she thinking?," "I wonder what lies behind that calm exterior?" As you initiated the reflective listening stage, you had to take inventory of your own motivation for listening by asking yourself a series of self-confronting questions: "Do I really want to be involved in this conversation?," "What past experiences have I had with the speaker that could positively or negatively affect my ability to listen?" Questioning skills were also inherent in the reflective listening stage when you followed each type of message — words, behaviors, and inferences — with a question for clarification: "Is that what you said?," "Did I describe your feelings accurately?," "Do you agree with my perception of the situation?"

In their most positive form, questions can (1) invite communication; (2) express lack of understanding; (3) clarify misperceptions or inaccurate information; (4) focus attention on specific thoughts, feelings, actions, and events; and (5) show concern and involvement. When used inappropriately, they can be threatening, interrupt the thought process, carry an accusatory or judgmental message, and generate defensiveness and hostility with the student.

Inventory questions are a unique subset of questions that stimulate introspection. When used effectively, they enable individuals to look inside themselves and to (1) stimulate communication related to thoughts, feelings, and behaviors; (2) clarify communication related to these personal states; (3) identify any discrepancies between their intended words and actions and how the messages are received by others; and (4) seek out potential alternatives and/or solutions. When students respond to inventory questions, they assume an active role in interpersonal communication. Inventory questions may be viewed as a process of shared problem solving, a way of identifying and bringing to the surface pieces of hidden behavior. The ultimate goal is to move students to a greater understanding of their behavior, assess the effects of this behavior, and determine if change is necessary.

Weinstein (1975)[17] states that the product of self-knowledge is to create more "response-ability," or more choices in the way people behave. In short, the better people understand the causes and consequences of their behavior, the greater their ability to control their actions. Maturity is reflective of continuous assessment, alteration, and reassessment of one's behaviors.

Descriptions of four types of inventory questions follow. These questions serve to (1) stimulate communication, (2) clarify information, (3) identify discrepancies, and (4) seek alternatives or solutions.

Level 1. Stimulate Communication. Inventory questions that stimulate communication are open invitations to talk. They give the speaker the opportunity to explore and discuss thoughts and feelings. They say to the student: "I am interested in you and concerned about what happens to you." Examples of inventory questions that stimulate communication are:

- "Can you tell me what happened?"
- "Can we talk about what's on your mind?"
- "How are you feeling about this?"

Remember that the purpose of these questions is to engage students in self-inquiry and to help them discuss specific actions or events and related feelings.

Consider the following vignette. Kevin, a student in your homeroom, has been sent to you by the playground monitor because he was involved in a fight. Which of the following inventory questions stimulates communication that can lead to further inquiry?

- "Kevin, whom were you fighting with this time?"
- "Kevin, can you tell me a little about what happened out on the playground?"
- "Kevin, why were you fighting?"

If you selected the first response, you may block all further communication. "Whom were you fighting with *this time*?" is accusatory and confrontative. If you selected the third response, it is unlikely that you will help Kevin disclose thoughts and feelings. Answering the question "why" often requires the student to analyze or intellectualize. Such questions can divert attention from real, immediate feelings and may cause the student to become defensive. Remember that inventory questions encourage individuals to reflect on "their behavior and their inner experiences with a minimum of obstructive self-judging, defensiveness, or ambitious striving for results."[18] If you selected the second response, you have increased the likelihood that Kevin will share thoughts and feelings with you. You have effectively stimulated communication.

Level 2. Clarify Information. Inventory questions at this level seek to expand and clarify thoughts, feelings, and actions, and enable students to begin recognizing patterns of behavior. Specifically, the goal of these questions is to (1) obtain more information, both factual and emotional; (2) relate specific examples, thus moving from vague generalizations to more concrete information; (3) clarify ambiguous terms or statements; and (4) focus on specific thoughts, feelings, and action as well as on patterns of behavior. Following are examples of inventory questions that clarify information.

- "Can you give me more information about what happened?"
- "Why don't you tell me more about what you were feeling?"
- "What did you mean when you said — ?" "Can you give me a specific example of when you felt that way?" "Can you say more about that?" "Has this ever happened before?"

- "Is this typical of the way you act/react?" "How do you usually react/act when this happens?" "What usually triggers this reaction?"

Let's continue with the preceding vignette and watch how the teacher uses clarifying questions to obtain more information and to help Kevin focus on specific feelings.

Kevin: Jack and I were fighting.
Teacher: Can you tell me specifically what happened?
Kevin: He called me a cheater and told me I played dirty ball.
Teacher: Can you say more?
Kevin: We were shooting baskets and I pushed him accidentally.
Teacher: And what were you thinking?
Kevin: It was an accident. I was all excited . . . and I just wanted to hit the basket.
Teacher: What did you say?
Kevin: Nothing. . . . I guess I just kicked him.
Teacher: You said that you were all excited, what else were you feeling?
Kevin: I just wanted to hit the basket this time. . . . I wanted to win. . . . I guess I got angry.
Teacher: Do you usually kick or fight when you get angry?

By effectively using inventory questions that clarify information, the teacher was able to receive a more accurate and comprehensive description of events that occurred. The teacher asked just one question at a time, did not ask questions that focused on "why" Kevin acted as he did, and was not accusatory or judgmental.

Level 3. Identify Discrepancies.   This level of inventory questions looks at the consequences and outcomes of specific behaviors or behavior patterns. It helps students determine if the outcomes of their actions are what they want or expect them to be and to identify any discrepancies that may exist. Inventory questions that identify discrepancies include these specific examples.

- "What was the outcome of your actions?"
- "Did things work out the way you wanted them to?"
- "What price did you pay for responding that way?"
- "How did it serve you to act this way?"

Let's continue with the next stage of the vignette. Here are sample questions that could help Kevin identify the results of his behavior.

- "What does kicking and fighting get you in the end?"
- "You wanted to win, but what was the result of the fight?"
- "You were angry, so you kicked Jack. How did that serve you?"

Notice that inventory questions identifying discrepancies are open-ended. These questions can be more confrontative than the others in this series. There are times, however, when this may be appropriate.

Level 4. Seek Alternatives or Solutions.   This level of inventory questions brings students to the next logical step. Once they realize that their behavior does not result in desirable consequences, students are ready to explore alternatives and consider new solutions.

This type of inventory question serves as a transition to the next cluster of skills in the taxonomy of interpersonal communications skills, Encouraging Alternative Behavior. Specific questions that can be used at this level include:

- "If you don't like the outcomes of your actions, in what other ways can you behave?"
- "If you had to do it all over again, how would you react?"
- "How could you change your behavior to achieve more positive outcomes?"
- "What else could you do to achieve your goal, to achieve more positive consequences?"

In our ongoing vignette, the teacher can explore with Kevin other strategies he could try when he gets excited and angry. These inventory questions can help Kevin become aware of choices and options.

YOUR TURN

Differentiating Among the Four Types of Inventory Questions: (1) Stimulating Communication, (2) Clarifying Information, (3) Identifying Discrepancies, (4) Seeking Alternatives or Solutions

Before you read further, test your skill by completing the following review exercise. Read the vignette and, in the spaces provided, code the type of inventory question. Use *SC* for stimulating communication, *CI* for clarifying information, *ID* for identifying discrepancies, and *PA* for seeking out potential alternatives or solutions. When you complete the review, check your responses with those provided.

As Mrs. Peterson walks down the hall, she overhears Mindy and Lisa arguing:

Mindy: Why did you tell me yesterday that you would go?

Lisa: I forgot that I already promised Sue I would go with her.

Mindy: Thanks a lot, FRIEND.

Lisa walks into the resource room and slumps into her chair.

_____ 1. *Mrs. Peterson:*   Lisa, you look so sad. Is anything wrong?
  Lisa: Nothing.

_____ 2. *Mrs. Peterson:*   Does it have anything to do with your conversation with Mindy?
  Lisa: Yeah, Mindy is mad at me because I can't go to the show with her today.

_____ 3. *Mrs. Peterson:*   Can you tell me what happened?
  Lisa: It's all so stupid. . . . I promised her I'd go to the show with her. . . . I forgot that I had already made plans to go with Sue.

_____ 4. *Mrs. Peterson:*   How did Mindy react?
  Lisa: Bad, I guess. I don't want Mindy to be mad.

_____ 5. *Mrs. Peterson:* What's your reaction to the situation?
　　　　　 Lisa: That I shouldn't have made two sets of plans again.

_____ 6. *Mrs. Peterson:* Has this happened before?
　　　　　 Lisa: Yeah.

_____ 7. *Mrs. Peterson:* Can you give me another example when you acted this way?
　　　　　 Lisa: Last week I did the same thing with Kathy.

_____ 8. *Mrs. Peterson:* So you make two different plans with two different friends. What usually happens? What does it get you in the end?
　　　　　 Lisa: I guess one friend ends up getting mad at me. Why don't I think sometimes, instead of just absentmindedly saying yes?

_____ 9. *Mrs. Peterson:* If you had it to do over again, what other ways could you act?

This dialogue was brief. One or two questions from each of the four types of inventory questions were enough. Remember, the teacher's questions merely guide the personal inquiry process.

The inventory process requires patient, supportive, and sensitive teachers who have mastered a series of specific, focused questions that they can use spontaneously. The entire interactive process necessitates a sensitivity in attending to students' nonverbal cues, sensing when to stop — stop questioning, stop probing. Teachers must protect their students from getting hurt, mocked, or ostracized by others.

Summary of effective inventory questions

Level 1: Stimulate communication. Questions at this level offer an open invitation to talk. They make students, parents, or colleagues aware of your interest and concern.

Level 2: Clarify information. Questions at this level seek to (1) obtain more information; (2) relate specific examples; (3) clarify ambiguous terms or statements; (4) focus on specific thoughts, feelings, and actions.

Level 3: Identify discrepancies. Questions at this level focus on the consequences and outcomes of specific behaviors; they aid in the identification of discrepancies that may exist between desired versus actual outcomes of one's behavior.

Level 4: Seek alternatives or solutions. Questions at this level focus on exploring and identifying productive behaviors that are more likely to achieve desired outcomes.

MASTERY TEST

OBJECTIVE 4 To differentiate among inventory questions that (a) stimulate communication, (b) clarify information, (c) identify discrepancies, and (d) seek alternatives or solutions

Read the following dialogue and code the underlined sentences according to the four different levels of inventory questions: *SC* = stimulating communication, *CI* = clarifying information, *ID* = identifying discrepancies, *PA* = seeking potential alternatives or solutions. To complete this test successfully, you must accurately code all eight inventory questions.

Mr. Cotter explained the rules of the game and then asked the students to divide themselves into four equally numbered teams. As they were selecting their teams, Mr. Cotter noticed Julia slipping quietly out the back door. She didn't return until all the teams were selected and the game was under way. Mr. Cotter motioned to Julia to meet him in the hall. Once outside he said:

_____ 1. *Mr. C.:* "I noticed that you left the room as soon as the kids started to select their teams, and you didn't come back until the game started. What made you leave? Do you want to talk about it?"

Julia: "I didn't want to stay."

_____ 2. *Mr. C.:* "Can you tell me more about that?"

Julia: "I didn't think anyone would pick me for the team. I never get picked for any team. Like yesterday when we had to play kickball, I probably would have been the last one picked. . . . Just because I'm new here, nobody picks me."

_____ 3. *Mr. C.:* "How did you act then?"

Julia: "I told Mr. Gold that I had to go to the lavatory."

Mr. C.: "So when the class is dividing themselves into teams, you usually leave before you get picked."

Julia: "I guess so."

_____ 4. *Mr. C.:* "Tell me Julia, what does running away get you? How does it serve you?"

Julia: "Well, if I can't stick around, then I don't have to be the last one picked."

_____ 5. *Mr. C.:* "What are some other consequences?"

Julia: "I guess I just end up sitting and watching the others play."

_____ 6. *Mr. C.:* "How do you feel when you watch the others play?"

Julia: "Well . . . I guess I feel left out."

_____ 7. *Mr. C.:* "So you leave before you can get picked and then feel left out when you have to sit back and watch. Did your behavior get you what you wanted?"

Julia: "No."

_____ 8. *Mr. C.:* "What other ways could you act so that you don't feel left out?"

Learning Activity 4.2

▦ *Practicing Inventory Questions*

You are now ready to practice the fourth and final interpersonal communication skill presented in this chapter. Review the checklist, become comfortable with the items, and establish the settings for practicing inventory questions, making sure that the situation is not too complex. Only a few people need be involved in the dialogues. Use only one or two questions from each of the inventory categories.

The final words of caution are worth repeating. Keep your practice settings simple, keep the number of people involved in the dialogue to a minimum, and use just one or two questions from each of the inventory categories.

Inventory Questioning Behavior Checklist: Observer's Assessment

	Frequently	*Occasionally*	*Never*
1. The teacher asked questions that stimulated communication related to the student's thoughts, feelings, and/or behaviors.	_____	_____	_____

Examples:

_____

_____

| 2. The teacher avoided questions that required the student to justify his or her thoughts and feelings. | _____ | _____ | _____ |

Examples:

_____

_____

| 3. The teacher asked questions that enabled the student to clarify his or her thoughts and feelings. | _____ | _____ | _____ |

Examples:

_____

_____

| 4. The teacher asked questions that helped the student to recognize patterns of behavior. | _____ | _____ | _____ |

Examples:

_____

_____

| 5. The teacher asked questions that helped the student see the consequences of his or her behavior. | _____ | _____ | _____ |

Examples:

_____

_____

6. The teacher asked questions that enabled the student to identify discrepancies between actual and desired outcomes of his or her actions.

   Examples:

   _____

   _____

7. The teacher asked the student questions that helped him or her to seek alternative behaviors.

   Examples:

   _____

   _____

Inventory Questioning Behavior Checklist: Self-Assessment

1. I asked questions to stimulate communication related to thoughts, feelings, and behaviors.

   I specifically asked: _____

2. I avoided asking questions that might cause the speaker to become defensive. Instead, I asked: _____

   _____

3. To obtain more information and help the speaker clarify thoughts and feelings, I asked: _____

   _____

4. To help the speaker recognize specific behavior patterns, I asked: _____

   _____

5. To help the speaker identify the consequences and/or outcomes of his or her behavior, I asked: _____

   _____

6. To help the speaker recognize discrepancies between the actual versus desired outcomes of behavior, I asked: _____

   _____

7. To help the speaker seek alternative behaviors, I asked: _____

   _____

Summary

You have now mastered the first two clusters in the interpersonal communications taxonomy. You have the skills for a meaningful pattern of communication and interaction between you and your students, as well as with their parents and your professional colleagues. The third cluster of skills, Encouraging Alternative Behaviors, will bring the process to the next logical point in the cycle. We encourage you to explore the skills inherent at this level of the hierarchy by referring to the original Weinstein and Fantini model mentioned on pages 194–195.

Stop for a moment and consider the hierarchical nature of the skills that you have practiced in this chapter. You have learned to observe both yourself and others, and have become aware of, and sensitive to, verbal and nonverbal behavior. Your students should also have become sensitized to these cues. You have learned to listen to both the intellectual and emotional content of your own messages and those sent by others. Your students should also have developed this skill. You have also learned to reflect, or describe to your students, the messages that they are sending through their words and actions. As a result, your students are gaining insight into themselves, and learning how their behaviors are perceived by others. You have also learned to ask inventory questions. These will help both you and your students to identify discrepancies between actual and desired behavior, and to explore potential alternatives and solutions. All the interpersonal communication skills will also serve you well in interaction with parents, community members, and colleagues in your school.

Through practice and genuine respect for yourself and others, you will move to the next stage, Encouraging Alternative Behavior. In essence, you will be saying to your students, "If you don't like the consequences of your behavior, you have the power to change."

▦ Answer Key for Your Turn Exercises

ANSWER KEY

Your Turn: Differentiating Among the Four Types of
            Inventory Questions

1. SC
2. CI
3. CI
4. CI
5. CI

6. ID
7. CI
8. ID
9. PA

▦ Answer Keys for Mastery Tests

ANSWER KEY

Mastery Test, Objective 1

1. (a) lack of eye contact
   (b) failure to use physical space in a manner conducive for communication
   (c) failure to use facial expression that stimulates interpersonal communication
2. (a) body posture (huddled)
   (b) facial expression (forlorn)
3. (a) used physical space more effectively by inviting Matthew to sit closer to the board and the teacher
   (b) established eye contact with Matthew

   (c) didn't interrupt Matthew while he was talking
   (d) attended to Matthew's nonverbal behavior (look of frustration)
4. (a) established eye contact
   (b) smiled (facial expression)
   (c) put his hand on Matthew's shoulder
   (d) established close physical proximity
   (e) used silence appropriately
   (f) used subsummary to capture the essence of Matthew's verbal and nonverbal messages

ANSWER KEY

Mastery Test, Objective 2

Give yourself 3 points for each item that matches those on the key. Give yourself 2 points for those items where your choices only partially match. (There is some similarity between the responses.) Give yourself 0 points if you missed altogether. If you received below 85, reread the preceding Learning Activity. Also share these statements with a friend and compare your perceptions.

Intellectual (Cognitive) (I'm Saying)	Emotional (Affective) (I'm Feeling)	Intellectual (Cognitive) (I'm Saying)	Emotional (Affective) (I'm Feeling)
1. I can do it myself.	I feel — angry, frustrated, annoyed, belittled, cocky, and/or independent.	6. I won't answer that.	I feel — confronted, angry, annoyed, irritated, obstinate, and/or arrogant.
2. I don't want to talk to anyone.	I feel — angry, depressed, upset, withdrawn, and/or isolated.	7. Stop following me around.	I feel — annoyed, put upon, and/or cornered.
3. I got an A.	I feel — surprised, amazed, delighted, and/or proud.	8. Trust me.	I feel — confident, secure, afraid, worried, and/or manipulating.
4. I can't do it.	I feel — frustrated, confused, and/or tired.	9. I'll do it later.	I feel — harried, annoyed, angry, and/or flippant.
5. I can't please him.	I feel — frustrated, manipulated, controlled, and/or pressured.	10. Let me try it.	I feel — eager, confident, and/or desperate.

ANSWER KEY

Mastery Test, Objective 3

1. WM
2. I
3. I
4. I
5. WM
6. I
7. B
8. I
9. B
10. WM

ANSWER KEY

Mastery Test, Objective 4

1. SC
2. CI
3. CI
4. ID
5. ID
6. CI
7. ID
8. PA

■ Notes

1. Gerald A. Weinstein and Mario F. Fantini, *Toward Humanistic Education: A Curriculum of Affect* (New York: Praeger, 1970).
2. Alfred Alschuler, Judith Evans, Gerald Weinstein, and Roy Tamashiro, "Search for Self-Knowledge," *Me Forum* (Spring 1975). University of Massachusetts Press.
3. *Ibid.*

4. J. E. Weigand, ed., *Developing Teacher Competencies* (Englewood Cliffs, NJ: Prentice-Hall, 1971), p. 247.
5. Carl Rogers, *On Becoming a Person* (Boston: Houghton Mifflin, 1961).
6. A. Mehrabian and M. Wiener, "Non-Immediacy Between Communication and Object of Communication in a Verbal Message," *Journal of Consulting Psychology* 30 (1966). See also E. Robbins and R. Haase, "Power of Nonverbal Cues in Counseling Interactions: Availability, Vividness or Salience, *Journal of Counseling Psychology* 32 (1985), 502–513.
7. Quoted in A. Woolfolk and D. Brooks, "The Influence of Teachers' Nonverbal Behaviors on Students' Perceptions and Performance," *The Elementary School Journal* 85 (1985): 513. See also T. Plax, P. Kearney, J. McCroskey, and Y. Richmond, "Power in the Classroom VI: Verbal Control Strategies, Nonverbal Immediacy and Affective Learning," *Communication Education* 35 (1986): 43–55.
8. Amy Halberstadt, "Race, Socioeconomic Status, and Non-Verbal Behavior," in Aaron Siegman and Stanley Feldstein, eds. *Multichannel Integrations of Non-Verbal Behavior* (Hillsdale, NJ: L Erlbaum Assocs., 1985).
9. A. Mehrabian, "Significance of Posture and Position in the Communication of Attitude and Status Relationships," *Psychological Bulletin* 71 (1969): 359–372.
10. Edward T. Hall, *The Hidden Dimensions* (Garden City, NY: Doubleday, 1966), p. 108.
11. J. Andersen, P. Andersen, M. Murphy, and M. Wendt-Wasco, "Students' Nonverbal Communication in the Classroom: A Developmental Study in Grades K–12," *Communication Education* 34 (1985): 292–307.
12. Belle Rose Ragins and Eric Sundstrom, "Gender and Power in Organizations: A Longitudinal Perspective," *Psychological Bulletin* 105 (1989): 51–88.
13. J. Pearson, *Gender and Communication* (Dubuque, IA: William C. Brown, 1985).
14. Gerald Miller, *Speech Communication: A Behavioral Approach* (Indianapolis: Bobbs-Merrill, 1966), p. 73.
15. Joel Davitz, ed., *The Communication of Emotional Meaning* (New York: McGraw-Hill, 1964), p. 195.
16. M. Sadker, "What's Your Gender Communications Quotient?," in M. Sadker, D. Sadker, J. Kaser, *The Communications Gender Gap* (Washington, DC: The Mid-Atlantic Center for Sex Equity, The American University, 1983), pp. 4–5.
17. Gerald Weinstein, introduction in *Discovering Your Teaching Self: Humanistic Approaches to Effective Teaching*, by Richard Curwin and Barbara Fuhrmann (Englewood Cliffs, NJ: Prentice-Hall, 1975), p. xix. See also J. Meyers and W. Nelson, "Cognitive Strategies and Expectations of Social Competence in Young Adolescents," *Adolescence* 82 (1986): 291–303.
18. Daniel Malamud and Solomon Machover, *Toward Self-Understanding: Group Techniques in Self-Confrontation* (Springfield, IL: Charles C. Thomas, 1970).

Additional Readings

Babad, Elisha, Frank Bernieri, and Robert Rosenthal. "Nonverbal and Verbal Behavior of Preschool, Remedial, and Elementary School

Teachers." *American Educational Research Journal* 24, No. 3 (Fall 1987): 405–415.

Blair, Timothy. *Emerging Patterns of Teaching*. Columbus, OH: Merrill, 1988.

Brammer, Lawrence M. *The Helping Relationship Process and Skills*. Englewood Cliffs, NJ: Prentice-Hall, 1973.

Brooks, Douglas, "The First Day of School." *Educational Leadership* 24 (1985): 63–70.

Brooks, Douglas, and Anita Woolfolk. "The Effects of Students' Nonverbal Behavior on Teachers." *The Elementary School Journal* 88, No. 1 (September 1987): 51–63.

Carkuff, Robert, and Richard Pierce. *The Art of Helping III*. Amherst, MA: Human Resource Press, 1977.

Curwin, Richard, and Barbara Fuhrmann. *Discovering Your Teaching Self*. Englewood Cliffs, NJ: Prentice-Hall, 1975.

Dusek, J. B., ed. *Teacher Expectancies*. Hillsdale, NJ: Erlbaum, 1985.

Eckman, Paul, and Wallace V. Friesen. *Unmasking the Faces*. Englewood Cliffs, NJ: Prentice-Hall, 1975.

Hall, Edward, and Mildred Hall. "Nonverbal Communication for Educators." *Theory into Practice* 26, Special Issue (Dec. 1987): 364–367.

Harrison, R., and J. Weimann. "The Nonverbal Domain: Implications for Theory, Research, and Practice." In J. M. Wiemann and R. P. Harrison, eds., *Nonverbal Interaction*, Vol. I. Beverly Hills, CA: Sage, 1983, pp. 271–286.

Kagan, Norman. *Interpersonal Process Recall. A Method of Influencing Human Interaction*. East Lansing, MI: Michigan State University Press, 1975.

Long, Lynette. *Listening/Responding. Human Relations Training for Teachers*. Monterey, CA: Brooks/Cole Publishing Company, 1978.

Long, Lynette, Louis Paradise, and Thomas Long. *Questioning Skills for the Helping Process*. Monterey, CA: Brooks/Cole Publishing Company, 1981.

Madden, Lowell. "Do Teachers Communicate with Their Students As if They Were Dogs?," *Language Arts* 65, No. 2 (February 1988): 142–153.

Rosenthal, R., ed. *Skill in Nonverbal Communication*. Cambridge, MA: Oeleschager, Gunn and Hain, 1979.

Sadker, Myra. "What's Your Gender Communications Quotient?" In Myra Sadker, David Sadker, and Joyce Kaser, *The Communications Gender Gap*. Washington, DC: The Mid-Atlantic Center for Sex Equity, The American University, 1983, pp. 4–5.

Tannen, Deborah. *You Just Don't Understand*. New York: William Morrow, 1990.

Wubbels, Theo, Mieke Brekelmans, and Herman Hoomayers. "Interpersonal Teacher Behavior in the Classroom." In Barry Fraser and Herbert Walberg, eds., *Educational Environments*. Oxford: Pergamon Press, 1991.

Classroom Management

8

■ Wilford A. Weber

OBJECTIVES

1 To describe the four stages of the analytic-pluralistic classroom management process

2 To describe the nature and dynamics of the authoritarian, intimidation, permissive, cookbook, instructional, behavior-modification, socioemotional-climate, and group-process approaches to classroom management

3 To analyze a given classroom situation and to describe and justify the managerial strategy or strategies most likely to be effective in facilitating and maintaining those classroom conditions deemed desirable

No other aspect of teaching is so often cited as a major concern by prospective, beginning, and experienced teachers as classroom management. No other aspect of teaching is more frequently discussed in the professional literature — or the faculty lounge. The reason is quite simple. Classroom management is a complex set of behaviors the teacher uses to establish and maintain classroom conditions that will enable students to achieve their instructional objectives efficiently — that will enable them to learn. Thus, effective classroom management is the major prerequisite to effective instruction. Classroom management may be considered the most fundamental — and the most difficult — task the teacher performs.

The teacher's competence in classroom management is largely a function of his or her understanding of the dynamics of effective classroom management. Therefore, the purpose of this chapter is to enable you to cope more effectively with classroom management problems by helping you to understand more fully the management dimension of teaching. Because no one best approach to classroom management has been found, eight different approaches are examined: the authoritarian, intimidation, permissive, cookbook, instructional, behavior-modification, socioemotional-climate, and group-process approaches. Your own teaching should be more effective if you understand the managerial process and the range of managerial strategies that characterize each of those eight approaches, and if you are able to select and apply those specific managerial strategies most likely to be effective in a given situation.

A search of the literature on teaching reveals a number of rather different definitions of the term *classroom management.* They differ because each represents a particular philosophical position and operational approach regarding classroom management. Each approach has its advocates and its practitioners; however, no one of these managerial approaches has been proved best. Therefore, you are discouraged from adopting any one position and from relying on only one managerial approach. Rather, you are encouraged to consider accepting a pluralistic definition of the term *classroom management.* Such a definition broadens the range of approaches from which to select managerial strategies having the potential to create and sustain conditions that facilitate effective and efficient instruction. Only the teacher who adopts a pluralistic operational definition — who draws from each of the eight approaches — is able to select from a full range that managerial strategy most likely to be effective, given an accurate analysis of a particular situation. A pluralistic approach does not tie the teacher to only one set of managerial strategies as he or she attempts to establish and maintain those conditions in which teachers can instruct and students can learn. The teacher is free to consider all strategies that appear workable.

A definition sufficiently broad to reflect a pluralistic approach might state: classroom management is that set of activities by which the teacher establishes and maintains those classroom conditions that facilitate effective and efficient instruction.

OBJECTIVE

1 To describe the four stages of the analytic-pluralistic classroom management process

Learning Activity 1

The previous section argued for a definition of classroom management that views it as a process — a set of activities — by which the teacher establishes and maintains those conditions that facilitate effective and efficient instruction. The purpose of this section is to expand on that position by providing a description of classroom management as a four-stage, analytic-pluralistic process in which the teacher (1) specifies desirable classroom conditions, (2) analyzes existing classroom conditions, (3) selects and utilizes managerial strategies, and (4) assesses managerial effectiveness.

Specifying Desirable Classroom Conditions

The classroom management process is purposive; that is, the teacher uses various managerial strategies to achieve a well-defined, clearly identified purpose — the establishment and maintenance of those particular classroom conditions the teacher feels will facilitate effective and efficient instruction with his or her students. Consequently, the first step in an effective classroom management process is the specification of those conditions the teacher deems desirable — the specification of "ideal" conditions. The teacher should develop a clear, thoughtful conceptualization of those conditions he or she believes will enable him or her to instruct effectively. In so doing, the teacher should recognize that the conditions identified as desirable will, to a large extent, reflect his or her personal philosophy. That is, the conditions the teacher deems desirable will reflect his or her personal view of teaching rather than any set of universally accepted and empirically validated truths. Additionally, the teacher should recognize the need to continually assess the utility of his or her conceptualization and to modify it as circumstances dictate.

The teacher who takes care to specify the classroom conditions he or she believes are desirable has two major advantages over the teacher who does not: (1) the teacher will be far less likely to view classroom management as a process in which he or she simply reacts to problems as they occur, and (2) the teacher will have a set of objectives — managerial objectives — toward which his or her efforts are directed and by which his or her accomplishments are evaluated. The teacher who has a clear understanding of his or her managerial objectives is far more likely to be effective than the teacher who does not.

Analyzing Existing Classroom Conditions

Having specified desirable classroom conditions, the teacher is in a position to analyze existing classroom conditions — to compare the "real" with the "ideal." Such an analysis allows the teacher to identify (1) discrepancies between existing conditions and desired conditions and decide which require immediate attention, which require eventual attention, and which require monitoring; (2) potential problems — discrepancies that are likely to arise if the teacher fails to take preventive measures; and (3) those existing conditions the teacher wishes to maintain, encourage, and sustain because they are desirable. Thus, the second stage of the process is based on the assumption that the effective teacher is one who is skilled at analyzing classroom interaction and particularly sensitive to what is happening in his or her classroom; that is, the teacher has an accurate understanding of what his or her students are doing — and not doing — and what they are likely to do. He or she is fully aware of "what's going on."

Selecting and Utilizing Managerial Strategies

When the teacher's analysis of existing conditions suggests the need for intervention, the teacher should carefully select and apply the managerial strategy or strategies having the greatest potential to achieve the goal — be it to solve a problem, prevent a problem, or maintain a desirable condition. The effective teacher understands the full range of managerial strategies implied by each of a variety of approaches to classroom management, and selects and applies the strategy or strategies most appropriate to a particular situation. The teacher is most likely to be effective if the strategy he or she selects is "situation specific" and "student specific." That is, the teacher makes a thoughtful, informed, reasoned decision based on an insightful understanding of the circumstances and the anticipated reaction of the student or students. For example, a teacher seeking to reinforce appropriate student behavior might publicly praise a student known to find public praise rewarding but avoid this strategy for a student known to find public praise punishing.

This selection process may be thought of as a "computer search," in which the teacher considers the strategies "stored" in his or her "computer bank" and selects that strategy or those strategies holding the greatest promise in promoting the conditions deemed desirable.

(4) *Assessing Managerial Effectiveness*

In the fourth stage of the managerial process, the teacher assesses his or her managerial effectiveness. From time to time the teacher should evaluate the extent to which his or her efforts are establishing and maintaining desirable conditions — the extent to which he or she is narrowing the gap between the "real" and the "ideal." This evaluation process focuses on two sets of behaviors: teacher behaviors and student behaviors. In the first case, the teacher evaluates the extent to which he or she is using those managerial behaviors he or she intends to be using. The teacher assesses whether the managerial strategies he or she is using are most likely to bring about those conditions deemed desirable. In the second case, the more important of the two, the teacher evaluates the extent to which his or her students are behaving in desirable ways. Here, the major emphasis is on the extent to which students are behaving appropriately — the extent to which they are doing what they are supposed to be doing. Teacher and student behavioral data may be collected from three sources: the teacher, the student, and an independent observer.

MASTERY TEST

OBJECTIVE 1   To describe the four stages of the analytic-pluralistic classroom management process

Briefly describe each of the four stages of the analytic-pluralistic classroom management process. When you have done so, compare your responses to those in the Answer Key at the end of the chapter.

OBJECTIVE   2 To describe the nature and dynamics of the authoritarian, intimidation, permissive, cookbook, instructional, behavior-modification, socioemotional-climate, and group-process approaches to classroom management

Earlier, the third stage of the analytic-pluralistic managerial process was described as a "computer search," in which the teacher selects and applies the managerial strategy or strategies that appear to have the greatest potential to be effective in a particular situation, given his or her analysis of that situation. It was emphasized that the teacher is most likely to be effective if the strategy he or she selects is "situation specific" and "student specific." The teacher must base his or her selection on an insightful understanding of both the situation and the student. In effect, the teacher must predict how that particular student will react to the teacher's intervention. That prediction should be based on what the teacher knows about that student, not on gender or ethnic stereotypes. For example, the teacher should publicly praise Mark because he *knows* that Mark feels rewarded by public praise and should avoid publicly praising Phil because he *knows* that Phil feels punished by public praise.

Earlier, it was also noted that this stage requires the teacher to understand the full range of managerial strategies implied by each of a variety of approaches to classroom management. The purpose of this section of the chapter is to increase your understanding of the authoritarian, intimidation, permissive, cookbook, instructional, behavior-modification, socioemotional-climate, and group-process approaches. It is not unreasonable to expect that a teacher might utilize strategies from a number of these approaches during a typical school day; however, primary attention will be given to the behavior-modification, socioemotional-climate, and group-process approaches because both the literature and research seem to point to their effectiveness. Somewhat less attention is given to the other five approaches. Limitations of space preclude an in-depth examination of any of the approaches. Consequently, you are encouraged to read the books listed in the Additional Readings section of this chapter.

Learning Activity 2.1

The Authoritarian Classroom Management Approach

The authoritarian approach to classroom management views the managerial process as one in which student behavior is controlled by the teacher. The approach places the teacher in the role of establishing and maintaining order in the classroom through the use of controlling strategies; the major goal of the teacher is to control student behavior. The teacher assumes responsibility for controlling the conduct of the student because the teacher "knows best." The teacher is "in charge." This is most often done by creating and enforcing classroom rules and regulations.

One should not view authoritarian strategies as intimidating. The teacher who draws from the authoritarian approach does not force compliance, demean the student, or use harsh forms of punishment. The authoritarian teacher acts in the best interests of the student. This position is perhaps best explained by Canter and Canter, advocates of an approach they have called "assertive discipline."[1] Canter and Canter argue that the teacher has the right to establish clear expectations, limits, and consequences; insist on acceptable behavior from his or her students; and follow through with an appropriate consequence when necessary. Canter and Canter take great pains to emphasize that assertive discipline is a humane approach. They argue that all students need limits, and that teachers have the right to set and enforce such limits.

Although it is an oversimplification, it is suggested here that the authoritarian approach offers five strategies that the teacher might wish to include in his or her repertoire of managerial strategies: (1) establishing and enforcing rules; (2) issuing commands, directives, and orders; (3) utilizing mild desists; (4) utilizing proximity control; and (5) utilizing isolation and exclusion.

Establishing and Enforcing Rules

The process of *establishing rules* is one in which the teacher sets limits by telling the student what is expected of him or her and why. Thus, it is a process that clearly and specifically defines the teacher's expectations concerning classroom behavior. Rules are statements — usually written — that describe and make public appropriate and inappropriate student behaviors. Rules are formalized guidelines that describe acceptable and unacceptable student behaviors; their purpose is to guide and limit student conduct. It is argued that well-defined rules are necessary if students are going to work within known boundaries. Rules that specify what is and is not acceptable are necessary if students are to know where they stand; students have a right to know "the rules of the game." In addition, they have a right to know the consequences of breaking the rules. Advocates of the authoritarian approach insist that the teacher should establish and enforce rules that are realistic, reasonable, well defined, limited in number, and clearly understood, and that he or she should do so beginning with the first day of the school year. They stress that no group can work together successfully without established standards of behavior — rules that are public and enforced.

Many recommendations have been made about the establishment of classroom rules. Space limitations allow only two major issues to be highlighted here. The first issue has to do with the extent to which students are involved in making the rules. The second issue, somewhat related to the first, has to do with the number of rules that should be established. There are various positions concerning student involvement in rule establishment. The polar positions are (1) students should have a central role in making rules because they are more likely to follow rules they have had a hand in developing — the role of the teacher is to guide the students' efforts to develop good rules; and (2) the teacher should make the rules because the teacher — not the students — has the responsibility to determine which student behaviors are acceptable and which are not — the role of the students is to follow the rules, not to make them.

A position somewhere between these extremes seems to be most attractive; that is, the teacher should first specify a limited number of nonnegotiable rules and then work with students to add additional rules deemed necessary. This viewpoint also incorporates what appears to be the most appealing position about the number of rules issue: Teachers should work to keep the number of rules to a minimum. The argument is that fewer rules, consistently enforced, are more likely to be effective than are many rules because a great number of classroom rules make enforcement impossible. When rules go unenforced, the teacher's ability to manage the classroom is greatly diminished. Thus, the teacher should establish a reasonable number of enforceable rules.

◼ Issuing Commands, Directives, and Orders

The use of *commands, directives, and orders* is the third authoritarian managerial strategy discussed here. A command is a statement the teacher uses to tell the student that he or she is supposed to do something the teacher wants him or her to do. Clearly, there are times when it is necessary and appropriate for the teacher to tell the student that he or she is supposed to do something the teacher wants him or her to do. The kindly kindergarten teacher who asks her students to move to the story center is issuing a command; the friendly French teacher who asks his students to open their texts to page 47 is issuing a command; and the businesslike calculus teacher who asks one of her students to distribute the midterm examinations is issuing a command. Even in the most democratically run classrooms, teachers issue commands. Advocates of this authoritarian strategy argue that the use of clearly stated, easily understood commands, directives, and orders is a perfectly acceptable way for the teacher to control student behavior so long as the teacher does not use force to compel the student to obey. They recommend that commands should describe what the student is expected to do in specific terms. One is hard pressed to disagree with this viewpoint.

Utilizing Mild Desists

A variety of recommendations have been made about the enforcement of classroom rules. Most typically, these recommendations have ranged from mild to harsh forms of punishment. Many who support the authoritarian viewpoint recognize that severe types of punishment have been shown to be ineffective in the classroom setting. They do point, however, to the effectiveness of a mild form of punishment — *mild desist behaviors.* The terms *mild desist, gentle desist, soft reprimand,* and *corrective* are used as labels for that managerial strategy in which the teacher reproves the student for behaving in an unacceptable way — for violating a rule. The teacher — in a kindly manner intended to promote more acceptable behavior, and not in a hostile manner intended to condemn the unacceptable behavior — informs the student that he or she is behaving inappropriately, should stop behaving inappropriately, and should return to behaving appropriately. The literature suggests that the use of mild desists is an effective strategy for helping the student who is exhibiting minor forms of misconduct — who is off-task — to get back on-task with a minimum of fuss. Those who support the use of this strategy are quick to remind others that mild desist behaviors are intended to be helpful, not hostile. They are verbal or nonverbal teacher behaviors intended to inform, not to indict.

Utilizing Proximity Control

A teacher may be described as utilizing *proximity control* when he or she moves closer to a student whom the teacher sees misbehaving or whom the teacher believes is on the verge of misbehaving. This sort of action is based on the assumption that the physical presence of the teacher will be sufficient to cause the student to refrain from misbehaving. Proximity control is intended to defuse a disruptive or potentially disruptive situation; it is not intended to be punitive or intimidating. Its primary function is to let the student know — by the teacher's presence — that the teacher is aware of the student's behavior. Much like the mild desist, its intent is to inform, not to indict.

Utilizing Isolation and Exclusion

Isolation, exclusion, inschool suspension, inschool detention, suspension, and other forms of exile are strategies that teachers and school administrators are encouraged to consider as a response to serious student misbehavior. Authors representing a wide range of philosophies support the use of various types of exile. All attest to the effectiveness of these strategies, and most view them as nonpunitive. On the other hand, Wallen and Wallen describe isolation as the "ultimate punishment," the most severe allowable form of punishment.[2] The growing use of isolation suggests that various forms of exile — particularly inschool suspension — are viewed as effective in dealing with more serious forms of student misbehavior.

Summary

Given the arguments presented here, teachers who build a repertoire of classroom management strategies would do well to consider the inclusion of at least five authoritarian managerial strategies: the establishment and enforcement of classroom rules; the use of commands, directives, and orders; the use of mild desists; the use of proximity control; and the use of isolation and exclusion.

Learning Activity 2.2

The Intimidation Classroom Management Approach

The intimidation classroom management approach — like the authoritarian approach — views classroom management as the process of controlling student behavior. Unlike the authoritarian approach, which stresses the use of humane teacher behavior, the intimidation approach emphasizes the use of intimidating teacher behaviors — harsh forms of punishment such as sarcasm, ridicule, coercion, threats, force, and disapproval, for example. The role of the teacher is viewed as one in which the teacher forces students to behave according to the teacher's dictates. The student behaves in a manner acceptable to the teacher out of a fear to do otherwise.

Although intimidation strategies are widely used, few authors who have written in the area of classroom management acknowledge that they believe the intimidation approach to be workable. On the contrary, it is often criticized in the literature. Its most articulate critics may be Johnson and Bany, who point to the ineffectiveness of "punitive and threatening practices" and "dominative and pressuring practices," strategies at the core of the intimidation approach.[3] They assert — and it is agreed here — that objective evaluation of intimidation managerial strategies leads to the conclusion that they are, for the most part, ineffective. Their use usually results in only temporary solutions followed by even greater problems, the most serious of which are student hostility and the destruction of teacher-student interpersonal relationships. At the very best, intimidation strategies deal only with a problem's symptoms, not with the problem itself.

Utilizing Harsh Desists

The literature suggests that teachers who wish to build a repertoire of effective classroom management strategies will find "slim pickings" in the intimidation approach. The one intimidation strategy that might be viewed as useful in certain situations is the *harsh desist*. A harsh desist or reprimand is a loud, verbal command issued in a situation in which the intent of the teacher is to immediately stop a serious student misbehavior. For example, the teacher who comes upon two students fighting in the hallway may yell "Stop!" in the hope that the students — hearing the voice of a teacher — would be afraid to continue to misbehave and break the rules in the presence of a teacher who could bring serious sanctions to bear. Obviously, this type of intimidating behavior would be best used only to *stop* the fight — to stop the misconduct at once. When the fighting has stopped, the continued use of intimidating teacher behaviors would not be as productive as other strategies. The viewpoint here is that the teacher who relies heavily on intimidation managerial strategies — who attempts to control student behavior through the use of intimidating teacher behaviors — is likely to be ineffective.

Learning Activity 2.3

The Permissive Classroom Management Approach

The permissive classroom management approach stresses the need to *maximize student freedom*. The major theme is that the teacher should allow students to do what they want whenever and wherever they want. The role of the teacher is to promote the freedom of students and thereby foster their natural development. In essence, the teacher is expected to interfere as little as possible. The teacher is to encourage students to express themselves freely so that they might reach their fullest potential. Frankly, the permissive approach has few advocates. It represents a point of view that most consider impossible to put into operation in the public school context. It fails to recognize that the school and the classroom are social systems, and as such make certain demands on those who are major actors in those systems. Students — and teachers — are expected to exhibit socially acceptable behavior, for to do otherwise is to risk violating the rights of others.

On the other hand, many who contend that the permissive approach in its "pure" form is not productive in school and classroom environments suggest that the teacher should give students an opportunity to "do their own thing" when it makes sense to do so. Students, they argue, must have the opportunity to be "psychologically free"; take "safe risks"; negotiate those aspects of the school experience that are negotiable; and to develop self-directedness, self-discipline, and self-responsibility. If the teacher does not encourage a measure of freedom when it is appropriate, those things are not likely to happen. Clearly, the teacher must find ways to provide the student with as much freedom as he or she can handle in a responsible manner. Those who would consider drawing on managerial strategies that are representative of the permissive approach would do well to consider the validity of such arguments.

Learning Activity 2.4

The Cookbook Classroom Management Approach

The fourth approach discussed here is the cookbook, or "bag-of-tricks," approach. This approach to classroom management — an ill-fitting combination of old wives' tales, folklore, and common sense — takes the form of recommendations touted as remedies for all managerial ills. Descriptions of the cookbook approach usually consist of lists of things a teacher should or should not do when confronted with various types of classroom management problems. These lists of dos and don'ts are commonly found in articles with titles like "Thirty Ways to Improve Student Behavior." Because these lists often have the appearance of being quick and easy recipes, this approach is known as the cookbook approach. The following are typical of the kinds of statements one might find on such a list:

Always reprimand a pupil in private.
Never raise your voice when admonishing a student.
Always be firm and fair when dealing with students.
Never play favorites when rewarding students.
Always be sure that a student is guilty before punishing him or her.
Always be sure that all students know all your rules and regulations.
Always be consistent in enforcing your rules.

Because the cookbook approach is not derived from a well-conceptualized base, it lacks consistency. Even though many suggestions put forward by advocates of the cookbook approach make a great deal of sense, there is no set of principles that permits the teacher to generalize to other problems. The cookbook approach tends to cause a teacher to be *reactive* in dealing with classroom management. In other words, the teacher who uses a cookbook approach usually is reacting to specific problems and using short-range solutions. It is more effective to be *proactive*, to anticipate problems, and to use long-range solutions. The cookbook approach does not foster this type of managerial behavior, which attempts to deal with (1) possible problems before they surface in the classroom and (2) causes rather than symptoms.

Another difficulty caused by acceptance of the cookbook approach is that when the specific prescription fails to achieve its intended goal, the teacher cannot posit alternatives because the cookbook approach deals in absolutes. If "such and such" happens, the teacher does "so and so." On the other hand, advocates of a pluralistic approach assert that if "such and such" happens, the teacher can do "this or this." And if one of those fails to work, it is simply a matter of reanalyzing the situation and selecting from a variety of other attractive alternatives. Teachers who operate from a cookbook framework put themselves at a disadvantage and are unlikely to be effective classroom managers.

A final word of caution: the cookbook approach should not be confused with either an eclectic approach or a pluralistic approach. The cookbook approach consists of ill-fitting bits and pieces of advice concerning the managerial behaviors the teacher is to use in particular situations. An eclectic approach is one in which the best aspects of a variety of managerial approaches are combined to create a well-conceptualized philosophically, theoretically, and/or psychologically sound whole from which the teacher selects that particular managerial behavior appropriate to a situation. As noted previously, a pluralistic approach is one in which the teacher selects from a wide variety of managerial approaches that managerial strategy or combination of strategies having the greatest potential, given an analysis of the situation. It is argued here that the wise teacher places value on those managerial approaches and strategies that are conceptually sound. He or she does not blindly follow a recipe.

Learning Activity 2.5

The Instructional Classroom Management Approach

The instructional approach to classroom management is based on the contention that carefully designed and implemented instruction will prevent most managerial problems and solve those it does not prevent. This approach argues that effective management is the result of high quality instructional planning. Thus, the role of the teacher is to carefully plan "good lessons" — learning tasks that are tailored to the needs and abilities of each student, provide each student with a reasonable opportunity to be successful, gain and hold the interest of each student, and motivate each student. The "war cry" of those who advocate the instructional managerial approach is: "Make your lessons interesting."

Advocates of the instructional approach to classroom management tend to view instructional teacher behaviors as having the potential to achieve two central managerial goals: (1) preventing managerial problems, and (2) solving managerial problems. It is argued here that well-planned and well-executed instructional activities make a major contribution to the first of these goals — the prevention of managerial problems — and little contribution to the second goal — the solving of managerial problems. There is considerable evidence to indicate that well-designed, well-implemented instructional activities are a primary factor in preventing managerial problems. In addition, there is overwhelming support for the contention that poorly designed, poorly implemented instructional activities are a major contributor to managerial problems. There is little evidence, however, to support the notion that instructional activities are effective in solving managerial problems once they have occurred. At best, it seems that instructional managerial behaviors are useful in dealing with only minor sorts of student misbehavior.

An examination of the arguments made by advocates of the instructional approach suggests that the teacher should consider the following instructional managerial strategies: (1) providing interesting, relevant, and appropriate curriculum and instruction; (2) employing effective movement management; (3) establishing classroom routines; (4) giving clear directions; (5) utilizing interest boosting; (6) providing hurdle help; (7) planning for environmental changes; (8) planning and modifying the classroom environment; and (9) restructuring the situation.

Providing Interesting, Relevant, and Appropriate Curriculum and Instruction

Davis states that "a well-planned curriculum implemented by a well-prepared teacher who presents a study topic so that it holds the interest of the students has traditionally been considered a deterrent to disruptive classroom behavior."[4] Kounin has reported research findings that are particularly relevant about this topic.[5] He found that the key to effective classroom management is the teacher's ability to prepare and conduct lessons that prevent inattention, boredom, and misbehavior. He found that successful teachers teach well-prepared, well-paced lessons that proceed smoothly with a minimum of confusion or loss of focus, waste little time moving students from one activity to another, and provide seat-work activities geared to the abilities and interests of students. Successful teachers, he found, are prepared and therefore able to exhibit what he called "smoothness" and "momentum." Such teachers employ effective movement management.

Employing Effective Movement Management

Effective movement management is evidenced by a teacher who is able to move students smoothly from one activity to the next (smoothness) and to maintain momentum within an activity (momentum). The ability to regulate the flow and pace of classroom activities is viewed by many as crucial to preventing student off-task behavior.

Kounin also found that unsuccessful teachers are inadequately prepared and therefore unable to exhibit smoothness and momentum; they exhibit "jerkiness" and "slowdowns." They do not move students smoothly from one activity to the next, nor do they maintain momentum within an activity. Instead, they display behaviors Kounin saw as contributing to jerkiness (*thrusts, dangles, truncations,* and *flip-flops*) and slowdowns (*overdwelling* and *fragmentation*). A *thrust* is an instance in which the teacher suddenly bursts into an activity with a statement or direction for which the group is not ready. A *dangle* is an instance in which the teacher leaves one activity dangling in midair to start another activity, and then returns to the first activity. A *truncation* is an instance in which the teacher simply leaves one activity dangling in midair and starts another activity. A *flip-flop* is an instance in which the teacher terminates one activity, starts a second, and then returns to the first. *Overdwelling* is an instance in which the teacher spends too much time giving explanations and/or directions. *Fragmentation* is an instance in which the teacher breaks down an activity into several unnecessary steps when it could have been appropriately handled as a whole.

Kounin's contention is that these teacher behaviors hinder smoothness and momentum, and contribute to jerkiness and slowdowns, which result in student inattention, boredom, and misbehavior. It is his position that unsuccessful teachers display ineffective behaviors primarily because they have not given adequate attention to planning and preparing the instructional activities they would have their students undertake. Since space does not permit a thorough description of Kounin's work, you are encouraged to refer to his 1970 book if you feel that his findings are of particular interest; that book has become something of a classic in the classroom management literature.

Establishing Classroom Routines

The process of *establishing classroom routines* is one in which the teacher — beginning with his or her first encounter with the classroom group — helps students understand what it is they are to do with regard to typical daily activities. Clear explanations of the teacher's expectations regarding classroom routines are viewed as a critical first step in effectively managing the classroom and developing a productive classroom group. It is a process that minimizes the potential for problems.

Giving Clear Directions

A number of authors emphasize the importance of giving *clear, concise directions*. Long and Frye argue that clear, simple instructions are fundamental to promoting desired behaviors.[6] Others argue that directions should be clear, precise, concise, to the point, and carefully sequenced. The effective classroom manager gives clearly understood directions. The teacher who says to his or her students, "Please open your books to the problems you worked for homework," is much more likely to create problems than is the teacher who says, "Please open your math book to page 47 so we can take a look at the six problems you did for last evening's homework." Obviously, students are far more likely to do what the teacher would like them to do if the teacher is clear in communicating what students are to do. Giving clear directions contributes to managerial effectiveness because it helps avoid problems that can result from poor directions.

Utilizing Interest Boosting

Interest boosting is a process in which the teacher makes a special effort to show genuine interest in a student's work when the student first begins to show signs of boredom or restlessness. The teacher might go to the student, look at his or her work, compliment his or her effort, and make suggestions for further improvements. In this way the teacher helps the student stay on-task and prevents misbehavior.

Providing Hurdle Help

Hurdle help is assistance given by the teacher to help the student cope with a frustrating problem just when the student really needs it to avoid exploding or giving up. The intent is to provide assistance before a situation gets out of hand. Hurdle help is a particularly useful way to prevent disruptive behavior.

Planning for Environmental Changes

The classroom management literature suggests that, to minimize managerial problems, the teacher should anticipate certain environmental changes and prepare the classroom group to deal with them. For example, students should be prepared for the possibility of a substitute teacher in the teacher's absence. Advance planning helps students know how to behave before potentially disruptive situations arise. Thus, managerial problems are prevented.

Planning and Modifying the Classroom Environment

A number of authors have pointed to the importance of a classroom environment that is cheerful and orderly, that is organized to maximize productivity and minimize misbehavior, and that is well designed with regard to the physical placement of students. These authors stress the need to plan and modify the classroom environment to prevent or eliminate certain types of unacceptable behaviors.

Restructuring the Situation

Situation restructuring is a managerial strategy in which the teacher, through the use of a simple cue — a sentence or two at most — initiates a new activity or causes an old activity to be performed in a different manner. Changing the nature of the activity, changing the focus of attention, or finding new ways of doing the same old thing appear to be effective in preventing managerial problems, particularly those that result from boredom.

Summary

In summary, the teacher should remember the following about instructional managerial strategies: (1) well-planned and well-conducted instructional activities are a key factor in preventing managerial problems, but not in solving them; (2) the teacher should design instructional activities that take into account the abilities and interests of each student; (3) the teacher should move students smoothly from one activity to the next, and should maintain momentum within an activity; (4) the teacher should establish classroom routines and give clear directions; (5) the teacher should use interest boosting and hurdle help; and (6) the teacher should plan the classroom environment, plan for environmental changes, and restructure the situation when necessary. The use of these instructional managerial strategies will prevent many managerial problems.

Learning Activity 2.6

The Behavior-Modification Classroom Management Approach

The behavior-modification approach is based on principles from behavioral psychology. The major principle underlying this approach is that behavior is learned. This applies both to appropriate and inappropriate behavior. Advocates of the behavior-modification approach contend that a student misbehaves for one of two reasons: (1) the student has learned to behave inappropriately, or (2) the student has not learned to behave appropriately.

The behavior-modification approach is built on two major assumptions: (1) there are four basic processes that account for learning, and (2) learning is influenced largely, if not entirely, by events in the environment. Thus, the major task of the teacher is to master and apply the four basic principles of learning that behaviorists have identified as influencing human behavior. They are positive reinforcement, punishment, extinction, and negative reinforcement.

Utilizing Positive Reinforcement, Punishment, Extinction, and Negative Reinforcement

Terrence Piper[7] provides an easily understood explanation of the four basic processes. He suggests that when a student behaves, his or her behavior is followed by a consequence. He argues that there are only four basic categories of consequences: (1) when a reward is introduced, (2) when a punishment is introduced, (3) when a reward is removed, or (4) when a punishment is removed. The introduction of a reward is called *positive reinforcement*, and the introduction of a punishment is simply called *punishment*. The removal of a reward is called either *extinction* or *time out*, depending on the situation. The removal of a punishment is called *negative reinforcement*.

Behaviorists assume that the frequency of a particular behavior is contingent (depends) upon the nature of the consequence that follows the behavior. Positive reinforcement, the introduction of a reward after a behavior, causes the reinforced behavior to increase in frequency. Rewarded behavior is thus strengthened, and is repeated in the future.

Example

Brad prepares a neatly written paper, which he submits to the teacher (student behavior). The teacher praises Brad's work and comments that neatly written papers are more easily read than those that are sloppy (positive reinforcement). In subsequent papers, Brad takes great care to write neatly (the frequency of the reinforced behavior is increased).

Punishment is the introduction of an undesirable or aversive stimulus (punishment) after a behavior, and causes the punished behavior to decrease in frequency. Punished behavior tends to be discontinued.

Example

Jim prepares a rather sloppily written paper, which he submits to the teacher (student behavior). The teacher rebukes Jim for failing to be neat, informs him that sloppily written papers are difficult to read, and tells him to rewrite and resubmit the paper (punishment). In subsequent papers, Jim writes less sloppily (the frequency of the punished behavior is decreased).

Extinction is the withholding of an anticipated reward (the withholding of positive reinforcement) in an instance where that behavior was previously rewarded. Extinction results in the decreased frequency of the previously rewarded behavior.

Example

Susie, whose neat work has always been praised by the teacher, prepares a neatly written paper, which she submits to the teacher (student behavior previously reinforced by the teacher). The teacher accepts and subsequently returns the paper without comment (withholding of positive reinforcement). Susie becomes less neat in subsequent papers (the frequency of the previously reinforced behavior decreases).

Time out is the removal of the student from the reward; it reduces the frequency of reinforcement and causes the behavior to become less frequent.

Example

The students in Ms. Clark's English class have come to expect that she will give them an opportunity to play a word game if their work is satisfactory. This is an activity they all enjoy. Ms. Clark notes that all their papers were neatly done except Jim's paper. She tells Jim that he will not be allowed to participate in the class game and must, instead, sit apart from the group (removal of the student from the reward). Subsequently, Jim writes less sloppily (the frequency of the behavior decreases).

Negative reinforcement is the removal of an undesirable or aversive stimulus (punishment) after a behavior, and it causes the frequency of the behavior to be increased. The removal of the punishment serves to strengthen the behavior and increase its tendency to be repeated.

Example

Jim is the one student in the class who consistently presents the teacher with sloppy papers. Despite the teacher's constant nagging, Jim's work becomes no neater. For no apparent reason, Jim submits a rather neat paper. Ms. Clark accepts it without comment — and without the usual nagging (the removal of punishment). Subsequently, Jim's work becomes neater (the frequency of the behavior is increased).

Utilizing Positive Reinforcement

In summary, the teacher can encourage appropriate student behavior by using positive reinforcement (the introduction of a reward) and negative reinforcement (the removal of a punishment). The teacher can discourage inappropriate student behavior by using punishment (the introduction of an undesirable stimulus), extinction (the withholding of an anticipated reward), and time out (the removal of the student from the reward). It must be remembered that these consequences exert influence on student behavior in accordance with established behavioral principles. If the teacher rewards misbehavior, it is likely to be continued; if the teacher punishes appropriate behavior, it is likely to be discontinued.

According to Buckley and Walker,[8] timing and frequency of reinforcement and punishment are among the most important principles in behavior modification. Student behavior that the teacher wishes to encourage should be reinforced immediately after it occurs; student behavior that the teacher wishes to discourage should be punished immediately after it occurs. Behavior that is not reinforced at once tends to be weakened; behavior that is not punished at once tends to be strengthened. Thus, the teacher's timing of rewards and punishment is important. "The sooner the better" should be the motto of those teachers who want to maximize their management effectiveness.

Of equal importance is the frequency with which a behavior is reinforced. Continuous reinforcement, reinforcement that follows each instance of the behavior, results in learning that behavior more rapidly. Thus, if a teacher wishes to strengthen a particular student behavior, he or she should reward it each time it occurs. While continuous reinforcement is particularly effective in the early stages of acquiring a specific behavior, once the behavior has been established, it is more effective to reinforce intermittently.

There are two approaches to intermittent reinforcement: an interval schedule and a ratio schedule. An *interval schedule* is one in which the teacher reinforces the student after a specified period of time. For example, a teacher using an interval schedule might reinforce a student every hour. A *ratio schedule* is one in which the teacher reinforces the student after the behavior has occurred a certain number of times. For example, a teacher using a ratio schedule might reinforce the student after every fourth occurrence of the behavior. For the most part, an interval schedule is best for maintaining a consistent behavior over time, while a ratio schedule is best for producing more frequent occurrence of a behavior.

Positive reinforcement has been defined as the introduction of a reward; extinction and time out have been defined as the removal of a reward. Punishment has been defined as the introduction of a punishment; negative reinforcement has been defined as the removal of a punishment. In other words, behavioral consequences have been discussed as either the introduction or the removal of rewards, or the introduction or removal of punishment. Therefore, let's take a closer look at the notions of reward and punishment.

By definition, a reward or reinforcer is any stimulus that increases the frequency of the behavior that preceded it; and, by definition, a punishment (or aversive stimulus) is anything that decreases the frequency of the behavior that preceded it. Different authors classify reinforcers differently. The behavior-modification literature is replete with labels. There is general agreement, however, that reinforcers may be classified into two major categories: (1) *primary reinforcers*, which are not learned and which are necessary to sustain life (food, water, and warmth are examples); and (2) *conditioned reinforcers*, which are learned (praise, affection, and money are examples). Conditioned reinforcers are of several distinct types, including *social reinforcers* — rewarding behavior by other individuals within a social context (praise or applause), *token reinforcers* — intrinsically nonrewarding objects that may be exchanged at a later time for tangible reinforcers (money or a system of check marks that can be traded in for free time or school supplies), and *activity reinforcers* — rewarding activities offered the student (outdoor play, free reading time, or being allowed to choose the next song).

Space limitations preclude a complete description of how various types of unconditioned and conditioned reinforcers can be used by the teacher to manage student behavior effectively. Many of the resources listed in the Additional Readings do that quite well. It is important to emphasize one point here: a reward is defined in terms of its ability to increase the frequency of the rewarded behavior. Thus, reward (and punishment) can be understood only in terms of an individual student. One student's reward may be another student's punishment. A response that the teacher intended to be rewarding may be punishing, and a response intended to be punishing may be rewarding. The latter is often the case. A common example occurs when a student misbehaves to get attention. The teacher's subsequent scolding rewards rather than punishes the attention-hungry student and, consequently, the student continues to misbehave to get the attention he or she seeks.

The above example suggests that the teacher must take great care in selecting a reinforcer that is appropriate to a particular student. While this is true, the selection process need not be difficult. Because reinforcers are idiosyncratic to the individual student, the student is in the best position to designate them. Thus, the best reinforcer is one selected by the student. Givener and Graubard[9] suggest three methods to identify individually oriented reinforcers: (1) obtain clues concerning potential reinforcers by observing what the student likes to do; (2) obtain additional clues by observing what follows specific student behaviors; that is, try to determine what teacher and peer behaviors seem to reinforce his or her behavior; and (3) obtain additional clues by simply asking students what they would like to do with free time, what they would like to have, and what they would like to work for.

Teachers who feel that it is important to reward appropriate student behavior do so in many ways. These range from "pats on the back" to "happy notes" informing a student's parents that the student has improved his or her conduct. Most teachers recognize that praise and encouragement are powerful social reinforcers. Additionally, behavior modification offers the teacher a number of managerial strategies that involve the use of reinforcement. Although much has been written about each of these strategies and their effectiveness, space allows only a brief description here.

Utilizing Modeling

Modeling is a process in which the student, by observing another person behaving, acquires new behaviors without himself being exposed to the consequences of the behavior. Modeling, as a managerial strategy, may be viewed as a process in which the teacher demonstrates, by his or her own actions, the values and behaviors he or she wants students to acquire and display.

Utilizing Shaping

Shaping is a procedure in which the teacher requires the student to perform a series of behaviors that approximate the desired behavior. Each time the student performs the required approximation or one a bit closer to the desired behavior, the teacher reinforces the student until the student is consistently able to perform the desired behavior. Thus, shaping is a behavior modification strategy used to encourage the development of new behaviors.

Utilizing Token Economy Systems

A *token economy system* usually consists of three elements intended to change the behavior of students: (1) a set of carefully written instructions that describe the student behaviors the teacher will reinforce, (2) a well-developed system for awarding tokens to students who exhibit the behaviors that have been specified as appropriate, and (3) a set of procedures that allows students to exchange tokens they have earned for "prizes" or opportunities to engage in special activities. The implementation and operation of a token economy requires a great investment of time and energy on the part of the teacher. Consequently, its most typical — and efficient — use is in situations where a large percentage of the students in a class are misbehaving and the teacher seeks to rapidly change the behavior of those students. A well-managed token economy can be an effective means for modifying the behavior of groups of students.

Utilizing Contingency Contracting

A *contingency contract* or behavioral contract, an agreement negotiated between the teacher and a misbehaving student, specifies the behaviors the student has agreed to exhibit and indicates what the consequences — the payoff — will be if the student exhibits those behaviors. A contract is a written agreement between the teacher and a student detailing what the student is expected to do, and what reward he or she will be given for doing those things. As in all contracts, both parties obligate themselves. The student is committed to behave in certain ways deemed appropriate, and the teacher is committed to reward the student when he or she does so. Contracting tends to be a somewhat time-consuming process. Therefore, it is usually reserved for those instances in which a student is exhibiting serious misbehaviors on a rather routine basis. Contracting can be an effective tool in such instances.

Utilizing Group Contingencies

Group contingencies consist of using a procedure in which the consequences — reinforcement or punishment — that each student receives depend not only on his or her own behavior, but also on the behavior of the members of his or her group. Usually, it involves an instance in which the rewards for each individual member of the class are dependent on the behavior of one or more or all of the other students in the class.

Reinforcing Incompatible Alternatives

Reinforcing an incompatible alternative involves a situation in which the teacher rewards a behavior that cannot coexist with the disruptive behavior the teacher wishes to eliminate.

Utilizing Behavioral Counseling

Behavioral counseling is a process involving a private conference between the teacher and the student — a conference intended to help the misbehaving student see that his or her behavior is inappropriate, and to plan for change. It is argued that such conferences help the student to understand the relationship between his or her actions and the resulting consequences, and to consider alternative actions likely to result in desired consequences.

▒ *Utilizing Self-Monitoring*

Self-monitoring (self-management, self-recording) is a strategy in which the student records some aspect of his or her behavior to modify that behavior. Self-monitoring systematically increases the student's awareness of a behavior he or she wishes to decrease or eliminate. Self-monitoring promotes self-awareness through self-observation.

▒ *Utilizing Cues, Prompts, and Signals*

A *cue* is a verbal or nonverbal prompt or signal — a reminder — given by the teacher when he or she feels the student needs to be reminded either to behave in a certain way or to refrain from behaving in a certain way. Thus, a cue can be used to encourage or discourage a given behavior. Unlike a reinforcer, a cue precedes a response; it "triggers" a behavior.

Having briefly discussed the use of rewards, let us now turn to the thorniest of dilemmas faced by advocates of the behavior-modification approach — the use of punishment to eliminate inappropriate behavior. This is a subject of great controversy, controversy that is far from resolution. While it appears that every author has a somewhat different opinion, three major viewpoints seem most prominent: (1) the appropriate use of punishment is highly effective in eliminating student misbehavior; (2) the judicious use of punishment in limited types of situations can have desirable immediate, short-term effects on student misbehavior, but the risk of negative side effects requires its use to be carefully monitored; and (3) the use of punishment should be avoided completely because student misbehavior can be dealt with just as effectively with other techniques that do not have the potential negative side effects of punishment.

Few authors present a viewpoint other than their own; however, Sulzer and Mayer[10] do help the reader examine the advantages and disadvantages of using punishment. They identify the following advantages: (1) punishment does stop the punished student behavior immediately, and it reduces the occurrence of that behavior for a long period of time; (2) punishment is informative to students because it helps students to discriminate rapidly between acceptable and unacceptable behaviors; and (3) punishment is instructive to other students because it may reduce the probability that other class members will imitate the punished behaviors. Disadvantages include: (1) punishment may be misinterpreted (sometimes a specific, punished behavior is generalized to other behaviors; for example, the student who is punished for talking out of turn may stop responding, even when appropriate to do so); (2) punishment may cause the punished student to withdraw altogether; (3) punishment may cause the punished student to become aggressive; (4) punishment may produce negative peer reactions; for example, students may exhibit undesirable behaviors (ridicule or sympathy) toward the punished student; and (5) punishment may cause the punished student to become negative about himself or herself or about the situation; for example, punishment may diminish feelings of self-worth or produce a negative attitude toward school.

In weighing the advantages and disadvantages of using punishment, Sulzer and Mayer conclude that alternative procedures for reducing student behaviors should always be considered. They contend that once a punishment procedure is selected, it should be employed with the utmost caution and its effects should be carefully monitored. They also suggest that the teacher anticipate and be prepared to handle any negative consequences that might arise. Finally, they recommend that teachers find desirable behaviors to reinforce at the same time they are withholding reinforcement or punishing undesirable behavior.

Other behaviorists also point to research that suggests punishment is largely ineffective in the classroom setting and argue against its use. As noted earlier, advocates of the authoritarian approach view mild forms of punishment (mild desists) as effective, whereas advocates of the intimidation approach view harsher forms of punishment as effective. Advocates of the socioemotional-climate approach argue for the effectiveness of another form of punishment — the application of logical consequences. Many behaviorists argue that the effective teacher is one who is able to modify inappropriate student behavior through the use of strategies other than punishment; they advocate the use of extinction and time out. Several other strategies are also advocated; these include overcorrection, response cost, negative practice, satiation, and fading.

Utilizing Overcorrection

Overcorrection is a mild form of punishment in which the teacher requires a disruptive student to restore the environment to a better condition than existed before his or her disruptiveness. The student is required to go beyond simple restitution and to make things better than they were before he or she misbehaved.

Utilizing Response Cost

Response cost is a procedure in which a specified reward is removed following an inappropriate behavior. The teacher arranges the rules of the classroom so that a particular cost — a fine — is levied for certain misbehaviors. Inappropriate behavior costs the student an already earned reward.

Utilizing Negative Practice

Negative practice is a process in which the student who exhibits an undesirable behavior is required by the teacher to repeatedly perform that behavior until it becomes punishing — to repeat that behavior to the point at which the behavior itself becomes aversive. Those who advocate the use of negative practice encourage teachers to use this procedure only to eliminate undesirable behaviors that can be repeated without causing additional harm or disruption.

Utilizing Satiation

Satiation — saturation — is the process of presenting a reinforcing stimulus at such a high rate that it is no longer desirable and becomes aversive. An "oversupply" of a particular reinforcer is presented so that the effectiveness of the reinforcer is diminished. In the typical situation, a teacher might insist that a misbehaving student continue to perform that misbehavior until he or she tires of doing it.

▨ *Utilizing Fading*

Fading is a process in which the teacher gradually eliminates the cues and prompts for a given kind of behavior. Supporting stimuli — cues and prompts — originally provided are gradually omitted until the student can perform the desired behavior without assistance.

▨ *Summary*

Clearly, this section on the behavior-modification approach cannot begin to describe in detail the many managerial strategies that constitute this approach. Should you feel the need for more information on this subject, books by Axelrod[11] and Clarizio[12] provide in-depth descriptions of behavior-modification strategies. Given the discussion in this section, the following seems to be an accurate summary of the lessons to be gained from the behavior-modification approach: (1) rewarding appropriate student behavior and withholding the rewarding of inappropriate behavior are effective in achieving better classroom behavior; (2) punishing inappropriate student behavior may eliminate that behavior, but may have serious negative side effects; and (3) rewarding appropriate behavior is probably the key to effective classroom management.

Learning Activity 2.7

The Socioemotional-Climate Classroom Management Approach

The socioemotional-climate approach to classroom management has its roots in counseling and clinical psychology and, consequently, places great importance on interpersonal relationships. It builds on the assumption that effective classroom management — and effective instruction — is largely a function of positive teacher-student relationships. Advocates of the socioemotional-climate approach emphasize that the teacher is the major determiner of interpersonal relationships and classroom climate. Consequently, the central managerial task of the teacher is to build positive interpersonal relationships and to promote a positive socioemotional climate.

Many of the ideas that characterize the socioemotional-climate approach may be traced to the work of Carl Rogers.[13] His major premise is that the facilitation of significant learning is largely a function of certain attitudinal qualities that exist in the interpersonal relationship between the teacher (the facilitator) and the student (the learner). Rogers has identified several attitudes that he believes are essential if the teacher is to have maximum effect in facilitating learning: realness, genuineness, and congruence; acceptance, prizing, caring, and trust; and empathic understanding.

▨ *Communicating Realness*

Realness is viewed by Rogers as the most important attitude the teacher can display in facilitating learning. Realness is an expression of the teacher being himself or herself; that is, the teacher is aware of his or her feelings, accepts and acts on them, and is able to communicate them when appropriate. The teacher's behavior is congruent with his or her feelings. In other words, the teacher is genuine. Rogers suggests that realness allows the teacher to be perceived by students as a real person, a person with whom they can relate. Thus, the establishment of positive interpersonal relationships and of a positive socioemotional climate is enhanced by the teacher's ability to display realness. Sincere expressions of enthusiasm or boredom are typical examples of realness.

Communicating Acceptance

Acceptance is the second attitude that Rogers views as important to teachers who are successful in facilitating learning. Acceptance indicates that the teacher views the student as a person of worth. It is nonpossessive caring for the learner. It is an expression of basic trust — a belief that the student is trustworthy. Accepting behaviors are those that make the student feel trusted and respected, those that enhance his or her self-worth. Through acceptance, the teacher displays confidence and trust in the ability and potential of the student. Consequently, the teacher who cares, prizes, and trusts the student has a far greater chance of creating a socioemotional climate that promotes learning than does the teacher who fails to do so.

Communicating Empathic Understanding

Empathic understanding is an expression of the teacher's ability to understand the student from the student's point of view. It is a sensitive awareness of the student's feelings, and it is nonevaluative and nonjudgmental. Expressions of empathy are all too rare in the classroom. When they occur, the student feels that the teacher understands what he or she is thinking and feeling. Rogers argues that clearly communicated, sensitively accurate empathic understanding greatly increases the probability that positive interpersonal relationships, a positive socioemotional climate, and significant learning will occur.

In summary, Rogers suggests there are certain conditions that facilitate learning, and most prominent among these is the attitudinal quality of the interpersonal relationship between the teacher and the student. He has identified three attitudes that are crucial to the rapport-building process: realness, acceptance, and empathy.

Ginott[14] has presented views similar to those of Rogers. His writing also stresses the importance of congruence, acceptance, and empathy, and gives numerous examples of how these attitudes may be manifested by the teacher. In addition, Ginott has emphasized the importance of *effective communication* in promoting positive teacher-student relationships. How the teacher communicates is viewed as being of decisive importance.

Utilizing Effective Communication

Ginott has written that the cardinal principle of communication is that the teacher talk to the situation, not to the personality and character of the student. When confronted with undesirable student behavior, the teacher is advised to describe what he or she sees, what he or she feels, and what needs to be done. The teacher accepts the student, but not the student's behavior; the teacher "separates the sin from the sinner." This notion has been called unconditional positive regard. (As you can see, it is identical to Rogers's notion of acceptance.) The teacher views the student as a person of worth, regardless of how the student behaves. In addition, Ginott has provided a list of recommendations describing ways in which the teacher might communicate effectively. Although a lengthy explanation of each is not possible here, a summary of these recommendations is:

1. Address the student's situation. Do not judge his or her character and personality because this can be demeaning.
2. Describe the situation, express feelings about the situation, and clarify expectations concerning the situation.
3. Express authentic and genuine feelings that promote student understanding.
4. Diminish hostility by inviting cooperation and providing students with opportunities to experience independence.
5. Decrease defiance by avoiding commands and demands that provoke defensive responses.
6. Recognize, accept, and respect the student's ideas and feelings in ways that increase his or her feelings of self-worth.
7. Avoid diagnosis and prognosis, which result in labeling the student, because this may be disabling.
8. Describe processes and do not judge products or persons. Provide guidance, not criticism.
9. Avoid questions and comments that are likely to incite resentment and invite resistance.
10. Avoid the use of sarcasm because this may diminish the student's self-esteem.
11. Resist the temptation to provide the student with hastily offered solutions; take the time to give the student the guidance needed to solve his or her own problem. Encourage autonomy.
12. Attempt to be brief; avoid preaching and nagging, which are not motivating.
13. Monitor and be aware of the impact one's words are having on students.
14. Use appreciative praise because it is productive; avoid judgmental praise because it is destructive.
15. Listen to students and encourage them to express their ideas and feelings.

This list cannot do justice to Ginott's views. The reader who desires a fuller explanation of these recommendations and who wishes to examine examples that support Ginott's suggestions is encouraged to refer to his last book, *Teacher and Child.*

Many of those who share Ginott's views about effective communication stress the importance of active listening and humor. *Active listening* is a process in which the teacher listens carefully to the student and then feeds back the message in an attempt to show that he or she understands what the student is trying to say. Advocates of this strategy argue that active listening creates a situation in which the student is more likely to feel understood and valued; some view it as a way to operationalize the concept of acceptance. *Humor* is a strategy that can be used to ease tension in an anxiety-producing situation, or to make a student aware of a lapse in behavior. Humor should be genial, kindly, and gentle, and should not be sarcastic or ridiculing because this endangers teacher-student relationships and student feelings of self-worth.

A third viewpoint that might be classified as a socioemotional approach is that of Glasser.[15] Although an advocate of teacher realness, acceptance, and empathy, Glasser does not give these primary emphasis. Rather, he stresses the importance of teacher involvement and the use of a managerial strategy called *reality therapy*.

Utilizing Reality Therapy

Glasser asserts that the single basic need that people have is the need for identity — feelings of distinctiveness and worthiness. He argues that to achieve a "success" identity in the school context, one must develop social responsibility and feelings of self-worth. Social responsibility and self-worth are the result of the student developing a positive relationship with others — both peers and adults. Thus, it is involvement that is crucial to the development of a success identity. Glasser argues that student misbehavior is the result of the student's failure to develop a success identity. He proposes an eight-step, one-to-one counseling process the teacher might use to help the student change his or her behavior. This process has been called *reality therapy* and is in many ways similar to behavior contracting, a behavior-modification strategy discussed in the previous learning activity. Glasser suggests that the teacher should:

1. Become personally involved with the student; accept the student, but not the student's misbehavior; indicate a willingness to help the student in the solution of his or her behavior problem.
2. Elicit a description of the student's present behavior; deal with the problem, do not evaluate or judge the student.
3. Assist the student in making a value judgment about the problem behavior; focus on what the student is doing to contribute to the problem and to his or her failure.
4. Help the student plan a better course of action; if necessary, suggest alternatives; help the student reach his or her own decision based on his or her own evaluation, thereby fostering self-responsibility.
5. Guide the student in making a commitment to the course of action he or she has selected.
6. Reinforce the student as he or she follows the plan and keeps the commitment; be sure to let the student know that you are aware that progress is being made.
7. Accept no excuses if the student fails to follow through with his or her commitment; help the student understand that he or she is responsible for his or her own behavior; alert the student of the need for a better plan; acceptance of an excuse communicates a lack of caring.
8. Allow the student to suffer the natural and realistic consequences of misbehavior, but do not punish the student; help the student try again to develop a better plan and expect him or her to make a commitment to it.

Glasser views the above process — reality therapy — as effective for the teacher who wishes to help the misbehaving student develop more productive behavior. In addition, Glasser proposes a similar process for helping a whole class deal with group behavior problems — the social problem-solving classroom meeting. As a managerial strategy, the classroom meeting is perhaps best thought of as a group-process managerial strategy. Therefore, it is described in Learning Activity 2.8, the next section of this chapter.

A fourth and final viewpoint that might be seen as a socioemotional-climate approach is that of Dreikurs.[16] While it is true that works by Dreikurs and his colleagues contain many ideas that have important implications for effective classroom management, there are two that stand out from the others: (1) an emphasis on the democratic classroom in which the students and the teacher share responsibility for both process and progress, and (2) a recognition of the impact that natural and logical consequences have on the behavior — and misbehavior — of students.

Developing a Democratic Classroom

A dominant theme in this approach is the assumption that student conduct and achievement are facilitated in a *democratic classroom*. The autocratic classroom is one in which the teacher uses force, pressure, competition, punishment, and the threat of punishment to control student behavior. The laissez-faire classroom is one in which the teacher provides little, if any, leadership and is overly permissive. Both the autocratic classroom and the laissez-faire classroom lead to student frustration, hostility, and/or withdrawal; both result in a devastating lack of productivity. True productivity can occur only in a democratic classroom — one in which the teacher shares responsibility with students. It is in a democratic atmosphere that students expect to be treated and are treated as responsible, worthwhile individuals capable of intelligent decision making and problem solving. And it is the democratic classroom that fosters mutual trust between the teacher and the students, and among students.

The teacher who attempts to establish a democratic classroom atmosphere must not abdicate his or her responsibilities as a leader. The effective teacher is not an autocrat, but neither is he or she an anarchist. The democratic teacher guides, the autocratic teacher dominates, and the laissez-faire teacher abdicates. The democratic teacher teaches responsibility by sharing responsibility.

The key to a democratic classroom organization is regular and frank group discussions. Here the teacher — acting the role of leader — guides the group in group discussions that focus on problems of concern. Three products of that process have been identified: (1) the teacher and the students have an opportunity to express themselves in a way that is sure to be heard, (2) the teacher and the students have an opportunity to get to know and understand one another better, and (3) the teacher and the student are provided with an opportunity to help one another. He notes that an essential by-product of such group discussions is the opportunity the teacher has to influence those values of his or her students that may differ from those considered more productive.

Although there is an emphasis on the importance of the teacher's developing a democratic socioemotional classroom climate, you will see in the next learning activity that these views on the value of shared leadership and group discussions are similar to those of the advocates of the group-process approach.

Employing Logical Consequences

The second major emphasis concerns the impact of consequences on student behavior. In the classroom setting, natural consequences are those that are solely the result of the student's own behavior. *Logical consequences* are those that are more or less arranged by the teacher, but are a logical outcome of the student's behavior. The natural consequence of the student's grasping a hot test tube is that he or she will burn his or her hand. The logical consequence of breaking the test tube is that the student will have to pay the cost of replacing it. To be considered a logical consequence, however, the student must view the consequence as logical. If it is viewed as punishment, the positive effect is lost. Although most behaviorists do not make a distinction between logical consequences and punishments, most advocates of the socioemotional-climate approach do. Dreikurs and Grey suggest five criteria they view as useful in distinguishing logical consequences from punishment:

1. Logical consequences express the reality of the social order, not of the person; punishment expresses the power of a personal authority; a logical consequence results from a violation of an accepted social rule.
2. Logical consequences are logically related to the misbehavior; punishment rarely is logically related; the student sees the relationship between the misbehavior and its consequences.
3. Logical consequences involve no element of moral judgment; punishment inevitably does; the student's misbehavior is viewed as a mistake, not a sin.
4. Logical consequences are concerned only with what will happen next; punishment is in the past; the focus is on the future.
5. Logical consequences are applied in a friendly manner; punishment involves either open or concealed anger; the teacher should try to disengage himself or herself from the consequences.

In summary, logical consequences express the reality of the social order, are intrinsically related to the misbehavior, involve no element of moral judgment, and are concerned only with what will happen next. On the other hand, punishment expresses the power of personal authority, is not logically related to the misbehavior, involves moral judgment, and deals with the past. As does Glasser, Dreikurs stresses the importance of the positive effect that the application of logical consequences has on the behavior of students. Both argue it is crucial that teachers help students understand the logical relationship between their behavior and the consequences of that behavior. Both also argue that it is important the teacher be able to use logical consequences appropriately — and avoid punishment — in helping students change their behaviors to those that are more desirable.

Summary

The teacher who is an effective classroom manager should include the following socioemotional-climate strategies in his or her behavioral repertoire: communicating realness, acceptance, and empathic understanding; utilizing effective communication; exhibiting unconditional positive regard and active listening; utilizing humor; utilizing reality therapy; developing a democratic classroom; and employing logical consequences. All are strategies that facilitate the establishment and maintenance of positive teacher-student interpersonal relationships and a positive socioemotional climate.

Learning Activity 2.8

The Group-Process Classroom Management Approach

The *group-process approach* — also known as the *sociopsychological approach* — is based on principles from social psychology and group dynamics. The major premise underlying the group-process approach is based on the following assumptions: (1) schooling takes place within a group context — the classroom group; (2) the central task of the teacher is to establish and maintain an effective, productive classroom group; (3) the classroom group is a social system containing properties common to all social systems, and the effective, productive classroom group is characterized by certain conditions that are compatible with those properties; and (4) the classroom management task of the teacher is to establish and maintain such conditions. While there is some disagreement concerning the conditions that characterize the effective, productive classroom group, you will examine the conditions described in three excellent sources: the work of Schmuck and Schmuck, Johnson and Bany, and Kounin. First let us focus on six properties identified by Schmuck and Schmuck[17] regarding classroom management: expectations, leadership, attraction, norms, communication, and cohesiveness.

Clarifying Expectations

Expectations are those perceptions that the teacher and the students hold regarding their relationships to one another. They are individual predictions of how self and others will behave. Therefore, expectations about how members of the group will behave greatly influence how the teacher and the students behave in relation to one another. The effective classroom group is one in which expectations are accurate, realistic, and clearly understood. The behavior of the teacher communicates to students what behavior the teacher expects of them, and the students, in turn, tend to conform to those expectations. Thus, if students feel the teacher expects them to misbehave, it is likely that they will misbehave; if students feel the teacher expects them to behave appropriately, it is more likely that they will behave appropriately.

Sharing Leadership

Leadership is best thought of as those behaviors that help the group move toward the accomplishment of its objectives. Thus, leadership behaviors consist of actions by group members; included are actions that aid in setting group norms, move the group toward its goals, improve the quality of interaction between group members, and build group cohesiveness. By virtue of their role, teachers have the greatest potential for leadership. In an effective classroom group, however, leadership functions are performed by both the students and the teacher. An effective classroom group is one in which the leadership functions are well distributed, and where all group members can feel power and self-worth in accomplishing academic tasks and in working together. When students share classroom leadership with the teacher, they are far more likely to be self-regulating and responsible for their own behavior. Thus, the effective teacher is one who creates a climate in which students perform leadership functions. The teacher improves the quality of group interaction and productivity by training students to perform goal-directed leadership functions and by dispersing leadership throughout the group.

Fostering Attraction

Attraction refers to the friendship patterns in the classroom group. Attraction can be described as the level of friendship that exists among members of the classroom group. The level of attraction is dependent on the degree to which positive interpersonal relationships have been developed. It is clear that a positive relationship exists between level of attraction and student academic performance. Thus, the effective classroom manager is one who fosters positive interpersonal relationships among group members. For example, the teacher attempts to promote the acceptance of rejected students and new members.

Promoting Productive Group Norms

Norms are shared expectations of how group members should think, feel, and behave. Norms greatly influence interpersonal relationships because they provide guidelines that help members understand what is expected of them and what they should expect from others. Productive group norms are essential to group effectiveness. Therefore, one important task of the teacher is to help the group establish, accept, and maintain productive group norms. Such norms provide a frame of reference that guides the behavior of members. The group, not the teacher, regulates behavior by exerting pressure on members to adhere to the group's norms. It is crucial that the teacher assist the group in the development of productive norms. This is a difficult task. Advocates of the group-process approach argue that productive norms can be developed — and unproductive norms changed — through the concerted, collaborative efforts of the teacher and the students using group discussion methods.

Encouraging Open Communication

Communication — both verbal and nonverbal — is dialogue between group members. It involves the uniquely human capability to understand one another's ideas and feelings. Thus, communication is the vehicle through which the meaningful interaction of members takes place, and through which group processes in the classroom occur. Effective communication means the receiver correctly interprets the message that the sender intends to communicate. Therefore, a twofold task of the teacher is to open the channels of communication so that all students express their thoughts and feelings freely and, frequently, to accept student thoughts and feelings. In addition, the teacher should help students develop certain communication skills — paraphrasing, perception checking, and feedback, for example (see Chapter 7, "Interpersonal Communication Skills").

■ *Fostering Cohesiveness*

Cohesiveness is the collective feeling that the class members have about the classroom group — the sum of the individual members' feelings about the group. Unlike attraction, cohesiveness emphasizes the individual's relation to the group as a whole instead of to individuals within the group. Schmuck and Schmuck note that groups are cohesive for a variety of reasons: (1) the members like one another, (2) there is high interest in a task, and (3) the group offers prestige to its members. Thus, a classroom group is cohesive when most of its members, including the teacher, are highly attracted to the group as a whole.

Cohesiveness occurs to the extent individual needs are satisfied by group membership. Schmuck and Schmuck assert that cohesiveness is a result of the dynamics of interpersonal expectations, leadership style, attraction patterns, and the flow of communication. The teacher can create cohesive classroom groups by open discussions of expectations, dispersion of leadership, the development of several friendship clusters, and the frequent use of two-way communication. Cohesiveness is essential to group productivity. Cohesive groups possess clearly established group norms — strong norms, not necessarily norms that are productive. Thus, the effective classroom manager is one who creates a cohesive group that possesses goal-directed norms.

To summarize the position taken by Schmuck and Schmuck, it can be said that they give importance to the teacher's ability to create and manage an effectively functioning, goal-directed classroom group. The implications of their position, as they suggest, are:

1. The teacher should work with students to clarify the interpersonal expectations held by individuals in the group, recognize the expectations he or she holds for each individual student and for the group, modify his or her expectations on the basis of new information, foster expectations that emphasize student strengths rather than weaknesses, and make a deliberate effort to accept and support each student.
2. The teacher should exert goal-directed influences by exhibiting appropriate leadership behaviors, helping students develop leadership skills, and dispersing leadership by sharing leadership functions with students, and by encouraging and supporting the leadership activities of students.
3. The teacher should display empathy toward students and help them develop an empathic understanding of one another, accept all students and encourage them to accept one another, provide opportunities for students to work collaboratively, and facilitate the development of student friendships and teacher-student rapport.
4. The teacher should help students resolve conflicts between institutional rules, group norms, and/or individual attitudes; use various problem-solving techniques and group discussion methods to help students develop productive, goal-directed norms; and encourage students to be responsible for their own behavior.
5. The teacher should exhibit effective communication skills and help students develop effective communication skills; foster open channels of

communication that encourage students to express their ideas and feelings freely and constructively; promote student interaction, which allows students to work with and get to know one another; and provide opportunities for students to discuss openly the group's processes.

6. The teacher should foster cohesiveness by establishing and maintaining a classroom group that is characterized by clearly understood expectations; shared, goal-directed leadership; high levels of empathy, acceptance, and friendship; and open channels of communication.

Although the views held by Johnson and Bany[18] are, in many ways, similar to those of Schmuck and Schmuck, they represent a contribution that warrants an examination here. Johnson and Bany describe two major types of classroom management activities — facilitation and maintenance. *Facilitation* refers to those management behaviors that improve conditions within the classroom; *maintenance* refers to those management behaviors that restore or maintain effective conditions. The teacher who manages the classroom effectively exhibits both facilitation and maintenance management behaviors.

Johnson and Bany have identified four kinds of facilitation behavior: (1) achieving unity and cooperation, (2) establishing standards and coordinating work procedures, (3) using problem solving to improve conditions, and (4) changing established patterns of group behavior. They have identified three kinds of maintenance behavior: (1) maintaining and restoring morale, (2) handling conflict, and (3) minimizing management problems. Although we cannot give a full description of these managerial behaviors — Johnson and Bany used over four hundred pages doing that — a brief explanation of each behavior is presented here.

Achieving classroom group unity and cooperation (cohesiveness) is a worthy and necessary goal if the teacher is to help the group be maximally effective. Because cohesiveness is largely dependent on group members liking one another and liking the group, the task of the teacher is to make group membership attractive and satisfying. Johnson and Bany assert that cohesiveness is dependent on the amount and frequency of student interaction and communication, the kind of structure that exists within the group, and the extent to which motives and goals are shared. It follows, then, that the teacher should encourage student interaction and communication by providing opportunities for students to work with one another and to discuss their ideas and feelings, accept and support all students while creating a structure within which each student develops a strong sense of belonging, and help students develop and recognize shared goals.

Establishing Standards and Coordinating Work Standards

Establishing standards and coordinating work procedures are among the most important — and the most difficult — of the teacher's responsibilities. Standards of conduct specify appropriate behaviors in given situations; work procedures are those standards that apply to interactive instructional processes. For example, a behavioral standard might involve the behavior prescribed for students as they stand in the cafeteria line, or as they pass out of the classroom during a fire drill. A work procedure might refer to the behavior expected of students when they are finished with seat-work assignments, or when they wish to ask the teacher a question. Clearly, effective instruction is dependent on the extent to which the teacher is able to establish appropriate standards, and the extent to which the teacher is able to facilitate student adherence to those standards. Johnson and Bany emphasize the importance of group decision methods as a means of establishing behavioral standards and gaining adherence to those standards. Standards that are accepted by the group become group norms. In a cohesive group, there is a great deal of pressure on members to conform to those norms. Thus, the effective classroom group is one in which desirable standards and work procedures are accepted group norms.

Using Group Problem-Solving Discussions

The use of group problem-solving discussions to improve classroom conditions is a strategy highly recommended by advocates of the group-process approach. The problem-solving process is viewed somewhat differently by different authors, but, for the most part, may be thought of as including: (1) identifying the problem, (2) analyzing the problem, (3) evaluating alternative solutions, (4) selecting and implementing a solution, and (5) obtaining feedback and evaluating the solution. The basic premise underlying this strategy is that students, given the opportunity, skills, and necessary guidance, can and will make responsible decisions regarding their classroom behavior. This premise suggests that the teacher should provide students with the opportunity to engage in group problem-solving discussions, foster the development of student problem-solving skills, and guide students in the problem-solving process.

Changing Established Patterns of Group Behavior

Changing established patterns of group behavior involves the use of planned-change techniques similar to those of group problem solving. The difference is that the purpose of the problem-solving process is to find a solution to a problem, while the purpose of the planned-change process is to gain acceptance of an already determined solution. Thus, the planned-change process is one of improving conditions by substituting appropriate goals for inappropriate goals. The group goals exert a strong influence on the behavior of group members, and when group goals are in conflict with those of instruction, students behave inappropriately. Therefore, it is necessary for the teacher to help the group replace inappropriate goals and behaviors with more appropriate ones, goals that satisfy group needs and are consistent with those of the school.

Johnson and Bany argue that group planning is the best process to use for changing inappropriate goals and behaviors to more appropriate ones. Their viewpoint is based on the assumption that such changes are much more likely to be accomplished and accepted if members of the group have participated in the decision to change. This suggests that the role of the teacher is to help students understand the goal to be achieved; involve students in discussions that result in an examination of various plans for achieving the goals, selecting a plan, and identifying tasks that need to be performed; implement the plan and perform the necessary tasks; and assess the plan's effectiveness. During the planned-change process, the teacher encourages group acceptance of externally established goals. Students are engaged in decisions regarding the strategies to be used in achieving those goals.

Simply put, the facilitation management behaviors of the teacher consist of: (1) encouraging the development of group cohesiveness; (2) promoting the acceptance of productive standards of conduct; (3) facilitating the resolution of problems through the use of group problem-solving processes; and (4) fostering appropriate group goals, norms, and behaviors. The intent of these facilitative management behaviors is the improvement of those classroom conditions that promote effective instruction. Maintenance management behaviors are intended to restore and maintain those classroom conditions. Descriptions of the three types identified by Johnson and Bany follow.

Maintaining and Restoring Morale

The ability to *maintain and restore morale* is important because the level of classroom group morale greatly influences group productivity. A group with high morale is far more likely to be productive than a group with low morale. Facilitation behaviors build morale; however, the effective teacher recognizes that many factors can cause morale to fluctuate. Thus, the teacher should understand the factors that influence morale and exhibit those behaviors that preserve high morale. Johnson and Bany note that morale is affected by the level of cohesiveness, the amount of interaction and communication, the extent to which members have shared goals, the extent to which the group's goal-directed efforts are hindered, and environmental conditions that cause anxiety and stress or otherwise affect the group adversely.

Thus, the task of the teacher may be viewed as twofold: (1) the teacher should act to rebuild morale — fostering cohesiveness, encouraging increased interaction and communication, and promoting shared goals; (2) the teacher should act to reduce anxiety and relieve stress — fostering cooperation rather than competition, exhibiting shared leadership, eliminating extremely frustrating and threatening situations, neutralizing disruptive influences, and clarifying stress situations through discussion. Crucial to the teacher's effectiveness is the extent to which the teacher is accepted and trusted by the students. The teacher cannot hope to be successful in restoring morale if students perceive him or her as part of the problem, or if his or her behavior creates new problems. The use of punishment is an all too common example of the latter.

Handling Conflict

Handling conflict in the classroom group is among the most difficult tasks a teacher faces. Hostile, aggressive student behaviors are emotion laden, disruptive, and irritating, especially when directed toward the teacher. But conflict and hostility must be viewed as a normal result of the interactive processes that occur in the classroom. It is not realistic to expect otherwise. Indeed, in the initial phases of a group's development, it is not unusual and can be constructive.

There are many causes of conflict. Primary among them is frustration. When the group is hindered or blocked in achieving its goal, the result is frustration. Feelings of frustration manifest themselves as hostility and aggression, or as withdrawal and apathy. The effective teacher should be able to recognize and deal with such problems quickly. Johnson and Bany suggest a process for resolving a conflict: (1) set guidelines for discussion, (2) clarify what happened, (3) explore differences in points of view, (4) identify the cause or causes of the conflict, (5) develop agreements regarding the cause or causes of the conflict and resolution of the conflict, (6) specify a plan of action, and (7) make a positive appraisal of group efforts. To prevent conflict, the teacher is encouraged to reduce frustrations as much as possible by allowing the group to set and reach reasonable goals.

If they are to minimize problems, teachers must understand their classroom group, and must be able to anticipate the influence various environmental factors will have on that group. In minimizing management problems, the effective teacher utilizes two major strategies: (1) facilitation and maintenance behaviors to establish and maintain an effectively functioning, goal-directed classroom group; and (2) continuous diagnosis and analysis of the health of the classroom group, and action on the basis of that diagnosis. For example, symptoms of disunity call for teacher behaviors intended to promote group cohesiveness. Symptoms of inappropriate norms call for teacher behaviors intended to change those norms to more appropriate ones. In addition, certain types of problems — the new student and the substitute teacher, for example — can and should be anticipated. The teacher should help the class prepare for such possibilities.

Effective classroom management, according to Johnson and Bany, involves the ability of the teacher to establish the conditions that enable the classroom group to be productive — and the ability to maintain those conditions. The latter involves the ability to maintain a high level of morale, resolve conflict, and minimize management problems. Implicit is the need to build effective communication, establish positive interpersonal relationships, and satisfy both individual and group needs. The overriding emphasis is on the ability of the teacher to use group methods of management. These behaviors determine the effectiveness of the group and the success of instruction.

So far in this section, we have presented two somewhat different viewpoints regarding the group-process approach to classroom management — the views of Schmuck and Schmuck and the ideas of Johnson and Bany. A brief examination of several additional ideas from the research of Kounin[19] and the work of Glasser[20] completes the overview presented in this section.

Utilizing Withitness, Overlapping, and Group-Focus Behaviors

As noted in Learning Activity 2.5, Kounin has conducted extensive research on the management dimension of teaching. Several concepts coming from his research were described as instructional managerial strategies. Here, three additional strategies — strategies relevant to the group-process approach — are described:

1. *Withitness behaviors* are those behaviors by which the teacher communicates to students that he or she knows what is going on, that he or she is aware of what students are doing — or not doing. Kounin concluded that withitness is significantly related to managerial success; that is, teachers who demonstrated withitness are more likely to have fewer and less serious student misbehaviors.

2. *Overlapping behaviors* are those behaviors by which the teacher indi-

cates that he or she is attending to more than one issue when there is more than one issue to deal with at a particular time. Kounin suggests that overlapping — when combined with withitness — is related to managerial success. The teacher who is able to pay attention to more than one issue at a time is more likely to be effective than the teacher who is unable to do so.

3. *Group-focus behaviors* are those behaviors teachers use to maintain a focus on the group — rather than on an individual student — during individual recitations. Kounin identified two aspects of group-focus behaviors: *group alerting*, which refers to the extent to which the teacher involves nonreciting students (maintains their attention and "keeps them on their toes"); and *accountability*, which refers to the extent to which the teacher holds students accountable and responsible for their task performances during recitations. Kounin found that group alerting and accountability are related to student behavior. He suggests that teachers who maintain a group focus are more successful in promoting student goal-directed behavior, and in preventing student misbehavior, than are teachers who do not.

In summarizing his studies, Kounin suggests there are certain teaching behaviors — withitness, overlapping, and group-focus behaviors — that are related to managerial success. He also notes that these techniques of classroom management apply to the classroom group and not merely to individual students. Thus, Kounin may be described as a staunch advocate of group management — a most interesting dimension of the group-process approach to classroom management.

Utilizing Classroom Meetings

Many behavior problems are best addressed through the use of the class as a problem-solving group under the guidance of the teacher. If each student can be helped to realize that he or she is a member of a working, problem-solving group, and that he or she has both individual and group responsibilities, it is likely that discussions of group problems will lead to the resolution of those problems. Without such help, students tend to evade problems, depend on others to solve their problems, or withdraw. The social–problem-solving *classroom meeting* is intended to provide the assistance students need in this regard. It is a viewpoint shared by most advocates of the group-process approach and best described by Glasser. He suggests three guidelines to enhance the potential effectiveness of social–problem-solving classroom meetings:

1. Any group problem may be discussed; a problem may be introduced by a student or the teacher.
2. The discussion should be directed toward solving the problem; the atmosphere should be nonjudgmental and nonpunitive; the solution should not include punishment or fault finding.
3. The meeting should be conducted with the teacher and students seated in a tight circle; meetings should be held often; meetings should not exceed 30 to 45 minutes, depending on the age of the students.

The reader who wishes to be more fully informed about these views should refer to Glasser's book, *Schools Without Failure.*

▓ *Summary*

In summary, it appears that the teacher who wishes to develop a behavioral repertoire that draws on the group-process approach should consider the advantages of the following strategies: fostering reasonable, clearly understood expectations; sharing leadership; fostering open communication; establishing and maintaining group morale and attraction; fostering group unity, cooperation, and cohesiveness; promoting productive group standards and norms; resolving conflicts through discussion; exhibiting withitness, overlapping, and group-focus behaviors; and employing problem-solving classroom meetings. This section provides an overview of the group-process approach. Space limitations preclude a more detailed treatment of the subject. It is recommended that the reader who wishes to explore this topic in more detail refer to the work of Schmuck and Schmuck, Johnson and Bany, Kounin, and Glasser. An excellent source of practical suggestions related to classroom group development is a book by Stanford.[21]

MASTERY TEST

OBJECTIVE 2

To describe the nature and dynamics of the authoritarian, intimidation, permissive, cookbook, instructional, behavior-modification, socioemotional-climate, and group-process approaches to classroom management

Learning Activities 2.1 through 2.8 presented brief descriptions of eight different approaches to classroom management. The following exercise provides you with an opportunity to assess your understanding of the basic principles of each of those approaches. Each of the following fifty statements takes a particular position with regard to the teacher and effective classroom management. Your task is to identify correctly the approach each statement represents. In the space provided in front of each statement, please place the code letters of that approach you feel the statement represents. Please use the following code:

    AU — authoritarian approach
    BM — behavior-modification approach
    CB — cookbook approach
    GP — group-process approach
    IN — instructional approach
    IT — intimidation approach
    PM — permissive approach
    SE — socioemotional-climate approach

When you have responded to all fifty statements, compare your responses to those presented in the Answer Key at the end of the chapter.

_____ 1. The teacher should recognize that a central role of the teacher is to maintain order and discipline in the classroom by controlling student behavior.

_____ 2. The teacher should recognize that classroom climate greatly influences learning, and that the teacher greatly influences the nature of that climate.

_____ 3. The teacher should reward acceptable student behavior and avoid rewarding unacceptable student behavior.

_____ 4. The teacher should recognize that an individualized curriculum can eliminate most classroom management problems.

_____ 5. The teacher should address the student's situation, not the student's character or personality, when dealing with a problem.

_____ 6. The teacher should not impose limits on students because this will keep them from reaching their full potential.

_____ 7. The teacher should understand that the use of logical consequences minimizes the potential for the negative side effects that can accompany other forms of punishment.

_____ 8. The teacher should understand that effective management begins with his or her ability to control each student through the use of force as necessary.

_____ 9. The teacher should always be fair and firm in dealing with students because consistency is important.

_____ 10. The teacher should help students understand, accept, and follow established rules and regulations.

_____ 11. The teacher should view a well-managed token system as an effective means of promoting appropriate student behavior.

_____ 12. The teacher should be tolerant of all forms of student behavior.

_____ 13. The teacher should allow students to suffer the natural and logical consequences of their behavior, unless those consequences involve physical danger.

_____ 14. The teacher should behave in ways that let the students know the teacher is aware of what is going on.

_____ 15. The teacher should recognize that a central role of the teacher is the establishment and maintenance of positive teacher-student relationships.

_____ 16. The teacher should understand that the use of punishment and the threat of punishment can be effective management tools when used appropriately.

_____ 17. The teacher should recognize that rewards are unique to the individual student.

_____ 18. The teacher should understand that appropriate classroom activities usually ensure appropriate student behavior because they decrease the potential for frustration and boredom.

_____ 19. The teacher should recognize that the appropriate use of mild desist behaviors can be both effective and efficient in controlling student behavior.

_____ 20. The teacher should treat students with respect and be committed to helping them develop self-responsibility and feelings of self-worth.

_____ 21. The teacher should never punish a student unless there is adequate evidence to establish guilt beyond a reasonable doubt.

_____ 22. The teacher should help students develop a high level of cohesiveness and productive norms.

_____ 23. The teacher should operate on the assumption that both appropriate and inappropriate student behaviors are learned.

_____ 24. The teacher should understand that disruptive students often misbehave because they have been given inappropriate learning tasks.

_____ 25. The teacher should recognize that the manner in which the teacher communicates with students is decisively important.

_____ 26. The teacher should use sarcasm carefully and only after positive interpersonal relationships have been established.

_____ 27. The teacher should always conduct himself or herself in a businesslike and dignified manner when interacting with students.

_____ 28. The teacher should observe and/or question students to obtain clues concerning potential rewards.

_____ 29. The teacher should understand that the use of classroom meetings and group problem-solving sessions can be an effective means for solving certain managerial problems.

_____ 30. The teacher should "separate the sin from the sinner" when dealing with a student who has behaved inappropriately.

_____ 31. The teacher should recognize that most classroom management problems can be avoided or solved by effective instructional practices.

_____ 32. The teacher should understand that it is important to help students develop communication, leadership, and group problem-solving skills.

_____ 33. The teacher should understand that effective classroom management is nothing more than the application of common sense.

_____ 34. The teacher should recognize that the proper use of sarcasm and ridicule can be effective in controlling student behavior.

_____ 35. The teacher should recognize that a central role of the teacher is to use a variety of instructional strategies to prevent and solve discipline problems.

_____ 36. The teacher should understand that it is important to establish and enforce reasonable expectations and rules.

_____ 37. The teacher should be fair but firm from the beginning because it is easier to relax control than it is to impose it once it has been lost.

_____ 38. The teacher should foster group cohesiveness by helping students perceive membership as attractive and satisfying.

_____ 39. The teacher should create discipline with lessons the children will find interesting and motivating.

_____ 40. The teacher should view teacher realness, acceptance, and empathy as keys to effective classroom management.

_____ 41. The teacher should understand that it is important to establish a physical and psychological environment in which the student is completely free to say and do anything he or she wants to.

_____ 42. The teacher should understand that well-planned lessons are an effective means of achieving order in the classroom.

_____ 43. The teacher should reinforce appropriate student behaviors in ways that recognize that rewards are unique to the individual student.

_____ 44. The teacher should understand that effective management is mostly a function of his or her ability to punish student misconduct when it occurs.

_____ 45. The teacher should recognize that he or she must often assume responsibility for controlling the behavior of the student.

_____ 46. The teacher should recognize that a central role of the teacher is to use tried-and-true techniques to prevent and solve discipline problems.

_____ 47. The teacher should recognize that rewarded behavior is likely to be continued, and that unrewarded behavior is likely to be discontinued.

_____ 48. The teacher should plan and use appropriate instructional activities to ensure appropriate student behavior.

_____ 49. The teacher should understand that effective classroom management is the result of the teacher's establishing and maintaining control.

_____ 50. The teacher should understand that effective classroom management is intended to help the classroom group become responsible for solving many of its own problems.

OBJECTIVE **3** To analyze a given classroom situation and to describe and justify the managerial strategy or strategies most likely to be effective in facilitating and maintaining those classroom conditions deemed desirable

Learning Activity 3.1

It was previously emphasized that the nature of the problem and its context should dictate the strategy that a teacher uses in attempting to solve the problem. In addition, a strong case has been made for the viewpoint that the teacher might appropriately employ any one of a number of strategies in attempting to solve a particular classroom management problem. Indeed, the effective teacher is one who is able to recognize several equally workable alternatives when confronted with the need to employ a managerial strategy. The following exercise is designed to give you an opportunity to practice that skill.

YOUR TURN

Recognizing Alternative Strategies

For each case study, please (1) describe the type of problem, (2) describe two different strategies a teacher might use in solving the problem, and (3) briefly explain and defend the choices you have made. Because of the wide range of possible responses, this learning activity does not have an answer key. After responding to all six case studies, you should analyze your answers. You might consider the extent to which your responses to a particular problem: (1) are really different approaches to the problem; (2) follow logically from the type of problem indicated; (3) deal with the problem's cause, and not just the symptoms; (4) would influence a majority of the class in a positive and productive way; (5) would have long-range benefit; and (6) most important, would promote those classroom conditions you deem desirable. If you are pleased with the results of your analysis, you can feel reasonably comfortable with your ability to consider alternative solutions to classroom management problems. If you are not pleased with your responses and feel that additional effort is required, you may find it helpful to review the information contained in Learning Activities 2.1 through 2.8.

1. Although you have no direct evidence that supports the assertion, Eddie has a reputation as a bully. He is large for his age and towers over most of his sixth grade classmates. Having attended to a chore that required you to leave your room for a few minutes, you return to find Eddie holding Harry, a much smaller boy, by the shirt. Eddie's clenched right hand is cocked as if he is about to deliver a sharp blow.
   a. Problem:
   b. Solution 1
      (1) Description:
      (2) Justification:
   c. Solution 2
      (1) Description:
      (2) Justification:

2. Having finished lunch, you hurry to the gym to set up the equipment necessary for your one o'clock physical education class. As you enter the gym, you find Phil and Allan, both seniors, smoking. Although school regulations forbid smoking and call for an automatic three-day suspension, some of your colleagues fail to enforce the regulation because they feel the punishment is too severe.
   a. Problem:
   b. Solution 1
      (1) Description:
      (2) Justification:
   c. Solution 2
      (1) Description:
      (2) Justification:

3. While your third grade class is working quietly at their seats, Cindy approaches your desk and in a near whisper says, "During recess someone took the pen I got for Christmas out of my desk. I think Ray took it because he's now using one just like it. I don't think he had it before. If I don't get it back, my mom is going to be awful mad."
   a. Problem:
   b. Solution 1
      (1) Description:
      (2) Justification:
   c. Solution 2
      (1) Description:
      (2) Justification:

4. Your eighth grade American history class is a delight to teach. They are bright and motivated. Although you have taught them for only three months, they have become your "all-time favorites." As you introduce the day's lesson, you notice immediately that they are angry and sullen. Recognizing that this is such unusual behavior for this group and that it is likely to inhibit your effectiveness that day, you decide to find out the reason for their feelings. Brenda, one of the class leaders, speaks out: "It's that Mr. Underhill. He gave us an exam that was totally unfair. It covered two chapters he hadn't even assigned and now he says he did. None of us did well on the exam; a 62 was the highest score. And he won't let us take a make-up. That's not fair." The rest of the class nods in agreement.

a. Problem:
b. Solution 1
   (1) Description:
   (2) Justification:
c. Solution 2
   (1) Description:
   (2) Justification:

5. At recess, you accompany your fifth grade class to the playground. You are watching a group of students skipping rope when you are attracted by noise coming from a group of boys in a cluster. As you approach them, you find eight or ten boys in a tight circle around another boy, Leslie McClendon. The boys in the circle are chanting, "Leslie is a girl's name. Leslie is a girl's name."
a. Problem:
b. Solution 1
   (1) Description:
   (2) Justification:
c. Solution 2
   (1) Description:
   (2) Justification:

6. A month into the school year, you assign small-group projects to your tenth grade biology students. You allow students to form their own groups of four or five. Although the class of thirty-four students consists of eighteen boys and sixteen girls (twenty white students and fourteen black students), you are surprised and disappointed to see that the groups the students form are composed of white boys, black boys, white girls, or black girls only. Not one of the eight groups is either sexually or racially integrated.
a. Problem:
b. Solution 1
   (1) Description:
   (2) Justification:
c. Solution 2
   (1) Description:
   (2) Justification:

Learning Activity 3.2

Thus far in this chapter, emphasis has been given to the notion that the effective classroom manager accurately identifies the nature of the problem and selects the managerial strategy that has the greatest potential for solving the problem. Accurate identification of the problem and selection of an appropriate strategy are crucial factors. Of equal importance is the matter of *timing*. *When* the teacher acts is often as important as *what* the teacher does. Even if the teacher decides not to act, that decision must be made quickly.

There are four such decisions to be made about the timing of an intervention. The teacher must (1) anticipate certain types of problems and act to prevent them from happening; (2) react immediately in instances requiring immediate action; (3) solve problems that do not require immediate action, but must be dealt with promptly; and (4) monitor the effectiveness of attempts to solve identified problems. The following exercise gives you an opportunity to practice the ability to react under the pressure of time — the ability to make effective decisions quickly.

YOUR TURN

Making Quick Decisions

Eight problems are briefly described. Your task is to describe what you would do in each case, and to justify the course of action you select. In this exercise, your response should also be timed so that you experience the pressure of having to make a decision within a limited amount of time. For each case, you will have two minutes to describe what you would do if faced with the problem described. The following procedures are recommended for this exercise.

Do *not* read the case studies yourself; have a partner read them to you instead. (You can do the same thing for him or her when you finish the exercise.) It will be most effective to become aware of the problems for the first time when — and only when — you are ready to do this exercise.

Have a partner select five to seven of the problems he or she feels are most relevant to your particular situation. Let him or her begin by reading the first problem and then pausing for exactly two minutes. At the end of that two-minute interval, he or she will read the second problem and make another two-minute pause. Then he or she will read the third problem, and so on, until all the problems have been read. You should write your solution — and only the solution, *not* the justification — to the first problem during the two-minute interval that follows each reading of a problem. At the end of the first pause, you should move on to the second problem, and so on, until you have responded to all the problems. Then go back and write justifications for each of the problems.

Your justifications ought to describe the reasoning behind your decisions. Additionally, you may find it helpful to describe the assumptions you made about the nature of the problem, and other alternatives you considered, and the condition you would be attempting to establish or re-establish. Having finished writing a justification for each response, carefully and thoroughly examine your responses and your justifications with a peer or group of peers. Or put your answers aside for a day or two. Then you might review your responses to determine how good you still feel about your answers. Obviously, this exercise has no right or wrong answers. For this reason, none are provided. The best answers are clearly those that make sense to you as you subject them to an objective analysis, and recognize the assumptions you have made about the problem and the managerial outcomes you would hope to achieve.

1. Jim is one of the brighter students in your third grade class, but he constantly misbehaves. He does nothing really serious, just a continuous series of minor incidents — talking out, laughing loudly, slamming his desk top, throwing wads of paper, and teasing fellow classmates, for example. Although these are not major misbehaviors, they are annoying and disruptive. In addition, the other students think these things are funny. They laugh and treat Jim's behavior as a joke. What do you do?

2. You are not sure of the problem, but the symptoms are obvious. Your seventh period algebra class is not working well. Assignments are generally late. The students are constantly complaining about your assignments, the fairness of tests, and everything in general. During class discussions, no one participates. No one volunteers to answer questions you believe many can answer. Little accidents such as pencils breaking, books falling on the floor, and an overturned waste basket seem frequent. What do you do?

3. Tom has been a member of your Spanish II class for nearly three weeks now, having transferred to Wilson High School after the Christmas break. Although he seems to be a nice young man, it is obvious that he

has not been accepted by his classmates. Small-group projects designed to involve Tom have not helped. Tom remains outside an otherwise cohesive group. The other students seem to ignore him, and he seems to ignore them; however, you have not seen any signs of hostility on anyone's part. What do you do?

4. Your fourth period social studies class has always been a bit more of a problem than your other tenth grade students. After six months, however, they now work quite well with one bothersome exception. Despite your telling them on numerous occasions that they are to wait until you dismiss them when the bell rings for them to go to fifth period lunch, they invariably get out of their seats and rush to the door, pushing and shoving into the hallway. As luck would have it, today Mr. Blake, the principal, was almost run over by your stampeding students. What do you do?

5. Your eighth grade history students are working quietly in groups of three or four. As you move around the room checking on the progress the groups are making on their projects, you hear constrained giggling from a far corner of the room. You look up in time to see Bill holding a penknife in his hand. Catching sight of you, Bill slips the knife into his desk. As you near Bill's desk, you notice that an obscene word has been carved in large letters on Bill's desk top. The carving is fresh; indeed, there are still wood chips on the desk. What do you do?

6. The flu kept you out of school for several days. Handling students after they have had a few days with a substitute teacher is generally something of a problem, and you do not really expect the first day back to go too smoothly. That expectation is reinforced by a note left for you by the substitute teacher. It reads: "I had nothing but trouble with all of your classes, but the first period business math is perhaps the worst group I've ever met. There isn't a polite person in that entire class. I don't know how you stand it. They gave me nothing but trouble. They are the most discourteous group I've ever met." The first period bell rings, and members of the business math class take their seats. What do you do?

7. When Linda's mother brought Linda to your kindergarten class on the first day of school, she warned you that Linda was "a very sensitive child." After only two weeks of school, you have some idea of the reason she felt the need to warn you. Linda displays a rare gift for temper tantrums. If she can't be first in line — temper tantrum. If she is not allowed to do what she wants — temper tantrum. And Linda's temper tantrums are complete with kicking, crying, screaming, and rolling on the floor. You have tried to ignore her outbursts, but now you find that the other children are making fun of Linda. Typical comments include: "There she goes again!" "What a baby she is!" "Grow up, crybaby!" What do you do?

8. Your ninth grade social studies class is the best you have ever had. They are both bright and well behaved. Class discussions are a delight; test scores are always high. On numerous occasions, you have praised the class for their accomplishments. The recent assignment of Barbara to the class, however, has created a problem. Barbara has had a miserable home life. She is the illegitimate daughter of a woman with a bad reputation in the community. Barbara herself has been in trouble with the law. Indeed, she has just been released from a school for delinquent girls, having served six months for shoplifting — a third such conviction. The principal has assigned her to your class because she is bright, and because he feels that she will be better behaved with "good students." Barbara has been in your class for only a few days when you begin to receive complaints that "things are missing." Pencils, pens, compacts, combs, lipsticks, and other things have begun to disappear. What do you do?

ANSWER KEY

Mastery Test, Objective 1

The four stages of the analytic-pluralistic classroom management process are (1) specifying desirable classroom conditions, (2) analyzing existing classroom conditions, (3) selecting and utilizing managerial strategies, and (4) assessing managerial effectiveness. If you have any reason to believe that your descriptions of these four stages are inadequate, you may want to refer to the appropriate section or sections of Learning Activity 2. Although it is important that you feel reasonably comfortable with your understanding of these four stages, subsequent learning activities are designed to provide the opportunity for more complete understanding.

ANSWER KEY

Mastery Test, Objective 2

The following answers might have been given for the items in this test. Some of your responses might not agree with those here. Where there is disagreement, you may want to analyze your position. As you do so, you should recognize that some managerial strategies may be representative of more than one approach, depending on your interpretation and preference. Thus, it is altogether possible for you to give a correct response that disagrees with the key. What is most important here is that you feel comfortable with your responses, even if you happen to disagree with the key. You should feel that you are familiar with the information presented in this section of the chapter

If you correctly identified at least forty-five of the statements, you can be fairly confident that you understand the basic principles of the eight managerial approaches described in this learning activity. If you did not

do as well as you would have liked, you may wish to review the information presented in Learning Activities 2.1 through 2.8 and/or study any of the resources listed under Objective 2 in the Additional Readings section of this chapter. When you are confident that you are familiar with each of the eight approaches, you are ready to move on to the next learning activity.

1. AU   2. SE   3. BM   4. IN   5. SE   6. PM   7. SE
8. IT   9. CB   10. AU   11. BM   12. PM   13. SE
14. GP   15. SE   16. IT   17. BM   18. IN   19. AU
20. SE   21. CB   22. GP   23. BM   24. IN   25. SE
26. CB   27. CB   28. BM   29. GP   30. SE   31. IN
32. GP   33. CB   34. IT   35. IN   36. AU   37. CB
38. GP   39. IN   40. SE   41. PM   42. IN   43. BM
44. IT   45. AU   46. CB   47. BM   48. IN   49. AU
50. GP

■ Notes

1. Lee Canter and Marlene Canter, *Assertive Discipline* (Los Angeles: Canter and Associates, 1979).
2. Carl J. Wallen and LaDonna L. Wallen, *Effective Classroom Management* (Boston: Allyn and Bacon, 1978), p. 214.
3. Lois V. Johnson and Mary A. Bany, *Classroom Management: Theory and Skill Training* (New York: Macmillan Co., 1970), pp. 45–49.
4. Jean E. Davis, *Coping with Disruptive Behavior* (Washington, DC: National Education Association, 1974), p. 21.
5. Jacob S. Kounin, *Discipline and Group Management in Classrooms* (New York: Holt, Rinehart & Winston, 1970).
6. James D. Long and Virginia H. Frye, *Making It Till Friday: A Guide to Successful Classroom Management* (Princeton, NJ: Princeton Book Company, 1977), pp. 35–36.
7. Terrence Piper, *Classroom Management and Behavioral Objectives: Applications of Behavioral Modification* (Belmont, CA: Lear Siegler/Fearon Publishers, 1974), pp. 10–18.
8. Nancy K. Buckley and Hill M. Walker, *Modifying Classroom Behavior: A Manual of Procedures for Classroom Teachers* (Champaign, IL: Research Press Company, 1970), p. 30.
9. Abraham Givener and Paul S. Graubard, *A Handbook of Behavior Modification for the Classroom* (New York: Holt, Rinehart & Winston, 1974), p. 8.
10. Beth Sulzer and G. Roy Mayer, *Behavior Modification Procedures for School Personnel* (Hinsdale, IL: Dryden Press, 1972), pp. 174–184.
11. Saul Axelrod, *Behavior Modification for the Classroom Teacher* (New York: McGraw-Hill, 1983).
12. Harvey F. Clarizio, *Toward Positive Classroom Discipline* (New York: John Wiley and Son, 1980).
13. Carl R. Rogers, *Freedom to Learn* (Columbus, OH: Charles E. Merrill, 1969).

14. Haim G. Ginott, *Between Parent and Child* (New York: Macmillan Co., 1965); *Between Parent and Teenager* (New York: Macmillan Co., 1969); and *Teacher and Child* (New York: Macmillan Co., 1972).
15. William Glasser, *Schools Without Failure* (New York: Harper and Row, 1969).
16. Rudolf Dreikurs and Loren Grey, *A New Approach to Discipline: Logical Consequences* (New York: Hawthorn Books, 1968); Rudolf Dreikurs and Pearl Cassel, *Discipline Without Tears* (New York: Hawthorn Books, 1972); and Rudolf Dreikurs, Bernice Bronia Grunwald, and Floyd C. Pepper, *Maintaining Sanity in the Classroom: Classroom Management Techniques* (New York: Harper and Row, 1982).
17. Richard A. Schmuck and Patricia A. Schmuck, *Group Processes in the Classroom* (Dubuque, IA: William C. Brown, 1979).
18. Johnson and Bany, *op. cit.*
19. Kounin, *op. cit.*
20. Glasser, *op. cit.*
21. Gene Stanford, *Developing Effective Classroom Groups* (New York: A & W Visual Library, 1980).

■ Additional Readings

Axelrod, Saul. *Behavior Modification for the Classroom Teacher.* New York: McGraw-Hill, 1983.

Buckley, Nancy K., and Hill M. Walker. *Modifying Classroom Behavior: A Manual of Procedures for Classroom Teachers.* Champaign, IL: Research Press Company, 1978.

Cangelosi, James S. *Classroom Management Strategies: Gaining and Maintaining Students' Cooperation.* New York: Longman, 1993.

Canter, Lee, and Marlene Canter. *Assertive Discipline.* Santa Monica, CA: Lee Canter and Associates, 1992.

Charles, C. M. *Building Classroom Discipline.* New York: Longman, 1992.

Clarizio, Harvey F. *Toward Positive Classroom Discipline.* New York: John Wiley and Sons, 1980.

Doyle, Walter. *Classroom Management.* West Lafayette, IN: Kappa Delta Pi, 1980.

Dreikurs, Rudolf, and Pearl Cassel. *Discipline Without Tears.* New York: Hawthorn Books, 1972.

Dreikurs, Rudolf, and Loren Grey. *A New Approach to Discipline: Logical Consequences.* New York: E.P. Dutton, 1990.

Dreikurs, Rudolf, Bernice Bronia Grunwald, and Floyd C. Pepper. *Maintaining Sanity in the Classroom: Classroom Management Techniques.* New York: Harper and Row, Publishers, 1982.

Duke, Daniel L. *Managing Student Behavior Problems.* New York: Teachers College, Columbia University, 1981.

Duke, Daniel L., ed. *Helping Teachers Manage Classrooms.* Alexandria, VA: Association for Supervision and Curriculum Development, 1982.

Duke, Daniel L., and Adrienne M. Meckel. *Teacher's Guide to Classroom Management.* New York: Random House, 1984.

Edwards, Clifford H. *Classroom Discipline and Management.* New York: Macmillan, 1993.

Emmer, Edmund T., Carolyn M. Evertson, Julie P. Sanford, Barbara S. Clements, and Murray E. Worsham. *Classroom Management for Secondary Teachers.* Englewood Cliffs, NJ: Prentice-Hall, 1989.

Evertson, Carolyn M., Edmund T. Emmer, Barbara S. Clements, Julie P. Sanford, and Murray E. Worsham. *Classroom Management for Elementary Teachers.* Englewood Cliffs, NJ: Prentice-Hall, 1989.

Ginott, Haim G. *Teacher and Child: A Book for Parents and Teachers.* New York: Macmillan Co., 1972.

Glasser, William. *Schools Without Failure.* New York: Harper and Row, 1969.

Grey, Loren. *Discipline Without Fear.* New York: Hawthorn Books, 1974.

Johnson, Lois V., and Mary A. Bany. *Classroom Management: Theory and Skill Training.* New York: Macmillan Co., 1970.

Jones, Fredric H. *Positive Classroom Discipline.* New York: McGraw-Hill, 1987.

Lehman, Jerry D. *Three Approaches to Classroom Management: Views from a Psychological Perspective.* Washington, DC: University Press of America, 1982.

Lemlech, Johanna Kasin. *Classroom Management: Methods and Techniques for Elementary and Secondary Teachers.* Prospect Heights, IL: Waveland Press, 1991.

Rinne, Carl H. *Attention: The Fundamentals of Classroom Control.* Columbus, OH: Merrill Publishing Company, 1984.

Schmuck, Richard, and Patricia A. Schmuck. *Group Processes in the Classroom.* Dubuque, IA: William C. Brown Company, 1979.

Stanford, Gene. *Developing Effective Classroom Groups.* New York: A & W Visual Library, 1980.

Stefanich, Greg. *The Cascade Model: A Dynamic Approach to Classroom Discipline.* Dubuque, IA: Kendall/Hunt, 1987.

Tanner, Laurel N. *Classroom Discipline for Effective Teaching and Learning.* New York: Holt, Rinehart & Winston, 1978.

Walker, James E., and Thomas M. Shea. *Behavior Modification: A Practical Approach for Educators.* St. Louis: C.V. Mosby Company, 1984.

Wallen, Carl J., and LaDonna L. Wallen. *Effective Classroom Management.* Boston: Allyn and Bacon, 1978.

Wolfgang, Charles H., and Carl D. Glickman. *Solving Discipline Problems: Strategies for Classroom Teachers.* Boston: Allyn and Bacon, 1986.

Cooperative Learning

9

■ Mary S. Leighton

OBJECTIVES

1   To list and explain the attributes of cooperative learning strategies that improve student achievement and to describe the ways these attributes may be embedded in a lesson

2   To describe the interpersonal activities that contribute to student achievement in learning teams

3   To form student learning teams that promote positive social interdependence

4   To describe and distinguish among Student Team Learning (Student Team Achievement Divisions and Teams-Games-Tournaments), Jigsaw, and Group Investigation strategies

5   To describe simple cooperative activity structures that can be integrated easily into regular lessons

6   To examine how physical, organizational, and instructional environments support effective use of cooperative learning strategies

The sixth grade reading and language arts class is working today on vocabulary. The class members have created a list of new and interesting words drawn from the novel they are now studying. The teacher, Ms. Harriman, helped the class to trim the original list to twenty words and then to find sentences in the novel that show how each word is used. She suggested that they try using the words in sentences about their own lives as a journal-writing exercise one day. The following day, teammates read sentences aloud to each other and made sure all understood how to use the words correctly.

As usual, Ms. Harriman has put study aids in each team's packet: a word-list; a guide that gives for each word the text sentence, a definition, and some examples of common usage; and four cards numbered 1 to 4. The Cougars — Isaac, Kate, Jose, and May — are old hands at team practice. May, assigned the role of materials manager for the week, fetches the team packet from the materials shelf and brings it to the team table. Each member draws a numbered card and glances at the chalkboard, where Ms. Harriman has written starting roles for each number. Isaac, having drawn 1, reaches for the wordlist, while Kate, with 4, takes the guide. Isaac reads the first question to May, number 2: "'[Muna] got no closer to those exalted figures than their horses' feed troughs.' What does 'exalted' mean?"[1] May responds promptly, "High class, important, rich." Kate checks May's explanation against the study guide and decides that the definition is acceptable. May spells the word correctly, and the action moves to the left. May becomes the questioner; Jose, the answerer; and Isaac, the checker.

Because this is Jose's first year in an English-language reading group, he asks for and gets extra help from his teammates, who have become adept in providing lots of examples from their daily routines to illustrate word meanings. Occasionally, they recruit the help of Raphael on the Pumas, because he can offer examples in Spanish too. Kate, whose extensive recreational reading makes her a star in this class, is another good resource for Jose, a peer with whom she previously had limited acquaintance. The Cougars finish their work early and use the extra time to try a practice test. Each is eager to make this week's quiz score higher than usual and thus contribute to the team's improvement points.

Ms. Harriman stops near the group to check its progress. She has had a private coaching session with Isaac, who is very assertive, to teach him how to exercise his irrepressible initiative (a mixed blessing, in her view!) on drawing out May, who is shy. Her observation shows that Isaac is making progress in this skill and that everyone is participating appropriately in the practice activity.

The class expects a quiz tomorrow. All group members' scores will be compared to their base scores, which are calculated by averaging their usual quiz scores in vocabulary; and the team will earn points when the comparison shows individual progress. Every team that reaches the Superteam standard of growth will be able to display the team's pennant on the library bulletin board next week. Those that meet the slightly lower Greatteam standard will display pennants on the classroom bulletin board. Since Ms. Harriman has been using this strategy, Isaac's quiz scores have risen from 70s to 80s and his interest in reading has visibly increased. Jose's scores too have improved dramatically, and by the end of the semester Ms. Harriman expects to see him reading on grade level in English, as he does already in Spanish. May smiles and participates more often in class discussions now, and her grades have risen to a solid B. Kate, always an A student but sometimes careless in her work, now often makes perfect scores on quizzes. For Kate's 100s and Jose's dramatic improvement, the team earns a lot of team points and is frequently included among the celebrated Superteams of the week. Equally important — at least from Kate and Jose's point of view — they are much more often recruited for playground games and lunchtime socializing than they used to be.

Scenarios like this one are not unusual in classrooms where teachers are using cooperative learning strategies. Students enjoy both academic and social success to a greater degree than they do in other classroom situations. Most effective cooperative learning strategies are flexible, orderly systems that usually involve formal presentation of information or other well-developed opportunities to learn; student discussion, practice, and peer coaching in learning teams that work together over periods of weeks or months; individual assessment of mastery; and public recognition of team success. These methods have proven effective in a wide range of content areas — including math, reading, language arts, social studies, and science — in grades 1 through 12. Their effectiveness is measured both in significantly improved achievement for students at all ability levels and in development of social skills that facilitate positive interdependence in the classroom and other environments (Slavin, 1983; Slavin, 1990; Slavin, 1991a and 1991b). Recent studies in adult, military, college, and graduate school settings — with strategies adapted to the advanced subject matter and learning competencies of mature students — show similar effects (summarized in Cooper, Prescott, Cook, Smith, Mueck, and Cuseo, 1990). Several projects show remarkable growth in literacy in second languages among both English- and non-English-speaking primary students in programs that make extensive use of cooperative learning.

The success of cooperative learning strategies in motivating students to learn derives from three important characteristics: group goals, individual accountability, and equal opportunities for success. *Group goals* are usually expressed in the form of rewards based on team success in academic tasks. Teams work to earn recognition for the improvement of each member over prior achievement levels. As in other classroom situations, all students are striving for mastery of targeted content, but their motivation to work hard is boosted by the possibility of winning team honors for reaching new levels of individual competence. *Individual accountability* involves assessing each student's mastery of content. Teammates practice together and coach each other, but individuals are tested in the usual ways to demonstrate their independent skill. They may take quizzes or create items for a portfolio or perform a task unaided. Their individual grades reflect their individual achievement. However, the learning gains of individual members form the basis of the team score, on which public team recognition is predicated. *Equal opportunities for success* are ensured by team scoring systems based on individual improvement over prior performance, rather than on reaching some norm-referenced or criterion-referenced level of achievement. Superteams are those whose members' growth is considerable, not those whose average test scores are highest. The low achiever's improvement from 50% one week to 60% the next contributes just as much to the team's score as the higher achiever's jump from 85% to 95%. Both members are thus seen as valuable teammates because they contribute to team improvement scores, yet the standards of real competence remain clear. These three characteristics empower cooperative learning as an incentive system, engaging all students actively and giving each the opportunity to see how effort multiplies the effects of ability to produce more satisfying academic outcomes.

This chapter describes several of the most widely used cooperative learning strategies as well as a few simple routines that can add a responsive, engaging dimension to any lesson. Whenever appropriate, descriptions will include context features that support cooperative learning indirectly. Inventive teachers devise their own variations on standard forms to match the content and circumstances of their own classrooms, and they experience positive outcomes of several kinds. However, research to date suggests that when improved achievement is the goal, incorporating group goals, individual accountability, and equal opportunities for success into teaching strategies is essential.

OBJECTIVE **1** To list and explain the attributes of cooperative learning strategies that improve student achievement and to describe the ways these attributes may be embedded in a lesson

Learning Activity 1

The General Context of Cooperative Learning

Teachers, students, and content all play vital roles in good lessons; the fundamental nature and importance of those roles is the same in effective cooperative learning as in other effective lesson formats. Lessons are most productive when

- Teachers control the lesson elements that students do not have the knowledge or skill to control.
- Students work hard.
- Lesson content is substantively adequate and worthy of students' time and effort.

Teachers provide the overview of content, that is, the structure of relevant knowledge and the processes of knowing. "Overview" in this instance is defined as a representation of content and process that is just beyond but within reach of the learner's current knowledge. For example, with primary students, having explored the roles, relationships, and responsibilities of members of families and the school, a teacher might launch the class into a study of town governance. Metaphors from family and school life might serve as organizers and illuminators of the general structure; observed discrepancies could illustrate the nature of differences and extensions with respect to familiar social systems. Given print materials, opportunities to interview, videotapes, or other sources of data that students can review independently, the teacher shifts from presenter to coach, guiding students through the lesson content as they become familiar with details of the new information. Teachers must know the general terrain of the curriculum and the present level of student understanding in order to determine what lesson content represents a reasonable, stimulating stretch for students and what presentation mode offers them the richest, most supportive opportunity to learn.

In the ordinary process of learning, students use perception, action, and conversation. Babies offer the most easily visible example of this phenomenon: For months and months they watch others closely. Increasingly they attempt to imitate what they see, discovering through practice how to move purposefully, speak intelligibly, and reach their self-selected goals. By two or three they begin to be able to learn from their own and others' speech. Alone in a room, they may chatter away, talking themselves through their play, in part because of continued reliance on vocalization to know what they are thinking and doing. While increased age brings increased ability to "hear" one's own thinking without speaking aloud, new learning continues to rely on expression to reveal both mastery and misconceptions. Teachers have traditionally relied on recitation formats to assess students' learning for just this reason. However, expression during the process of learning, in the company of other novices, performs the important function of revealing both to the learner and to his or her peers the nature and extent of their mastery. Whether adults or children, novices frequently think they know something until they try to explain it; then, even before the other listeners can comment, the speakers hear the limitations of their own knowledge. If they do not, the other listeners generally do. Learners need to express their knowledge as it is developing, both to confirm and to correct its adequacy. Good cooperative learning strategies engage students in sharing how they think, examining their knowledge themselves, gaining insight from the critiques of their peers, and enlarging their conceptual understanding by hearing how others understand the same content.

Like other lessons, those using cooperative learning strategies to engage students depend ultimately on the adequacy of the content itself — both the knowledge and the processes of developing it — to promote growth. If the initial presentation of new content is muddled or shallow, if the practice exercise offers too fragmented a view of substance, if meaningful interaction over content is sacrificed for rote learning, then the lesson is doomed no matter how deftly the cooperative learning incentive system is implemented.

The concepts and activities explained in this chapter show how to motivate students to work hard together so that each one makes the most of his or her ability. To lead to measurable gains in achieving mastery of targeted skills and content, however, cooperative learning must operate in a context where teachers provide accessible and engaging opportunities to learn and the content is substantively compelling.

Essential Features of Cooperative Learning

What distinguishes effective cooperative learning from other activities that depend on small-group work is its particular combination of group goals or team rewards, individual accountability, and equal opportunities for success. Informal small-group work is common in classrooms; for example, teachers may ask students to review or discuss with two or three classmates materials first presented in a lecture or film. Such a format may lend interest to a class period by breaking up large blocks of instruction and stimulating the flow of recall and new insights. However, without some forms of team reward and individual accountability to shape the work, small-group assignments do not lead predictably to better achievement for all. Without an incentive structure that rewards individual growth and thus motivates students to take an interest in each member's learning, small-group assignments may become the burden of the smartest student in each group.

Team rewards function as effective supports for providing peer assistance; the opportunity to earn a team reward — even if it is largely symbolic — encourages students to invest time in coaching teammates. Under ordinary conditions, a bright student might be able to finish a page of practice exercises in a few minutes and spend the remainder of the allotted time reading or getting into mischief. A low-achieving student might not work at all, thus ensuring continued failure. Team rewards offer a payoff for the able students to help the less able and thereby create incentives for the less able students to work harder. The combination of harder work and explanations rendered in possibly more accessible peer terms generates success for the low achievers. What do the high achievers get? For one thing, the act of coaching itself seems to be related positively to improved achievement (Webb, 1988). Able students' mastery of skills and concepts also grows when they act as coaches for teammates.

Furthermore, by supporting mutual assistance among peers and generating interaction over academic tasks, team rewards stimulate students to forge new social bonds. Bright students whose academic interests and gifts might have been viewed ambivalently by classmates become assets to the learning team. In addition, students whose popularity may have caused others to overlook their academic shortfalls begin to feel pressure to improve their achievement. The productive contacts students experience on learning teams spill over into nonacademic spheres of school life. The coaching required for a team to earn an academic pennant causes its members to cross the boundaries of neighborhood, social class, culture, or ethnicity that may keep them apart in other settings. Cross-group social cohesiveness improves measurably on the playground and in the larger community (Slavin, 1979; 1990).

Individual accountability ensures that all students take the learning task seriously, and that no single student's mastery obscures the failure of another. In cooperative methods that emphasize individual accountability, the only way the group can succeed is to ensure that every member of the group has learned the lesson. To achieve the highest levels of mastery, students focus their energy on explaining ideas to one another, asking questions, monitoring progress on assignments, and assessing understanding. They know that the team score is based on the average of individual growth, measured individually.

When teachers grade the products of group work collectively, so that all members receive the same grade, very often one or two bright, ambitious members carry out the assignment. The others merely "hitchhike" to the completion point. Though the bright students will grumble about the unfair distribution of effort, they sensibly choose to assure their high grade by doing the work themselves, and the less able students — eager to improve their own grades — sensibly let them. Academically productive cooperative learning strategies use collective task structures to generate the individual effort that promotes individual competence. More and less able students work hard enough to experience the real progress that offers intrinsic satisfaction as well as higher grades.

Equal opportunities for success make it clear that growth, not absolute achievement, is the foundation of recognition. In learning teams, *success* means improving one's own past performance to a predetermined extent. The student whose test grade moves from last week's 40% to this week's 55% contributes exactly the same value to the team's score as the student whose grade goes from 80% to 95%. Within the system of team recognition, progress is the key to success. In most cooperative learning situations, success is not limited to one team. Rather, it is defined as reaching a preset level of improvement, for example, having an average team gain score of 20. The concept of "first prize" is replaced by the concept of "personal best." Every team that reaches the highest standards of growth is rewarded. Students are thus motivated to invest in the improvement of each team member.

Offering equal opportunities for success does not imply changing grading standards. Team success requires harnessing the members' combined energy to boost everyone to maximum achievement, whatever "maximum" might mean for each individual. Grading, on the other hand, usually means evaluating achievement — or some combination of effort and achievement — on the basis of a standard other than progress alone. Teachers who use cooperative learning methods to motivate students to work hard usually employ conventional grading systems. The high achiever's test score of 93% earns a report card grade of A, while the low achiever's 75% earns a C, although the low achiever's steady rise from 50% to 75% over the marking period may have contributed most to the team's regular Superteam awards. Cooperative learning does not lower legitimate standards of excellence; however, it does create conditions under which more students reach those standards.

In an effectively functioning cooperative learning lesson, students at every ability level are experiencing challenge and making good academic progress. Carefully controlled studies reveal that when lesson structures elicit the engagement of all group members, even the most gifted students grow measurably faster than gifted students in homogeneous classes (Slavin, 1991b). If the lesson provides a good opportunity to learn content, heterogeneous learning teams make more of that opportunity available to more students. Ability differences may still result in different levels of mastery, but the improved effort of all students in an effective cooperative learning structure means that all students will learn more. Furthermore, the social interaction over lesson content can promote critical thinking and development of advanced skills and knowledge among all students (Davidson and Worsham, 1992).

Typical Cooperative Learning Lessons

Widely used and well-researched forms of complex cooperative learning structures have four components: the presentation of content; skill practice or concept development activities in heterogeneous learning teams; assessment of individual student mastery; and team recognition or rewards.

Presentation of Content

Using any format that assures adequate quantity and quality, the teacher presents the content of the lesson. As in any strategy, the adequacy of this component establishes the potential extent of the learning. Students learn only if they have the opportunity to learn. Teacher presentation of content or teacher control of presentation ensures the completeness and accuracy of what is available for learning. In a straightforward lesson about a math computation skill, for example, the teacher might explain and demonstrate the skill and lead students through whole-class guided practice. In analyzing the characters of a novel, the teacher might brainstorm with students some of the questions they will use to guide group research. In developing a learning center where groups will explore a topic, the teacher uses materials and tasks that represent the topic effectively. Student team learning is *not* a self-instruction model, but a model in which students help each other learn content that has been presented effectively and clearly. Whether the teacher chooses the role of lecturer, guide, critic, or coach, he or she takes responsibility for the adequacy of lesson content. The teacher provides the resources, materials, and experiences that students need to understand lesson content.

Student Discussion and Practice in Learning Teams

Two factors contribute to the productivity of learning teams. The first factor is *the academic task structure*. The academic tasks and the procedures for completing them are designed to involve each member actively in learning. In many forms of successful cooperative learning, team members engage in group practice, discussion of material, individual practice, and peer coaching. Students attempt practice problems together and individually, explain their solutions, comment on each other's problem solving, and share insights about the nature of the problem and its relation to familiar issues. In preparing for a test about characters in a novel, they might pool collections of details supporting a particular assertion. In developing individual essays about self-selected topics related to the same novel, team members might share ideas about each other's topics, provide feedback about particular features of essay drafts, and trade proofreading services. The task structure engages them in conversation about skills, applications, and meaning and provides an audience for their work.

The second factor responsible for the productivity of learning teams is *heterogeneity*. Productive teams are microcosms of the larger class. Each team has males and females; high, middle, and low achievers; and members of any subgroups of the class (for example, special education students; racial, ethnic, or language minority students). Teams composed of members of pre-existing social groups may tend to slide off-task or interact over the nonacademic issues that form the basis of their voluntary association. Teams formed for the purpose of academic work and composed of members with different perspectives and abilities are more likely to pursue the academic goals. Evidence suggests that their success in this pursuit creates new, enduring, and positive social ties outside of class (Slavin, 1979; 1990).

Assessing Individual Student Mastery

Without assistance from team members, each student must demonstrate mastery of the lesson content in an individual assessment. While some engaging task structures include filling out worksheets together or creating collective products, the team's goal is for each student to perform well independently. Asking for and giving coaching help to teammates is the norm; asking for and giving answers is seen to be a shortcut to individual failure. Teachers' decisions about whether to reteach or move on to the next lesson, how to assign course grades, and how to interpret each student's academic achievement are based on individual test scores, performances, or portfolio items — that is, evidence of individual mastery.

Team Recognition and Reward

In many cooperative learning methods, all teams that reach a preset standard of individual gain averages are publicly recognized; terms such as "Superteam," "Greatteam," and "Goodteam" are used to convey the concept of collective achievement. The recognition is mostly ceremonial, accompanied by appropriate fanfare. Some teachers offer elaborate (photocopied) certificates, sometimes with small additional prizes — for example, Superteams may be given a "no homework" pass, extra recess, or some other token. For the most part, however, praise and honor serve as the coin of this academic realm. Occasionally, recognition comes from the team's public display of expertise, for example in a presentation. Outstanding individual progress may be recognized as evidence of effective teamwork, as well as of individual effort. If Jose makes a spectacular showing in the weekly vocabulary test, his team will be honored for its contribution to his learning.

MASTERY TEST

OBJECTIVE 1 To list and explain the attributes of cooperative learning strategies that improve student achievement and to describe the ways these attributes may be embedded in a lesson

Scenarios

Now that you have read something about the factors that generate improved achievement in cooperative learning strategies, see if you can distinguish between strategies that have those critical factors and other group strategies. Among the group activities described below, some will probably stimulate improved achievement and others will not (although they may be appealing for other reasons). For those missing a critical factor, explain what is missing — team rewards, individual accountability, equal opportunities for success, or generic essential lesson features such as sound presentation or task structure — and suggest how it might be included.

_____ 1. During Multicultural Month, Señor Gomez visits each class in the primary grades to read aloud children's stories set in Mexico. The school is in the center of a large city, and most of the children live in apartments. The story he reads to the third graders is about Elida, an eight-year-old girl who lives on a farm in a remote area of the country. When he finishes the story, he has the students sit in their regular, heterogeneous learning teams and write words and phrases describing the life of a typical Mexican child. He reviews their work and tests them individually, rewarding teams that reach preset standards of growth. Is this academically productive cooperative learning?

_____ 2. Mrs. McGrath presents a thorough explanation of long division and leads several brave students through practice problems on the chalkboard. Then she hands out a sheet of twenty problems to all members of the class and directs them to work silently and independently in their learning teams. The team captain will have a copy of the answer key. As each team member finishes the page, he or she gets the answer key from the captain, checks his or her work, and recomputes the problems that have errors. When the lesson on long division — of which this is one segment — is completed, the students will take tests individually, and teams will earn awards for reaching preset standards of growth. Is this academically productive cooperative learning?

_____ 3. Ms. Mustard has assigned each of her three reading groups (advanced, on-grade, and remedial) to choose a single book from her list and make a class presentation about it. Each group will receive a collective grade for its report. Is this academically productive cooperative learning?

_____ 4. Mr. Pickle's social studies class has been investigating the contributions of men and women to the development of the first thirteen American colonies. On Friday, he will give a test on where and when the men and women lived and what each contributed. He has assigned students to heterogeneous, four-member teams to review the material they have covered. After grading the tests, Mr. Pickle will post on the "Notable Historians" bulletin board the names of the teams (and members) whose scores average gains of 10 or more points. Is this academically productive cooperative learning?

_____ 5. Ms. Juniper taught a lesson on dividing decimal numbers. She assigned students to work on practice problems in heterogeneous, four-member teams. At the end of the lesson, Ms. Juniper administered the test. She rewarded teams on the basis of the team test grade average; Greatteams averaged in the 80s and Superteams averaged in the 90s. Is this academically productive cooperative learning?

_____ 6. Mr. Herman has been lecturing and showing films about the structure of DNA, a major component of genes. Before he started the unit, he calculated base scores representing each student's usual achievement in his course. After he finished presenting the material, he assigned students to study together in heterogeneous learning teams, using a study guide. After administering the unit test in the regular way, he calculated gain scores for each student by comparing the unit test score with the base score. On a special awards bulletin board, he posted the names of the individual students who made exceptional progress. Is this academically productive cooperative learning?

True/False Statements

Indicate whether the following conditions are essential for academic productivity in cooperative learning strategies (true) or not (false). If a statement is false, revise it to make it true.

_____ 1. In the first stage of the lesson, students usually conduct independent research on the topic of study.

_____ 2. Productive learning teams are made up of members who have a lot in common, such as gender or membership in a voluntary social group.

_____ 3. Students' participation in learning teams in the classroom usually translates to more cooperative social interactions elsewhere.

_____ 4. Academic progress in cooperative learning activities is measured by having the team take a test together to build team spirit.

_____ 5. If a student does exceptionally well on a test after working with a learning team, the teacher may recognize the team in public.

_____ 6. Team rewards are usually based on earning high grades on a test; for example, teams earn rewards by scoring an average of 90%.

OBJECTIVE   **2** To describe the interpersonal activities that contribute to student achievement in learning teams

Learning Activity 2

Cooperative learning strategies are strengthened by their reliance on the social aspect of learning (Corno, 1987; Trimbur, 1985). In other strategies, students listen to a lecture, or "interact" with a text or worksheet in preparation for a test. These are strangely solitary activities to be carried on in the tempting arena of a peer-filled classroom. We can assume that the students' interest in academic competence and the possible public recognition for high achievement will be motivating to some extent, especially for students with hopes of success. These motivations run counter, however, to most students' social drive. Students like to socialize. In addition, acquiring academic competence often involves skills better nurtured in group work, where modeling and feedback occur more frequently than in independent work. In other strategies, students are asked to sacrifice highly desirable interaction with peers. In cooperative learning strategies, they are given a structure in which they can and do interact with each other productively. Lessons are organized to harness the impulse to chat, develop new interaction patterns and directions, and improve learning opportunities for students at all achievement levels by use of peer coaching.

Cooperative learning methods use the students' desire for social interaction to drive the academic agenda. The part of each lesson that demands accuracy and completeness — presentation of material — is controlled by the teacher, who is the resident expert on content. The part of the lesson that may be managed by students is controlled by the group task structure. Using practice questions, discussion, texts, and other resources, group members review the content, rehearse procedures, critique each other's performance, and coach toward mastery. Students who need clarification ask peers who can give it. Students who learn the content from the original presentation learn even more in the process of retelling (Webb, 1988). Research clearly shows that both high and low achievers gain in achievement. Conversation about content under these circumstances becomes a social event. Participation in the social event is, by virtue of the assigned group task, academic.

The academic tasks in cooperative learning methods may be simple or complex, but all are structured to encourage each group member to bring all others to mastery. Some feature of the task engages the members in mutual coaching and pursuit of earning the group reward. Assessment of mastery is still individual — the goal of schooling is to produce knowledgeable individuals, after all — but in cooperative learning methods, individual growth in achievement is calculated to determine the group score. Groups gain recognition when each member shows optimal growth, no matter what the starting score was. Effective cooperative learning strategies thus harness the drive toward competence and public recognition to the drive for successful social interaction. Only when every student improves notably does the team earn rewards.

Fostering productive teamwork involves teaching prerequisite group process skills and, in some cases, adopting new classroom management strategies. Many teachers begin by posting guidelines developed jointly with students. Such guidelines might include the following:

1. Work *quietly* together on team assignment.
2. Ask for and give explanations, not answers.
3. Listen carefully to teammates' questions.
4. Ask teammates for help if you need it.
5. Work at the pace that is right for your team.
6. Help each other stay on-task; don't talk about or work on other things.
7. Remember that the team's work is finished only when every member knows the material.
8. Ask the teacher for help only after you have asked everyone on your own team.

In classrooms of diverse students, however, teachers cannot assume that everyone knows how to follow such rules. In some families, working "quietly" may mean total silence — seldom useful in this group-based learning activity — while in others, asking for help from peers may be construed as cheating. Many students will initially feel that the teacher is the only acceptable authority in the class, and they will consequently deluge the teacher with questions about both process and content that peers could answer with equal accuracy and greater speed. Concepts of good manners and respectful behavior vary greatly among different American subgroups, and their importance relative to other social values also varies in interesting ways. Assuming that all students have the prerequisite skills and a similar understanding of rules regarding their use will be counterproductive and lead to frustration and embarrassment. In addition, recent analyses of the learning demands that adults face at work (for example, Resnick, 1988) reveal that the skills recommended for productive participation in cooperative learning activities continue to be useful outside school. Therefore, time invested during a lesson in teaching students how to work together may pay great dividends in both the near and the long-term future.

For these reasons, teachers will find it useful to demonstrate how to work in groups and to engage students in rehearsal, practicing to the point of mastery in the same way and with the same patient persistence they would use to teach any new, difficult content. Such practice will contribute to the creation of a classroom culture accessible to all students, not mistakenly assumed to be familiar to students whose experience has not, in fact, prepared them. Once the skills have been demonstrated and practiced, teachers nurture them by circulating among learning teams and shaping behaviors in unobtrusive ways. When they can do so without interrupting ongoing work, teachers can reinforce effective group process by publicly praising good examples. Some post charts where they list instances of cooperative student behavior observed during a lesson.

In addition, teachers must cultivate their own supportive behaviors, which in some cases are quite different from the behaviors that work well in more directed lesson activities. For example, after students have been dispatched to work on teams, teachers should respect their need for concentration and keep whole-class communications to an absolute minimum. When conferring with individual teams, teachers should speak in a voice audible only to the team. When responding to questions, teachers should model coaching and explaining, whenever appropriate. For many teachers, the hardest new skill to learn is turning individual student questions back to the team instead of answering them immediately, when students are engaged in team activities. Once the initial presentation of new material in a lesson is complete, answering student questions is one way that other students can improve understanding and retention. Furthermore, once directions have been given, students are usually capable of repeating them for peers; those who listened will be impatient with those who did not, and they will generate peer pressure for classmates to listen more carefully when the teacher gives directions in the first place.

By creating lesson structures that rely on students to manage independent practice and engage them in meaningful, substantively valuable interactions about lesson content, teachers promote productive effort among students at every ability level. When students work hard in the socially appealing task structures of cooperative learning, they improve achievement in basic skills, content, and critical thinking. This positive outcome reinforces a principle underlying most human enterprises: hard work on tasks related to the goal produces better outcomes.

MASTERY TEST

OBJECTIVE 2   To describe the interpersonal activities that contribute to student achievement in learning teams

Student Types

All of the imaginary students listed below have what might be considered a "fatal flaw" when they are working in traditional, teacher-centered lesson formats. Use points made in Learning Activity 2 to explain how each student could benefit from a cooperative learning lesson format.

_____   1.   Charlie loves to liven up classtime by whispering a continuous flow of off-task commentary to his neighbors.

_____   2.   Sherrie is afraid to raise her hand in class (although she often knows the answer) and has not made many friends yet.

_____ 3. Casey is seldom chosen for sports teams because he is a very slow learner. He spends some time every day working with the resource teacher on reading and math.

_____ 4. Wanda usually finishes her exercises ahead of everyone else and then irritates the teacher with excessive demands for attention. Wanda's scores are in the low 90s, although she does not work very hard.

_____ 5. Kim is a new immigrant. She understands English pretty well but seldom participates in class activities, because she is not sure how to act. In her family, respectful silence is expected of children when adults are speaking.

_____ 6. Jesse was the terror of the third grade, but a Big Brother he met this summer while staying in a homeless shelter has persuaded him to mend his ways in school. Jesse wants to turn over a new leaf, beginning by figuring out how to interact with classmates without getting into fights.

Teacher Types

Each of the imaginary teachers below has a habit that seems useful when he or she is using teacher-centered instructional methods but will not work well in a cooperative learning lesson. Use points made in Learning Activity 2 to explain how each teacher should adjust behavior to use cooperative learning effectively.

_____ 1. Ms. Butler, having trained as an opera singer before becoming a teacher, projects her voice so effectively that she can get the whole class's attention no matter how noisily engaged they are in a project.

_____ 2. Mr. O'Hara prides himself on his patience. He willingly answers questions about task directions until every student in the room is able to get to work. Although his directions are always clear from the beginning, he sometimes spends half of the period repeating himself.

_____ 3. Ms. Murphy understands that Joey's reticence makes it hard for him to answer a question in front of the class, so she seldom calls on him for answers or comments.

_____ 4. Mr. Rogers is famous in his school for having the quietest, most orderly classroom. During language arts, you can hear a pin drop while his students are working on their essays or writing answers to questions about a novel they have just read.

OBJECTIVE   **3** To form student learning teams that promote positive social interdependence

Learning Activity 3

The teams that are most productive in academic achievement and that facilitate growth of social skills are those whose members represent the diversity of the larger class group. The dynamic, task-oriented interchanges that characterize the most effective learning teams arise from two conditions. First, members of heterogeneous learning teams reflect the diversity of the whole class. Differences in perception, learning style, prior knowledge, ability, native language, assertiveness, sociability, and verbal skills — to name a few — that may characterize students with different backgrounds serve as resources to the team. Second, learning teams formed across the usual social boundaries have primarily the learning task itself to bind them together. Students who share membership in voluntary groups — for example, as close neighbors, church members, or cultural groups — are bound by existing habits of interaction over the content of that prior association. They will be inclined to pursue familiar conversations or activities. At least initially, learning team members have only academic work as the basis for their interaction. As they will do later in adult work situations, team members use social skills to create a productive unit, whether or not they also become friends elsewhere.

To form learning teams, the teacher first computes the current achievement level of each student in the whole class and ranks students by achievement. A simple way to do this is to average the last three performance scores in the content area in which the team will work. For example, to form learning teams for math, one averages the last three math test scores. It is important to use achievement measures that give a reliable indication of typical end-of-lesson performance. (Teachers are sometimes tempted to use pretest scores, but they are not suited for this purpose because they are intended to reflect entering ability, not final achievement.) The teacher then sorts students by achievement into the top 25%, the bottom 25%, and the middle 50%. Other characteristics that may affect group participation — such as race, gender, handicapping condition, or language minority status — are noted for each student.

Using this information, the teacher forms groups of four or five by first choosing one or two students from each ability group, then attending to the array of other characteristics. For example, in a class of twenty-eight with seventeen boys and eleven girls, eight minority students, two students with physical handicaps, and one student with a learning disability, every team should have one high, one low, and two average achievers. Every team should have at least one girl, and no team should have more than two. Every team should have at least one minority student, and three teams should include a student with a disability. If the class had thirty students, an additional student of average ability should be added to each of two groups of four. For students in the intermediate grades and above, groups of four are ideal, a fifth being added only when necessary. For younger students, groups of two or three may work a little better; a foursome can be created for some projects by pairing pairs. For adults, groups as large as six may be productive.

Three predictable possibilities require teachers to adapt this team formation formula. First, where several language minority students with different levels of English proficiency are members of the same class conducted in English, it may be useful to place two on a team — one with better English skills to provide support for a second with more limited English. Second, where relations between two members of a class are actively hostile, discretion is the better part of valor; they should not initially be assigned to the same teams. Ultimately, they will acquire the group process skills to work together, but it is not wise to force the issue in the early days. Third, occasionally a student will simply refuse to work in any group at all. While initial resistance is not rare, most reluctant students can be persuaded to try out teamwork by the judicious application of modest incentives. Some students need a few days or even weeks to see how well the system works with their classmates before they will join a team. Very few students hold out for long. Most teachers find that permitting a student to work alone poses no real problems. In that case, the student would *not* be entitled to rewards offered for group work but should receive the report card grade and other recognition that might otherwise be earned by his or her solitary efforts. Such students should be offered regular invitations to join teams, and if they do, the scoring formula should reflect concern with fairness to those already on the team.

Learning teams stay together for several weeks (about four to six), long enough to complete a project or a related series of tasks. They are re-formed when work or conditions change. For example, a student who has been functioning as a low achiever may gain sufficient strength to be re-classified as an average or even high achiever; or the class may finish a unit of study, providing an opportunity for reorganization. Periodic changes in team membership give students ongoing practice in using so-cial skills to create productive work groups and further experience in forg-ing alliances with new, formerly unfamiliar classmates. The balance to be struck is between the benefits of such change and the benefits of remaining on a team long enough to develop insights about teammates that enable teams to make best use of diverse talents.

YOUR TURN

Balancing Learning Teams

Use the grades on the following class list to form a master list of students ranked by achievement. Then form three learning teams balanced according to achievement, gender, and ethnicity.

Name	Quiz 1	Quiz 2	Quiz 3	Gender	Ethnicity
Alvin	70	73	75	M	White
Andy	76	79	70	F	Black
Carol	62	64	65	F	Other
Danielle	74	85	80	F	White
Eddy	98	94	100	M	Other
Edgar	79	82	85	M	White
Jack	40	49	50	M	White
Mary	91	100	85	F	Black
Sarah	100	97	100	F	White
Stan	82	73	80	M	Other
Tammy	91	94	85	F	White
Travis	67	64	75	M	Black

MASTERY TEST

OBJECTIVE 3
To form student learning teams that promote positive social interdependence and academic success

Use the following class list and grades to form a master list in which students are ranked by prior achievement, with gender and special characteristics noted. Use your masterlist to form heterogeneous learning teams.

Team Formation

_____   1. Rank students in order of achievement, according to test scores.

_____   2. Form four- or five-member teams balanced by achievement, gender, and ethnicity.

Name	Test Scores	Gender	Ethnicity
Alice	78, 90, 67	F	White
Auggie	65, 85, 70	M	Other
Bernard	45, 70, 56	M	White
Colette	83, 90, 79	F	Black
Carl	87, 65, 84	M	Black
Danny	89, 87, 91	M	White
Debra	54, 72, 65	F	Other
Elizabeth	87, 92, 85	F	White
Ed	84, 72, 75	M	Other
Fred	56, 35, 65	M	Black
Gertrude	98, 97, 93	F	White
Hattie	78, 86, 79	F	Other
Isaac	86, 46, 74	M	White
Jenny	55, 46, 75	F	White
Keith	75, 80, 64	M	Black
Kim	98, 99, 97	M	Other
Laurie	34, 78, 65	F	Other
Mike	78, 73, 80	M	White
Ned	89, 83, 76	M	White
Olivia	74, 82, 79	F	Black
Peter	92, 91, 93	M	Black
Zelda	67, 43, 54	F	White

OBJECTIVE 4
To describe and distinguish among Student Team Learning (Student Team Achievement Divisions — STAD — and Teams-Games-Tournaments — TGT), Jigsaw II, and Group Investigation strategies

Learning Activity 4.1

Student Team Learning

Two extensively used forms of Student Team Learning are Student Teams Achievement Divisions (STAD) and Teams-Games-Tournaments (TGT; Slavin, 1990). Each begins with teacher presentation of lesson content to the whole class. Then students divide into previously assigned, heterogeneous, four- or five-member learning teams. The teams work together on teacher-selected or teacher-constructed study questions or practice exercises, coaching each other to mastery. After presentation and team practice in STAD, the teacher ends the lesson with a mastery test taken by students individually. For each student the teacher calculates an improvement score, comparing a base score (typical past achievement) with the new score. The improvement score for each student is averaged with the improvement scores of teammates to form a team improvement score. Teams that achieve a preset standard of improvement earn public recognition.

In TGT, the teacher ends the lesson with a tournament. Students leave learning teams and compete at tournament tables with two others at the same achievement level. For instance, three students who are customarily the three top scorers in multiplication compete at one table. Those who usually rank four, five, and six compete at another table. The questions at each table come from the same set, but the rate of accuracy needed to be the winner at each table differs. For example, the winner at the high achievers' table might have answered nineteen out of twenty questions correctly, defeating the two competitors, who answered only seventeen and eighteen right. The winner at the low achievers' table might have answered twelve out of twenty correctly, compared with nine and eleven correct answers for the competitors. Players at each table earn points to bring home to the learning team. The number of points earned is determined by the player's relative score at the tournament table: top, middle, or bottom. At the end of the tournament, each individual's tournament points are credited to the learning team. The winning team is the one with the highest average number of tournament points per member to its credit.

STAD and TGT are particularly effective with content that consists of quantifiable information or basic skills. Significant gains in achievement have been found in studies dealing with language arts, English, math, social studies, and science. All students in class are attempting mastery of the same content. Within groups, students act as peer tutors and coaches. For example, in a third grade spelling lesson, one aspect of student coaching might be giving and taking practice tests. In a senior high school social studies class, students might be searching through text material to form a comparison list for analyzing types of government. The teacher's role, apart from initial presentation of content, is to operate as a consultant to the groups.

Team scoring generates the basis for determining eligibility for recognition, but *does not* change the nature of conventional grading standards. A team member whose 75% represents significant enough improvement to earn the highest team improvement score may nevertheless receive a report grade of C. The teammate whose score of 93% represents maintenance but no improvement, and who earns therefore a lower improvement score, still receives a report card grade of A. In STAD and TGT, the task and reward structures lead to more time on-task, more efficient use of learning time, and more active engagement (Slavin, 1986). While their overall effectiveness usually leads to higher grades, they do not influence the achievement standards, or the nature or amount of content to be covered.

STAD and TGT have five elements.

1. *Team Formation.* Heterogeneous learning teams are formed as described in Objective 3.
2. *Presentation of Content.* Lesson presentation in STAD or TGT may involve lecturing, showing a film, or directing students to common resource materials such as texts or supplementary readings. Teachers have generally found it most effective to include three components in their presentation: (a) *introduction,* including a simple statement of the lesson goal and perhaps an attention-getting device, as well as a brief review of prerequisite skills; (b) *development,* emphasizing meaning; focusing on demonstration, explanation, and informal assessment; and maintaining a brisk pace; and (c) *guided practice,* requiring all students to attempt answers and calling on a random selection of respondents to sustain attention (Slavin, 1986). In this component, the teacher assures that students have an excellent opportunity to learn content.
3. *Team Practice.* To practice effectively, students need a set of study questions, worksheets, or other materials to guide their discussion. They should have access to an answer sheet, if appropriate, to check accuracy and understanding. In general, team practice includes an initial round of collective responses — group practice — followed by individual practice, with group checking and explaining. For example, the team might first practice a spelling list aloud, taking turns, then give each other practice tests. Or the team might work through two word problems aloud before settling down to working independently and then comparing answers. Preparation for this part of the strategy involves creating or finding appropriate study materials. When students first begin to work in learning teams, they may need a review of process skills that will facilitate work, as explained earlier. Many teachers find that rewarding well-behaved and productive teams with quiet attention communicates most powerfully to the other teams the expectations for student behavior.
4. *Assessment and Scoring.* For STAD, the final test is based on the same material as the study questions. It may take any reliable and valid form. Student grades for the test reflect whatever system the teacher uses; for instance, A might be given for scores 90 to 100, B for scores 80 to 89, and so on. Improvement scores, however, are based on a special formula, which may be established in various ways. One formula often used is:

*Posttest Score**	*Improvement Points*
10 or more below base score*	0
Within 10 points (+/−) of base score	10
11–20 points above base score	20
More than 20 points above base score or a perfect score	30

*Base scores and test scores are expressed in percentages.

Improvement points are calculated for each student, and teammates' improvement points are averaged. Teams whose collective improvement amounts to average gains of predetermined levels are eligible for certificates. For example:

Goodteams = Average improvement points 5–10
Greatteams = Average improvement points 11–20
Superteams = Average improvement points more than 20

For TGT, students leave learning teams after practice and report to tournament tables. At each tournament table, three students with comparable levels of previous achievement are grouped. The test questions in STAD are equivalent to tournament questions in TGT. At each table, students take turns asking questions and earning points for correct answers. One student is the reader and has the question list with numbered questions. On the tournament table is a face-down stack of numbered cards, each with the number of a test question on it. The reader draws a numbered card from the stack, reads the question of that number, and answers. The next student to the left (for this round, called the first challenger) either passes or challenges by offering a different answer. The remaining student (for this round, called the second challenger) either passes or challenges by offering an answer different from the other two. The second challenger is also the checker. When all players have answered or passed, the second challenger/checker reads the answer aloud from the answer sheet. If the reader answered correctly, the reader keeps the number card; if the reader was wrong, there is no penalty. If a challenger was right, he or she keeps the number card. If a challenger was wrong, he or she must return a previously won card (if already in possession) to the stack. If no one gives the right answer, the card is returned to the stack. When a round is ended, play moves one person to the left. (The first challenger becomes reader, the reader becomes checker, and so on.) The game is over when the number stack is used up (that is, all cards have been won) or when the teacher calls time. It takes about ten minutes to tally tournament scores at each table and to determine tournament points. Tournament points are awarded according to the following table (Slavin, 1986).

Calculating Tournament Points

For a Four-Player Game

Player	No Ties	Tie for Top	Tie for Middle	Tie for Low	3-Way Tie for Top	3-Way Tie for Low	4-Way Tie	Tie for Low and High
Top Scorer	60 points	50	60	60	50	60	40	50
High Middle Scorer	40 points	50	40	40	50	30	40	50
Low Middle Scorer	30 points	30	40	30	50	30	40	30
Low Scorer	20 points	20	20	30	20	30	40	30

For a Three-Player Game

Player	No Ties	Tie for Top Score	Tie for Low Score	3-Way Tie
Top Scorer	60 points	50	60	40
Middle Scorer	40 points	50	30	40
Low Scorer	20 points	20	30	40

For a Two-Player Game

Player	No Ties	Tied
Top Scorer	60 points	40
Low Scorer	20 points	40

These scores are credited to the players' learning team, and the learning team with the highest average tournament score per member wins the tournament.

5. *Recognition.* Recognition of team achievement appears in a class newsletter, bulletin board, or other arena appropriate for the grade level. One popular and simple recognition activity is to award certificates to members of winning teams.

YOUR TURN

Student Team Learning

1. Use the following class list (from the Mastery Test for Objective 3) to form homogeneous tournament teams of three or four for TGT.

Name	Test Scores	Gender	Ethnicity
Alice	78, 90, 67	F	White
Auggie	65, 85, 70	M	Other
Bernard	45, 70, 56	M	White
Colette	83, 90, 79	F	Black
Carl	87, 65, 84	M	Black
Danny	89, 87, 91	M	White
Debra	54, 72, 65	F	Other
Elizabeth	87, 92, 85	F	White
Ed	84, 72, 75	M	Other
Fred	56, 35, 65	M	Black
Gertrude	98, 97, 93	F	White
Hattie	78, 86, 79	F	Other
Isaac	86, 46, 74	M	White
Jenny	55, 46, 75	F	White
Keith	75, 80, 64	M	Black
Kim	98, 99, 97	M	Other
Laurie	34, 78, 65	F	Other
Mike	78, 73, 80	M	White
Ned	89, 83, 76	M	White
Olivia	74, 82, 79	F	Black
Peter	92, 91, 93	M	Black
Zelda	67, 43, 54	F	White

2. The content of a lesson that could be adapted to the student team learning approach follows. Develop a worksheet for completion in STAD learning teams based on this lesson. Write a ten-item short-answer test based on your worksheet.

When calculating the total amount in a problem that involves a percentage gain, change the percent to a decimal, multiply the decimal times the original number, and add the result to the original number. For example: Last year it rained 30 inches and this year it rained 10% more. How many inches did it rain this year?

(a) 10% = .10 (b) .10 × 30 = 3 (c) 30 + 3 = 33

3. Imagine that the students in the following teams earned the corresponding scores on the posttest you wrote for item 2 on page 301. Use the improvement point formula on page 299 to determine which team(s) qualified for Goodteam, Greatteam, and Superteam awards.

Team A Member	Base Score (%)	Posttest (%)
Alice	90	92
Eliz.	80	95
Keith	70	69
Peter	40	49

Team B Member	Base Score (%)	Posttest (%)
Auggie	95	85
Ed	85	90
Hattie	65	70
Olivia	50	55

Team C Member	Base Score (%)	Posttest (%)
Bernard	90	100
Gertrude	85	94
Jenny	65	76
Ned	55	85

Team D Member	Base Score (%)	Posttest (%)
Collette	95	84
Fred	80	70
Zelda	70	60
Mike	50	59
Debra	40	48

Team E Member	Base Score (%)	Posttest (%)
Laurie	95	90
Kim	70	81
Isaac	60	73
Carl	60	72
Danny	45	52

4. The students in teams A through E in question 3 competed in a tournament. Students were assigned to tournament tables on the basis of their usual achievement, and earned the following scores at their tables. (Next to each participant's name is the score earned by answering tournament questions. All teams had the same 30 questions.) First, determine the tournament points for each student, according to the table on page 300. Then determine which of the teams A through E won the tournament by adding up the tournament points earned by each member.

Table 1		*Table 2*		*Table 3*		*Table 4*	
Peter	15	Olivia	19	Hattie	20	Keith	25
Debra	17	Ned	17	Jenny	22	Zelda	24
Danny	14	Mike	20	Isaac	22	Kim	21
				Carl	24		

Table 5		*Table 6*		*Table 7*	
Elizabeth	22	Auggie	25	Gertrude	27
Ed	27	Laurie	26	Bernard	25
Fred	25	Colette	28	Alice	21

5. Describe the kind of team recognition that might be suitable for the students at the grade level you would like to teach.

Learning Activity 4.2

Jigsaw II

Jigsaw II is designed to promote interdependence. Students participate in expert groups and learning teams. In expert groups, students gather information about one aspect of complex content and become experts in this aspect of content. Then they return to their learning teams and share their expertise with their teammates, each of whom has likewise become expert in a different aspect of the content. Teammates coach each other toward mastery of the complex body of information by sharing expertise. All class members are then tested on all aspects of the content. For example, imagine that the class is using the Jigsaw II approach to gain an overview of the geographical features of Latin America. All students read through the same study materials, view the same films, or listen to the same lectures. Some students are focused on gathering information about, for example, the waterways, while others are focused on mountain ranges, agriculture, or areas of limited productivity such as deserts. These students have been given study guides with questions to facilitate data collection in the area to which they have been assigned. In a four-member learning team, each member has a different focus area. After presentation of material, the students who share the same focus gather in expert groups. They review the study questions and generate an inclusive response set. Together they identify all the information presented that is relevant to their area of expertise. The experts then return to their learning teams. Each learning team in the Latin American geography example has one expert each on waterways, mountains, agriculture, and areas of limited production. The group members present to each other the information from their special areas. The various experts on each learning team discuss the entire body of information. They may use a general study guide to help them integrate their findings. At the end of the lesson, all students take the same test about Latin America's geography.

Jigsaw II has six elements.

1. *Learning Team Formation.* Heterogeneous learning teams are formed, as with STAD and TGT. Each team has four or five members.
2. *Expert Team Formation.* One member of each team is assigned to a heterogeneous expert group. These groups may have six to eight members — as many as required by the number of areas of expertise planned and the number of learning teams.
3. *Presentation and Development of Expertise.* Members of each expert group are given a study guide that directs their attention toward certain information in the presentation. All students read the same material, for example the text chapter or in some other way share the same presentation, which includes information from all expert areas. As they listen to or view the presentation, students take notes on the material of particular relevance to their assigned expert area. After the presentation or reading, students from each expert group meet to review information in their area.

4. *Sharing Expertise in Learning Teams.* Experts return to their original learning teams, with at least one expert in each area on each team. They use an overview or study guide designed to elicit all the relevant information from each expert to direct their work. They coach each other to ensure mastery of all expert areas by all students on the learning team.

5. *Assessment and Scoring.* All students are tested individually on the content of all expert areas. Learning team improvement scores are calculated comparing base score with test score, as with STAD and TGT.

6. *Recognition.* Recognition of learning team achievement appears in the newsletter or on the bulletin board, or certificates are awarded.

Jigsaw I

Jigsaw I is the original form of the Jigsaw strategy (Aronson, 1978). In the original form, expert groups were the only ones to get information about their special topics. This limited dissemination of information — each learning team member was dependent on the experts in the learning team for information because it was not available except through the experts. Many teachers found Jigsaw I difficult to implement because it often requires development of special curriculum materials. Jigsaw I is a powerful strategy, however, when students will be doing research or can use materials that are normally organized by expert areas. To implement this variation, step 3 (Presentation and Development of Experts) is changed slightly: teachers simply assign study questions that lead each expert group to different information sources. When the expert groups have developed their unique information base, they bring it to their respective learning teams, as in step 4 above. Testing and recognition are the same as in Jigsaw II.

YOUR TURN

Jigsaw

Several general topics are listed. For each topic, write at least four subtopics that might be suitable for study by expert groups in Jigsaw.

1. Geographical features of a region

2. Analysis of "The Legend of Sleepy Hollow" (or some other story)

3. Explanation of the elements of a desert community

4. Major ethnic groups in the former Soviet Republics of eastern Europe and Asia.

Learning Activity 4.3

Group Investigation

Unlike STAD, TGT, and Jigsaw, the Group Investigation strategy (Sharan and Sharan, 1987) does not presume a clearly defined set of facts or skills to be mastered. Instead, it uses potential breadth and depth of rather generally defined topics for students to find and describe specific areas of interest. In Group Investigation, students are likely to learn as much about the structure of inquiry as about the facts of a case. For example, a teacher might use the Group Investigation strategy when the curriculum calls for study of local history and permits choice of which topics to pursue in detail. Given a goal such as "Students will be able to describe features of daily life in this region in the eighteenth century," a great variety of inquiry approaches might be appropriate. Analysis of a work of literature might also include a number of different kinds of inquiry. Accuracy, logical thinking, and coherent synthesis of information are important in Group Investigation, but the content to be mastered by students is a matter of their choice, given the domain of learning implied by the general subject or curricular goal.

The productivity of students in Group Investigation depends to a great extent on their skills in group process. In the other cooperative learning strategies discussed previously, the amount to be learned was set by the teacher, and the learning activities were based on the expectation of a predetermined amount of content coverage. The relative simplicity of the work assigned to the group stimulates the development of the requisite skills in interaction. In Group Investigation, success depends more on how well students listen to each other, support work, and use each other's contributions, because the group's task is complex. For this reason, Group Investigation works best with students who have completed some team-building exercises and demonstrated ability and willingness to work in a group. Strengthening group process skills is part of the planned outcomes of Group Investigation, but some skills are required at the outset.

Teams are formed as a function of both individual interest in a particular subject and representation of the diversity of the whole group within one subgroup. For example, the Group Investigation strategy might be used in social studies to undertake inquiry into the causes of the American Revolution. First, students would be divided into temporary brainstorming groups of three or four, each charged with generating a list of questions one might ask in relation to study of the Revolution. The whole class would compile a composite list of questions, which would be sorted into categories. Learning teams would include those who are particularly interested in investigating each category of questions. The teacher's role is to guide the formation of teams so that, to the extent possible, each team includes a fair sampling of students.

The learning teams review the questions in their category and pull together those questions most amenable to investigation. They set the goals for their work and divide the tasks among themselves. Then they begin to study the topic they have chosen. When their studies are complete, they present their findings to the class. A representative from each learning team is delegated to a central coordinating committee to ensure that team reports are presented in orderly fashion and work is equitably distributed within each team.

Evaluation may be designed by the teacher alone or in collaboration with a representative student group. The content on which students are evaluated must reflect the priorities established by the original choice of inquiry topics and by the presentations themselves. Students may be assessed individually on the basis of either the sum of the whole class presentations or the particular material developed within each group. In the Group Investigation strategy, individual accountability may take many forms, unlike most other cooperative learning strategies. Group recognition is also different, deriving from the celebrity of participating as one of a panel of experts, rather than from tangible awards such as Superteam certificates.

Group Investigation involves six steps.

1. *Identification of Topics.* This usually means presenting to the students the curricular goals or subjects that permit choice among several options for study. Such topics include, for example, complex historical events, literary analysis, science (ecological systems, environmental problems), and citizenship issues. After writing a brief statement of the topic on the board, the teacher asks students to list by themselves the questions they think relevant to the topic. After a few minutes, students in pairs or foursomes compare lists and come up with one list that includes all the different ideas. The whole class reassembles, and each small group reports the list of questions. With teacher assistance, students identify the categories into which the questions fall. All the ideas are listed under categories of study. In history, for instance, ideas might fall into categories such as types of work, architecture, explorations, clothing, food, art, games, schooling, and farming practices. These categories represent the topics to be addressed by the teams.

2. *Formation of Learning Teams.* Four- or five-student learning teams are formed on the bases of interest in each topic and heterogeneity. Some categories may not attract any volunteers; these can be dropped. Others may attract a large number of interested students; these can be subdivided further to form teams that will work on different aspects of the topic. The first team task is to discuss its topic more extensively and answer the question, "What do we want to study?" The members list relevant questions, and decide which member will pursue which line of inquiry for what purpose. They also identify useful resources, set timelines, and meet with the teacher to set a plan of action.

3. *Investigating the Selected Topics.* Students carry out the work they have planned. With the help of the teacher, they gather information, decide what it means, and contribute their perceptions to teammates. In some situations it is useful to provide support for planning and implementing their work by means of a worksheet, including the following items:

Study Question:
Names of Team Members:
Topics to be covered in work:
Resources for learning:
Scope of work or assignment for each team member:

4. *Preparing Presentations.* Students prepare a report to be made to the class. With the teacher as coordinator of all reports, team members decide what is to be presented and how it might be presented most effectively. Members choose or assign presentation tasks, including preparation of appropriate media support and definition of presentation priorities. In cooperation with other groups, members set criteria for presentation to be met by all.

5. *Making Presentations to the Class.* Students present the final report to the whole class, taking care to tie their part of the investigation to the parts undertaken by other groups and to attend to the presentation guidelines set by the class. Presentations should include audience participation and feedback.

6. *Evaluating the Work.* Evaluation is based on predetermined criteria appropriate to the learning tasks. For instance, if the understanding at the outset was that the whole group was responsible for mastering some of the information presented by all, the teacher might help with preparation of a regular test, with items selected by each group on the basis of the group's assessment of their importance. Other evaluation should focus on self- and peer-perceptions of the quality and amount of work done by each, and on evidence of higher-order thinking.

YOUR TURN

Group Investigation

1. Following are some learning goals typically found in school curricula. Some are well suited for the Group Investigation strategy, and some are better taught by other means. Write *GI* next to those particularly appropriate for Group Investigation.

   _____ Spell 100 on-grade spelling words.

   _____ Use the multiplication facts with accuracy.

   _____ Explain the causes of the Civil War.

   _____ Recite the first ten amendments to the Constitution.

   _____ Given their conventional abbreviations, name the elements on the periodic tables.

   _____ Describe the relevance of *The Scarlet Letter* to the morality of the colonial era.

   _____ Tell how pollutants affect the local environment.

   _____ Describe ten people who contributed to the welfare of this community in the last fifty years.

2. Choose two of the examples listed in number 1 that you think are suitable for Group Investigation. For each, write five questions that pertain to their study.

3. Imagine that you are working with the group of students listed on page 297. Auggie, Colette, Debra, Ed, Fred, Hattie, Kim, Mike, Olivia, and Peter all volunteer to work on a Group Investigation topic, Important Local Citizens in the Early Twentieth Century. Sort these students into two groups and define a subtopic for each.

MASTERY TEST

OBJECTIVE 4   To describe and distinguish among Student Team Learning (Student Team Achievement Divisions and Teams-Games-Tournaments), Jigsaw, and Group Investigation strategies

1. Read the following list of brief lesson descriptions and determine which include all the features that characterize effective cooperative learning strategies. For those that do not include all the essential features, tell which feature is missing.
   a. The Bluebird, Redbird, and Yellowbird reading groups meet daily with the teacher. Members of each group often ask each other for help on seat-work, with the encouragement of the teacher. At the end of each grading period, all students take a common reading test, and the high scorers' names are posted prominently. Is this effective cooperative learning?
   b. Everyone in the class uses the same speller, but students do their spelling exercises in teams that have good, average, and poor spellers. They ask for and get help from their peers. Every Friday afternoon, each member of each team meets with two students from other teams to have a mini spelling bee. (The three students had test scores from the previous week that were similar.) Students earn points for being the top, middle, or low speller in their mini bee. After the spelling bee, students return to their home team and add up team scores. The team with the highest score gets a certificate. Is this effective cooperative learning?

2. The following are activities or characteristics of student work groups. Some are typical of groups participating in effective cooperative learning; others are irrelevant or perhaps even inimical to learning. Circle the letter in front of those that support cooperative learning.
   a. High achievers tell everyone how to fill in the blanks.
   b. Team members ask for and get explanations.
   c. Everyone in a group belongs to the same social crowd.
   d. Group members talk to each other about academic tasks.
   e. Group members discuss nonacademic issues of common interest during group time.
   f. Minority students are grouped together.
   g. Two students with hearing impairments are put in the same group to simplify communication.
   h. Team scores are based on the improvement points earned by each member.
   i. Average achievers are all put together.
   j. Low achievers are put in a remedial-level team.
   k. The grade earned on a worksheet or project completed collectively is the grade recorded for each member.
   l. Students are tested individually, and individual scores form the basis for recognition.

3. The following class list includes the average of the last three test scores (given as a percentage) in one subject for each student, and information about student characteristics. Form teams whose composition will stimulate positive social interdependence and academic success.

Name	Average (%)	Gender	Ethnicity
Ann	87	F	White
Bud	67	M	White
Doris	81	F	Other
Frank	96	M	Black
George	56	M	White
Melissa	45	F	White
Nan	65	F	Black
Paul	85	M	Black
Victor	97	M	White

4. Briefly summarized plans for several kinds of lessons follow. Some are just lessons that use small groups for some tasks, while others use Student Team Learning, Jigsaw, or Group Investigation strategies. For each lesson description, write the name of the strategy used: *STL, Jigsaw, Group Investigation,* or *small groups.*

   a. After a lecture by the teacher on adding two-digit numbers, students break up into previously-assigned heterogeneous groups to discuss their worksheets and coach each other on how to find answers. When the final test scores are posted, groups whose members showed average gains of 10 points or more over base scores are given certificates.

   b. Prior to intensive study of the Civil War era, groups of four or five students (selected for their range of academic differences) are each given a topic to research: Dates of Important Battles, Confederate Military Leaders, Union Military Leaders, Civilian Leaders of the North, Civilian Leaders of the South, Weapons, and Geography. After reviewing their research materials, each group sends its members back to their usual work teams to report on what they learned. Each work team has one member from each group of specialists. The whole class takes a quiz that covers all topics. Recognition is given to the work teams that score well on the quiz.

   c. In a class with three reading groups — excellent, average, and below-level readers — a teacher uses a different novel with each group to introduce literary terms. Groups meet separately to discuss their books and to study concepts such as plot, characterization, setting, rising action, and climax. At the end of the lessons, the teacher administers to all the students a single test covering these concepts. Students who earn high scores are rewarded.

   d. One curricular goal for a group of students in science is to list some of the important elements in the ecosystems of their immediate environment, a farming community set in a low mountain range. The teacher leads students in a discussion that identifies many aspects of their environment. Students sort these ideas into categories and sign up to work with groups, one group assigned to each category. After a period of research and planning, students present findings to the class, and their knowledge of the environment is tested.

5. Using content and a student audience related to your own experience or goals, describe three lessons: one using Student Team Learning (STAD or TGT), Jigsaw, and Group Investigation. Briefly summarize the key components of each.

OBJECTIVE **5** To describe simple cooperative activity structures that can be integrated easily into regular lessons

Learning Activity 5

Complex lesson formats such as Student Team Learning are among the broad array of approaches to instruction that constitute the repertoire of good teachers. Circumstances will often require using other strategies in which, for the most part, students are all attending to the same instructional event at once — a lecture, demonstration, or film, for example. Several very simple tactics can assure that students maintain engagement and integrate lesson content with their prior knowledge. Three are described below; Kagan (1989) and others have collected and tested ideas for many more that promote active learning even in lesson formats that are relatively passive in nature.

Think-Pair-Share (TPS)

During a lesson in which the teacher is lecturing or demonstrating, he or she can develop comprehension or practice questions to serve as checkpoints during the period. When such questions are addressed to a single person, only that person gains from the opportunity to express developing comprehension and receive feedback on its adequacy. Using Think-Pair-Share (Lyman, 1992), every student experiences the practice opportunity and gets some kind of feedback. Here is how it works: The teacher explains some simple pairing scheme at the beginning of class, for example, having students count off in duplicate — 1,1; 2,2; 3,3; 4,4; and so on. If necessary, the last group may be a threesome or the teacher may take a partner. Before beginning the activity, the teacher also explains the think-pair-share strategy. At appropriate points during the lesson, the teacher poses a question and calls for a short "think-time," perhaps ten seconds or more, depending on the nature of the question. During this think-time, students must remain silent, forming their own answers. At a signal, usually just a simple word — "share" — or the sounding of a timer's bell, students turn to their partners and exchange answers, taking a minute to explain their thinking and resolve any differences. At the end of share-time, the teacher asks a pair to report. Depending on the lesson and the time available, the teacher may discuss the item further, invite other pairs to comment, or simply move along to the next lesson segment. If students are already sitting in their regular four-member teams and the lesson warrants further discussion, the activity may be extended to become "think-pair-square-share" — that is, after individual response and partner sharing, two partnerships compare and discuss responses together before the teacher reconvenes the whole class for discussion.

3 by 3 by 3

A slightly simpler and more flexible version of Think-Pair-Share, "3 by 3 by 3,"[2] works especially well with older students — including adults — during otherwise conventional large-group lessons, such as lectures. It requires no prior planning, no special instruction for students, and has been used successfully even in college lecture classes with hundreds in attendance. The teacher presents a lesson segment, for instance the first 10 or 15 minutes of a lecture or film, and then pauses. Students are directed to form groups of three with those sitting nearby; brainstorm at least three ideas, facts, or issues that have been raised during the previous segment of the lesson; and write down questions they wish the teacher to answer. They have three minutes to complete this activity. At the end of three minutes, the teacher may ask for questions or simply continue the lesson, stopping again for a 3 by 3 by 3 whenever necessary or desirable. As in TPS, the teacher may direct the group's discussion by posing a problem. If time does not permit dealing with the students' questions during the class period, the teacher collects written questions at the end of the period and deals with them later. In the normal course of events, many questions raised early in the period are answered either by peers during the three-minute discussions or later in the lecture as the topic unfolds. Students hand in only those questions that remain unanswered at the end of the period.

Numbered Heads Together

Numbered Heads Together[3] makes drills and quick reviews of facts engaging and productive for the whole class, and it may add depth to students' participation in more complex academic work as well. Numbered Heads is easiest to use with existing learning teams, although it also adapts easily to situations where teams are formed on an *ad hoc* basis for a single lesson. It has four components: (1) students receive a number; (2) the teacher poses a question; (3) students make sure everyone knows the answer; (4) the teacher calls on a number to answer.

Numbering students involves assigning students to four-member teams, using five-member teams only as needed, and giving each student on the team a number. In classes where learning teams are already in place, a set of numbered cards may be kept in each team's materials packet; students each draw a number when playing this game. Numbers 4 and 5 on the team may trade off answering when the number 4 is drawn (as described below). After students play this game once or twice, they establish routines for numbering off. In the example at the beginning of this chapter, Isaac, Jose, Kate, and May use the numbers in their team packet for a variety of tasks.

When the teams are settled and students numbered, the *teacher poses a question;* this activity is best suited for low-inference, high-convergence questions, such as "How do you find the answer to 25 times 31?" or "What are the main industries of Kansas?" or "What is the shape of a DNA molecule?" or "What is the meaning of the word 'exalted'?"

After the question is posed, the teams put their *heads together*, often literally, to discuss their responses quietly. Team members figure out what the answer is and then make sure that each person knows it, whether it is a fact or a process.

At the teacher's signal, teams stop conferring. The teacher calls a number at random — some use a spinner to assure randomness — and the student on each team with that number raises a hand or stands up. During this stage of the game, the teacher must enforce absolute silence among teammates in order to maintain conditions that support effective coaching during the assigned "heads together" time. Depending on the circumstances and the nature of the questions, teachers may opt for either of two respondent selection tactics at this point. They may call on one of the identified team representatives at random, taking care to give approximately equal numbers of response opportunities to all teams over the course of the lesson. Or they may have all of the identified representatives — one from each team — respond simultaneously, by writing the answer on a piece of scrap paper or the chalkboard, joining a choral response, or signaling in some predetermined way. The team receives a point for each correct response made by its randomly selected representative.

Some enterprising student teachers worked out a Jeopardy-like variation on Numbered Heads, using items from study guides developed for secondary students in various subjects. They created "answer grids" with columns of categories related to unit topics and rows of items of increasing difficulty with increasing point value. They reproduced these grids on either large chart paper or overhead projector transparencies, obscuring the answers with removable covers. In the class sessions scheduled for unit review, they assigned numbers to members of existing learning teams and provided each team with a supply of scrap paper and a marker. The order of play went like this: At the beginning of the game, the teacher gave the answer to the first easy question in the first column and gave the signal for "heads together." After teams had conferred, the teacher used a spinner to choose a number. After the number was called, strict silence was enforced while on each team the team with that number wrote the question in marker on scrap paper. (Breaking the silence resulted in a team's losing the opportunity to answer.) At a signal, all respondents put markers down and revealed to the teacher what they had written. Those who offered the correct question earned the designated number of points for their teams. The teacher allowed one of the winners to choose the next category. Winning teams earned one "late homework pass" for each member.

Like more elaborate cooperative learning strategies that are used over a longer period, Numbered Heads Together provides an incentive for students to harness their interest in socializing to an academic agenda, to invest in the learning of their teammates, and to work hard themselves. Furthermore, most students really enjoy playing. However, it does not address some of the underlying problems that erode the motivation of less able students. If one team's Number 2 student happens to be very bright academically and another team's Number 2 is learning disabled, neither the teams nor the individuals experience equal opportunities for success in competition with each other. In addition, the quick pace of the game and necessarily short "heads together" time make it practical for students to give answers rather than explanations to each other. For these reasons, Numbered Heads is best used as a small part of an incentive system generally driven by rewards for making progress and achieving "personal bests."

YOUR TURN

1. Describe a lesson using Think-Pair-Share or 3 by 3 by 3 that is appropriate for a subject in the grade level at which you hope to teach. Explain what you hope to cover during the lesson period, where you will pause for students to confer, and what question or assignment you will give them to focus their discussion.

2. Imagine that your class is organized into six learning teams; four teams have four members and two teams have five members. You have developed a list of twenty terms related to the unit on which the class is working and are preparing students for a quiz on those terms. Write a plan for a lesson using Numbered Heads Together as a review strategy. Include the following elements: (1) a list of terms related to a real unit of study; (2) a strategy for assigning numbers to team members; (3) a set of simple game rules expressed appropriately for the targeted grade level; (3) your strategy for calling on respondents; (4) the scoring system; and (5) potential obstacles to successful implementation and proposed solutions.

MASTERY TEST

OBJECTIVE 5   To describe simple cooperative activity structures that can be integrated easily into regular lessons

Listed below are ten brief descriptions of lessons that teachers have chosen to offer as whole-class, teacher-centered activities. Most of them would benefit from investing part of the lesson time in simple cooperative structures such as TPS, Numbered Heads Together, or 3 by 3 by 3. In a few cases, the teacher is making a big mistake in planning — the lesson would be easier to teach and more effective if offered in a Student Team Learning (STL) format. For each lesson, indicate which simple structure could be used effectively or whether the whole-class format should be dropped altogether in favor of an STL strategy.

1. The second grade teacher is reading aloud *The Story of Ping* to her class of twenty-five during their regular half-hour story time.

2. During a one-hour period, the American history class is watching a forty-five-minute segment of a film series on the Civil War to learn more about its effect on the lives of ordinary soldiers.

3. The Spanish-language teacher has introduced and explained the new vocabulary in the chapter, and today after a quick review he will give students practice in comprehension and use by telling them a story using the words and asking occasionally for responses to questions about content.

4. After spending several days in hands-on experiences with manipulatives, the fifth grade teacher plans to spend a period demonstrating how to add and subtract fractions.

5. The computer specialist plans to spend one class session in the lab giving students an overview of new software, a practice that experience has taught her works most efficiently. In the next class session, they will try it out for themselves, with her help.

6. The students have worked on a variety of team and whole-class activities in their study of the mid-Atlantic states. In preparation for the district's standardized test for this unit, the teacher wants to spend a period reviewing the basic facts that everyone needs to know.

7. The fourth grade math class will spend today working all together on computation problems, mixed operations, as a prerequisite for beginning a problem-solving unit tomorrow. The teacher wants to be able to check everyone's understanding and provide additional instruction if it seems necessary.

8. The sixth grade class is working on essays based on family stories, and in the process of discussing drafts, the teacher has discovered that almost everyone is confused about the placement of quotation marks. He plans to spend twenty minutes of today's class giving the whole class an explanation of quotation marks, using examples paraphrased from their stories for guided practice.

9. Students have asked many questions about the history of settlement in North America, especially about the precolonial eras, but the syllabus for this course does not allow much time for exploration of the topic. The teacher has decided to devote one class to aspects of the historiography of the pre-Columbian period, responding to students' evident interest in knowing how the stories that make up history texts are put together.

10. The class has just finished reading *The Sign of the Chrysanthemum,*[4] the story of Muna, an orphaned boy living in twelfth-century Japan. The teacher plans to spend the period working with the whole class to create character descriptions based on details found in the novel.

OBJECTIVE   **6** To examine how the physical, organizational, and instructional environments support effective use of cooperative learning strategies

Learning Activity 6

Some typical teaching activities look easy from the outside — the hard parts of giving a lecture or writing a test happen in private, as preparation, and the visible performance appears deceptively simple. Cooperative learning, however, is a complex activity that may seem daunting from the start. One learns eventually that developing the perfect lecture or test is also quite a complex undertaking, but one sees at the very beginning that cooperative learning strategies require careful planning. Those who use cooperative learning routinely discover in the long term that their early investment of time pays off — the students soon become active learners, applying their own energy to lessons, moving forward with their own momentum. On the other hand, in teacher-centered strategies, the teacher is often doing the lion's share of the work, pulling the class along; students have only to listen, take notes, and fill in blanks. To be successful in adding cooperative learning strategies to their professional repertoires, teachers must address the physical, organizational, and instructional aspects of environment that bear on implementation.

Physical Environment

A classroom's physical arrangement can either support easy use of learning teams or get in the way. The ideal arrangement includes several elements. First, desks, chairs, or tables should be set up for students in groups of four (or five). Students are always sitting in teams, whether or not a given lesson calls for teamwork. In most cases, desks can be adjusted to face the front when the activity requires it, and individual work can be completed as easily with students seated in clusters as otherwise. As a practical matter, in the history of education, arranging desks in rows facing front has by itself never been able to extinguish all student chatter. Seeing the students arranged in teams will prompt teachers more often spontaneously to use strategies like TPS, Numbered Heads, or less formal discussion options to promote students' reflection on and application of new ideas, as the content and pace of a lesson permit.

Second, the room should have areas designated for displays and supplies. An awards display site suitable for the grade level of the students should be prominent. If it is a room used by more than one class, there should be enough space for each. Team supplies — team packets, pennants, work-in-progress — and other materials should be easily available. If the room has general use areas, such as a library corner, policies should establish how they may be used during team time.

Third, the arrangements for desks, supplies, and teamwork should minimize the class's impact on others sharing open space areas or in immediately adjacent rooms. Thoughtfully designed physical arrangements have enabled cooperative learning strategies to be used successfully even in schools where large open spaces serve several classes. The trick is to use area rugs, furniture, floor space, and tightly clustered workgroups to keep noise levels low.

Finally, if the new ways of using furniture, space, or supplies result in different demands on custodial staff, teachers should alert them to the change and find out how to facilitate reasonable maintenance. For instance, diligent custodians might routinely straighten the desks back into rows each night, thinking it their responsibility, if they are not advised of the change. New learning tasks might at first cause undue messiness, which students must learn to manage.

Organizational Environment

Trial and error have shown teachers many ways to gain the support of coworkers as they begin implementing cooperative learning strategies. Starting to learn and apply these methods with a colleague has been a real asset to adoption. Peers can plan together, share resources, critique new ideas, observe each other, and generally provide the moral support that can help each through the first tentative steps.

Teachers report that principals and other supervisors can offer important assistance. Supervisors who have participated in cooperative learning training can, of course, provide insightful feedback on new plans and practices. Those who have little background in this area will need a briefing, so that they know what to expect if they drop in to visit. They can be offered a small observation "assignment" for their next planned visit. For example, they can take verbatim data on a team discussion or document the participation of mainstreamed special education or language minority students in teamwork. Such data are difficult for a teacher to collect, and they are very useful for reflecting on a lesson. Supervisors who have not been alerted to the new practices may mistake the lively buzz of conversation in a properly functioning team activity for off-task chat. Taking a proactive stance in explaining how the lesson is supposed to work and soliciting supervisors' input can promote their productive participation in implementation.

In a similar fashion, colleagues who are unfamiliar with cooperative learning strategies may be curious about what is happening in a newly cooperative classroom. Definitions of acceptable noise levels may have to be renegotiated. Explanations of the incentive value of team scoring may need to be offered. Some teachers will have the misconception that team points are substitutes for individual achievement; qualms of those who have such misconceptions can often be relieved by giving them the right information. Field experience has already taught every first-year teacher that good practicing teachers do not all agree on what belongs in a complete professional repertoire. Some features of cooperative learning — the hum of teamwork is the most notorious — raise questions that are usually resolved in early conversations with colleagues. Converts are most often won by the evidence of the effectiveness of cooperative learning strategies in achieving academic and social goals with every student.

Teachers often inform parents when they begin using cooperative learning to enlist their support and understanding. Parents of the highest and lowest achievers may have questions. Bright students' parents worry that cooperative learning strategies will make their children the workhorses of the teams and that working with a group of less able students will hold their children back. Teachers will need to explain how the scoring system requires every child to work hard to earn team points and to review the data that show how much the brightest students gain in real achievement in such settings. Less able students' parents worry that their children will not be able to keep up. While limited ability may still lead to only more modest achievement, the record is clear that in cooperative learning groups less able students gain significantly. Their individual achievement rises because they are working harder. Furthermore, they gain in popularity and acceptance because their progress (not their ultimate achievement level) contributes to the team score. Some of the structures of cooperative learning are unfamiliar to parents, and they will appreciate an explanation. Because positive outcomes are evident very soon after implementation begins and so many students eventually earn higher grades based on better performance, parents can become champions of the new strategy. Parent volunteers, appropriately oriented to the principles of cooperative learning, can be of great help in managing materials and supporting productive teamwork during lessons.

Instructional Environment

Whatever complex or simple cooperative learning strategy a teacher is using in a particular lesson, productivity will be increased if students share common expectations about how to proceed. The environment created by general social and behavioral expectations influences instruction. As discussed earlier, teaching prerequisite skills is the first step in initiating cooperative activities. In addition to teaching such things as how to talk in a voice that only one's group can hear or how to give an explanation instead of an answer, preparation may include team-building exercises.

The first team assignment is to choose a name — even high school students and adults in workshops enjoy this task. It may be appropriate for teams that will be together for several weeks to create a team poster or pennant that "flies" at their workplace whenever they are working together. Some teachers use part of the poster for *ad hoc* awards, for example, stickers earned for winning a game of Numbered Heads Together or for demonstrating exemplary skill in group process. Team posters can also serve as displays for weekly team scores. (The actual grades, of course, would not be displayed, but the team's improvement point scores reflect only gains.)

Teachers can use several tactics to teach group process skills in the course of a real learning task. For example, roles can be given to each student, by number, as was the case in the opening story of this chapter, or as a weekly assignment. Depending on the age level and the task, each team might need a materials manager, a task manager, a questioner, a checker, a note-taker, and/or a reporter, to name a few common roles. The materials manager gets supplies for a task from the supply shelf, returns homework or other papers from the teacher, and collects things to be given to the teacher. The note-taker records important points from a group discussion. The reporter uses the note-taker's records to tell the whole class what the team said. The set of roles is flexible, to meet the demands of different lessons and subjects.

Role assignment rotates — everyone learns how to lead, record, report, manage, and so on. In the beginning, students might need what Kagan (1989) calls "gambits" to help them fill their roles. The purpose of gambits is to provide a formula for communication that enables a child to take an unfamiliar leadership role and make it work. A gambit for the note-taker might be, "Do you want me to write that down?" A gambit for a task manager might be, "Our job for this period is to finish the exercise. Can we do the next problem?"

Another tactic that facilitates team communications is "talking chips" (Kagan, 1989). A talking chip is any object that every student has — a pencil, a book, a ruler, or even an actual chip from the math manipulative box. During a group discussion, when a team member speaks, he or she puts the chip in the middle. He or she may not speak again until every other team member has spoken and all the chips are in the middle. At that point, they retrieve their chips and start again. This tactic helps teams develop more equitable discussion habits in otherwise relatively unstructured tasks.

The purpose of activities such as these is to ensure that every student has the knowledge and the inclination to use appropriate group process skills during team learning periods. However, from the first time teachers use cooperative learning strategies, they must balance attention to lesson content with attention to group process skills. In properly functioning team learning activities, students learn how shared norms of civility can contribute to attaining a worthy end; in school, the worthy end is academic. If cooperative learning activities focus too exclusively on group process, students may benefit in the social skills arena but forfeit the academic gains they have a right to demand from schoolwork. On the other hand, if they do not receive instruction in how to work cooperatively, their squabbling may itself impede access to substantive learning opportunities.

To sustain and nurture a productive instructional environment, teachers must help students remain aware how their civility contributes to their academic progress, creating social and academic achievements that are intrinsically satisfying.

Teachers have found that two management practices are particularly helpful in implementing cooperative learning strategies. The first is using what this chapter has called team packets — an envelope or storage file that serves many purposes: Teachers can collect and return homework papers by means of the packet, which is handled by the team's materials manager. Packets can hold teams' works-in-progress, practice exercises, team score sheet, team pennant, number cards for numbered heads, and any other handouts or supplies that the teacher may place in the packet before class, for easy distribution by team members. The second practice is adopting a "zero noise signal," which is any signal that can be perceived by the whole class. Teachers use this signal on the very rare occasions when they must interrupt teams' deliberations to make an announcement of general interest, restore more reasonable noise levels, or for some other reason have everyone's attention. The signal may be raising one hand while catching the eye of the nearest team, each member of which then silently raises a hand until the whole class has noticed and is waiting in silence. Some teachers find that flicking the lights or ringing a small bell works. The most important aspect of this signal is that it must work almost instantly, to keep down time to a minimum. Rehearsing purposefully with a stopwatch and setting class goals for speedy compliance help most classes learn to respond to the signal effectively. However, teachers should not overuse the signal; working teams ought not be disturbed. Students will not be inclined to take their own teamwork seriously if the teacher is continually interrupting them.

MASTERY TEST

OBJECTIVE 6   To examine how the physical, organizational, and instructional environments support effective use of cooperative learning strategies

In the interests of refreshing his professional repertoire, Mr. Wills attended a three-day workshop on cooperative learning strategies at the staff development center. He is now eager to put his new knowledge into practice. He is working with Ms. Deyo, his school's master teacher, to plan the first lessons and reflect on his practice in the first few months. He has prepared a list of problems that require some action and will discuss them with Ms. Deyo after school today. Read the list and propose solutions consistent with the recommendations in Learning Activity 6.

1. The individual student tables in his classroom have been arranged in rows since time immemorial.

2. Ms. Jones, the custodian, has been tidying the desks into rows after school since time immemorial.

3. Neither the principal nor the grade-level lead teacher has ever used (or apparently heard of) cooperative learning. The principal often comes in for informal visits.

4. Mr. Zack, across the hall, runs a very orderly and silent classroom and already thinks Mr. Wills is an easy grader.

5. Alison's mother and father, both successful attorneys with a civil law practice, are grooming her for a fast-track Ph.D. program in an Ivy League school. They fret constantly about perceived slights to her considerable intellectual gifts.

6. Mr. Wills' students are sometimes uneasy about taking leadership roles in academic work; some appear unable to participate productively in group work.

Cooperative Learning Implementation Checklist

The key to successful use of cooperative learning strategies is organization. Planning, preparing materials, and maintaining a low-profile but helpful presence will ensure that students make the academic and social gains that have been proven in research. The following checklist might be helpful in introducing many of the strategies described in this chapter.

I. Before Teaching
　1. Write the lesson objectives.
　2. Write a team study worksheet that has problems, questions, or discussion items derived from lesson objectives. Frame the first few items to promote discussion among all members.
　3. Write a test or quiz based on the objectives and the team study worksheet.
　4. Form four- or five-member heterogeneous learning teams.
　5. Develop and post simple guidelines and reward systems. For example, design an awards bulletin board or certificates.
　6. Post improvement point scoring formula and team score sheets.

II. At the Beginning of a Cooperative Learning Exercise
　7. Announce team membership.
　8. Arrange desks to facilitate group interaction.
　9. Give teams time to name themselves.
　10. Post and review guidelines for effective teamwork.
　11. Rehearse teamwork skills that are new or unfamiliar.

III. Teaching the Lesson
　12. State lesson objective. Win student attention.
　13. Review prerequisite skills.
　14. Emphasize meaning, demonstration.
　15. Check student understanding and provide guided practice.
　16. Remind teams to start work by doing a few worksheet items together aloud and explaining answers.
　17. Circulate from team to team to provide help.
　18. Quietly praise teams that work productively.
　19. Use team names often.
　20. Maintain tolerable noise level.
　21. Model effective listening, questioning, and helping techniques.
　22. Redirect student questions to teammates if necessary.

IV. After the Lesson
　23. See that tests are checked, and improvement points and team scores calculated as soon as possible.
　24. Be prepared to announce Superteams, Greatteams, and Goodteams at the promised time.
　25. If mentioning individual improvement, credit team help.
　26. Use student feedback to make adjustments to lesson or procedures if necessary.

Many teachers find it helpful to start using cooperative learning at the same time as a colleague. Cooperative partners can offer support, coaching, and new ideas.

■ Answer Keys for Your Turn Exercises

ANSWER KEY

Your Turn: Balancing Learning Teams

Answers will vary. Teams should have two males and two females; an equitable racial mixture; and one high, one low, and two middle achievers. One possible set of teams is:

Team A: Sarah — female, white, high achiever; Andy — female, black, middle achiever; Stan — male, other, middle achiever; Jack — male, white, low achiever.

Team B: Eddy — male, other, high achiever; Tammy — female, white, middle achiever; Alvin — male, white, middle achiever; Carol — female, other, low achiever.

Team C: Mary — female, black, high achiever; Edgar — male, white, middle achiever; Danielle — female, white, middle achiever; Travis — male, black, low achiever.

ANSWER KEY

Your Turn: Student Team Learning

1. Answers will vary. One possible set of teams is: Peter, Debra, Danny; Olivia, Ned, Mike; Hattie, Jenny, Isaac, Carl; Keith, Zelda, Kim; Elizabeth, Ed, Fred; Gertrude, Bernard, Alice; Auggie, Laurie, Colette.
2. Answers will vary. The worksheet should have several problems of the form in the question (for example, weight gain, mark-up, cost with tax, tax increase, salary increase, output increase). The test should have ten similar items. When discussing worksheet construction, emphasize the need for some questions to distribute mastery demonstrations among team members. For example, write the first items so that one team member converts the problem's percent to a decimal, a second calculates the percentage, and a third adds the original number and amount of gain.
3. Results are:

Team A

Member	Base Score (%)	Post-test (%)	Improvement Points
Alice	90	92	10
Eliz.	80	95	20
Keith	70	69	10
Peter	40	49	10

Average Improvement Points: 12.5

Team B

Member	Base Score (%)	Post-test (%)	Improvement Points
Auggie	95	85	0
Ed	85	90	10
Hattie	65	70	10
Olivia	50	55	10

Average Improvement Points: 7.5

Team C

Member	Base Score (%)	Post-test (%)	Improvement Points
Bernard	90	100	30
Gertrude	85	94	10
Jenny	65	76	20
Ned	55	85	30

Average Improvement Points: 22.5

Team D

Member	Base Score (%)	Post-test (%)	Improvement Points
Colette	95	84	0
Fred	80	70	0
Zelda	70	60	0
Mike	50	59	10
Debra	40	48	10

Average Improvement Points: 4

Team E

Member	Base Score (%)	Post-test (%)	Improvement Points
Laurie	95	90	20
Kim	70	81	10
Isaac	60	73	20
Carl	60	72	20
Danny	45	52	10

Average Improvement Points: 16

Superteam — Team C; Greatteam — Teams A and E; Goodteam — Team B.

4. The tournament points are:

Table 1				Table 2		
Peter	15	40		Olivia	19	40
Debra	17	60		Ned	17	20
Danny	14	20		Mike	20	60

Table 3				Table 4		
Hattie	20	20		Keith	25	60
Jenny	22	40		Zelda	24	40
Isaac	22	40		Kim	21	20
Carol	24	60				

Table 5				Table 6		
Elizabeth	22	20		Auggie	25	20
Ed	27	60		Laurie	26	40
Fred	25	40		Colette	28	60

Table 7		
Gertrude	27	60
Bernard	25	40
Alice	21	20

Tournament winner is learning team D — Colette, Fred, Zelda, Mike, and Debra.

5. Answers will vary.

ANSWER KEY

Your Turn: Jigsaw

Answers will vary. Examples are:

1. Mountains, waterways, deserts, farming; varieties of watersheds; types of farming or agricultural use; desirable use opportunities.
2. Plot, characters, setting, style.
3. Producers, consumers, decomposers; flora, fauna, habitats.
4. Russians, Georgians, Ukranians, Serbians, Cossacks, etc.

ANSWER KEY

Your Turn: Group Investigation

Learning goals that are well suited for the Group Investigation strategy:

1. Explain the causes of the Civil War.
   Describe the relevance of *The Scarlet Letter* to the morality of the colonial era.
   Tell how pollutants affect the local environment.
   Describe ten people who contributed to the welfare of this community in the last fifty years.
2. Answers will vary.
3. Answers will vary. Groups should be heterogeneous.

ANSWER KEY

Your Turn: Simpler Cooperative Lesson Structures

1. Answers will vary. They should include selection of content that is most appropriately covered in a whole-class format in the first place; reasonable teaching segments, in light of the students; questions suitable for either sharing (TPS) or discussion; and plans for following up in 3 by 3 by 3, if questions raised are not to be addressed during class.

2. Answers will vary. The terms selected should be central to the content of the unit of study; the strategy for assigning numbers should be manageable; game rules should emphasize expected behavior; the scoring system should be fair; and the list of problems and solutions should show perceptive forethought about the circumstances that would affect implementation in a real-world situation.

▥ Answer Keys for Mastery Tests

ANSWER KEY

Mastery Test, Objective 1

SCENARIOS

1. No, because he presents a lesson with content very unfamiliar to the students and indeed arguably not presenting the life of a typical Mexican child, does not assess students' initial understanding, and provides inadequate followup to correct misperceptions. Even if the cooperative learning strategy appears to work well, students have too little information to generate reliable, new learning.
2. No, because learning improves when students talk to each other about problems, explaining how they worked and critiquing each other's results. There is no opportunity in this scene for peer coaching.
3. No, because there is no individual accountability. Each student could write a separate report, developed with the assistance of the team, or present an individually developed segment of the team's report.
4. Yes. Teams are recognized; mastery is tested individually; team scores are based on improvement.
5. No. Students have unequal opportunities for success, because team rewards are based on absolute achievement rather than improvement. Teammates with very low initial achievement have little chance of reaching a score of 80 or 90 in a week. Team recognition should be based on average improvement.
6. No. Teams receive no credit for their efforts to support individual learning; team rewards are missing. Recognition should be based on average team improvement.

TRUE/FALSE STATEMENTS

1. False. The teacher normally directs study at the beginning.
2. False. Teams are heterogeneous with respect to gender, ability, race, and other differences that occur in the class as a whole.
3. True.
4. False. Students take tests individually.
5. True.
6. False. Team rewards are always based on average gain scores.

ANSWER KEY

Mastery Test, Objective 2

1. Cooperative learning strategies harness students' sociability to the academic tasks of the lesson.
2. Cooperative learning task structures require each student to participate in a small-group session that's less intimidating for shy students.
3. Casey's improvement in grades will enable him to make a contribution to team success, even if he does not earn a passing grade.
4. Wanda's talents will be used and expanded by her participation in teamwork; she will get some positive attention from teammates; her scores may rise even higher.
5. The teacher's direct instruction on procedures, combined with opportunities to ask teammates for further clarification, will help Kim.
6. Rehearsing new behaviors gives Jesse a chance to get along better with classmates.

TEACHER TYPES

1. Ms. Butler must learn to speak softly so that only the team to which she is speaking hears her during group time.
2. Mr. O'Hara must refer questions about material already presented once to the whole class to the learning teams. Students will not rely on each other or themselves if they are allowed to rely on him for repetition of procedural or substantive information.
3. Ms. Murphy must set up learning team task structures that will engage Joey in explaining and answering aloud in the relative safety of the small group, so that he can benefit as the other students do from articulating his ideas.
4. Mr. Rogers must get used to a noisier environment during the times he is using cooperative learning. Students who are quietly discussing their topics and sharing ideas for essay development make a certain amount of noise.

ANSWER KEY

Mastery Test, Objective 3

Team Formation Exercise

Name	Test Scores	Gender	Ethnicity	Average	
Kim	98, 99, 97	M	Other	98	
Gertrude	98, 97, 93	F	White	96	
Peter	92, 91, 93	M	Black	92	High
Danny	89, 87, 91	M	White	89	
Elizabeth	87, 92, 85	F	White	88	
Colette	83, 90, 79	F	Black	84	
Ned	89, 83, 76	M	White	83	
Hattie	78, 86, 79	F	Other	81	Average
Carl	87, 65, 84	M	Black	79	
Olivia	74, 82, 79	F	Black	78	
Alice	78, 90, 67	F	White	78	Fifth Members
Ed	84, 72, 75	M	Other	77	
Mike	78, 73, 80	M	White	77	
Keith	75, 80, 64	M	Black	73	
Auggie	65, 85, 70	M	Other	73	Average
Isaac	86, 46, 74	M	White	69	
Debra	54, 72, 65	F	Other	64	
Laurie	34, 78, 65	F	Other	59	
Jenny	55, 46, 75	F	White	59	
Bernard	45, 70, 56	M	White	57	Low
Zelda	67, 43, 54	F	White	55	
Fred	56, 35, 65	M	Black	52	

Possible Teams:

Team A: Kim — male, other; Colette — female, black; Mike — male, white; Isaac — male, white; Laurie — female, other.

Team B: Gert — female, white; Hattie — female, other; Keith — male, black; Bernard — male, white.

Team C: Peter — male, black; Ned — male, white; Debra — female, other; Jenny — female, white.

Team D: Danny — male, white; Carl — male, black; Ed — male, other; Alice — female, white; Zelda — female, white.

Team E: Elizabeth — female, white; Olivia — female, black; Auggie — male, other; Fred — male, black.

Answers may vary. Male and female; white, black, and other; and high, average, and low achievers should be mixed.

ANSWER KEY

Mastery Test, Objective 4

1. a No, there is no team recognition or equal opportunity for success.
   b. Yes.
2. b, d, h
3. Answers will vary. Each team should have 1 high, 2 average, and 1 low achiever; 1 or 2 girls; and 1 or 2 white students.
4. a. STL b. Jigsaw c. small group d. GI
5. Answers will vary.

ANSWER KEY

Mastery Test, Objective 5

Answers may vary. There is no hard-and-fast rule about when to use TPS and 3 by 3 by 3, although TPS usually works better with younger students.

1. Think-Pair-Share would provide engaging opportunities for students to check comprehension or predict events.
2. The teacher could use 3 by 3 by 3 to elicit comments and questions.
3. Whole-class instruction offers most students little opportunity for practice. A team activity involving development of dialogues in Spanish using the key vocabulary would involve everyone more actively, and the teacher could correct grammar and pronunciation by circulating from group to group to monitor.
4. Think-Pair-Share could be used for guided practice problems throughout the lesson.
5. The teacher could use 3 by 3 by 3 for periodic comprehension checks, to make sure students are following her as well as they can at this stage.
6. Numbered Heads Together would make this review period exciting and engaging.
7. Numbered Heads Together could keep everyone on-task.
8. He could use TPS to involve students in punctuating examples he writes on the board or on an overhead transparency.
9. She could use 3 by 3 by 3 two or three times during her lecture to maintain students' attention and encourage them to apply what she is saying to the information provided in their texts.
10. The goal of becoming familiar with characters in a novel by finding hints in the text can be reached much more efficiently by using Student Team Learning strategies or Jigsaw. This is a potentially interesting learning task that will seem boring as a lecture or whole-class discussion, even if the teacher uses TPS or 3 by 3 by 3.

ANSWER KEY

Mastery Test, Objective 6

1. Rearrange them in team clusters of four or five.
2. Tell Ms. Jones the plan. Enlist her help.
3. Give the principal a short description of cooperative learning. Invite him to join a team in the second or third week, and have the children explain teamwork to him. (Details of this answer may vary.)
4. Explain the new strategy and its history of positive academic impact. Keep the door closed if necessary until the students learn how to talk in soft voices during teamwork.
5. Give them information about the considerable benefits to gifted children who participate in cooperative learning.
6. Assign roles and gambits. Have teams model how to use them.

Notes

1. K. Paterson, *The Sign of the Chrysanthemum* (New York: Harper and Row, 1973).
2. *3 by 3 by 3* stands for 3 students, 3 ideas, 3 minutes.
3. Kagan (1989) credits this game to Russ Frank, a teacher in Diamond Bar, California.
4. K. Paterson, *The Sign of the Chrysanthemum* (New York: Harper and Row, 1973).

▇ Additional Readings

Aronson, E., et al. *The Jigsaw Classroom.* Beverly Hills, CA: Sage Publications, 1978.

Calderon, M. *Cooperative Learning for Limited English Proficient Children.* Baltimore, MD: Center for Research on Effective Schooling for Disadvantaged Students, 1990.

Cooper, J. L., S. Prescott, L. Cook, L. Smith, R. Mueck, and J. Cuseo. *Cooperative Learning and College Instruction: Effective Use of Student Learning Teams.* Carson, CA: California State University Foundation on Behalf of the California State University Institute for Teaching and Learning, 1990.

Corno, L. "Teaching and Self-regulated Learning." In D. C. Berliner and B. V. Rosenshine, *Talks to Teachers.* New York: Random House, 1987.

Davidson, N., and T. Worsham, eds. *Enhancing Thinking Through Cooperative Learning.* New York: Teachers College Press, 1992.

Duran, R. "Cooperative Learning for Language Minority Students." Paper presented at the Annual Meeting of the American Anthropolical Association, November 1991.

Kagan S. *Cooperative Learning Resources for Teachers.* San Juan Capistrano, CA: Resources for Teachers, 1989.

Lyman, F. "Think-Pair-Share, Thinktrix, Thinklinks, and Weird Facts: An Interactive System for Cooperative Thinking." In Davidson and Worsham, eds., *Enhancing Thinking Through Cooperative Learning.* New York: Teachers College Press, 1992.

Resnick, L. "Learning in School and Out." In *Educational Researcher* 16, No. 9 (December 1987): 13–20.

Sharan, S., and Y. Sharan. "Group Investigation: A Strategy for Expanding Cooperative Learning." Paper presented at the First Annual Mid-Atlantic Conference on Cooperative Learning, Annapolis, MD, 1987.

Slavin, R. E. "Effects of Biracial Learning Teams on Cross-Racial Friendships." *Journal of Educational Psychology* 71 (1979): 381–387.

Slavin, R. E. "When Does Cooperative Learning Increase Student Achievement?" *Psychological Bulletin* 94 (1983): 429–445.

Slavin, R. E. "An Introduction to Cooperative Learning Research." In R. E. Slavin et al., eds., *Learning to Cooperate, Cooperating to Learn.* New York: Plenum, 1985.

Slavin, R. E. *Using Student Team Learning.* Baltimore, MD: Center for Research on Elementary and Middle Schools, The Johns Hopkins University, 1987.

Slavin, R. E. *Cooperative Learning: Theory, Research, and Practice.* Englewood Cliffs, NJ: Prentice-Hall, 1990.

Slavin, R. E. "Synthesis of Research on Cooperative Learning." *Educational Leadership* 48, No. 5 (February 1991): 71–82.

Slavin, R. E. "Are Cooperative Learning and 'Untracking' Harmful to the Gifted?" *Educational Leadership* 48, No. 6 (March 1991): 68–71.

Trimbur, J. "Collaborative Learning and Teaching Writing." In B. W. McClelland and T. R. Donovan, *Perspectives on Research on Scholarship in Composition.* New York: Modern Languages Association, 1985.

Webb, N. "Small Group Problem-Solving: Peer Interaction and Learning." Paper presented at the annual meeting of the American Educational Research Association, New Orleans, 1988.

Evaluation | 10

■ Terry D. TenBrink

1 To define *evaluation,* and to describe each of the four stages in the evaluation process

2 To select appropriate information-gathering instruments when seeking to make classroom evaluations

3 To write effective test items for evaluating achievement

4 To develop checklists and rating scales for evaluating student products and performances

5 To describe how to use information to evaluate; that is, to grade, judge student progress, judge changes in student attitudes, and judge the effectiveness of your own instruction

6 To select and use standardized instruments

Educational evaluation is useful only if it helps the educator (administrator, teacher, student) make sound educational judgments and decisions. In this chapter, you will learn about some of the basic principles of evaluation as applied to classroom problems. This chapter can be helpful when you are faced with the task of evaluating your students. I would encourage you, however, to go beyond this introductory level of understanding. Purchase a basic text on classroom evaluation techniques. Practice your test-writing skills whenever possible. Learn from your mistakes as you begin to evaluate your own students, and learn to use evaluation as a necessary and important teacher tool. Use evaluation to help you teach better and to help your students learn better.

OBJECTIVE

1 To define *evaluation,* and to describe each of the four stages in the evaluation process

Learning Activity 1.1

Stated most simply, to evaluate is to place a value upon — to judge. Forming a judgment is not an independent action. To judge, one must have information. The act of judging depends on this prerequisite act of obtaining information. The act of forming a judgment is itself prerequisite to an action one step further: decision making. So, *evaluation*, the process of forming judgments, depends on information gathering and leads to decision making. Picture it this way:

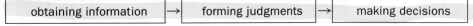

| obtaining information | → | forming judgments | → | making decisions |

Or this way:

> *Evaluation* is the process of obtaining information and using it to form judgments that, in turn, are used in decision making.

The definition clearly specifies the interrelationships among the various stages in the evaluation process; and yet, it also clearly indicates the centrality of forming judgments. If you have not formed a judgment, you have not evaluated.

It is important for you to understand the *total* evaluation process. So, let's expand this definition. So far, it is obvious that evaluation involves at least three stages: obtaining information, forming judgments, and using those judgments in decision making. By adding a preparation stage and enlarging a bit on the last stage, we come up with the following four stages:

The evaluation process

Stage 1: Preparing for evaluation
Stage 2: Obtaining needed information
Stage 3: Forming judgments
Stage 4: Using judgments in making decisions
and preparing evaluation reports

Let's look at a rather typical teaching-learning situation. Notice how this teacher goes through these four stages as she attempts to make her instruction more effective.

Stage 1. Preparing for Evaluation.   Bonnie, a third grade teacher, has become concerned about Billy. He seems to be having trouble keeping up in reading. Bonnie wonders how long he will be able to function within the reading group he is in. She wonders whether or not she should move him to a slower group. Perhaps there is something she can do to help — some extra work, for example, or some extra attention. She decides she needs more information before she can accurately judge Billy's level of achievement in reading. After determining the kind of information she needs (for example, information about the kind of errors made when reading orally, Billy's use of various word attack skills, Billy's interests), Bonnie determines when and how to obtain that information.

Stage 2. Obtaining Needed Information.   Over a period of several days Bonnie obtains a great deal of information about Billy. She gives him a standardized reading test, listens to him read orally, carefully records the errors he makes, and observes him throughout the day, watching for patterns of behavior that might indicate particular attitudes toward various subjects.

Stage 3. Forming Judgments.   After analyzing all the information she has obtained, Bonnie comes to the following conclusions:

Billy is not capable of reading material written at a third grade level.
Billy reads comfortably only that material written on a second grade level or lower.
Billy's primary weakness lies in the area of word attack skills.
Billy does not have a comprehension problem. He understands what is read to him.
Billy likes the children in his reading group.
Billy enjoys the stories in the third grade reader.

Stage 4. Using Judgments in Making Decisions and Preparing Evaluation Reports.   On the basis of her judgments Bonnie decides that she should keep Billy in his present reading group. She also decides to take the following action:

Prepare a checklist of word attack skills.
Systematically teach Billy those skills on a one-to-one basis.
Continue to have the stories read to Billy so that he will not fall behind on his comprehension skills.
Have Billy check off each word attack skill as he demonstrates competence in using it.

Having made these decisions, Bonnie writes a brief summary of her judgments, noting the actions she anticipates making. She files this in her own files for future reference. She also calls in Billy's parents and shares her findings with them. She asks them to cooperate, give Billy lots of encouragement and praise, and support him as he struggles to make up the deficiencies she has discovered.

Note the key features of each of the stages

1. *Stage 1. Preparation.* Determine the kind of information needed and decide how and when to obtain it.
2. *Stage 2. Information Gathering.* Obtain a variety of information as accurately as possible.
3. *Stage 3. Forming Judgments.* Judgments are made by comparing the information to selected criteria.
4. *Stage 4. Decision Making and Reporting.* Record significant findings and determine appropriate courses of action.

Learning Activity 1.2

Talk to a teacher about how he or she decides what to teach, when to teach, and how to teach. Probe for specific answers. Try to identify the various stages in the evaluation process as that teacher explains his or her decision making to you. Could you use the terminology of this chapter to explain what the teacher has done?

MASTERY TEST

OBJECTIVE 1   To define *evaluation,* and to describe each of the four stages in the evaluation process

1. Give a brief definition of *evaluation.*
2. List the four stages in the evaluation process. Describe briefly what goes on in each stage. Use examples from the classroom to clarify your descriptions.

 **2**   To select appropriate information-gathering instruments when seeking to make classroom evaluations

Learning Activity 2

The first step in preparing to evaluate is determining what you will be evaluating, and what kind of information you will need to make that evaluation.[1] Once that has been determined, you are ready to choose a tool for obtaining that information. There are two steps involved: (1) determine the information-gathering technique you want to use, and (2) select the type of instrument that should be used.

Step 1. Choose an Appropriate Technique

There are four different techniques classroom teachers use to obtain information about themselves and their students: inquiry, observation, analysis, and testing. To inquire is to ask. Whenever you wish to know someone's opinions, feelings, interests, likes and dislikes, etc., ask that person. Effective teachers always ask their students how they feel about what is going on. They know the value of information gained through inquiry. Observations are made by teachers whenever they look, listen, feel, or use any other senses to find out what is going on in the classroom. Observations of student performances, habit patterns, and interpersonal interactions all provide the teacher with helpful information. Analysis is the process of breaking something down into its component parts. For example, a teacher might analyze a math assignment to discover the kinds of errors students are making, or a vocational education teacher might analyze a coffee table made by a woodworking student to evaluate the project according to the design, overall construction, and finish of the table. Testing is being used whenever there is a common situation to which all students respond (for example, a test question), a common set of instructions governing the students' responses, a set of rules for scoring the responses, and a description (usually numerical) of each student's performance — a score.

The following chart compares these four techniques. Study the chart and then try to do the exercise that follows.

Summary of the Major Characteristics of the Four Information-Gathering Techniques*

	Inquiry	Observation	Analysis	Testing
Kind of information obtainable	Opinions Self-perceptions Subjective judgments Affective (especially attitudes) Social perceptions	Performance or the end products of some performance Affective (especially emotional reactions) Social interaction psychomotor skills Typical behavior	Learning outcomes during the learning process (intermediate goals) Cognitive and psychomotor skills Some affective outcomes	Attitude and achievement Terminal goals Cognitive outcomes Maximum performance
Objectivity	Least objective Highly subject to bias and error	Subjective, but can be objective if care is taken in the construction and use of the instruments	Objective but not stable over time	Most objective and reliable
Cost	Inexpensive, but can be time-consuming	Inexpensive but time-consuming	Fairly inexpensive Preparation time is somewhat lengthy but crucial	Most expensive, but most information gained per unit of time

*Terry D. TenBrink, *Evaluation: A Practical Guide for Teachers* (New York: McGraw-Hill, 1974), p. 140. © 1974 by McGraw-Hill Book Co. Used with the permission of the McGraw-Hill Book Company.

YOUR TURN

Choosing an Evaluation Technique

For each of the following questions, decide on the evaluation technique that would probably be most helpful. Use the following key: *A*, inquiry; *B*, observation; *C*, analysis; *D*, testing.

1. What kind of errors does Sally make when reading aloud?

2. How well can Sammy read?

3. What is George's attitude toward math?

4. Why isn't Ernest completing his workbook during spelling?

5. What is the average reading level of this class?

6. Who does Johnny have as friends?

7. What mistakes are most common in long division problems?

8. How well did the students learn the concepts in Chapter 7?

9. How well does Mary interact with her classmates during recess?

10. What are Kevin's primary handwriting errors?

Step 2. Select the Best Instrument to Obtain the Information You Need

Once you have selected an appropriate information-gathering technique, you should choose the type of information-gathering instrument to be used. An information-gathering technique is a *procedure* for obtaining information. An information-gathering instrument is a *tool* we use to help us gather information. We will briefly examine four basic types of instruments: tests, checklists, rating scales, and questionnaires.

A *test* is an instrument that presents a common situation to which all students respond, a common set of instructions, and a common set of rules for scanning the students' responses. Tests are used primarily for determining aptitude and achievement. When we want to know how much a student knows, or how well he or she can perform certain skills, a test is an appropriate instrument to use. Most classroom tests are constructed by the teacher, and are referred to as *teacher-made tests* or *classroom tests* to distinguish them from *standardized tests*. The instructions on standardized tests have been carefully standardized so that everyone taking the test does so under similar conditions. Most standardized tests are developed and sold by test publishers, and have been carefully developed, tried out, revised, standardized, and evaluated for reliability and validity.

A *checklist* is basically a list of criteria (or "things to look for") for evaluating some performance or end product. One uses a checklist by simply checking off those criteria that are met. For example, one could use a checklist to be certain that a student goes through all the routines in an exercise program, or a list of criteria for an effective speech could be checked as an indication of what a student did correctly when making a speech to inform. Whenever it is helpful to know whether an important characteristic is present in a performance (or is found in some end product), a checklist would be an appropriate instrument to use.

If we wish to rate the quality of a performance or end product, a *rating scale* would be the instrument to use. We might judge a speech, for example, by whether or not gestures were used. But if we want to determine the quality of those gestures (whether they were good, fair, poor, etc.), a rating scale should be used. A rating scale provides a scale of values that describe someone or something being evaluated. Questionnaires are especially useful for getting at opinions, feelings, and interests. They can be used when we are not certain about the type of responses we might get.

The advantages and disadvantages of each type of instrument are highlighted for you in the following table. Again, study the table carefully, and then take "your turn" at trying to select an appropriate instrument.

Advantages and Disadvantages of Each Type of Information-Gathering Instrument

Type of Instrument	Advantage	Disadvantage
Standardized tests: used when accurate information is needed.	Usually well developed and reliable. Include norms for comparing the performance of a class or an individual.	Often not measuring exactly what had been taught. Expensive. Limited in what is measured.
Teacher-made tests: used routinely as a way to obtain achievement information.	Usually measure exactly what has been taught. Inexpensive. Can be constructed as need arises.	No norms beyond the class are available. Often unreliable. Require quite a bit of time to construct.
Checklists: used to focus observations.	Helpful in keeping observations focused on key points or critical behaviors.	Measure only presence or absence of a trait or behavior.
Rating scales: used to judge quality of performance.	Allow observational data to be used in making quality as well as quantitative judgments.	Take time and effort to construct. Can be clumsy to use if too complex.
Questionnaires: used to inquire about feelings, opinions, and interests.	Keep inquiry focused and help teacher to obtain the same information from each student.	Take time and effort to construct. Difficult to score — no right answers and therefore hard to summarize the data.

YOUR TURN

Selecting an Information-Gathering Instrument

Read each of the following classroom situations. First decide what technique is being used (inquiry, observation, analysis, testing), and then write down which instrument you would use and why. Compare your answers with those of your peers and those found in the answer key.

1. A second grade teacher wants to find out if her pupils now understand how to form the vowels in cursive writing.

2. A high school social studies teacher wants to know how his students feel about the outcome of the latest elections.

3. A fourth grade teacher wants to know how well his class compares to other fourth grade classes in their achievement of the basics: reading, writing, arithmetic.

4. An eighth grade teacher just finished teaching her students to compute the volume of a cube, and wants to know how well her students learned this skill.

5. A music teacher wants to rank-order her clarinet players so that she can assign them chairs in the band.

6. A shop teacher wants to make sure that all his students follow the safety precautions when operating a radial arm saw.

MASTERY TEST

OBJECTIVE 2   To select appropriate information-gathering instruments when seeking to make classroom evaluations

For each of the situations described in the following questions, determine the best technique and/or instrument to be used.

1. A fifth grade teacher wants to ask all her students how they feel about each of the subjects they are studying.
   a. Testing — classroom test
   b. Observation — questionnaire
   c. Inquiry — rating scale
   d. Inquiry — questionnaire

2. A high school math teacher wants to know if her class is ready to go on to the next unit. To measure the students' level of achievement, she should use a:
   a. Classroom test
   b. Standardized test
   c. Checklist
   d. Rating scale

3. The school superintendent wants an overall picture of the level of achievement for each class in the school system.
   a. Checklist
   b. Classroom test
   c. Standardized test
   d. Rating scale

4. A speech teacher is trying to improve her ability to judge impromptu speeches.
   a. Analysis
   b. Observation
   c. Testing
   d. Inquiry

5. An English teacher examines each student's theme carefully so she can get an idea about each person's particular strengths and weaknesses in writing.
   a. Analysis — checklist
   b. Analysis — test
   c. Inquiry — checklist
   d. Inquiry — test

6. To determine academic aptitude for placement in special programs, one should use a:
   a. Rating scale
   b. Checklist
   c. Classroom test
   d. Standardized test

OBJECTIVE   **3** To write effective test items for evaluating achievement

Learning Activity 3.1

The first step in test construction is to determine what it is you are trying to test, and what kind of item would be best suited to testing that type of information. Most classroom tests are used to measure learning outcomes. The best statements of learning outcomes are instructional objectives. As you may recall from the discussion in Chapter 3, instructional objectives define clearly, in observable terms, the achievement we expect of our students, and the importance of well-chosen verbs in writing instructional objectives was emphasized. The verb should describe precisely the kind of response you expect the student to make to a particular subject matter content. If the verb used in an instructional objective does that, it is a relatively simple matter to determine the type of test item you should use. For example, suppose you are trying to find out if your students have mastered the following objectives:

To list the names of the first ten presidents of the United States
To describe the major contributions of Washington and Lincoln
To explain the changes that occur when a different political party takes
   control of Congress

The first objective obviously calls for a short-answer question in which the student is asked to list names. The other two objectives would best be tested with an essay question because the student would have to describe or explain — not the kind of thing they could do on an objective test such as true/false or multiple choice. What kinds of learning outcomes are best measured with objective-test items (true/false, matching, multiple choice)? These types of items are best suited for measuring learning outcomes for which the student must be able to choose among alternatives. For example:

To choose the word that best describes the author's feelings
To select the sentence that best represents the democratic position
To identify the emotive language in a paragraph
To determine which of several experiments would most likely provide the
   information needed by a particular researcher

Note that each of these objectives could readily be measured with an objective test; however, it is possible to measure some of them with another type of item. For example, the third objective in the list (to identify emotive language) could be measured with a variety of test items:

1. *True/False:* The statement underlined in the paragraph above is emotive language.
2. *Multiple Choice:* Which of the following sentences (as numbered in the paragraph above) represents emotive language?
   (a) Sentence 2   (c) Sentence 6
   (b) Sentence 3   (d) Sentence 9
3. *Short Answer:* Pick out three emotive statements from the paragraph above and write them on your paper.

You can readily see that the first step in selecting the type of item to use is to examine the instructional objectives. There is often still room for choice, however; some objectives can be measured by more than one item type. Consequently, other things must be taken into account. The following table highlights the advantages and disadvantages of the major types of test items. Study this table carefully, and then try the exercise "Your Turn."

Advantages and Disadvantages of Different Types of Test Items

Type	Advantages	Disadvantages
Short answer	Can test many facts in a short time. Fairly easy to score. Excellent format for math. Tests recall.	Difficult to measure complex learning. Often ambiguous.
Essay	Can test complex learning. Can evaluate thinking process and creativity.	Difficult to score objectively. Uses a great deal of testing time. Subjective.
True/False	Tests the most facts in shortest time. Easy to score. Tests recognition. Objective.	Difficult to measure complex learning. Difficult to write reliable items. Subject to guessing.
Matching	Excellent for testing associations and recognition of facts. Although terse, can test complex learning (especially concepts). Objective.	Difficult to write effective items. Subject to process of elimination.
Multiple choice	Can evaluate learning at all levels of complexity. Can be highly reliable, objective. Tests fairly large knowledge base in short time. Easy to score.	Difficult to write. Somewhat subject to guessing.

YOUR TURN

Selecting the Type of Item

For each learning outcome, determine the type of test item you would use and briefly state your reason.

1. To explain the value of using strong, active verbs in writing paragraphs.

2. To list the steps to take when processing a film.

3. To select, from among alternatives, the best way to introduce a new topic.

4. To discuss the implications of the new morality.

5. To write down the names of a least five generals from World War II.

6. To choose the most likely cause of a given kind of engine malfunction.

7. To recognize each of the major parts of speech.

Writing Test Items

▨ Writing Essay Questions

The secret to effective item writing is to be as clear and concise as possible. Don't try to trick the students. Test each learning outcome (instructional objective) in as straightforward a manner as possible. When reading a test question, a student should understand exactly what is being asked. If the student knows the material, he or she should be able to answer the question correctly.

The objectivity that comes from an item written in this way is especially difficult to attain when writing and grading essay questions. By following the simple guidelines listed, however, you should be able to produce well-written essay questions.

Guidelines for Writing Essay Questions

1. Make certain that your question really tests the learning outcome of interest.
2. Each essay item should include:
   (a) A clear statement of the problem
   (b) Any restrictions on the answer
3. For each item, construct a model answer. It should include:
   (a) The content of an ideal answer
   (b) Any important organizational features one might expect in an ideal answer

Once you are certain that an essay is the type of item you wish to use, you need to formulate the question so that every student reading it will have the same understanding about what is expected in the answer. Every student need *not* be able to answer the question; however, every student should know what the question is asking. That criterion for a well-written essay question will be easier to meet if you:

1. Use clear, concise language.
2. Are precise about any restrictions you want to place on the answer.

Examine the following sets of questions. Note that the questions that are easiest to understand are shorter, contain simpler language, involve simple sentence structures, and do not include extraneous verbiage.

Set A

Clear: Describe a wedge, and list three or four of its uses.
Not so Clear: Explain what a wedge is and its function with a few examples.
Downright confusing: Produce a descriptive paragraph concerning the wedge and its functional utility.

Set B

Clear: Explain why certain chemicals should always be mixed in a certain order.
Ambiguous: Exploding chemicals can be dangerous, which should not happen. How do you avoid this?
Impossible: Sometimes reactions occur that are potentially volatile when the proper order of mixing certain chemicals is not maintained. Can you explain this?

Using clear, concise language is not enough. An effective essay question must also indicate the level of specificity you expect in the answer. It must let the student know whether opinions are acceptable, whether or not arguments must be substantiated, and, if so, whether or not references are needed. It should provide the student with an indication of just how much freedom he or she has in responding. Take, for example, the following essay item:

Discuss the various properties of water.

The language of this item is certainly clear and concise. But what kind of response would be acceptable? Would "water tastes good and gets you wet when you fall in it" be an acceptable answer? Maybe. Only the author of the question knows. Look at the following alternative ways of writing this item. Each one imposes slightly different restrictions on the student's answers, and each one is better than our original item because of those added restrictions.

Describe what happens to water when it is exposed to extreme temperatures.
List the chemical properties of water.
List the nutritional properties of drinking water.
Why does the taste of water vary so greatly from one location to another?
List and briefly describe five ways that water helps to sustain life.

Note that each of these items clearly calls for a different kind of response. Note too the variety of ways one can restrict or shape a student's response. Now try your hand at writing essay items by doing the following exercise.

YOUR TURN

Writing Essay Items

Write two essay questions. One should be an open-ended question. The second should place restrictions on the response the student is asked to make.

1. Write an open-ended question with little restrictions.

2. Write an essay question that somehow restricts or limits the student's response in one or more of the following ways.
   (a) Limit the amount of time to answer, or the number of words that can be used in the answer.
   (b) Limit the topic to certain, specified subtopics.
   (c) Ask the student to focus on one aspect of the topic.
   (d) Restrict the response to only one point of view.

Well-written essay items will help make it easier for the students to respond *and* easier for the teacher to grade. The biggest problem with essay tests is that they are difficult to grade objectively. That problem can be greatly reduced if a model answer is developed and used as a guide when the students' answers are graded. There are two major considerations when writing a model answer.

1. All important content should be included in a model answer.
2. Any important organizational features that would be expected in a comprehensive answer should be specified.

YOUR TURN

Constructing a Model Answer

Write two or three essay questions with various degrees of freedom. Then write a model answer for each question.

First, a model answer should contain any content you hope to find in the students' answers. When comparing a student's answer to the model answer, you should only have to check through the student's answer to see whether or not it includes the items listed as important content in the model answer. Facts, concepts, principles, and acceptable problem solutions are the kinds of things one should list in a model answer. Two examples of model answers follow. The first is for an essay question calling primarily for factual material; the second calls for a specific type of answer, but allows the student some freedom in the particular content to be discussed.

Example of a Model Answer for a Factual Essay Question

Question: Describe the steps to take when developing black and white film.
Model Answer: Student answers should include the following information.
Step 1: In darkened room (red light only), load film onto developing reel, grasp film by edges, check to see that film surfaces are not touching each other.
Step 2: Place reel in developing tank and cover with light-tight lid.
Step 3: Wet down the film, etc.

Example of a Model Answer for an Essay Question Allowing Some Freedom of Content

Question: Defend *or* refute the following statement: Civil wars are necessary to the growth of a developing country. Cite reasons for your argument, and use examples from history to help substantiate your claim.
Model Answer: All answers, regardless of the position taken, should include (1) a clear statement of the position, (2) at least five logical reasons, (3) at least four examples from history that *clearly* substantiate the reasons given.

Note that in the second example, the student has great freedom to choose what to discuss, but restrictions are placed instead on the *type* of information to be included in the answer. For some essay questions, the order in which topics are included in the answer may be important. Other questions may call for a carefully developed logic, and the specific content is less important. Just remember this basic rule: a model answer should highlight the features that best reflect the learning outcome being measured by the essay question.

Writing Multiple-Choice Questions

Multiple-choice questions are perhaps the most frequently used type of test item. To make it easier to talk about these items, labels have been developed for each part of such an item:

```
STEM ──────→ Which of the following words is misspelled?
                  (a) Geography
CORRECT ──────→ *(b) Filosophy
ALTERNATIVE       (c) History ←────→ DISTRACTORS
                  (d) Filament
```

The multiple-choice item is the most versatile of all item types. You can ask questions at almost all levels of understanding, and do so with a high degree of reliability. To be both a reliable and a valid measure of a learning outcome, however, a multiple-choice item should meet the following criteria:

1. Present a single problem or question
2. Measure a learning outcome that can be tested by selecting a right or best answer from among several alternatives
3. Include alternatives that are terse — most of the item's information occurs in the stem
4. Include alternatives that are similar in wording, writing style, length, etc.
5. Include alternatives that follow logically and grammatically from the stem
6. Include distractors that are plausible but not correct.

Let's examine a few multiple-choice items to see if they meet the criteria listed. Then you will have an opportunity to evaluate items, and try writing some of your own.

Examples of Multiple-Choice Items

Poor Item: Alternatives too lengthy, question unclear.

1. Frozen foods
    (a) Can be quick-frozen and then stored at zero degrees and only then for specified periods of time
    (b) Are tastier than any other kind of processed foods
    (c) Should always be washed and blanched before being packed for freezing
    (d) Can be stored at 28° or less if they are properly packaged and sealed

Improved: Question clarified, alternatives shortened.

1. What is most important to a long shelf life for frozen foods?
    (a) Zero° temperature
    (b) Air-tight packages
    (c) Blanching foods before freezing
    (d) Selection of food for freezing

Poor Item: Alternatives do not follow grammatically from stem.

1. The constituents of air that are essential to plant life are
    (a) Oxygen and nitrogen
    (b) Carbon monoxide

(c) Nitrogen and iodine
(d) Water

Improved: All alternatives are plural, stem shortened.

1. Which of the following pairs are essential to plant life?
   (a) Oxygen and nitrogen
   (b) Carbon oxide and iodine
   (c) Polyethyl and water
   (d) Water and carbon monoxide

Improved: All alternatives are singular.

1. Which of the following is essential to plant life?
   (a) Nitrogen
   (b) Carbon monoxide
   (c) Polyethylene
   (d) Iodine

YOUR TURN

Evaluating and Writing Multiple-Choice Questions

Choose a subject with which you are familiar and write five multiple-choice questions. Try to write at least two of them at a level of learning higher than just the memorization of facts.

Writing True/False Items

True/false items are often criticized because they are so susceptible to guessing on the student's part. Certain kinds of learning outcomes, however, lend themselves naturally to a true/false format. If the items are carefully written to make them as reliable as possible, it would seem reasonable to include a few true/false items in a test.

The most important rule to remember when writing true/false items is that each item must be clearly true or clearly false. Look at the following examples.

1. Squares have only three sides and two right angles.
2. Liquids always flow in the direction of gravitational pull.
3. Complete sentences include both a subject and predicate.
4. Cities are built on major traffic routes.
5. Our moon reflects the light of the sun.
6. Extroverts are outgoing and always popular.

Note that items 3 and 5 are clearly true, and that only item 1 is clearly false. Item 2 is basically true, but "always" is extremely strong language. Might there be some exceptions? And what about item 4? It is a reasonable generalization, to be sure, but not true in every case. Finally, item 6 is partially true (outgoing, yes, but not always popular). Does the part that is false make the whole statement false? The problem with item 6 can often be avoided by remembering a second rule: each true/false statement must present one and only one fact. For example, we could improve item 1 by making two items from it:

(a) Squares have a total of three sides.
(b) Squares have only two right angles.

A final rule to remember when constructing a true/false item is: do not try to trick the students. Don't take a perfectly true statement, for example, and insert a "not" or other qualifying word that would make the statement false.

Good Item: The sun is closer to the earth at the equator.
Good Item: The sun is farther from the earth at the equator.
Bad Item: The sun is not closer to the earth at the equator.

Don't lift a statement out of context, hoping that the student will remember reading it and think it true because it is familiar.

Poor: Nouns modify nouns.
Improved: Although they do not normally do so, in some situations nouns can modify nouns, for example, baseball bat.

There are many other ways to trick students. You'll know it when you are doing it. Avoid the temptation. Always ask yourself, "Am I measuring an important learning outcome in a straightforward manner?"

YOUR TURN

Writing True/False Items

Try the following exercise. Remember the three rules cited in the text, and also remember to avoid (1) using statements lifted directly from the "book," (2) double negatives, and (3) long, complex statements.

A professor has just assigned several children's books to his literature class and wants to spot-check whether or not they remember the stories they have read. Write six to eight true/false items about the story "Little Red Riding Hood."

■ *Writing Matching Items*

Matching items are written as a group of items divided into two lists. The student's task is to match each item from one list with an item from the other list. A well-written set of matching items will illustrate some particular relationship between pairs of items from the two lists. A common use of the matching exercise, for example, is to test the relationship between a term and its definition. Other relationships that might be tested with a matching exercise are:

1. Historical events and dates
2. Novels and their authors
3. Tools and their uses
4. Problems and their solutions
5. Elements and their symbols
6. Causes and their effects
7. Drawings and their interpretations

Relationships like these are relatively easy to test with a matching exercise. Simply make two lists and write a clear set of instructions, telling the student the kind of relationship you are testing (the rationale, or basis, for matching). Try your hand at writing a matching exercise as instructed in the next exercise. Make sure that you keep the following points in mind.

Points to Remember When Writing a Matching Exercise

1. An obvious, natural relationship must exist between the items in the two lists.
2. The basis for matching must be made clear to the student.
3. One of the lists should be approximately 50% longer than the other list (which makes it difficult to obtain correct matches by the process of elimination).
4. The shorter list should not contain more than seven or eight items.

YOUR TURN

Writing a Matching Exercise

Write a matching exercise to measure elementary science facts (for example, properties of water, uses of elementary tools, weather conditions and their signs). Your shorter list should include five items to be matched with items from a seven-item list. Make certain that you have written clear instructions to the pupils.

Learning Activity 3.2

As an optional learning exercise, you may find it helpful to examine a variety of test items, judging them in light of the criteria set down in the last few pages. Ask your instructor to help you locate both standardized and teacher-made tests for you to examine. For each item, ask yourself what makes the item an effective or ineffective one. Also ask: "What is the writer of this item really trying to measure?" This activity can be done individually or in small groups, but any findings should be shared with others in a general class discussion.

MASTERY TEST

OBJECTIVE 3   To write effective test items for evaluating achievement

Write a set of objectives for a unit of instruction. (Choose the subject matter and grade level.) Next, develop a test designed to find out whether students have mastered the objectives. You may wish to put your items on index cards to file for future use.

OBJECTIVE   **4** To develop checklists and rating scales for evaluating student products and performances

There are many times when tests will not give you the information you need. You want to rate a student's musical performance, judge a speech contest, or grade an art project. You are on a committee evaluating textbooks for possible adoption. These and similar situations represent the kind of evaluation problem best solved through the use of checklists or rating scales.

Developing Checklists

Checklists provide a systematic way of checking whether or not important characteristics are present in someone's performance (or in a product that someone has produced). Note the key consideration: are some characteristics of this performance or product so important that it is valuable simply to know whether or not they are present? When the answer to that question is yes, a checklist is what you are looking for. The kinds of performances and products that might be evaluated through the use of checklists are:

Performances	*Products*
Playing a musical instrument	Drawings and paintings
Singing	Sculptures
Speaking	Maps
Participating in a discussion	Wood products
Leading a discussion	Handicrafts
Conducting an experiment	Outlines
Working through a math problem	
Conducting a library search	
Painting in oils	
Sculpturing	

When developing a checklist for evaluating a performance, your focus will be on behaviors; in developing one for use with products, it will be on observable features or characteristics. Note this difference by comparing the following two checklists. The first has been designed to evaluate a student while he is doing an oil painting (performance). The second has been designed to evaluate an oil painting after a student has completed it (product). How are these lists similar? How are they different?

Example: Evaluating a Student's Oil Painting

Performance	*Product*
_____ General layout sketched out first	_____ Overall layout pleasing
_____ Background wash painted over the large areas	_____ Colors crisp and clean
_____ Colors mixed on canvas	_____ Composition appropriate to subject
_____ Paints "worked" little, to keep them crisp	_____ Sufficient details, but not overdone
_____ Brushes and painting knives selected carefully to produce the desired textures	

The process of developing a checklist is relatively simple. First, list the important behaviors or characteristics. Second, add any common errors to the list. Finally, arrange the list so that it is easy to use.

Listing the important behaviors of a performance is not as easy as listing the important characteristics of a product. That is because when we are good performers, we are often unaware of the things we do that make our performance good. It is especially difficult for a motor-skill performer to verbalize what he or she does when performing. Try to list, for example, the steps you take to balance a bicycle and move it forward. One way to deal with this problem is to watch a good performer and list all the things you observe that person doing. Later, pick out the most important behaviors and include them in your final checklist.

The common errors are most easily listed after you have had an opportunity to watch a beginning performer, or to examine a beginner's early products. Note that a checklist is especially useful as a diagnostic tool when it includes common errors. If you anticipate using a checklist only as a final check on performance, there is no need to include common errors.

A well-designed checklist should meet the following criteria.

1. The list should be relatively short.
2. Each item should be clear.
3. Each item should focus on an observable characteristic or behavior.
4. Only important characteristics or behaviors should be included.
5. The items should be arranged so that the total list is easy to use.

Developing Rating Scales

Checklists help us determine the presence or absence of a list of behaviors or characteristics. Rating scales help us determine the quality of a behavior or characteristic. It is helpful to know, for example, that a speaker uses gestures. It is even more helpful to be able to judge the quality of those gestures. A rating scale is used to evaluate that quality of performance. It helps you answer the question: "How well does the speaker gesture?"

A rating scale is developed by taking a list of behaviors or characteristics (as one might use in a checklist) and constructing a qualitative scale for evaluating each behavior or characteristic.

Example: A Rating Scale for Rating Discussion Leaders*

Directions: Rate the discussion leader on each of the following characteristics by placing an X anywhere along the horizontal line under each item.

1. To what extent does the leader encourage discussion?

Discourages discussion by negative comments	Neither discourages nor encourages discussion	Encourages discussion by positive comments

---

*Excerpted from Terry D. TenBrink, *Evaluation: A Practical Guide for Teachers* (New York: McGraw-Hill, 1974), pp. 276–277. © 1974 by McGraw-Hill Book Co. Used with the permission of the McGraw-Hill Book Company.

2. How well does the leader keep the discussion on the right track?

Lets the discussion wander	Only occasionally brings the discussion back on target	Does not let discussion wander from the main topic	

3. How frequently does the leader ask controversial questions?

Never asks controversial questions	Occasionally asks controversial questions	Continually asks controversial questions	

4. How does the leader respond to inappropriate comments?

Ridicules the one who made the comment	Treats inappropriate comments the same as appropriate ones	Discourages inappropriate comments	

This rating scale would help an observer focus on specific, observable aspects of each behavior. Each time the scale was used, the same things would be examined. This would help improve the reliability of evaluating a performance, and would reduce the errors due to observer bias.

Developing a rating scale involves the same steps used to develop a checklist, plus the step of defining a scale for each characteristic. This added step is sometimes difficult, but it will be easier if you first define the extreme ends of each scale and then describe the midpoints. Defining the extremes is easiest if you can think of some real-life examples. Suppose, for example, that you are developing a rating scale for evaluating the social development of third graders. Among the many characteristics you feel are important is that of sharing with friends. To define the extreme ends, think first of a child you know who exemplifies this characteristic. This child shares readily with all her friends in an unselfish manner. Imagine this child as she shares with others. See her in your mind. Write down what you see her do; describe her sharing. That description defines the positive end of your scale. To define the extreme negative or low end of the scale, think of a child who is poor at sharing and describe that child's behavior. Now you have the basis for the description at the low end of the scale. By examining these two extremes, you will be able to imagine fairly easily what someone would be like who falls in the middle, and the midpoints of the scale should be easy to define. A completed scale for the characteristic of sharing might look something like:

Sharing with Friends

Complains when a friend has other friends. Won't let others borrow possessions.	Shares occasionally, but is somewhat possessive of friends and possessions.	Encourages others to share friends and possessions.	

Note that at this point, we have placed no numbers on the scale. For purposes of scoring, one might number the points along the scale. The lowest point could be assigned 1, the highest, 5. A scale without the numbers is *descriptive*; one with numbers is a *numerical-descriptive* scale. Removing the description and simply using numbers would produce a *numerical* scale. Numerical scales are usually not helpful unless the characteristic can be easily quantified (for example, number of times the child shares toys in one day: 0, 1 or 2, 2–4, 4–6, 6 or more).

Following these suggestions should help you produce some reasonably effective rating scales. There are many, much more sophisticated techniques for producing scales, however, and these are discussed in some of the references listed at the end of this chapter.

Space does not allow a complete treatment of the topic of rating-scale development and use. However, several of the questions teachers ask most often about rating scales follow, along with brief answers. Read these carefully, and ask your instructor for more detailed explanations of any that interest you.

Questions Teachers Often Ask About Rating Scales

Question: "What advantage is there to using a rating scale? Isn't it easier to construct a checklist that is effective?"

Answer: Whenever you need to know simply if a characteristic is present or absent, the checklist is a better tool. Checklists simply record quantitative information, however, and are not helpful for judging the quality of a performance or product.

Question: "Do I have to have a rating scale in front of me when I evaluate performances? Can't I keep the information that I think is important in my head?"

Answer: After you have used a particular rating scale many times, you may be able to evaluate effectively without having the scale in front of you. Even in that situation, however, the scale offers you a convenient way to record the information you have observed. Having an instrument in front of you while you are observing helps you to focus on the important characteristics, and greatly reduces observer bias.

Question: "How many points should a rating scale have? Is a five-point scale best? Is a three-point scale okay?"

Question: Generally speaking, you will get your most reliable results if you use a five- to seven-point scale. Also, scales with an odd number of points (five or seven) are usually better than those with an even number of points (four or six).

Question: "Can students use rating scales to help evaluate each other?"

Answer: Definitely. If the scale is well designed and if there are clear instructions for the observer, students can rate each other. Student evaluations can be used quite successfully in the performing arts. Well-designed scales can also be used by students to evaluate their own take-home projects, art projects, etc.

MASTERY TEST

OBJECTIVE 4   To develop checklists and rating scales for evaluating student products and performances

1. Select one of the following (or similar) student products, and develop a checklist that lists the most important criteria for evaluating that product.
   (a) Soap sculpture
   (b) Relief map
   (c) Pencil sketch
   (d) Book report
   (e) Model of a village
   (f) Educational game
   (g) Cursive handwriting
   (h) Health poster

2. Use the following format as a guide to develop a rating scale that you might find useful in your own teaching.
   (a) Name the performance or social-personal trait to be evaluated.
   (b) List the major steps to take, or important characteristics to be considered, in the evaluation.
   (c) Select four or five items from the list in number 1 and produce a scale for each item, describing the extremes first and then the midpoints. (You may decide to have more than four or five items in your full scale, but do at least four or five for purposes of this exercise.)

OBJECTIVE

5 To describe how to use information to evaluate; that is, to grade, judge student progress, judge changes in student attitudes, and judge the effectiveness of your own instruction

To evaluate is to judge, to place a value on. When we assign grades, determine that a child is functioning below grade level, evaluate a child's progress, or evaluate a teacher's effectiveness, we are judging. The basic question we will answer in this section of the chapter is: "How can one use information that has been obtained (through observation, tests, etc.) to evaluate, to form judgments?" Let's take a look at the process of forming judgments in general, and then examine more carefully several specific kinds of classroom judgments (for example, grading, judging student progress, judging changes in student attitudes, and judging the effectiveness of teaching).

Forming Judgments

The process of forming judgments is well known to all of us because we use it many times each day. We judge the value of a car we want to buy, the quality of a restaurant, the value of a television show, the neatness of our classroom, the warmth of our home, the friendliness of our neighbors, etc. Each time we make these judgments, we use the same basic process. We compare information we have about what we are judging to some referent. For example, we say that a restaurant is bad because the food is not nearly as good as Mom's. We decide that it's cold in the house because the thermometer reads below 65°. We determine that a car is too expensive because other, similar cars are selling for less, or we may feel that it's too expensive because it's $500 more than we can afford to spend. In each case, we compare information we have to some referent. The following chart, which illustrates this process for a variety of judgments, breaks each judgment down into two parts: (1) information used, and (2) the referent to which the information is compared.

Common Judgments

Judgment	Information	Compared to	Referent
Peter is my best speller.	Peter's spelling test scores		The spelling scores of his classmates
Sally reads above grade level.	Sally's reading achievement score		The average reading score of students at her grade level
This book is the best one I've seen on teaching math.	My perusal of the book		My perusal of other math books
Bobby has an above average I.Q.	Bobby's I.Q. score		The average I.Q. test score of students Bobby's age
The class is ready to move to the next unit in the math book.	The math achievement scores		The level of math achievement deemed necessary to do the work in the next unit
George is too tall for the Navy.	George's height		Navy's maximum height limit
Elaine has made a great deal of progress on learning to study in her seat.	The number of times Elaine left her seat today		The number of times Elaine left her seat one day last week

Note that different kinds of referents are used in the examples in the table. We frequently compare information we have with some referent or norm (for example, the food in the restaurant compared to food in most other restaurants we have dined in, or the number of problems George got correct compared to the average number correct by the class as a whole). This kind of judgment is based on a *norm-referenced approach.*

Whenever we want to determine whether the persons or things we are judging meet some minimal criterion or standard, we specify that criterion carefully and use it as our basis for comparison. For example, a car is judged to be too expensive when we compare its price to the amount we can afford to spend. The amount we can afford to spend is our criterion, and the kind of judgment we make using such a standard is called a *criterion-referenced judgment.* Criterion-referenced judgments allow us to judge a student's work independently of how well or how poorly the other students have done. It is an important type of judgment when using a mastery-learning approach to classroom teaching.

A third type of judgment that is quite useful is called a *self-referenced judgment.* When making this type of judgment, the individual (or thing) being judged serves as his or her own (self) referent. For example, we judge Sam's performance to be very good. Compared to what he was doing yesterday, today's performance was very good. Whenever we are concerned about student progress, we should make self-referenced judgments. Self-referenced judgments should also be used for diagnosing a student's strengths and weaknesses. To answer the question "How are Sarah's math skills compared to her reading skills?" is to make a self-referenced judgment.

Whenever you need to select a few students from among a larger group, you will need to make norm-referenced judgments. Comparing a student to a norm group such as other classmates is helpful whenever you need to make comparisons among several individuals to judge their relative merit (for example, who is the best math student). To select one student and not another (as in choosing a class leader) requires you to be able to compare those two students on certain characteristics. That requires norm-referenced judgments. These types of judgments should always be used when you need to compare students.

Criterion-referenced judgments, on the other hand, are most helpful when making decisions about the kind of assignment to give a student, or the level of achievement at which to begin a student. In other words, whenever a certain specified standard of performance or achievement is necessary before an action can be taken, criterion-referenced judgments are most useful. When making decisions that rely on information about a student's progress or about his or her relative aptitude in different subjects, self-referenced judgments are in order.

YOUR TURN

Types of Judgments

Answer the following questions to see how well you understand the basic process of forming judgments of different types.

1. What is the heart of the *process* of forming judgments?
   (a) Information
   (b) Comparisons
   (c) People
   (d) Statistics

2. To make a judgment is to place a _____ on.
   (a) Mark
   (b) Number
   (c) Value

3–6. For each of the following situations, determine the kind of judgment being made. Use the following key: A, norm-referenced; B, criterion-referenced; C, self-referenced.

___A___ 3. A third grade teacher discovers that her class scored above the national average on a math achievement test. *NR*

___A___ 4. A high school biology teacher selected his best students to help him set up the experiments for the next day. *NR*

___C___ 5. Misty's teacher was really pleased because of her progress in reading. Her gains since last year are obvious. *SR*

___B___ 6. Four of the students who took the algebra aptitude test failed to get a high enough score, and they were not allowed to take beginning algebra. *CR*

Types of Judgments

▓ Grading

Assigning grades has forever been a task teachers dislike. There seems to be no fair way to do it, and any grading system used seems subject to all kinds of interpretation problems. (See articles on grading listed under Additional Readings at the end of this chapter.) The next few paragraphs will not resolve the problems of grading, but they should help you understand better the alternatives available to you.

One of the most common questions teachers get from students concerning grading policy is: "Are you going to grade on the curve?" Whether grades are fitted to a normal curve or just curved to make a reasonable distribution, the basic idea behind grading on a curve is the same: making norm-referenced judgments, a common form of assigning grades. The class as a whole is used as a norm group, and the class average usually serves as the referent against which all other grades are judged. Usually the average score is assigned a grade of C, and some proportion of scores on either side of that average are also assigned grades of C (the C range usually includes 30 percent to 50 percent of the class). After that, grades are assigned by selecting some cut-off points so that a certain (usually smaller) percentage of students fall into the B and D ranges. Finally, those left fall into the A and F ranges, as their scores deviate above or below C. What do you think are the advantages and disadvantages of this form of grading? List them on a separate sheet of paper, and then compare your answers later on with the information in the table below. Remember that whenever you grade someone's work by comparing it to someone else's (or to the average of some group), you are using a norm-referenced approach, and all the disadvantages of that type of approach apply.

Another way to assign grades is to establish certain cut-off points for each grade. These cut-off points serve as criteria against which a given student's performance is judged. A common way in which this approach is used is for a teacher to assign points for every assignment and every test. Next, the teacher determines how many total points a student must get to get an A, B, etc. Each assignment or test can be graded that way. The total number of points for the marking period can be added together and compared to cut-off totals in the same way to assign report card grades. This could be called criterion-referenced grading. True criterion-referenced evaluation is a bit more complex, however, than what we have just described because the cut-off scores should be determined on the basis of some meaningful external criterion. What do you think are the advantages and disadvantages of this kind of criterion-referenced grading?

Teachers often find themselves wanting to give a student a high grade for having made so much improvement. Grading on the basis of improvement is a popular kind of self-referenced grading. Comparing a student to himself or herself is a desirable, humane way to grade; however, this kind of grading has many disadvantages. Can you think of some of them? After writing down your ideas, study the following table.

Advantages and Disadvantages of Different Types of Grading

Type of Grading	Advantages	Disadvantages
Norm-referenced	1. Allows for comparisons among students. 2. Classes can be compared to other classes. 3. Allows teacher to spot students who are dropping behind the class.	1. If whole class does well, some students still get poor grades. 2. If class as a whole does poorly, a good grade could be misleading. 3. Does not allow individual progress or individual circumstances to be considered. 4. The whole class (or large portions of it) must be evaluated in the same way. 5. Everyone in class (or norm group) must be evaluted with the same instrument under the same conditions.
Criterion-referenced	1. Helps teacher decide if students are ready to move on. 2. Criteria are independent of group performance. 3. Works well in a mastery-learning setting. 4. Each individual can be evaluated on different material, depending on his or her level of achievement.	1. It is difficult to develop meaningful criteria (therefore arbitrary cut-off scores are often used). 2. Presents unique problems in computing the reliability of criterion-referenced tests. 3. Makes it difficult to make comparisons among students.
Self-referenced	1. Allows you to check student progress. 2. Makes it possible to compare achievement across different subjects for the same individual.	1. All measures taken on an individual must be taken with similar instruments under similar circumstances. 2. Does not help you to compare an individual with his or her peers.

Using an appropriate referent (norm, criterion, or self) is a first, and important, step toward making sure that grades given are appropriate and meaningful. However, there are a number of other very important factors to consider when assigning grades. Recent concerns over grading practices have brought several of these considerations to the forefront.[2] (See Additional Readings at the end of this chapter for other articles describing various grading practices.)

In the next few paragraphs, several of the common grading practices currently being questioned by parents, educators, and evaluation experts will be discussed. The issues raised here are very important, but solutions to the problems are not always simple. In some cases experts disagree about the best way to handle a given problem. Therefore, this chapter will familiarize you with the problems and indicate which grading practices you should avoid where possible. You should study these problems further on your own, talk further with your instructor about them, or enroll in a test and measurement course that will provide you with some of the measurement and statistics concepts needed to understand the various solutions to these problems.

Inconsistency in the use of grading scales is a problem that plagues virtually every school district in the country and affects education at all levels, kindergarten through graduate school. A student in one class might receive a grade of B for a score of 80%, while in another class that 80% might merit an A or a C! Grading scales differ from class to class, from school to school, from school district to school district, and may even differ from test to test within the same classroom by the same teacher.

A second, very troubling problem, is the practice of averaging grades. Averaging scores can produce inaccurate results because the procedure for obtaining those averages does not consider the difficulty level of the tests or assignments that make up each individual score. This problem can be overcome by converting test scores to standard scores and then averaging the standard scores (see a tests and measurement book such as the one by Gilbert Sax listed under Additional Readings for a discussion of standard scores).

Another problem, not so easily solved, occurs when an extreme score is averaged along with other scores. Suppose, for example, a student has all scores in the A range except one, which he failed (perhaps he was ill, misunderstood a major concept, or studied the wrong material). That one low score could bring his average to a B or a C depending on how many scores were being averaged. Here is a student who probably knows the material as well (and maybe better) than the other students receiving a grade of A. However, because of one test or one assignment, that student receives a much lower grade at report card time.

Assigning zeros for unfinished work or as a disciplinary measure ("You talked out of turn — zero for today!") is another very unfair practice. A zero, when averaged with other grades, is given tremendous weight. A zero, when averaged in with several grades in the A range, could easily drop the average to a D or F range. In such a case, a student whose tested knowledge is at the A level is given a failing, or close to failing, grade because he missed a test or was being disciplined (in most cases for a behavior that had nothing to do with academic ability).

Pop quizzes, testing obscure facts, and other strategies for catching students off guard is another practice that produces grades that reflect something other than academic achievement. Furthermore, these kinds of testing practices usually produce short, unreliable, and invalid measures. Although teachers rarely pay any attention to the reliability or validity of their tests, the impact of measurement error on final grades must be accounted for. A teacher may carefully add up and average a large number of scores, only to end up with an inaccurate grade because of the inaccuracies in the individual scores being averaged. The author has personally analyzed hundreds of teacher-made tests of such low reliability (and, consequently, such high measurement error) that the distribution of grades would have been just as accurate had they been assigned randomly!

Measurement error should be clearly understood by every classroom teacher and every school administrator. Unfortunately, courses teaching these concepts are not always a mandatory part of the teacher preparation curriculum. The tests and measurement and evaluation books listed under Additional Readings at the end of the chapter discuss the concept of measurement error. You are encouraged to read those discussions carefully.

One final grading practice that you need to avoid is the practice of averaging every piece of a student's work into the final grade. Students are given assignments so that they can learn new knowledge or gain a new skill. These assignments frequently represent practice exercises. They offer the students an opportunity to try out a skill, to make some errors, and then, with appropriate feedback from the teacher, learn from those errors.

Is it really fair to average those grades in with tests given *after* the students have had sufficient time and practice to reach a reasonable level of proficiency?

When the author taught writing skills to junior and senior high school students, he encouraged them to experiment with different sentence structures, different styles of prose, and so forth. Early attempts were often a disaster but soon students would learn from their mistakes and would become very good at using their new skills in subsequent writing assignments. Surely any risk-taking behavior and any exploring of new ideas would have been penalized had those early attempts been graded and the scores averaged in with their later, well-written essays.

Assigning grades is more complex than we would like it to be. However, it is important that we do everything we can to make the process fair and the results as meaningful as possible.

Some of the recent attempts to involve students in the process of establishing criteria for grades are very promising and worth considering. Read, for example, Doris Sperling's excellent article in the February 1993 *Educational Leadership*.[3]

Judging Student Progress

Teachers have an ongoing concern about the amount of progress their students are making. If students are making a reasonable amount of progress, the methods, materials, etc., are probably working. If no progress or too little progress is being made, some changes may need to be made somewhere in the instructional program.

A judgment of student progress is, of course, a self-referenced judgment, and thus all the disadvantages of that type of judgment will hold. It is especially important that progress in achievement be measured the same way each time progress is checked. Suppose that you were trying to check a student's progress in reading. It would be best if you could use the same type of test each time progress was checked (alternate forms of the same standardized tests, observations of oral reading, using the same type of checklist or rating scale, etc.).

The following suggestions should help you evaluate student progress. Study them carefully, and then discuss with your classmates ways in which these suggestions could be carried out at various grade levels for different subjects.

Suggestions for Evaluating Student Progress

1. Determine ahead what student characteristics or skills you are going to keep track of (don't suddenly ask, halfway through the semester, "Has any progress been made?").
2. Establish a baseline (achievement level, behavior patterns, etc.) early in the semester.
3. Choose and/or develop instruments (tests, rating scales, etc.) in advance that you can use throughout a student's progress.
4. Describe the changes you expect will occur as your students progress. This description will help you focus your evaluation on appropriate behaviors and achievements.
5. Obtain information often enough so that you can see any progression that might be occurring, and so a single bad sample of information won't throw your evaluation off.

▇ *Evaluating Changes in Attitude*

Most psychologists would define *attitude* as a predisposition to act in a negative or positive way toward some object or person. Note that the attitude is a *predisposition*, which is not observable or measurable; however, it is a predisposition to *act*, and that is observable. This means that to measure attitudes, one must focus on the actions or behaviors of students. Of course, the difficult part is discerning what any given action or pattern of actions means (what the attitude is that is producing the actions).

Usually a teacher becomes concerned about attitude change when he or she discovers that one or more students have a bad attitude. Common among these are negative attitudes toward a given subject, a negative attitude toward the teacher, or feelings of prejudice toward minority students in the class. The important thing to remember when you first become aware of a negative attitude is that there must have been some behaviors that led you to discover that attitude. The student(s) must have said something (speech is an observable behavior), done something, or refused to do something that made you aware of the attitude. Your first step, therefore, is to try to determine what specific behaviors led you to believe that there was an attitude that needed changing.

Once you have determined the behaviors associated with an attitude you think should change, your next step is to systematically obtain information about the frequency of occurrence of those behaviors. These data will serve as the baseline (the referent) against which you will judge any future changes in attitude.

When you are sure that the behaviors you observed are frequent and do indeed represent an inappropriate attitude, you are ready to set down a plan for observing any possible changes in attitude (as they would be reflected in changes in behaviors). There are two important things to consider at this point. First, be certain that you make frequent observations so that you can feel confident that the behavior you are observing is representative and not isolated. Second, look for the behaviors when the student is in the presence of or thinking about the object of his or her inappropriate attitude (for example, look for disruptive behaviors during math if the student dislikes math).

Finally, when the information is obtained, you must judge whether or not the attitude has changed. Remember the disadvantage of making self-referenced judgments. Differences between any two sets of observations may not mean too much. If you find over a period of time (and attitudes usually take considerable time to change) that the undesirable behaviors are decreasing and the desirable ones increasing, an attitude change is probably occurring.

You can use a rating scale to help you summarize the data from your observations. Suppose that you were trying to see if a student's attitude toward math were improving. You might develop a rating scale that would look something like this.

Hates math		*Tolerates math*		*Loves math*
1	2	3	4	5

Complains about math, puts off doing assignments, turns in sloppy math papers	Says, "Don't care about math grade"; does assignment but delays some, never chooses math over other subjects	Says, "I like math"; gets right at assignments; does extra-credit work; chooses math over other subjects

Note that the behaviors characteristic of different attitudes have been placed under the two endpoints and the midpoint of the scale. Each time we observed our student react to math, we could determine which set of behaviors his or her actions were most like and mark an X on the scale accordingly. Several scales each marked in turn over a semester would give us a picture of any progress the student was making.

In summary, the basic steps involved in evaluating a student's change in attitude are:

1. Determine the behaviors associated with the attitude you think should change.
2. Systematically obtain information about the frequency of occurrence of these behaviors.
3. Decide if the behaviors occur frequently enough and consistently enough to represent an inappropriate attitude.
4. Set down a plan for observing any possible changes in attitude over time.
5. Decide whether the attitude has changed by comparing the information obtained at two or more different times.
6. Record your findings, possibly using a rating scale.

Evaluating Instruction

Most teachers have a genuine desire to know whether or not their instruction is effective. They also fear that they, or their principal, will find out that it is not effective. Principals, fellow teachers, students, and parents are all going to judge the quality of instruction. Therefore, it is advantageous for the teacher to have well-documented evidence of his or her teaching effectiveness.

Besides accountability, of course, teachers are concerned about improvement. They are always wanting information to help them upgrade their courses. So let's explore briefly some of the options available to teachers who wish to evaluate their own teaching. The information provided here will help you start thinking about evaluating instruction, but it in no way pretends to make you an excellent evaluator. Several books on program evaluation are cited in the references at the end of this chapter. Later, you may have an opportunity to enroll in a program-evaluation course. In the meantime, here are a few basic suggestions.

There are two primary considerations in evaluating your own instruction. First, you must determine the kind of information you will obtain about the effectiveness of your instruction. Second, you must determine an appropriate referent for judging the effectiveness of your instruction.

There are at least three kinds of information that can be used to determine the effectiveness of your instruction. The first is information about your own behaviors as a teacher. If you feel, for example, that effective instruction occurs when teachers do certain things (for example, provide behavioral objectives for their students, interact a great deal with their students, or ask certain types of questions during instruction), obtaining information about whether or not you do these things is a place to begin in the evaluation of your teaching. Many teacher-effectiveness rating scales do focus on such teacher behaviors. Although this kind of information can be helpful to you as you check your own progress as a teacher, it may be misleading about the *effectiveness* of instruction. A teacher's doing certain things doesn't necessarily ensure either effective teaching or improved learning.

A more popular (and slightly better measure) of teaching effectiveness comes from student ratings of teacher effectiveness. There are a number of fairly well-developed instruments that allow the students to evaluate their teachers. If you decide to design one of your own, focus on those characteristics of effective teachers that seem to make a difference. Even open-ended questions ("What did you like best about this class?" or "What could be done to make this class more effective?") can sometimes give the teacher useful information.

Of course, the ultimate test of teaching effectiveness is how well the students learn. There are several problems, however, with using learner achievement as a measure of teaching effectiveness. First, students may learn well despite the teacher. Second, it is difficult to know what would have happened had a teacher used a different approach; even though the students learned well, could they have learned better? Suppose that a class does poorly. Were there extenuating circumstances? Were the textbooks poorly written? Would the students have done that poorly had another teacher taught the lesson? These last questions are not easy to answer, but they do suggest an important solution to the many problems of evaluating instructional effectiveness. That solution is to evaluate the various *components* of the instructional process separately, rather than trying to obtain an overall measure. Suppose, for example, that we were developing a rating scale for students to evaluate the instruction in a high school English class. Instead of focusing all our questions on the teacher, we would also ask questions about some of the other components of instruction in that classroom. We might ask the students for their opinions about the textbook, workbook, library assignments, small-group discussions, tests, etc.

A second major consideration when evaluating instruction is the choice of an appropriate referent. You must decide to what you are going to compare your teaching. Will you compare it to other teachers (for example, by comparing your students' standardized achievement scores to the scores of other classes in your school district)? Will you judge your teaching effectiveness by some predetermined criterion (for example, "At least 80% of my students should score at or above grade level on the *Iowa Test of Basic Skills*)? Will you use a self-referenced approach (for example, comparing the student ratings from this semester with those of the previous two semesters)? All three types of referents are legitimate. You simply need to decide which would be most useful in improving your teaching. A discussion of this issue with your peers may help to clarify your own thinking.

MASTERY TEST

OBJECTIVE 5   To describe how to use information to evaluate; that is, to grade, judge student progress, judge changes in student attitudes, and judge the effectiveness of your own instruction

1. What is the major advantage of grading on a curve?
   (a) Allows comparisons among students
   (b) Produces more accurate judgments
   (c) Allows for differences in individuals

   For each of the following, determine the kind of grading that is involved. Use the following key: *A,* norm-referenced; *B,* criterion-referenced; *C,* self-referenced.

2. A teacher gives George a D because his scores were far below the class average.

3. A high school biology teacher promises an A to anyone scoring above 90% on the test.

4. Ms. Kelly tells Jane's parents that she reads well above grade level, as judged by her scores on a standardized test.

5. "I think your language arts grade will soon be up to the same high level as your math grade."

6. What is the biggest problem in judging student progress?
   (a) Deciding when to measure progress
   (b) Getting similar measurements from one time to the next

7. What type of judgment is being made when a teacher evaluates a student's progress?
   (a) Norm-referenced
   (b) Criterion-referenced
   (c) Self-referenced

8. What is being measured or observed in the evaluation of attitude changes?
   (a) Feelings
   (b) Ideas
   (c) Predispositions
   (d) Behaviors

9. What can be used to measure success in teaching?
   (a) Student performance
   (b) Student ratings of the teacher
   (c) Observations of the teacher's behaviors
   (d) All of the above
   (e) None of the above

▓ *Alternative Learning Activities*

1. Take a poll among your peers, and ask them to list all the things they dislike about the way they have been graded throughout their educational careers. Find out what they think would be the most equitable way to grade. Share these findings with your classmates, and discuss the implications for your own teaching.
2. Ask as many parents as you can what kind of information they would like to have about their children's progress in school. Get them to be as specific as possible.
3. Once you have written effective test questions, you still need to put some of them together in a test format. Ask a teacher you know to tell you some of the important things to consider when putting a test together (for example, make sure the ditto-master produces clear copy).

OBJECTIVE   6 To select and use standardized instruments

Learning Activity 6

What Are Standardized Tests?

Standardized tests are especially helpful when you need highly reliable information to make a wide variety of educational decisions. Although standardized instruments are usually commercially prepared, their most important characteristic is their "standardization." A *standardized test* has a standard set of procedures that must be followed each time the test is used. There is a fixed set of questions that must be administered according to a carefully specified set of directions, within certain time limitations. Standardized tests have usually been administered to a norm group, and the performance of that group is summarized in a manual so that you can compare the performance of your group to that of the norms. There are three major types of standardized instruments.

1. Aptitude tests
2. Achievement tests
3. Interest, personality, and attitude inventories

Aptitude tests attempt to predict how well someone might do in some area of human endeavor: intelligence tests measure general academic ability, creativity tests measure the ability to be creative, etc. Besides these more general aptitude measures, there are numerous academic subject aptitude tests that measure ability to learn those subjects (math aptitude, writing aptitude, music aptitude etc.).

Achievement tests measure how well an individual has achieved in some specific area. There are general achievement tests with subtests covering several different subjects (for example, the *Iowa Tests of Basic Skills*) and those that measure achievement more in-depth in a given subject (for example, *Gates-MacGinitie Reading Tests*). Most achievement tests are graded by grade levels, and scores are often reported as grade equivalency scores.

Interest, personality, and attitude inventories are not technically tests because there is usually no single right answer to any given question. These instruments seek to measure typical rather than maximum performance. Inventories that measure interest, study habits, learning style, and attitudes toward academic pursuits are especially helpful to school counselors as well as to teachers.

Selecting Standardized Tests

There are four major considerations when selecting a standardized test:

1. Will it give me the information I need?
2. Will the information be reasonably reliable?
3. Is the test easy to administer, score, and interpret?
4. Is the cost within our budget?

Will It Give Me the Information I Need?

To ask this question is to ask if the test is valid for my purpose(s). The validity of a test is an estimate of how well it measures what it is supposed to measure. Obviously, if a test is not valid — it does not provide you with the information you need — then look for another test.

There are many ways to determine the validity of a test. Perhaps the most important of these is *content validity*, which is simply a judgment about how well the items in a test measure what the test has been designed to measure. If you obtain a specimen set of a test you are considering, you can examine the items and compare what they measure with your perception of what you want to measure. If you are examining an achievement test, for example, you could compare the test items to your classroom objectives. By comparing several achievement tests, you could select the one that most closely measures the learning outcomes specified by those objectives.

Predictive validity is an estimate of how well a test predicts scores on some future test or performance. *Concurrent validity* estimates how well a test approximates a score on another test that was designed to measure the same variables. Both tests are given at the same time and their scores are correlated. Predictive validity estimates are generally lower than concurrent validity estimates, so always compare the same kind of validity estimates.

The manuals that accompany a standardized test will usually also provide validity estimates in the form of coefficients of validity. These coefficients will be reported as a number from 0 to 1 (1 being the highest). By comparing tests measuring the same thing, you can get a feel for what size number might represent a reasonable validity coefficient for that type of test. It is important, however, that you compare tests on the same type of validity.

Will the Information Be Reasonably Reliable?

A test is reliable when it measures consistently. Reliability is computed several different ways, and the resulting coefficients, like validity coefficients, will be numbers ranging from 0 to 1. Reliability coefficients are generally higher than validity coefficients. Perhaps the most useful reliability estimates are *internal consistency measures* — they estimate how consistently the test measures from item to item. These are usually reported using one or more Kuder Richardson formulas: KR20, KR21. *Test-retest reliability* estimates how consistently a test measures from one time to the next. *Alternate form reliability* is an estimate of how closely two forms of the same test measure the same thing. Always compare tests by comparing similar reliability coefficients.

Is the Test Easy to Administer, Score, and Interpret?

These factors are not as easy to assess when selecting a test, but there are a number of things you should look for. Are the directions for administering the test easy to follow? Are the examples used appropriate, and would they make sense to your students? Are the guidelines for timing clear? Is there an adequate explanation about how to handle student questions? Are the answer sheets easy to use? Is hand scoring a reasonable option? Is machine scoring available, and if so, how much does it cost? What other information (summary statistics, local norms data, response patterns, score interpretation) would be available through the scoring service? Are there adequate charts and/or explanations to help you interpret the data? The answers to these questions can be found by examining specimen sets, or by reading critiques of the test published in journals or in the *Mental Measurements Yearbooks.*

Is the Cost Within Our Budget?

When determining the cost of a test, make certain you consider the cost of each of the following: test booklets, manuals, answer sheets, scoring services, training time (for teachers who will administer the test, if such training seems necessary), report forms (for reporting results to parents), and cost/time involved in interpreting the results.

Sources of Information About Tests

There are valuable sources of information that can help you answer your questions about selecting a standardized test. Read the following descriptions carefully so you will know where to turn for the information you need.

Mental Measurements Yearbooks

There is probably no better, single source of information about specific standardized tests than the *Mental Measurements Yearbooks.*[4] Besides basic descriptive information (author, publication date, forms available, types of scores reported, administration time, prices, scoring services available, etc.), these yearbooks provide critical reviews by measurement experts. A bibliography of journal articles that review a given test is also included.

Tests in Print

Tests in Print[5] summarizes information that has appeared in previous *Mental Measurements Yearbooks*. It allows one to make a quick check of pertinent information when narrowing down choices among several tests. A more detailed analysis can be done using the *Mental Measurements Yearbooks.*

Professional Journals

There are numerous journals that contain reviews of tests. To locate those articles not referenced in the *Mental Measurements Yearbooks*, refer to references such as the *Psychological Abstracts* or the *Education Index.*

Specimen Sets

There is no substitute for a careful examination of the tests themselves. Read the administration and technical manual, try taking the test, get a feel for its ease of use, look at the answer sheets, etc. You can order specimen sets from most test publishers at a nominal cost, or you can often find them at the testing center or library on a college or university campus.

Using Standardized Tests

Administration

The most important thing to remember when administering a standardized test is that the scores will be difficult, if not impossible, to interpret unless the directions for administering the test are followed exactly. Read those directions carefully ahead of time. For most standardized tests, timing is critical. Be certain that you time the test carefully, and that there is a way to hand out and collect the tests so that all students have the same amount of time. For example, ask students to leave their booklets closed until you say open them, and then to close them when you call time and leave them closed on their desk until you pick them up.

Students will have questions during the explanation of the directions and during the test. Handle these questions carefully. Each student must understand the directions, and clarification should be made. If there seems to be ambiguity in the questions themselves, or students don't seem to understand what is being asked, you should help them understand what is being asked of them, but you should do nothing that would give away the answer.

Questions can often be minimized if students are prepared in advance for the test. Respond honestly to their questions about how the test is to be used. Reassure them that standardized tests are designed so that almost no one gets all the answers correct. Tell them to do their best, but not to worry if there are some questions they cannot answer.

Scoring

Most standardized tests are objective and are not too difficult to score manually. A scoring template is usually provided. There are several advantages, however, to using the publisher's scoring service when it is available. The scoring will be accurate. You will often get charts and graphs showing the distribution of the scores for your class. Summary statistics are usually made available, and you can ask for summary data for several classes within your school (or school district). Finally, some services will help you develop local norms.

MASTERY TEST

OBJECTIVE 6 To select and use standardized instruments

1. What is the most important characteristic of standardized tests?

2. Write down, in your own words, the four questions you need to answer when trying to select a standardized test.

3. Which statistical estimate would be important if you were trying to determine if a test measures what it says it does?
   a. Reliability
   b. Validity
   c. Usability
   d. None of the above

4. Which one of the following sources will give you the most information about a specific standardized test?
   a. *Mental Measurements Yearbooks*
   b. *Tests in Print*

5. What is the most important thing to remember about administering a standardized test?

6. Briefly explain how a teacher should handle questions that students ask about a standardized test they are taking.

Answer Keys for Your Turn Exercises

ANSWER KEY

Your Turn: Choosing an Evaluation Technique

1. B
2. D or B
3. A
4. B or A
5. D

6. A or B
7. C
8. D
9. B
10. C or A

ANSWER KEY

Your Turn: Selecting an Information-Gathering Instrument

1. Observation is the best choice because to find out *how* the pupils form their letters, you must watch them forming them.
2. Feelings are best discovered by inquiry. This teacher should ask his students how they feel.
3. Achievement is best measured through testing.
4. Whenever you want a measure of maximum performance of a cognitive skill, test.

5. Observing their performance and perhaps analyzing what she hears — that's the answer to this music teacher's evaluation problem.
6. Observation is best, preferably without the students knowing that they are being watched.

ANSWER KEY

Your Turn: Selecting the Type of Item

1. *Essay:* To "explain," the student needs considerable freedom to respond.
2. *Short answer:* No freedom here, just the steps.
3. *Multiple choice:* Selection from among alternatives is being called for.
4. *Essay:* To discuss requires freedom to respond.
5. *Short answer:* This objective calls for just a list, no explanation.

6. *Multiple choice:* This requires choosing among alternatives or *matching,* with types of malfunctions in one column and the possible causes in another.
7. *Multiple choice:* An example of this type of item might be: "The underlined word represents which of the following parts of speech" or *matching,* with words in one column and parts of speech in the other.

ANSWER KEY

Your Turn: Writing Essay Items

1. *An open-ended question:* This question should allow the student a great deal of freedom to respond, but it should be quite clear about what is being asked. You can see from the following samples that open-ended questions can be difficult to grade because each student may choose to restrict his or her own answer in a different way.

   Sample Questions

   (a) Discuss ways you might reduce your anxiety when preparing to make a contemporaneous speech.
   (b) What could you do to reduce the number of germs on medical instruments if you have no sterilization equipment?
   (c) Discuss the pros and cons of the draft registration.
   (d) Convince me that it is important to understand the history of the English language.

2. *A restricted essay question:* Again, make certain that your question has been clearly written. Check to see that your question limits the answers in a way that will help the student to respond (the student will know how to answer *if* he or she knows the information being asked for).

   Sample Questions

   (a) List and explain each of the steps we discussed for setting up an experiment.
   (b) In no more than ten lines, describe a typical Eskimo village from the early 1900s.
   (c) Cite five reasons for having a 55 mph speed limit. Defend one of your reasons with supporting evidence.

ANSWER KEY

Your Turn: Constructing a Model Answer

Check your model answer against the criteria for model answers. Compare your model answers with those of your peers. If you are uncertain about your answers, ask your instructor to check them.

ANSWER KEY

Your Turn: Evaluating and Writing Multiple-Choice Questions

Check your items against the criteria for effective multiple-choice items. In addition, exchange your items with a classmate and evaluate each other's items.

ANSWER KEY

Your Turn: Writing True/False Items

Compare your questions to those of your classmates and to the following examples. The content of your questions may be different from the examples, but they should not violate the rules for writing effective true/false items.

_____ 1. Little Red Riding Hood was on her way to the store when she met the wolf.

_____ 2. The wolf was friendly to Little Red Riding Hood at first.

_____ 3. The basket Little Red Riding Hood carried contained food for her grandmother.

_____ 4. The wolf followed Little Red Riding Hood to her grandmother's.

_____ 5. Little Red Riding Hood immediately recognized the wolf when she found him in her grandmother's bed.

_____ 6. The wolf was finally caught and killed.

ANSWER KEY

Your Turn: Writing a Matching Exercise

Check your work according to the criteria for matching exercises. Ask a friend to read your instructions to see if they are clear.

ANSWER KEY

Your Turn: Types of Judgments

1. B
2. C
3. A

4. A
5. C
6. B

Answer Keys for Mastery Tests

ANSWER KEY

Mastery Test, Objective 1

1. Evaluation is the process of obtaining information and forming judgments to be used in decision making.
2. (a) *Preparing for evaluation.* In this stage, you need to determine the judgments and decisions you anticipate making (for example, when to begin Unit 2, what assignments to give, where to place Johnny). Next, you must decide what information you will need to make those judgments and decisions (for example, how quickly the students are moving through Unit 1, what the students' interests are, how well Johnny reads). Finally, you will decide when and how to obtain the information needed (for example, weekly, through quizzes; first week of class, using an interest inventory; second week of class, using a standardized test of reading and observing students during oral reading).

(b) *Obtaining needed information.* Involves asking students (inquiry), observing students (watching students setting up an experiment), or testing students (giving a multiple-choice test of history facts).
(c) *Forming judgments.* In this stage, you compare the information with some referent and make a value judgment. Grades reflecting achievement and predictions about how well a student might be expected to do are both common examples of classroom judgments.
(d) *Using judgments in decisions and preparing evaluation reports.* Deciding what action to take (for example, move Johnny to a slower reading group) and reporting the evaluation results that led to that decision comprise the major tasks of the final stage of evaluation. Note that the emphasis is on the *use* of judgments.

ANSWER KEY

Mastery Test, Objective 2

1. d
2. a
3. c

4. b
5. a
6. d

ANSWER KEY

Mastery Test, Objective 3

Evaluate your test against these criteria:
1. The test clearly measures the objectives.
2. The items are clear and concise (unambiguous).
3. The type of items used represents the most direct way to measure the objectives.

4. The readability of the items is appropriate for the grade level you selected.
5. Any necessary instructions to the students are clearly stated.

ANSWER KEY

Mastery Test, Objective 4

1. *Developing checklists:* Your checklist should be clear, concise, and easy to use. If possible, try using it. Ask someone who is an expert at the performance to check your list to see if you have included only the important behaviors.

2. *Constructing rating scales:* Check your scale against the criteria for an effective rating scale. Share your scale with classmates, and ask them if they feel that they would be able to use it successfully.

ANSWER KEY

Mastery Test, Objective 5

1. a
2. A
3. B
4. A
5. C

6. b
7. c
8. d
9. d

ANSWER KEY

Mastery Test, Objective 6

1. Validity. If a test does not measure what you need measured, it is not valid for your use. It is of no use to you, even if it is extremely reliable.
2. a. Will it give me the information I need?
   b. Will the information be reasonably reliable?
   c. Is the test easy to administer, score, and interpret?
   d. Is the cost within our budget?

3. b
4. a
5. To follow exactly the instructions for administering the test.
6. The teacher should try to clarify and help students understand what is being asked of them, but should do nothing that would give away the answer.

▦ Notes

1. For more details, see T. D. TenBrink, *Evaluation: A Practical Guide for Teachers* (New York: McGraw-Hill Book Company, 1974).
2. R. L. Canady and P. R. Hotchkiss, "It's a Good Score: It's Just a Bad Grade," *Phi Delta Kappan* (September 1989): 68–71.
3. D. Sperling, "What's Worth an 'A'? Setting Standards Together," *Educational Leadership* 50 No. 5 (February 1993): 73–75.
4. J. J. Kramer and J. C. Conoley (ed.), *Eleventh Mental Measurements Yearbook*, (Lincoln, NE: University of Nebraska Press, 1992).
5. J. V. Mitchell (ed.), *Tests in Print III* (Lincoln, NE: University of Nebraska Press, 1983).

▦ Additional Readings

Ahmann, J. S., and M. D. Glock. *Evaluating Student Progress: Principles of Tests and Measurements,* 6th ed. Boston: Allyn and Bacon, 1981.

Anderson, K. E., and F. C. Wendel. "Pain Relief: Make Consistency the Cornerstone of Your Policy on Grading," *American School Board Journal* 175 (October 1988): 36–37.

Austin, S., and R. McCann. "Here's Another Arbitrary Grade for Your Collection: A Statewide Study of Grading Policies." Philadelphia, PA: Research for Better Schools, Inc., 1992, p. 41.

Bloom, B. S., T. J. Hastings, and G. F. Madaus. *Handbook of Formative and Summative Evaluation of Student Learning.* New York: McGraw-Hill Book Company, 1971.

Carlson, K. W. "Grading the Gradebooks," *InCider* 5 (Feb 1987): 66–75.

Duke, D., and R. L. Canady. "Evaluating Student Performance," *School Policy.* New York: McGraw-Hill, Inc., 1991.

Ebel, R. L., and D. A. Frisbie. *Essentials of Educational Measurement,* 5th ed. Englewood Cliffs, NJ: Prentice-Hall, Inc., 1990.

Evans, E. D., and R. A. Engelbert. "Student Perceptions of School Grading," *Journal of Research and Development in Education* 21 (Win 1988): 45–54.

Gribbin, A. "Making Exceptions When Grading and the Perils It Poses," *Journalism Educator* 46 (Win 1992): 73–76.

Gronlund, N. E., and R. L. Linn. *Measurement and Evaluation in Teaching,* 6th ed. New York: Macmillan Co., 1989.

Haley, B. "The Grading System: Does an 'A' Really Equal Learning?" *NASSP Bulletin* 72 (Apr 1988): 35–41.

Lyman, H. B. *Test Scores and What They Mean,* 5th ed. Englewood Cliffs, NJ: Prentice-Hall, 1990.

Madgic, R. F. "The Point System of Grading: A Critical Appraisal," *NASSP Bulletin* 72 (Apr 1988): 29–34.

Mehrens, W. A., and I. J. Lehmann. *Measurement and Evaluation in Education and Psychology,* 4th ed. San Diego: Harcourt Brace Jovanovich, 1991.

Nottingham, M. "Grading Practices — Watching Out for Land Mines," *NASSP Bulletin* 72 (Apr 1988): 24–28.

Oosterhof, A. C. "Obtaining Intended Weights When Combining Students' Scores. NCME Instructional Module," *Educational Measurement: Issues and Practices* 6 (Win 1987): 29–37.

Ornstein, A. C. "The Nature of Grading," *Clearing House* 62 (Apr 1989): 365–69.

Popham, W. J. *Educational Evaluation,* 3rd ed. Boston: Allyn and Bacon, 1992.

Sax, G. *Principles of Educational and Psychological Measurement and Evaluation,* 3rd ed. Belmont, CA: Wadsworth Publishing Co., 1989.

Stufflebeam, D. I., et al. *Educational Evaluation and Decision Making.* Itasca, IL: F. E. Peacock Publishers, 1971.

TenBrink, T. D. *Evaluation: A Practical Guide for Teachers.* New York: McGraw-Hill Book Company, 1974.

Terwilliger, J. S. *Assigning Grades to Students.* Glenview, IL: Scott, Foresman, and Company, 1971.

Thorndike, R. *Measurement and Evaluation in Psychology and Education,* 5th ed. New York: Macmillan Co., 1990.

Walsh, W. B., and N. E. Betz. *Tests and Assessment,* 2nd ed. Englewood Cliffs, NJ: Prentice-Hall, Inc., 1990.

Wittrock, M. C., and D. E. Wiley (eds.). *The Evaluation of Instruction: Issues and Problems.* New York: Holt, Rinehart and Winston, 1970.

Appendix A

The Question Master Game

Preparation for the Game

1. Cut out the cards on the following pages and stack them in three piles: Chance Cards, Question About Questions Cards, and Classification Cards.
2. Read the directions.
3. Turn to the game board and begin.

The Question Master

Directions

Object:

The object of the game is to become the first teacher in your neighborhood to reach that magic circle of the select few (to wit, the Question Master Circle).

Players:

2 to 6

Moves:

You move along the board from the space marked "Start" by rolling a die. If you don't have any dice, then simply make and cut out cards numbered from 1 to 6, and each player can select a card from the pile on his or her turn. If you are a professional game player, use your spinner.

Pieces:

Use anything that fits on the spaces (different coins, buttons, small pieces of paper with your initials, chess pieces, etc.).

Spaces:

Classification. When you land on a space marked with a C, *another* player selects a card from the pile of Classification Cards and reads the question to you. You must then classify the question on the appropriate level of Bloom's *Taxonomy*. The correct answer is printed on the card. If you are correct, you can stay on that space. If you are *incorrect*, you must go back *three* spaces.

Question. When you land on a space marked with a Q, *another* player selects a card from the pile of Question About Questions Cards. If you answer the question correctly (correct answers are also written on the card), you stay on that space. If you answer incorrectly, you must go back *three* spaces.

Ah, the whims of fortune. If you land on this space, select a card from the Chance pile and follow the instructions.

An arrow signifies a different route that must be followed when you land on this space. The first of these is a shorter route; the second is a longer route.

You lose one turn if you land on this space.

If you land on a space marked Gym, Principal's Office, Lunch Room, or Detention Hall, then you have no questions to answer or classify. You may also be sent to these locations by a Chance Card.

The Question Master: You need *not* land on the last space (Question Master) by exact count.

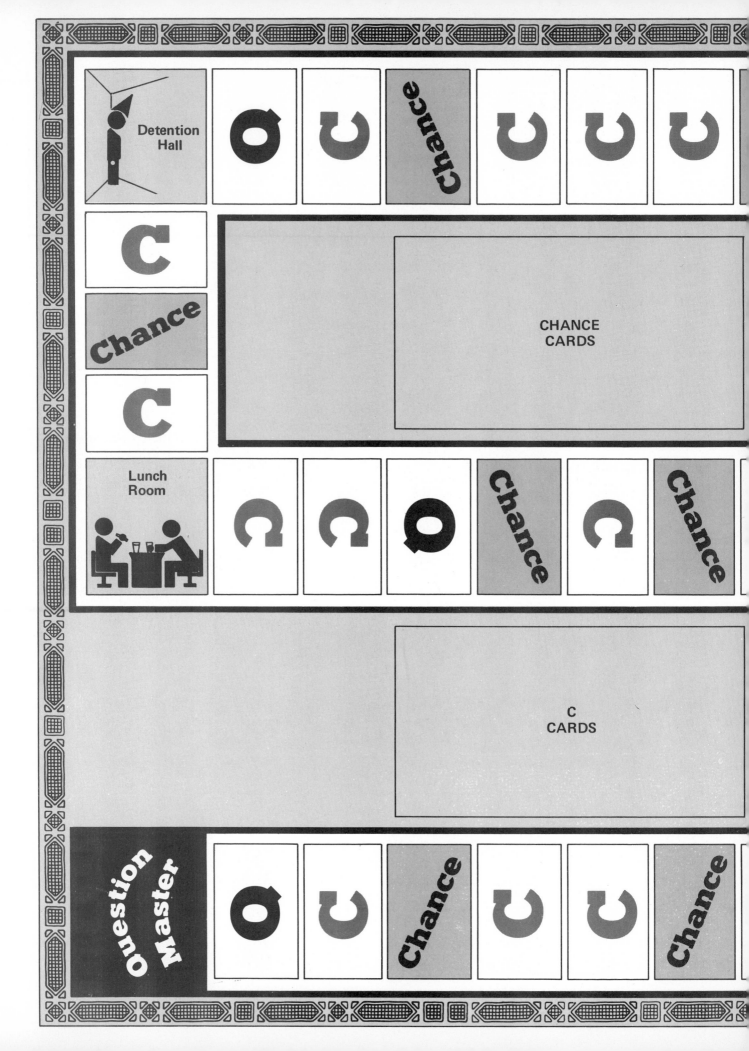

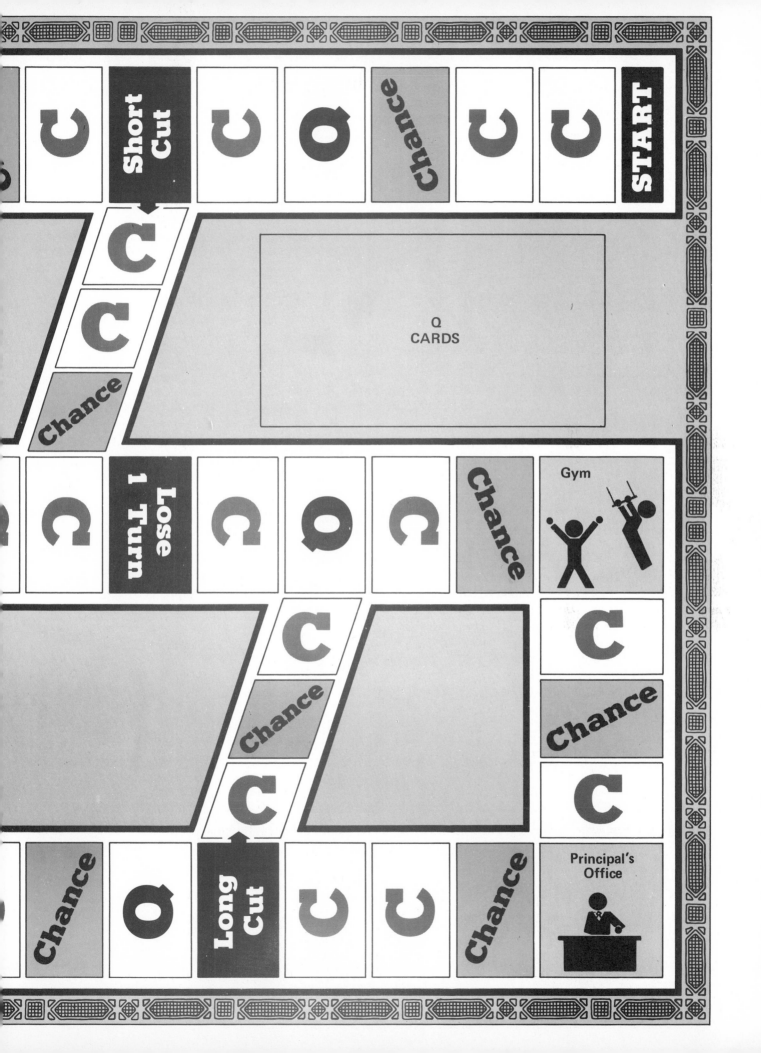

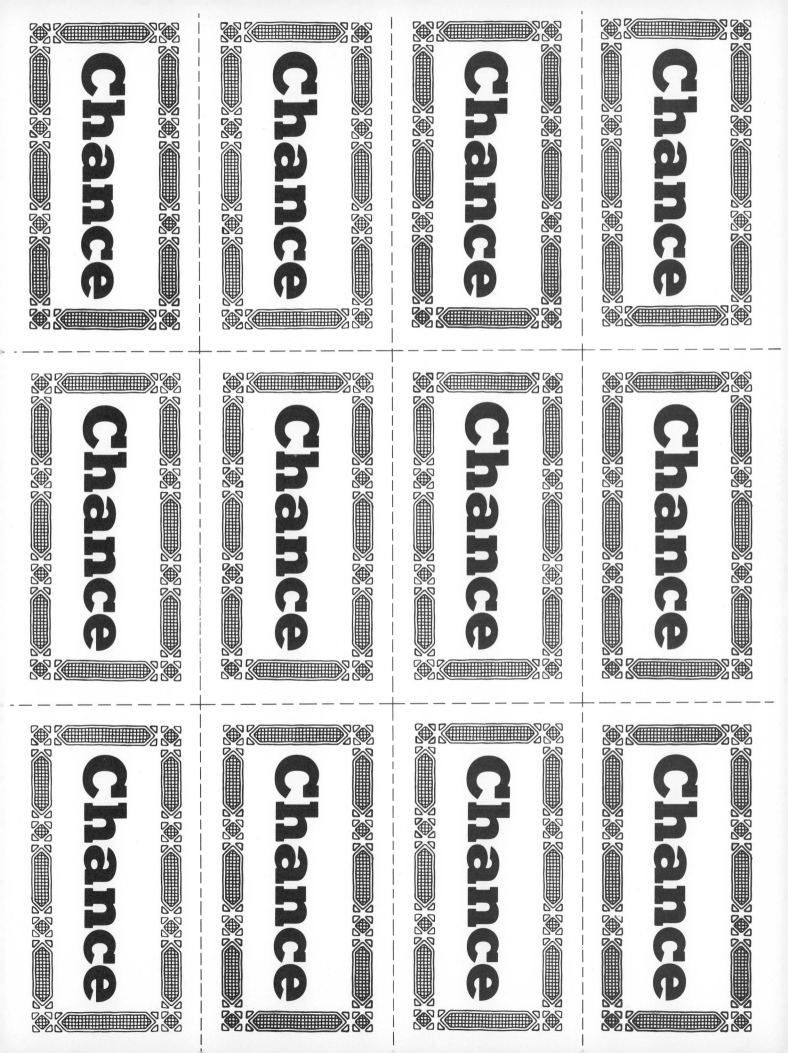

Chance Card

Students just selected you as their best teacher. Roll the dice to determine how many spaces you can move ahead.

Chance Card

You forgot to lock your cabinet, and your prize Hopi Indian Kit is gone. Go back 3 spaces.

Chance Card

Promotion. Move ahead six spaces if you can re-cite the 6 levels of Bloom's *Taxonomy* backwards within ten seconds. GO.

Chance Card

Two more students fell asleep when you asked a question. Move back 2 spaces.

Chance Card

You have been using only memory questions in class and your students do not really understand the material. Go back 3 spaces.

Chance Card

Teacher of the Year Award. Move ahead 4 spaces.

Chance Card

You've just been assigned to stay after school with kids who were behavior problems. Go to detention hall.

Chance Card

Your evaluation report just came back and you will be getting tenure. Live it up. Take another turn.

Chance Card

You've just been passed by for merit. Move back 3 spaces.

Chance Card

The principal is coming to observe you and you forgot your lesson plans. Go back 3 spaces.

Chance Card

Your car ran out of gas on your way to work. Lose one turn.

Chance Card

The principal smiled at you and said you were doing a fine job. Stay where you are.

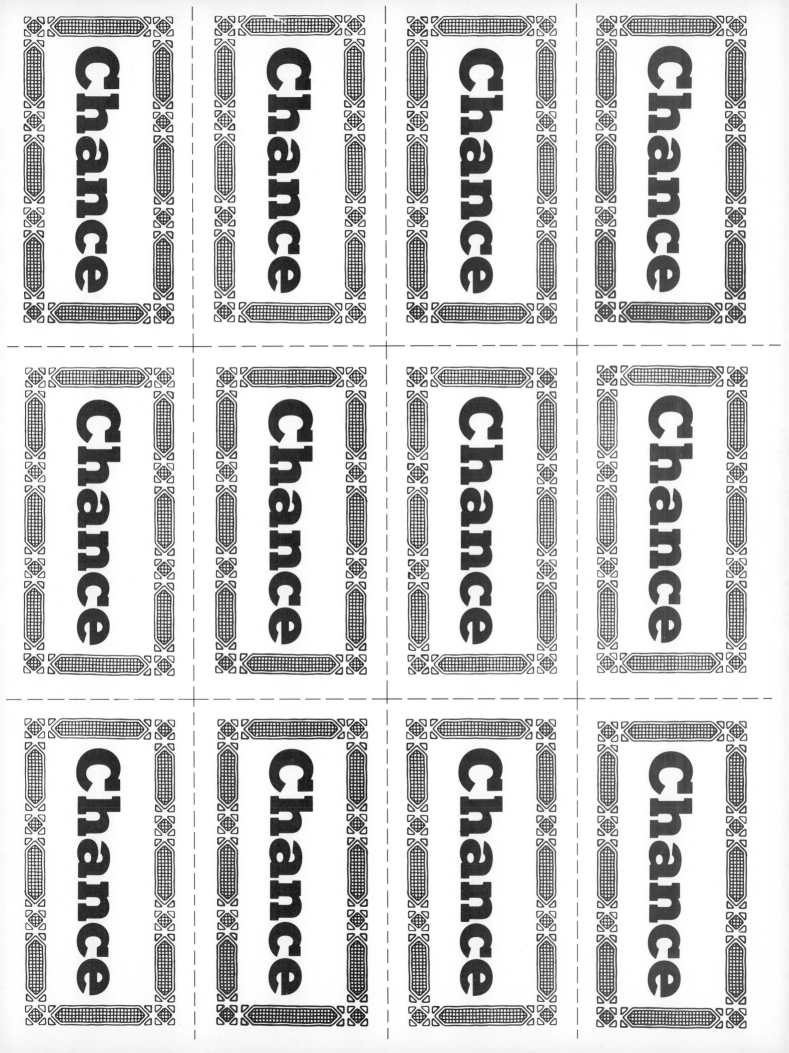

Chance Card

TGIF (Thank God It's Friday). You made it to Friday. Move ahead one space.

Chance Card

You've just been assigned lunch room duty. Move directly to the lunch room.

Chance Card

Christmas Vacation — get your battery recharged. Move ahead 5 spaces.

Chance Card

June is here and everyone has spring fever. Lose one turn.

Chance Card

You are being considered for assistant principal. Go directly to the principal's office and wait — for three turns before going on.

Chance Card

Congratulations! You are now the new basketball coach. Go directly to the gym.

Chance Card

Your attendance reports are missing and the principal would like you to recall who was absent during the last week. Go to the principal's office. Lose two turns.

Chance Card

Your higher order questions are really making a difference and student grades are improving. Go ahead five spaces.

Chance Card

Faculty meeting this afternoon. Lose one turn.

Chance Card

Inservice workshop this afternoon. Go ahead 4 spaces.

Chance Card

The parents of your students are so pleased with your effective classroom questions that they have taken an ad out in the local newspaper thanking you. Take another turn.

Chance Card

You stayed up last night until 2:00 a.m. grading student papers, and you forgot to take them to school this morning. Lose one turn.

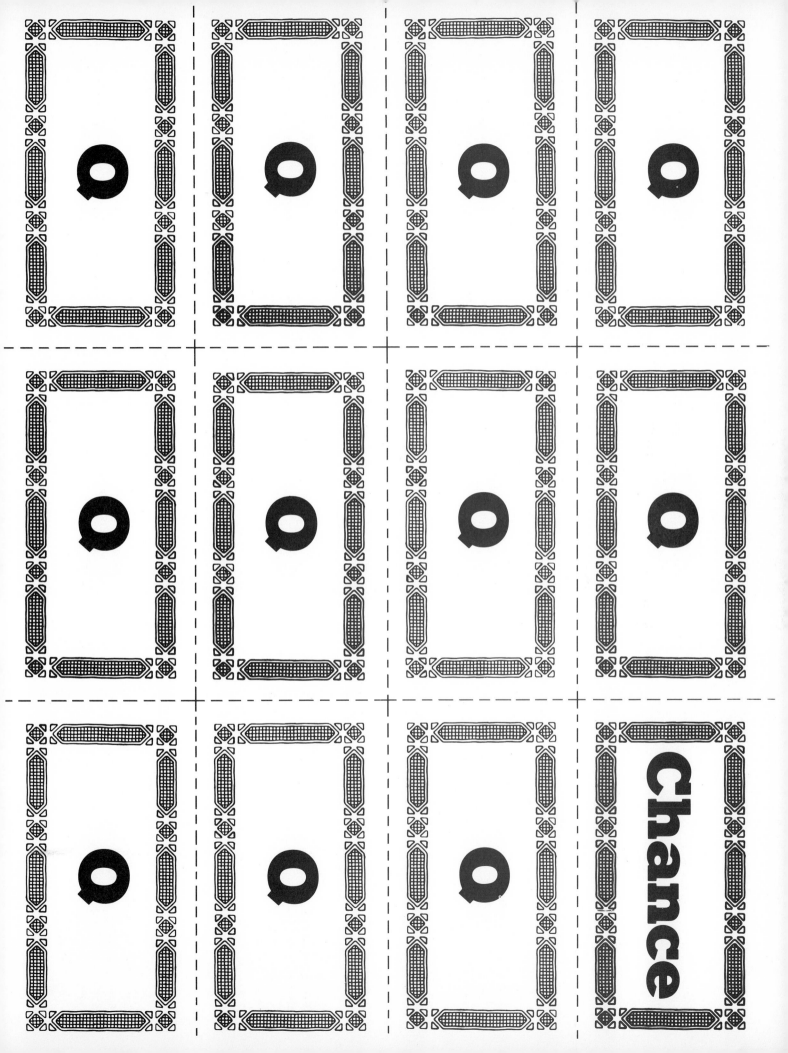

Question About Questions Cards

Analysis questions call for higher order thinking. True or false?

Answer: True

Question About Questions Cards

Which of the following is *not* a process required by analysis questions? (a) identifying evidence to support a statement (b) making a statement based on evidence (c) explaining motives or causes (d) making predictions.

Answer: (d)

Question About Questions Cards

A "why" question suggests a question asked on the analysis level. True or false?

Answer: True

Question About Questions Cards

Synthesis questions require students to do all of the following *except* (a) make predictions (b) solve problems (c) construct original communications (d) evaluate ideas, solutions to problems, and aesthetic works.

Answer: (d)

Question About Questions Cards

A student who is asked to interpret a cartoon is functioning on a (a) knowledge (b) comprehension (c) application (d) analysis level

Answer: (b)

Question About Questions Cards

Application level questions generally have more than one one possible answer. True or false?

Answer: False

Question About Questions Cards

If you were asked to use a particular process in order to solve a problem, what level of the *Taxonomy* would you be operating on?

Answer: application

Question About Questions Cards

When you are asked to solve mathematical problems, you are usually working at what level of the *Taxonomy*?

Answer: application

Chance Card

Your use of higher order questions has made this your best year of teaching. Take an extra turn.

Question About Questions Cards

Most of the questions asked by teachers are on what level of thinking?

Answer: Lower order or memory or knowledge level

Question About Questions Card

Memory questions are lower order and not useful. Teachers would be better off if they did not use them. True or false?

Answer: False. Although overused, they are essential for other levels of thinking to occur.

Question About Questions Card

Comprehension questions require students to (a) repeat information exactly (b) make comparisons (c) make judgments (d) offer opinions, beliefs, and values.

Answer: (b)

Classification Card

Who wrote *Romeo and Juliet?*

Answer: knowledge

Classification Card

What did King John say in the next chapter?

Answer: knowledge

Classification Card

How are these two solutions similar?

Answer: comprehension

Classification Card

How would you state the main idea of this poem?

Answer: comprehension

Classification Card

What is the capital of Maryland?

Answer: knowledge

Classification Card

Who is the governor of Wisconsin?

Answer: knowledge

Classification Card

Who wrote *Pollution: The Last Chapter?*

Answer: knowledge

Classification Card

When was the charter written?

Answer: knowledge

Question About Questions Cards

Synthesis questions require original and creative thought from students. True or false?

Answer: True

Question About Questions Cards

Which level of the *Taxonomy* would you be functioning at if you drew a self-portrait?

Answer: synthesis

Question About Questions Cards

What level of the *Taxonomy* is a question that asks you to describe what you think the United States will be like in the year 2000?

Answer: synthesis

Question About Questions Cards

Your new assignment is to judge an all-male beauty contest. You will be asked to decide on a winner. What level of the *Taxonomy* will you be working on?

Answer: evaluation

Classification Card

What does this chart mean?

Answer: comprehension

Classification Card

What is the message of this political cartoon?

Answer: comprehension

Classification Card

How does yesterday's class discussion compare with your textbook account of the American Revolution?

Answer: comprehension

Classification Card

Using the process we discussed yesterday, solve this problem.

Answer: application

Classification Card

How does the geography of Maine compare with the geography of Mexico?

Answer: comprehension

Classification Card

Considering your two reading assignments, what characteristics do Vietnam and Thailand have in common?

Answer: comprehension

Classification Card

In your own words, what were the main ideas in your homework assignment?

Answer: comprehension

Classification Card

Describe yesterday's discussion in your own words.

Answer: comprehension

Classification Card

What is the meaning of democracy? (The students have previously been given the definition.)

Answer: knowledge

Classification Card

How is ecology defined? (The students have previously been given the definition.)

Answer: knowledge

Classification Card

What was the topic of yesterday's discussion?

Answer: knowledge

Classification Card

Give the textbook definition of the feminist movement.

Answer: knowledge

Classification Card

What would society be like if marriage were against the law?

Answer: synthesis

Classification Card

Should the United States stop foreign aid?

Answer: evaluation

Classification Card

Who was our greatest President?

Answer: evaluation

Classification Card

How would people respond if Congress enacted a law that forced people to wear seat belts?

Answer: synthesis

Classification Card

Which solution is best?

Answer: evaluation

Classification Card

Do you believe that he's telling the truth?

Answer: evaluation

Classification Card

Which song do you prefer?

Answer: evaluation

Classification Card

Who is your favorite movie star?

Answer: evaluation

Classification Card

Locate Memphis by latitude and longitude on a map.

Answer: application

Classification Card

Should people be allowed to marry at any age?

Answer: evaluation

Classification Card

Which party do you prefer: Democrats or Republicans?

Answer: evaluation

Classification Card

If Harry takes two hours to mow a lawn and Harriet takes one hour, how long would it take if they both mowed the lawn?

Answer: application

Classification Card

Using any land area in the world, choose a site you consider an ideal location for a city.

Answer: synthesis

Classification Card

What would be the effects of a woman being elected President?

Answer: synthesis

Classification Card

How many answers to this problem can you think of?

Answer: synthesis

Classification Card

Compose a letter to a friend who is having problems in his studies.

Answer: synthesis

Classification Code

Why is New York called "The Empire State"?

Answer: analysis

Classification Card

Why did Myra refuse to give her diary to the publisher?

Answer: analysis

Classification Card

What evidence can you cite to support your argument?

Answer: analysis

Classification Card

What is the tone of the article?

Answer: analysis

Classification Card

Do you like modern art?

Answer: evaluation

Classification Card

Do you prefer Picasso, Chagall, or Miro?

Answer: evaluation

Classification Card

Solve $x^2 + 14 = 18$.

Answer: application

Classification Card

Using the rules of punctuation that we have learned, find the error in the following sentence.

Answer: application

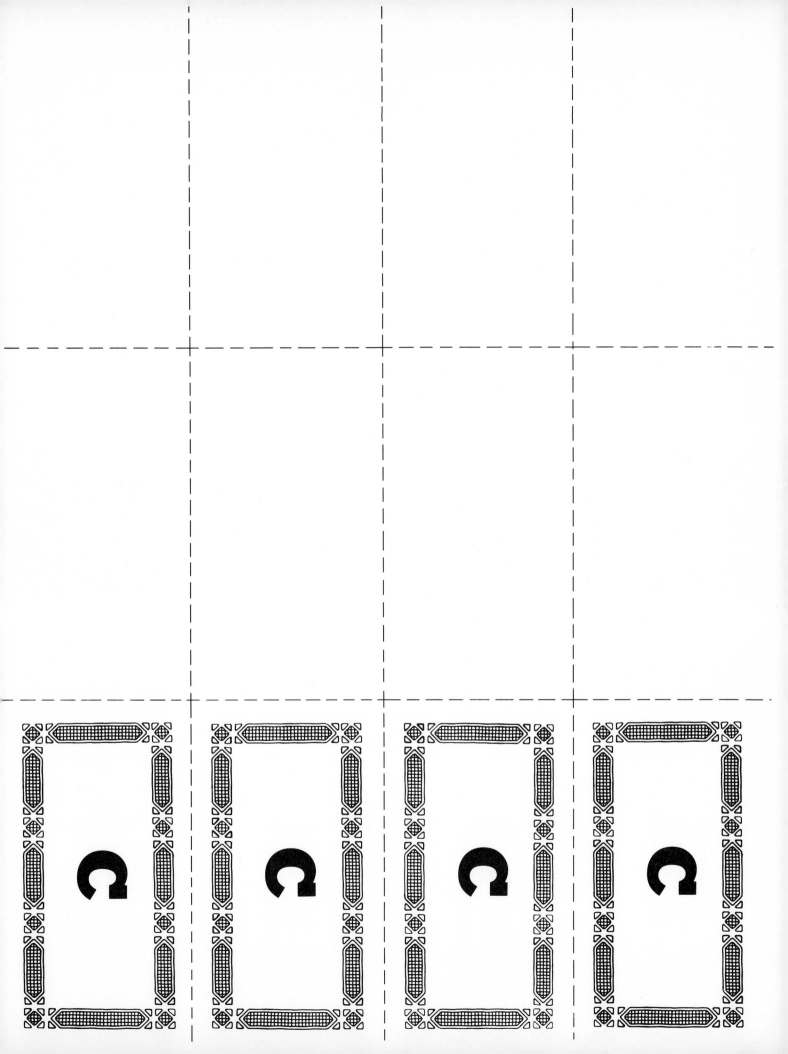

Classification Card

Draw a picture of your favorite building.

Answer: synthesis

Classification Card

How can we make foreign aid more effective?

Answer: synthesis

Classification Card

How can we determine the weight of this object without a standard scale?

Answer: synthesis

Classification Card

What should we call our pet?

Answer: synthesis

Appendix B

Concept Cards

soldier	rhythm	haiku
family	translation	set (in mathematics)
love	intensity (in color)	distance
justice	well done (in cooking)	direction
vertebrae	coordination	melody
amoeba	transportation	accent
vowel	heredity	waste
mass media	photosynthesis	airplane

cloud	map	hypotenuse
polygon	symmetry	square feet
moisture	counterpoint	preposition
gravity	hue	adverb
wood	resource	debate
mass	personality	idiomatic phrase
vapor	off key	exercise
democracy	harmony	sprint
slavery	exponent	curve ball
		pocket (in football)

Glossary

Abstract concepts. Those concepts that can be acquired only indirectly through the senses.

Active listening. Differentiating between the intellectual and emotional content of a message, and making inferences about the feelings experienced by the speaker.

Advance organizers. Informing students of the way in which new information is organized.

Affective objectives. Objectives that deal primarily with emotion and feeling.

Analysis questions. Questions that require the student to break down a communication into its constituent parts, such that the relative hierarchy of ideas is made clear and/or the relations between the ideas expressed are made explicit.

Application questions. Questions requiring the student to apply a rule or process to a problem to determine the correct answer.

Attending behavior. Use of verbal and nonverbal cues by the listener that demonstrate he or she is listening with care and empathy to what is being said.

Attitude. A predisposition to act in a positive or negative way toward persons, ideas, or events.

Attraction. Friendship patterns in the classroom group.

Base score. A percentage score calculated for each student by averaging scores of three recent tests of equal weight to show the student's relative achievement standing in a class and to serve as the point of comparison with later test scores. Base scores are designed to provide a relatively stable indicator of a student's typical performance in a content area.

Checklist. A list of criteria for evaluating a performance or end product.

Classroom diversity. The condition typical of many contemporary classrooms, based on extensive variety of ethnic/cultural/linguistic backgrounds students bring to the classroom.

Classroom management. The set of teacher behaviors by which the teacher establishes and maintains conditions that facilitate effective and efficient instruction — conditions that promote on-task behavior.

Closure. Actions and statements by teachers that are designed to bring a lesson presentation to an appropriate conclusion.

Cohesiveness. The collective feeling that the class members have about the classroom group; the sum of the individual members' feelings about the group.

Comprehension questions. Questions requiring the student to select, organize, and arrange mentally the materials pertinent to answering the question.

Concept map. A procedure for organizing and graphically displaying ideas relevant to a given topic, so that relationships among the ideas are clarified.

Concepts. Categories into which our experiences are organized, and the larger network of intellectual relationships brought about through categorization.

Concrete concepts. Those concepts that can be perceived directly through one of the five senses.

Conditioned reinforcers. Reinforcers that are learned.

Conjunctive concepts. Concepts that have only a single set of qualities or characteristics to learn.

Convergent thinking. Thinking that occurs when the task, or question, is so structured that several people will arrive at similar conclusions or answers, and the number of possible appropriate conclusions is limited (usually one conclusion).

Criterial (or critical) attributes. The basic characteristics of a concept.
Criterion-referenced judgments. Judgments made by comparing the information you have about an individual with some performance criterion; that is, some description of expected behavior.

Decision. A choice among alternative courses of action.
Desist behaviors. Behaviors the teacher uses in an effort to stop student misbehavior.
Diagnostic procedures. Procedures to determine what pupils are capable of doing with respect to given learning tasks.
Disjunctive concepts. Concepts that have two or more sets of alternative conditions under which the concept appears.
Divergent thinking. Thinking that occurs when the task, or question, is so open that several people will arrive at different conclusions or answers, and the number of possible appropriate conclusions is fairly large.

Effective teacher. One who is able to bring about intended learning outcomes.
Enactive medium. A representational medium for acquiring concepts by enacting or doing the concept.
Equal opportunities for success. In cooperative learning activities, calculations of team achievement must be designed to assure that equal individual *improvement* results in equal individual *contribution* to the team score, in spite of differences among teammates in absolute achievement. Students with low entering achievement must be assured the chance to become as valuable to their team as those with high entering achievement, in order to assure that the team is motivated to support the work of all members.
Evaluation. The process of obtaining information and using it to form judgments that, in turn, are to be used in decision making.
Evaluation questions. Questions requiring students to use criteria or standards to form judgments about the value of the topic or phenomena being considered.
Expectations. Those perceptions that the teacher and the students hold regarding their relationships to one another.
Explaining behavior. Planned teacher talk designed to clarify any idea, procedure, or process not understood by a student.
Extinction. Withholding of an anticipated reward in an instance where that behavior was previously rewarded; results in the decreased frequency of the previously rewarded behavior.

Facts. Well-grounded, clearly established pieces of information.
Feedback. Information about the effects or consequences of actions taken.
Fine-tuning. Making small adjustments in the planned procedures for a lesson during teaching of the lesson.

Goals. General statements of purpose.
Group-focus behaviors. Those behaviors teachers use to maintain a focus on the group, rather than on an individual student, during individual recitations.
Group investigation. A cooperative learning strategy in which students brainstorm a set of questions on a subject, form learning teams to find answers to questions, and make presentations to the whole class.

Heterogeneous learning teams. In cooperative learning, working groups of four or five are formed of students whose differences in entering achievement levels, gender, and ethnicity reflect the variety in the whole class.

Iconic medium. A representational medium for acquiring concepts by viewing a picture or image of the concept.
Improvement scores. In cooperative learning, team scores are calculated by comparing the entering achievement levels (see **base scores**) with the test scores of

each individual. Differences of a given amount translate into "improvement points" and are added to create a team "improvement score" according to a predetermined formula. Improvement scores are the basis of team rewards.

Individual accountability. In cooperative learning, outcome measures are designed to assure that the achievement of each student is measured independently and that individual achievement provides the basis for earning team rewards.

Inference. A conclusion derived from, and bearing some relation to, assumed premises.

Inquiry. Obtaining information by asking.

Instructional event. Any activity or set of activities in which students are engaged (with or without the teacher) for the purpose of learning.

Instructional grouping. Dividing a class of pupils into small subunits for purposes of teaching. Groups can be formed according to achievement or interest, depending on instructional purpose.

Instructional objectives. Statements of desired changes in student's thoughts, actions, or feelings that a particular course or educational program should bring about.

Instructional strategies. Plans for managing the learning environment to provide learning opportunities and meet objectives. Strategies involve the methods used, along with concerns for motivating, sequencing, pacing, and grouping.

Interval schedule. A type of intermittent reinforcement in which the teacher reinforces the student after a specified period of time.

Inventory questions. Questions asking individuals to describe their thoughts, feelings, and manifested actions.

Jigsaw. A cooperative learning strategy in which students participate first in expert groups, where they learn about a particular aspect of a subject, and then return to learning teams (each having one or more experts of each kind) where the experts in turn teach teammates, who eventually share the knowledge mastered by each expert group.

Judgment. Estimate of present conditions or prediction of future conditions. Involves comparing information to some referent.

Knowledge questions. Questions requiring the student to recognize or recall information.

Leadership. Those behaviors that help the group move toward the accomplishment of its objectives.

Lecture. Planned teacher talk designed to convey important information in an effective and efficient manner.

Measurement error. The error that occurs when any measurement is made. Theoretically, it is the difference between the "true" score and any given obtained score.

Movement management behaviors. Those behaviors that the teacher uses to initiate, sustain, or terminate a classroom activity.

Noncriterial (or noncritical) attributes. Features that are frequently present in concept illustrations, though they are not an essential part of the concept.

Norm-referenced judgments. Judgments made by comparing the information you have about an individual with information you have about a group of similar individuals.

Norms. Shared expectations of how group members should think, feel, and behave.

Novice. A person who is inexperienced in performing a particular activity.

Observation. The process of looking and listening, noticing the important elements of a performance or a product.

On-task behavior. Student behavior that is appropriate to the task.

Overlapping behaviors. Those behaviors by which the teacher indicates that he or she is attending to more than one issue when there is more than one issue to deal with at a particular time.

Peer teaching. A procedure that provides teachers an opportunity to practice new instructional techniques in a simplified setting, teaching lessons to small groups of their peers (other prospective or experienced teachers).

Primary reinforcers. Reinforcers that are unlearned and necessary to sustain life.

Probing questions. Questions following a response that require the respondent to provide more support, be clearer or more accurate, or offer greater specificity or originality.

Professional development. The process of acquiring specialized knowledge and skills, as well as an awareness of the alternative actions that might be appropriate in particular situations.

Punishment. Use of an unpleasant stimulus to eliminate an undesirable behavior.

Questionnaire. A list of written questions that can be read and responded to by the student or other respondent.

Rating scales. Instruments that provide a scale of values describing someone or something being evaluated.

Ratio schedule. A type of intermittent reinforcement in which the teacher reinforces the student after the behavior has occurred a certain number of times.

Referent. That to which you compare the information you have about an individual to form a judgment.

Reflection. Giving direct feedback to individuals about the way their verbal and nonverbal messages are being received.

Reinforcement. The process of using reinforcers; in general, any event that increases the strength of a response. A reward for the purpose of maintaining an already acquired behavior is called *positive reinforcement*. Strengthening a behavior through the removal of an unpleasant stimulus is called *negative reinforcement*.

Relational concepts. Concepts that describe relationships between items.

Repertoire. A set of alternative routines or procedures, all of which serve some common purpose, and each of which serves some additional, unique purpose. A person who has a repertoire of procedures available is recognized as being practiced and skillful in use of these procedures, and sensitive in selecting the appropriate procedure to use in any given situation.

Review closure. A type of closure technique whose main characteristic is an attempt to summarize the major points of a presentation or discussion.

Routine. An established pattern of behavior.

Self-referenced judgments. Judgments made by comparing information you have about an individual to some other information you have about that same individual.

Set induction. Actions and statements by the teacher that are designed to relate the experiences of the students to the objectives of the lesson.

Standard score. A derived score expressed on a uniform standard scale. When a raw score is converted to a standard score, its relationship to other scores in the distribution does not change.

Standardized test. A test that has a fixed set of questions that must be administered according to a specified set of directions and within time limitations.

Steering group. A group of pupils within the class who are carefully observed by the teacher to determine whether the class is understanding the content being discussed in the lesson.

STAD (Student-Teams-Achievement-Divisions). A cooperative learning strategy in which teacher presentation is followed by team practice and individual testing, with individual improvement scores contributing to team scores and rewards.

Symbolic medium. A representational medium for acquiring concepts through symbols such as language.

Synthesis questions. Questions requiring the student to put together elements and parts to form a whole. Include producing original communications, making predictions, and solving problems for which a variety of answers are possible.

Systems design. A self-correcting and logical methodology of decision making to be used for the design and development of constructed entities; particularly in this book, instructional systems.

Target mistakes. The teacher stopping the wrong student or desisting a less serious deviancy.

Taxonomy. A classification system; used here in reference to a classification system of educational objectives or skills.

Teaching skill. A distinct set of identifiable behaviors needed to perform teaching functions.

Team packet. In cooperative learning, an envelope or box or file used to expedite distribution and collection of lesson materials.

Team rewards. In cooperative learning, four- or five-member learning teams win certificates and other forms of public recognition on the basis of individual improvement scores.

Terminal goals. Goals one can expect to reach at the end of a given learning experience.

Test. An instrument that presents a common situation to which all students respond, a common set of instructions, and a common set of rules for scanning the students' responses. Used primarily for determining aptitude and achievement.

TGT (Teams-Games-Tournaments). A cooperative learning strategy in which teacher presentation is followed by team practice and individual mastery is tested in "tournaments," with two or three students of matched achievement, rather than tests. Team rewards are based on "tournament points" earned by various teammates at their respective tournament tables.

Theoretical knowledge. Concepts, facts, and propositions that make up much of the content of the disciplines.

Time out. The removal of a reward from the student or the removal of the student from the reward.

Topic-associating narrative style. A style of storytelling involving movement from topic to topic, rather than focusing on and developing a single theme.

Topic-centered narrative style. A style of storytelling involving development of a single theme through description of related events.

Unit plan. A plan for a sequence of several lessons dealing with the same general topic.

Wait time. The amount of time the teacher waits after asking a question before calling for the answer.

Withitness behaviors. Behaviors by which the teacher communicates to students that he or she knows what is going on.

Zero noise signal. In cooperative learning, an action that communicates a need for silence and immediate attention, to permit the teacher to provide additional whole-group directions during a team activity.

Index